Attention Deficit Disorder
SOURCEBOOK

Health Reference Series

First Edition

Attention Deficit Disorder
SOURCEBOOK

*Basic Consumer Health Information about Attention
Deficit/Hyperactivity Disorder in Children and Adults,
Including Facts about Causes, Symptoms, Diagnostic
Criteria, and Treatment Options Such as Medications,
Behavior Therapy, Coaching, and Homeopathy*

*Along with Reports on Current Research Initiatives,
Legal Issues, and Government Regulations, and
Featuring a Glossary of Related Terms, Internet
Resources, and a List of Additional Reading Material*

Edited by
Dawn D. Matthews

Omnigraphics

615 Griswold Street • Detroit, MI 48226

Bibliographic Note

Because this page cannot legibly accommodate all the copyright notices, the Bibliographic Note portion of the Preface constitutes an extension of the copyright notice.

Edited by Dawn D. Matthews

Health Reference Series

Karen Bellenir, *Managing Editor*
David A. Cooke, MD, *Medical Consultant*
Elizabeth Barbour, *Permissions Associate*
Dawn Matthews, *Verification Assistant*
Carol Munson, *Permissions Assistant*
Laura Pleva Nielsen, *Index Editor*
EdIndex, Services for Publishers, *Indexers*

* * *

Omnigraphics, Inc.

Matthew P. Barbour, *Senior Vice President*
Kay Gill, *Vice President—Directories*
Kevin Hayes, *Operations Manager*
David P. Bianco, *Marketing Consultant*

* * *

Peter E. Ruffner, *President and Publisher*
Frederick G. Ruffner, Jr., *Chairman*
Copyright © 2002 Omnigraphics, Inc.
ISBN 0-7808-0624-7

Library of Congress Cataloging-in-Publication Data

Attention deficit disorder sourcebook : basic consumer health information about attention deficit/hyperactivity disorder in children and adults, including facts about causes, symptoms, diagnostic criteria, and treatment options such as medications, behavior therapy, coaching, and homeopathy; along with reports on current research initiatives, legal issues, and government regulations, and featuring a glossary of related terms, internet resources, and a list of additional reading material / edited by Dawn D. Matthews.-- 1st ed.
　　　p. cm. -- (Health reference series)
　　Includes index.
　　ISBN 0-7808-0624-7 (library binding : acid-free paper)
　　　1. Attention-deficit hyperactivity disorder. 2. Attention-deficit disorder in adolescence.
　　3. Attention-deficit disorder in adults. I. Matthews, Dawn D. II. Health reference series (Unnumbered)

RJ506.H9 A885 2002
616.85'89--dc21

2002072093

∞

Printed in the United States

Table of Contents

Part II: Diagnosis and Treatment

Part III: Help for Parents and Teachers

Part IV: AD/HD Facts for Specific Populations

Part V: Adults with AD/HD

Part VI: Additional Help and Information

Preface

About This Book

Attention deficit disorder (ADD) is an often-used name for attention deficit/hyperactivity disorder (AD/HD), a complex condition diagnosed in approximately 3% to 5% of school-aged children. The most common symptoms of AD/HD—hyperactivity, inattention, and impulsivity—usually appear before age six and may get worse over time. The individual with AD/HD is so easily distracted by outside stimuli that completing a task or learning something new is challenging. Not everyone who is hyperactive, inattentive, or impulsive has AD/HD, but a pattern of characteristic behaviors distinguish it from other conditions.

This *Sourcebook* contains information about the symptoms, diagnosis, and causes of AD/HD. The most common treatments, including medication therapy, behavior therapy, and AD/HD coaching, are discussed, and facts about alternative therapies are provided. A section on educational issues offers tips about creating Individual Education Programs (IEPs), solving parent/teacher conflicts, and protecting the educational rights of children with AD/HD. Information is also included for gifted children, teenagers, and college students. A section for adults with AD/HD provides advice for improving social skills, maintaining close relationships, and finding an AD/HD-friendly job. In addition, this book contains a glossary of related terms, a list of support groups, internet resources, and suggested additional reading.

How to Use This Book

This book is divided into parts and chapters. Parts focus on broad areas of interest. Chapters are devoted to single topics within a part.

Part I: Introduction provides an overview of the issues related to attention deficit/hyperactivity disorder. It discusses the link between drug and alcohol use during pregnancy and the occurrence of AD/HD in children. A chapter with information about distinguishing AD/HD from other conditions is also included.

Part II: Diagnosis and Treatment contains information about medication management of AD/HD and the long-term effects of stimulant medications on the brain. Information about behavior therapy, AD/HD coaching, and homeopathic therapy is provided. A chapter discussing unproven treatments offers help to people exploring alternatives to traditional therapy.

Part III: Help for Parents and Teachers provides guidelines for parenting children with AD/HD and playing an active role in guiding their educational efforts. Information about the relationship between nutrition and learning is also presented.

Part IV: AD/HD Facts for Specific Populations focuses on issues that are relevant to specific groups, including gifted children, females, teenagers, college students, substance abusers, and youth in the juvenile justice system.

Part V: Adults with AD/HD addresses some of the many issues faced by adults with AD/HD. It provides helpful advice for improving social skills, maintaining close relationships, and finding an AD/HD-friendly job.

Part VI: Further Help and Information contains a glossary of related terms, a list of support groups and organizations, internet resources, and suggested additional reading.

Bibliographic Note

This volume contains documents and excerpts from publications issued by the following U.S. government agencies: National Institutes of Health (NIH); National Institute of Mental Health (NIMH); National Institute on Drug Abuse (NIDA); National Parent Information Network (NPIN); and the U.S. Department of Education.

In addition, this volume contains copyrighted documents from the following organizations and individuals: About.com, Inc.; ADHD Living Guide.com; American Optometric Association; Children and Adults with Attention-Deficit/Hyperactivity Disorder (CHADD); James J. Crist, Ph.D.; Donald J. Getz, O.D., FCOVD, FAAO; Henry Holt and Co.; Peter S. & Patricia H. Latham; George T. Lynn, M.A.; Mental Health Sanctuary; Kathleen G. Nadeau, Ph.D.; National Attention Deficit Disorder Association; Judith Reichenberg-Ullman; Schwab Learning; Lisa Simmons; Susan Vogel, Ph.D.; and Teens with Problems.

Full citation information is provided on the first page of each chapter. Every effort has been made to secure all necessary rights to reprint the copyrighted material. If any omissions have been made, please contact Omnigraphics to make corrections for future editions.

Acknowledgements

Special thanks go to the many organizations, agencies, and individuals who have contributed materials for this *Sourcebook* and to Karen and Bruce Bellenir and Liz Barbour for their ongoing help and support.

Note from the Editor

This book is part of Omnigraphics' *Health Reference Series*. The *Series* provides basic information about a broad range of medical concerns. It is not intended to serve as a tool for diagnosing illness, in prescribing treatments, or as a substitute for the physician/patient relationship. All persons concerned about medical symptoms or the possibility of disease are encouraged to seek professional care from an appropriate health care provider.

Our Advisory Board

The *Health Reference Series* is reviewed by an Advisory Board comprised of librarians from public, academic, and medical libraries. We would like to thank the following board members for providing guidance to the development of this series:

Dr. Lynda Baker,
Associate Professor of Library and Information Science,
Wayne State University, Detroit, MI

Nancy Bulgarelli,
William Beaumont Hospital Library, Royal Oak, MI

Karen Imarisio,
Bloomfield Township Public Library, Bloomfield Township, MI

Karen Morgan,
Mardigian Library, University of Michigan-Dearborn,
Dearborn, MI

Rosemary Orlando,
St. Clair Shores Public Library, St. Clair Shores, MI

Medical Consultant

Medical consultation services are provided to the *Health Reference Series* editors by David A. Cooke, M.D. Dr. Cooke is a graduate of Brandeis University, and he received his M.D. degree from the University of Michigan. He completed residency training at the University of Wisconsin Hospital and Clinics. He is board-certified in Internal Medicine. Dr. Cooke currently works as part of the University of Michigan Health System and practices in Brighton, MI. In his free time, he enjoys writing, science fiction, and spending time with his family.

Health Reference Series *Update Policy*

The inaugural book in the *Health Reference Series* was the first edition of *Cancer Sourcebook* published in 1989. Since then, the *Series* has been enthusiastically received by librarians and in the medical community. In order to maintain the standard of providing high-quality health information for the layperson the editorial staff at Omnigraphics felt it was necessary to implement a policy of updating volumes when warranted.

Medical researchers have been making tremendous strides, and it is the purpose of the *Health Reference Series* to stay current with the most recent advances. Each decision to update a volume will be made on an individual basis. Some of the considerations will include how much new information is available and the feedback we receive from people who use the books. If there is a topic you would like to see added to the update list, or an area of medical concern you feel has not been adequately addressed, please write to:

Editor
Health Reference Series
Omnigraphics, Inc.
615 Griswold Street
Detroit, MI 48226

The commitment to providing on-going coverage of important medical developments has also led to some format changes in the *Health Reference Series*. Each new volume on a topic is individually titled and called a "First Edition." Subsequent updates will carry sequential edition numbers. To help avoid confusion and to provide maximum flexibility in our ability to respond to informational needs, the practice of consecutively numbering each volume has been discontinued.

Part One

Introduction

Chapter 1

Attention Deficit/Hyperactivity Disorder (AD/HD): An Overview

Imagine living in a fast-moving kaleidoscope, where sounds, images, and thoughts are constantly shifting. Feeling easily bored, yet helpless to keep your mind on tasks you need to complete. Distracted by unimportant sights and sounds, your mind drives you from one thought or activity to the next. Perhaps you are so wrapped up in a collage of thoughts and images that you don't notice when someone speaks to you.

For many people, this is what it's like to have attention deficit/ hyperactivity disorder, or AD/HD. They may be unable to sit still, plan ahead, finish tasks, or be fully aware of what's going on around them. To their family, classmates or coworkers, they seem to exist in a whirlwind of disorganized or frenzied activity. Unexpectedly—on some days and in some situations—they seem fine, often leading others to think the person with AD/HD can actually control these behaviors. As a result, the disorder can mar the person's relationships with others in addition to disrupting their daily life, consuming energy, and diminishing self-esteem.

AD/HD, once called hyperkinesis or minimal brain dysfunction, is one of the most common mental disorders among children. It affects 3 to 5 percent of all children, perhaps as many as 2 million American

"Attention Deficit Hyperactivity Disorder," National Institute of Mental Health, NIH Pub. No. 96-3572, 1996. Despite the date of this document, readers seeking to understand the issues surrounding attention deficit/hyperactivty disorder will find helpful background information and a review of related topics in this chapter.

3

children. Two to three times more boys than girls are affected. On the average, at least one child in every classroom in the United States needs help for the disorder. AD/HD often continues into adolescence and adulthood, and can cause a lifetime of frustrated dreams and emotional pain.

But there is help...and hope. In the last decade, scientists have learned much about the course of the disorder and are now able to identify and treat children, adolescents, and adults who have it. A variety of medications, behavior-changing therapies, and educational options are already available to help people with AD/HD focus their attention, build self-esteem, and function in new ways.

In addition, new avenues of research promise to further improve diagnosis and treatment. With so many American children diagnosed as having attention deficit disorder, research on AD/HD has become a national priority. During the 1990s—which the President and Congress have declared the Decade of the Brain—it is possible that scientists will pinpoint the biological basis of AD/HD and learn how to prevent or treat it even more effectively.

Understanding the Problem

Mark, age 14, has more energy than most boys his age. But then, he's always been overly active. Starting at age 3, he was a human tornado, dashing around and disrupting everything in his path. At home, he darted from one activity to the next, leaving a trail of toys behind him. At meals, he upset dishes and chattered nonstop. He was reckless and impulsive, running into the street with oncoming cars, no matter how many times his mother explained the danger or scolded him. On the playground, he seemed no wilder than the other kids. But his tendency to overreact—like socking playmates simply for bumping into him—had already gotten him into trouble several times. His parents didn't know what to do. Mark's doting grandparents reassured them, "Boys will be boys. Don't worry, he'll grow out of it." But he didn't.

At age 17, Lisa still struggles to pay attention and act appropriately. But this has always been hard for her. She still gets embarrassed thinking about that night her parents took her to a restaurant to celebrate her 10th birthday. She had gotten so distracted by the waitress' bright red hair that her father called her name three times before she remembered to order. Then before she could stop herself, she blurted, "Your hair dye looks awful!"

In elementary and junior high school, Lisa was quiet and cooperative but often seemed to be daydreaming. She was smart, yet couldn't improve her grades no matter how hard she tried. Several times, she failed exams. Even though she knew most of the answers, she couldn't keep her mind on the test. Her parents responded to her low grades by taking away privileges and scolding, "You're just lazy. You could get better grades if you only tried." One day, after Lisa had failed yet another exam, the teacher found her sobbing, "What's wrong with me?"

Although he loves puttering around in his shop, for years Henry has had dozens of unfinished carpentry projects and ideas for new ones he knew he would never complete. His garage was piled so high with wood, he and his wife joked about holding a fire sale.

Every day Henry faced the real frustration of not being able to concentrate long enough to complete a task. He was fired from his job as stock clerk because he lost inventory and carelessly filled out forms. Over the years, afraid that he might be losing his mind, he had seen psychotherapists and tried several medications, but none ever helped him concentrate. He saw the same lack of focus in his young son and worried.

What Are the Symptoms of AD/HD?

The three people you've just met, Mark, Lisa, and Henry, all have a form of AD/HD—attention deficit hyperactivity disorder. AD/HD is not like a broken arm, or strep throat. Unlike these two disorders, AD/HD does not have clear physical signs that can be seen in an x-ray or a lab test. AD/HD can only be identified by looking for certain characteristic behaviors, and as with Mark, Lisa, and Henry, these behaviors vary from person to person. Scientists have not yet identified a single cause behind all the different patterns of behavior—and they may never find just one. Rather, someday scientists may find that AD/HD is actually an umbrella term for several slightly different disorders.

At present, AD/HD is a diagnosis applied to children and adults who consistently display certain characteristic behaviors over a period of time. The most common behaviors fall into three categories: inattention, hyperactivity, and impulsivity.

Inattention. People who are inattentive have a hard time keeping their mind on any one thing and may get bored with a task after only a few minutes. They may give effortless, automatic attention to activities and things they enjoy. But focusing deliberate, conscious attention to organizing and completing a task or learning something new is difficult.

For example, Lisa found it agonizing to do homework. Often, she forgot to plan ahead by writing down the assignment or bringing home the right books. And when trying to work, every few minutes she found her mind drifting to something else. As a result, she rarely finished and her work was full of errors.

Hyperactivity. People who are hyperactive always seem to be in motion. They can't sit still. Like Mark, they may dash around or talk incessantly. Sitting still through a lesson can be an impossible task. Hyperactive children squirm in their seat or roam around the room. Or they might wiggle their feet, touch everything, or noisily tap their pencil. Hyperactive teens and adults may feel intensely restless. They may be fidgety or, like Henry, they may try to do several things at once, bouncing around from one activity to the next.

Impulsivity. People who are overly impulsive seem unable to curb their immediate reactions or think before they act. As a result, like Lisa, they may blurt out inappropriate comments. Or like Mark, they may run into the street without looking. Their impulsivity may make it hard for them to wait for things they want or to take their turn in games. They may grab a toy from another child or hit when they're upset.

Not everyone who is overly hyperactive, inattentive, or impulsive has an attention disorder. Since most people sometimes blurt out things they didn't mean to say, bounce from one task to another, or become disorganized and forgetful, how can specialists tell if the problem is AD/HD? To assess whether a person has AD/HD, specialists consider several critical questions: Are these behaviors excessive, long-term, and pervasive? That is, do they occur more often than in other people the same age? Are they a continuous problem, not just a response to a temporary situation? Do the behaviors occur in several settings or only in one specific place like the playground or the office? The person's pattern of behavior is compared against a set of criteria and characteristics of the disorder. These criteria appear in a diagnostic reference book called the *DSM* (short for the *Diagnostic and Statistical Manual of Mental Disorders*).

According to the diagnostic manual, there are three patterns of behavior that indicate AD/HD. People with AD/HD may show several signs of being consistently inattentive. They may have a pattern of being hyperactive and impulsive. Or they may show all three types of behavior.

According to the *DSM*, signs of inattention include:

- becoming easily distracted by irrelevant sights and sounds
- failing to pay attention to details and making careless mistakes
- rarely following instructions carefully and completely
- losing or forgetting things like toys, or pencils, books, and tools needed for a task

Some signs of hyperactivity and impulsivity are:

- feeling restless, often fidgeting with hands or feet, or squirming
- running, climbing, or leaving a seat, in situations where sitting or quiet behavior is expected
- blurting out answers before hearing the whole question
- having difficulty waiting in line or for a turn

Because everyone shows some of these behaviors at times, the *DSM* contains very specific guidelines for determining when they indicate AD/HD. The behaviors must appear early in life, before age 7, and continue for at least 6 months. In children, they must be more frequent or severe than in others the same age. Above all, the behaviors must create a real handicap in at least two areas of a person's life, such as school, home, work, or social settings. So someone whose work or friendships are not impaired by these behaviors would not be diagnosed with AD/HD. Nor would a child who seems overly active at school but functions well elsewhere.

Can Any Other Conditions Produce These Symptoms?

The fact is, many things can produce these behaviors. Anything from chronic fear to mild seizures can make a child seem overactive, quarrelsome, impulsive, or inattentive. For example, a formerly cooperative child who becomes overactive and easily distracted after a parent's death is dealing with an emotional problem, not AD/HD. A chronic middle ear infection can also make a child seem distracted and uncooperative. So can living with family members who are physically abusive or addicted to drugs or alcohol. Can you imagine a child trying to focus on a math lesson when his or her safety and well-being are in danger each day? Such children are showing the effects of other problems, not AD/HD.

In other children, AD/HD-like behaviors may be their response to a defeating classroom situation. Perhaps the child has a learning disability and is not developmentally ready to learn to read and write at the time these are taught. Or maybe the work is too hard or too easy, leaving the child frustrated or bored.

It's also important to realize that during certain stages of development, the majority of children that age tend to be inattentive, hyperactive, or impulsive—but do not have AD/HD. Preschoolers have lots of energy and run everywhere they go, but this doesn't mean they are hyperactive. And many teenagers go through a phase when they are messy, disorganized, and reject authority. It doesn't mean they will have a lifelong problem controlling their impulses.

AD/HD is a serious diagnosis that may require long-term treatment with counseling and medication. So it's important that a doctor first look for and treat any other causes for these behaviors.

What Causes AD/HD?

Understandably, one of the first questions parents ask when they learn their child has an attention disorder is "Why? What went wrong?"

Health professionals stress that since no one knows what causes AD/HD, it doesn't help parents to look backward to search for possible reasons. There are too many possibilities to pin down the cause with certainty. It is far more important for the family to move forward in finding ways to get the right help. Scientists, however, do need to study causes in an effort to identify better ways to treat, and perhaps some day, prevent AD/HD. They are finding more and more evidence that AD/HD does not stem from home environment, but from biological causes. When you think about it, there is no clear relationship between home life and AD/HD. Not all children from unstable or dysfunctional homes have AD/HD. And not all children with AD/HD come from dysfunctional families. Knowing this can remove a huge burden of guilt from parents who might blame themselves for their child's behavior.

Over the last decades, scientists have come up with possible theories about what causes AD/HD. Some of these theories have led to dead ends, some to exciting new avenues of investigation. One disappointing theory was that all attention disorders and learning disabilities were caused by minor head injuries or undetectable damage to the brain, perhaps from early infection or complications at birth. Based on this theory, for many years both disorders were called minimal brain damage or minimal brain dysfunction. Although certain types of head injury can explain some cases of attention disorder, the theory was rejected because it could explain only a very small number of cases. Not everyone with AD/HD or LD has a history of head trauma or birth complications.

Another theory was that refined sugar and food additives make children hyperactive and inattentive. As a result, parents were encouraged to stop serving children foods containing artificial flavorings, preservatives, and sugars. However, this theory, too, came under question. In 1982, the National Institutes of Health (NIH), the Federal agency responsible for biomedical research, held a major scientific conference to discuss the issue. After studying the data, the scientists concluded that the restricted diet only seemed to help about 5 percent of children with AD/HD, mostly either young children or children with food allergies.

AD/HD is not usually caused by too much TV, food allergies, excess sugar, poor home life, or poor schools. In recent years, as new tools and techniques for studying the brain have been developed, scientists have been able to test more theories about what causes AD/HD.

Using one such technique, NIMH scientists demonstrated a link between a person's ability to pay continued attention and the level of activity in the brain. Adult subjects were asked to learn a list of words. As they did, scientists used a PET (positron emission tomography) scanner to observe the brain at work. The researchers measured the level of glucose used by the areas of the brain that inhibit impulses and control attention. Glucose is the brain's main source of energy, so measuring how much is used is a good indicator of the brain's activity level. The investigators found important differences between people who have AD/HD and those who don't. In people with AD/HD, the brain areas that control attention used less glucose, indicating that they were less active. It appears from this research that a lower level of activity in some parts of the brain may cause inattention.

The next step will be to research why there is less activity in these areas of the brain. Scientists at NIMH hope to compare the use of glucose and the activity level in mild and severe cases of AD/HD. They will also try to discover why some medications used to treat AD/HD work better than others, and if the more effective medications increase activity in certain parts of the brain. Researchers are also searching for other differences between those who have and do not have AD/HD. Research on how the brain normally develops in the fetus offers some clues about what may disrupt the process. Throughout pregnancy and continuing into the first year of life, the brain is constantly developing. It begins its growth from a few all-purpose cells and evolves into a complex organ made of billions of specialized, interconnected nerve cells. By studying brain development in animals and humans, scientists are gaining a better understanding of how the brain works when the nerve cells are connected correctly and incorrectly. Scientists at NIMH and other research institutions are tracking clues to determine what might prevent nerve cells from forming the proper connections. Some of the factors they are studying include drug use during pregnancy, toxins, and genetics.

Research shows that a mother's use of cigarettes, alcohol, or other drugs during pregnancy may have damaging effects on the unborn child. These substances may be dangerous to the fetus's developing brain. It appears that alcohol and the nicotine in cigarettes may distort developing nerve cells. For example, heavy alcohol use during pregnancy has been linked to fetal alcohol syndrome (FAS), a condition that can lead to low birth weight, intellectual impairment, and certain physical defects. Many children born with FAS show much the same hyperactivity, inattention, and impulsivity as children with AD/HD.

Drugs such as cocaine—including the smokable form known as crack—seem to affect the normal development of brain receptors. These brain cell parts help to transmit incoming signals from our skin, eyes, and ears, and help control our responses to the environment. Current research suggests that drug abuse may harm these receptors. Some scientists believe that such damage may lead to AD/HD.

Toxins in the environment may also disrupt brain development or brain processes, which may lead to AD/HD. Lead is one such possible toxin. It is found in dust, soil, and flaking paint in areas where leaded gasoline and paint were once used. It is also present in some water pipes. Some animal studies suggest that children exposed to lead may develop symptoms associated with AD/HD, but only a few cases have actually been found.

Other research shows that attention disorders tend to run in families, so there are likely to be genetic influences. Children who have AD/HD usually have at least one close relative who also has AD/HD. And at least one-third of all fathers who had AD/HD in their youth bear children who have AD/HD. Even more convincing: the majority of identical twins share the trait. At the National Institutes of Health, researchers are also on the trail of a gene that may be involved in transmitting AD/HD in a small number of families with a genetic thyroid disorder.

Getting Help

In third grade, Mark's teacher threw up her hands and said, "Enough!" In one morning, Mark had jumped out of his seat to sharpen his pencil six times, each time accidentally charging into other children's desks and toppling books and papers. He was finally sent to the principal's office when he began kicking a desk he had overturned. In sheer frustration, his teacher called a meeting with his parents and the school psychologist.

But even after they developed a plan for managing Mark's behavior in class, Mark showed little improvement. Finally, after an extensive assessment, they found that Mark had an attention deficit that included hyperactivity. He was put on a medication called Ritalin to control the hyperactivity during school hours. Although Ritalin failed to help, another drug called Dexedrine did. With a psychologist's help, his parents learned to reward desirable behaviors, and to have Mark take time out when he became too disruptive. Soon Mark was able to sit still and focus on learning.

Because Lisa wasn't disruptive in class, it took a long time for teachers to notice her problem. Lisa was first referred to the school evaluation team when her teacher realized that she was a bright girl with failing grades. The team ruled out a learning disability but determined that she had an attention deficit, AD/HD without hyperactivity. The school psychologist recognized that Lisa was also dealing with depression.

Lisa's teachers and the school psychologist developed a treatment plan that included participation in a program to increase her attention span and develop her social skills. They also recommended that Lisa receive counseling to help her recognize her strengths and overcome her depression.

When Henry's son entered kindergarten, it was clear that he was going to have problems sitting quietly and concentrating. After several disruptive incidents, the school called and suggested that his son be evaluated for AD/HD. As the boy was assessed, Henry realized that he had grown up with the same symptoms that specialists were now finding in his son. Fortunately, the psychologist knew that AD/HD can persist in adults. She suggested that Henry be evaluated by a professional who worked with adults. For the first time, Henry was correctly diagnosed and given Ritalin to aid his concentration. What a relief! All the years that he had been unable to concentrate were due to a disorder that could be identified, and above all, treated.

How Is AD/HD Identified and Diagnosed?

Many parents see signs of an attention deficit in toddlers long before the child enters school. For example, as a 3-year-old, Henry's son already displayed some signs of hyperactivity. He seemed to lose interest and dart off even during his favorite TV shows or while playing games. Once, during a game of catch, he left the game before the ball even reached him!

Like Henry's son, a child may be unable to focus long enough to play a simple game. Or, like Mark, the child may be tearing around out of control. But because children mature at different rates, and are very different in personality, temperament, and energy level, it's useful to get an expert's opinion of whether the behaviors are appropriate for the child's age. Parents can ask their pediatrician, or a child psychologist or psychiatrist to assess whether their toddler has an attention disorder or is just immature, has hyperactivity or is just exuberant.

Seeing a child as "a chip off the old block" or "just like his dad" can blind parents to the need for help. Parents may find it hard to see their child's behavior as a problem when it so closely resembles their own. In fact, like Henry, many parents first recognize their own disorder only when their children are diagnosed.

In many cases, the teacher is the first to recognize that a child is hyperactive or inattentive and may consult with the school psychologist. Because teachers work with many children, they come to know how average children behave in learning situations that require attention and self-control. However, teachers sometimes fail to notice the needs of children like Lisa who are quiet and cooperative.

Types of Professionals Who Make the Diagnosis

School-age and preschool children are often evaluated by a school psychologist or a team made up of the school psychologist and other specialists. But if the school doesn't believe the student has a problem, or if the family wants another opinion, a family may need to see a specialist in private practice. In such cases, who can the family turn to? What kinds of specialists do they need? Table 1.1. lists the professionals who can and cannot make a diagnosis of AD/HD.

The family can start by talking with the child's pediatrician or their family doctor. Some pediatricians may do the assessment themselves, but more often they refer the family to an appropriate specialist they know and trust. In addition, state and local agencies that serve families and children, as well as some volunteer organizations can help identify an appropriate specialist.

Knowing the differences in qualifications and services can help the family choose someone who can best meet their needs. Besides school psychologists, there are several types of specialists qualified to diagnose and treat AD/HD. Child psychiatrists are doctors who specialize in diagnosing and treating childhood mental and behavioral disorders. A psychiatrist can provide therapy and prescribe any needed medications. Child psychologists are also qualified to diagnose and treat AD/HD. They can provide therapy for the child and help the family develop ways to deal with the disorder. But psychologists are not medical doctors and must rely on the child's physician to do medical exams and prescribe medication. Neurologists, doctors who work with disorders of the brain and nervous system, can also diagnose AD/HD and prescribe medicines. But unlike psychiatrists and psychologists, neurologists usually do not provide therapy for the emotional aspects of the disorder. Adults who think they may have AD/HD can also seek a psychologist, psychiatrist, or neurologist. But at present, not all specialists are skilled in identifying or treating AD/HD in adults.

Within each specialty, individual doctors and mental health professionals differ in their experience with AD/HD. So in selecting a specialist, it's important to find someone with specific training and experience in diagnosing and treating the disorder.

Steps In Making a Diagnosis

Whatever the specialist's expertise, his or her first task is to gather information that will rule out other possible reasons for the child's

Table 1.1. Professionals Who Can Make the Diagnosis

Specialty	Can Diagnose AD/HD	Can Prescribe Medications, If Needed	Provides Counseling or Training
Psychiatrists	yes	yes	yes
Psychologists	yes	no	yes
Pediatricians or Family Physicians	yes	yes	no
Neurologists	yes	yes	no

13

behavior. In ruling out other causes, the specialist checks the child's school and medical records. The specialist tries to sense whether the home and classroom environments are stressful or chaotic, and how the child's parents and teachers deal with the child. They may have a doctor look for such problems as emotional disorders, undetectable (petit mal) seizures, and poor vision or hearing. Most schools automatically screen for vision and hearing, so this information is often already on record. A doctor may also look for allergies or nutrition problems like chronic caffeine highs that might make the child seem overly active.

Next the specialist gathers information on the child's ongoing behavior in order to compare these behaviors to the symptoms and diagnostic criteria listed in the *DSM (Diagnostic and Statistical Manual of Mental Disorders)*. This involves talking with the child and if possible, observing the child in class and in other settings.

The child's teachers, past and present, are asked to rate their observations of the child's behavior on standardized evaluation forms to compare the child's behaviors to those of other children the same age. Of course, rating scales are subjective—they only capture the teacher's personal perception of the child. Even so, because teachers get to know so many children, their judgment of how a child compares to others is usually accurate.

The specialist interviews the child's teachers, parents, and other people who know the child well, such as school staff and baby-sitters. Parents are asked to describe their child's behavior in a variety of situations. They may also fill out a rating scale to indicate how severe and frequent the behaviors seem to be.

In some cases, the child may be checked for social adjustment and mental health. Tests of intelligence and learning achievement may be given to see if the child has a learning disability and whether the disabilities are in all or only certain parts of the school curriculum. In looking at the data, the specialist pays special attention to the child's behavior during noisy or unstructured situations, like parties, or during tasks that require sustained attention, like reading, working math problems, or playing a board game. Behavior during free play or while getting individual attention is given less importance in the evaluation. In such situations, most children with AD/HD are able to control their behavior and perform well.

The specialist then pieces together a profile of the child's behavior. Which AD/HD-like behaviors listed in the *DSM* does the child show? How often? In what situations? How long has the child been doing them? How old was the child when the problem started? Are the behaviors seriously interfering with the child's friendships, school activities, or home life? Does the child have any other related problems? The answers to these questions help identify whether the child's hyperactivity, impulsivity, and inattention are significant and long-standing. If so, the child may be diagnosed with AD/HD.

Adults are diagnosed for AD/HD based on their performance at home and at work. When possible, their parents are asked to rate the person's behavior as a child. A spouse or roommate can help rate and evaluate current behaviors. But for the most part, adults are asked to describe their own experiences. One symptom is a sense of frustration. Since people with AD/HD are often bright and creative, they often report feeling frustrated that they're not living up to their potential. Many also feel restless and are easily bored. Some say they need to seek novelty and excitement to help channel the whirlwind in their minds. Although it may be impossible to document when these behaviors first started, most adults with AD/HD can give examples of being inattentive, impulsive, overly active, impatient, and disorganized most of their lives.

Until recent years, adults were not thought to have AD/HD, so many adults with ongoing symptoms have never been diagnosed. People go for decades knowing that something is wrong, but not knowing what it is. Psychotherapy and medication for anxiety, depression, or manic-depression fail to help much, simply because the AD/HD itself is not being addressed. Yet half the children with AD/HD continue to have symptoms through adulthood. The recent awareness of adult AD/HD means that many people can finally be correctly diagnosed and treated.

A correct diagnosis lets people move forward in their lives. Once the disorder is known, they can begin to receive whatever combination of educational, medical, and emotional help they need. An effective treatment plan helps people with AD/HD and their families at many levels. For adults with AD/HD, the treatment plan may include medication, along with practical and emotional support. For children and adolescents, it may include providing an appropriate classroom setting, the right medication, and helping parents to manage their child's behavior.

What Are the Educational Options?

Children with AD/HD have a variety of needs. Some children are too hyperactive or inattentive to function in a regular classroom, even with medication and a behavior management plan. Such children may be placed in a special education class for all or part of the day. In some schools, the special education teacher teams with the classroom teacher to meet each child's unique needs. However, most children are able to stay in the regular classroom. Whenever possible, educators prefer to not to segregate children, but to let them learn along with their peers.

Children with AD/HD often need some special accommodations to help them learn. For example, the teacher may seat the child in an area with few distractions, provide an area where the child can move around and release excess energy, or establish a clearly posted system of rules and reward appropriate behavior. Sometimes just keeping a card or a picture on the desk can serve as a visual reminder to use the right school behavior, like raising a hand instead of shouting out, or staying in a seat instead of wandering around the room. Giving a child with AD/HD extra time on tests can make the difference between passing and failing, and gives them a fairer chance to show what they've learned. Reviewing instructions or writing assignments on the board, and even listing the books and materials they will need for the task, may make it possible for disorganized, inattentive children to complete the work.

Many of the strategies of special education are simply good teaching methods. Telling students in advance what they will learn, providing visual aids, and giving written as well as oral instructions are all ways to help students focus and remember the key parts of the lesson. Students with AD/HD often need to learn techniques for monitoring and controlling their own attention and behavior. For example, Mark's teacher taught him several alternatives for when he loses track of what he's supposed to do. He can look for instructions on the blackboard, raise his hand, wait to see if he remembers, or quietly ask another child. The process of finding alternatives to interrupting the teacher has made him more self-sufficient and cooperative. And because he now interrupts less, he is beginning to get more praise than reprimands.

In Lisa's class, the teacher frequently stops to ask students to notice whether they are paying attention to the lesson or if they are thinking about something else. The students record their answer on a chart. As students become more consciously aware of their attention, they begin to see progress and feel good about staying better focused. The process helped make Lisa aware of when she was drifting off, so she could return her attention to the lesson faster. As a result, she became more productive and the quality of her work improved.

Because schools demand that children sit still, wait for a turn, pay attention, and stick with a task, it's no surprise that many children with AD/HD have problems in class. Their minds are fully capable of learning, but their hyperactivity and inattention make learning difficult. As a result, many students with AD/HD repeat a grade or drop out of school early. Fortunately, with the right combination of appropriate educational practices, medication, and counseling, these outcomes can be avoided.

Right to a Free Public Education

Although parents have the option of taking their child to a private practitioner for evaluation and educational services, most children with AD/HD qualify for free services within the public schools. Steps are taken to ensure that each child with AD/HD receives an education that meets his or her unique needs. For example, the special education teacher, working with parents, the school psychologist, school administrators, and the classroom teacher, must assess the child's strengths and weaknesses and design an Individualized Education Program (IEP). The IEP outlines the specific skills the child needs to develop as well as appropriate learning activities that build on the child's strengths. Parents play an important role in the process. They must be included in meetings and given an opportunity to review and approve their child's IEP. Chapter 26 of this Sourcebook contains further information about IEPs.

Many children with AD/HD or other disabilities are able to receive such special education services under the Individuals with Disabilities Education Act (IDEA). The Act guarantees appropriate services and a public education to children with disabilities from ages 3 to 21. Children who do not qualify for services under IDEA can receive help under an earlier law, the National Rehabilitation Act, Section 504, which defines disabilities more broadly. Qualifying for services under the National Rehabilitation Act is often called 504 eligibility. Chapter 30 contains further discussion on AD/HD under the Individuals with Disabilities Act (IDEA).

Because AD/HD is a disability that affects children's ability to learn and interact with others, it can certainly be a disabling condition. Under one law or another, most children can receive the services they need.

Some Coping Strategies for Teens and Adults with AD/HD

When necessary, ask the teacher or boss to repeat instructions rather than guess. Break large assignments or job tasks into small, simple tasks. Set a deadline for each task and reward yourself as you complete each one. Each day, make a list of what you need to do. Plan the best order for doing each task. Then make a schedule for doing them. Use a calendar or daily planner to keep yourself on track.

Work in a quiet area. Do one thing at a time. Give yourself short breaks. Write things you need to remember in a notebook with dividers. Write different kinds of information like assignments, appointments, and phone numbers in different sections. Keep the book with you all of the time. Post notes to yourself to help remind yourself of things you need to do. Tape notes on the bathroom mirror, on the refrigerator, in your school locker, or dashboard of your car—wherever you're likely to need the reminder.

Store similar things together. For example, keep all your Nintendo disks in one place, and tape cassettes in another. Keep canceled checks in one place, and bills in another. Create a routine. Get yourself ready for school or work at the same time, in the same way, every day. Exercise, eat a balanced diet and get enough sleep.

Part V of this *Sourcebook* contains more information for adults with AD/HD, and teens with AD/HD will find further helpful information in Chapter 33.

What Treatments Are Available?

For decades, medications have been used to treat the symptoms of AD/HD. Three medications in the class of drugs known as stimulants seem to be the most effective in both children and adults. These are methylphenidate (Ritalin), dextroamphetamine (Dexedrine or Dextrostat), and pemoline (Cylert). For many people, these medicines dramatically reduce their hyperactivity and improve their ability to focus, work, and learn. The medications may also improve physical coordination, such as handwriting and ability in sports. Recent research by NIMH suggests that these medicines may also help children with an accompanying conduct disorder to control their impulsive, destructive behaviors.

Ritalin helped Henry focus on and complete tasks for the first time. Dexedrine helped Mark to sit quietly, focus his attention, and participate in class so he could learn. He also became less impulsive and aggressive. Along with these changes in his behavior, Mark began to make and keep friends.

Unfortunately, when people see such immediate improvement, they often think medication is all that's needed. But these medicines don't cure the disorder—they only temporarily control the symptoms. Although the drugs help people pay better attention and complete their work, they can't increase knowledge or improve academic skills. The drugs alone can't help people feel better about themselves or cope with problems. These require other kinds of treatment and support.

For lasting improvement, numerous clinicians recommend that medications should be used along with treatments that aid in these other areas. There are no quick cures. Many experts believe that the most significant, long-lasting gains appear when medication is combined with behavioral therapy, emotional counseling, and practical support. Some studies suggest that the combination of medicine and therapy may be more effective than drugs alone. NIMH is conducting a large study to check this.

Use of Stimulant Drugs

Stimulant drugs, such as Ritalin, Cylert, and Dexedrine, when used with medical supervision, are usually considered quite safe. Although they can be addictive to teenagers and adults if misused, these medications are not addictive in children. They seldom make children high or jittery. Nor do they sedate the child. Rather, the stimulants help children control their hyperactivity, inattention, and other behaviors.

Different doctors use the medications in slightly different ways. Cylert is available in one form, which naturally lasts 5 to 10 hours. Ritalin and Dexedrine come in short-term tablets that last about 3 hours, as well as longer-term preparations that last through the school day. The short-term dose is often more practical for children who need medication only during the school day or for special situations, like attending church or a prom, or studying for an important exam. The sustained-release dosage frees the child from the inconvenience or embarrassment of going to the office or school nurse every day for a pill. The doctor can help decide which preparation to use, and whether a child needs to take the medicine during school hours only or in the evenings and on weekends, too.

Nine out of 10 children improve on one of the three stimulant drugs. So if one doesn't help, the others should be tried. Usually a medication should be tried for a week to see if it helps. If necessary, however, the doctor will also try adjusting the dosage before switching to a different drug.

Other types of medication may be used if stimulants don't work or if the AD/HD occurs with another disorder. Antidepressants and

19

other medications may be used to help control accompanying depression or anxiety. In some cases, antihistamines may be tried. Clonidine, a drug normally used to treat hypertension, may be helpful in people with both AD/HD and Tourette's syndrome. Although stimulants tend to be more effective, clonidine may be tried when stimulants don't work or can't be used. Clonidine can be administered either by pill or by skin patch and has different side effects than stimulants. The doctor works closely with each patient to find the most appropriate medication.

Sometimes, a child's AD/HD symptoms seem to worsen, leading parents to wonder why. They can be assured that a drug that helps rarely stops working. However, they should work with the doctor to check that the child is getting the right dosage. Parents should also make sure that the child is actually getting the prescribed daily dosage at home or at school—it's easy to forget. They also need to know that new or exaggerated behaviors may also crop up when a child is under stress. The challenges that all children face, like changing schools or entering puberty, may be even more stressful for a child with AD/HD.

Some doctors recommend that children be taken off a medication now and then to see if the child still needs it. They recommend temporarily stopping the drug during school breaks and summer vacations, when focused attention and calm behavior are usually not as crucial. These drug holidays work well if the child can still participate at camp or other activities without medication. Children on medications should have regular checkups. Parents should also talk regularly with the child's teachers and doctor about how the child is doing. This is especially important when a medication is first started, re-started, or when the dosage is changed.

The Medication Debate

As useful as these drugs are, Ritalin and the other stimulants have sparked a great deal of controversy. Most doctors feel the potential side effects should be carefully weighed against the benefits before prescribing the drugs. While on these medications, some children may lose weight, have less appetite, and temporarily grow more slowly. Others may have problems falling asleep. Some doctors believe that stimulants may also make the symptoms of Tourette's syndrome worse, although recent research suggests this may not be true. Other doctors say if they carefully watch the child's height, weight, and overall development, the benefits of medication far outweigh the potential side effects. Side effects that do occur can often be handled by reducing the dosage. It's natural for parents to be concerned about whether taking a medicine is in their child's best interests. Parents need to be clear about the benefits and potential risks of using these drugs. The child's pediatrician or psychiatrist can provide advice and answer questions.

Another debate is whether Ritalin and other stimulant drugs are prescribed unnecessarily for too many children. Remember that many things, including anxiety, depression, allergies, seizures, or problems with the home or school environment can make children seem overactive, impulsive, or inattentive. Critics argue that many children who do not have a true attention disorder are medicated as a way to control their disruptive behaviors.

Medication and Self-Esteem

When a child's schoolwork and behavior improve soon after starting medication, the child, parents, and teachers tend to applaud the drug for causing the sudden change. But these changes are actually the child's own strengths and natural abilities coming out from behind a cloud. Giving credit to the medication can make the child feel incompetent. The medication only makes these changes possible. The child must supply the effort and ability. To help children feel good about themselves, parents and teachers need to praise the child, not the drug.

It's also important to help children and teenagers feel comfortable about a medication they must take every day. They may feel that because they take medicine they are different from their classmates or that there is something seriously wrong with them. C.H.A.D.D. (which stands for Children and Adults with Attention Deficit Disorders), a leading organization for people with attention disorders, suggests several ways that parents and teachers can help children view the medication in a positive way:

- Compare the pills to eyeglasses, braces, and allergy medications used by other children in their class. Explain that their medicine is simply a tool to help them focus and pay attention.

- Point out that they're lucky their problem can be helped. Encourage them to identify ways the medicine makes it easier to do things that are important to them, like make friends, succeed at school, and play.

Myths about Stimulant Medication

- Myth: Stimulants can lead to drug addiction later in life.

- Fact: Stimulants help many children focus and be more successful at school, home, and play. Avoiding negative experiences now may actually help prevent addictions and other emotional problems later.

- Myth: Responding well to a stimulant drug proves a person has AD/HD.

- Fact: Stimulants allow many people to focus and pay better attention, whether or not they have AD/HD. The improvement is just more noticeable in people with AD/HD.

- Myth: Medication should be stopped when the child reaches adolescence.

- Fact: Not so. About 80 percent of those who needed medication as children still need it as teenagers. Fifty percent need medication as adults.

Treatments to Help People with AD/HD and Their Families Learn to Cope

Life can be hard for children with AD/HD. They're the ones who are so often in trouble at school, can't finish a game, and lose friends. They may spend agonizing hours each night struggling to keep their mind on their homework, then forget to bring it to school. It's not easy coping with these frustrations day after day. Some children release their frustration by acting contrary, starting fights, or destroying property. Some turn the frustration into body ailments, like the child who gets a stomachache each day before school. Others hold their needs and fears inside, so that no one sees how badly they feel.

It's also difficult having a sister, brother, or classmate who gets angry, grabs your toys, and loses your things. Children who live with or share a classroom with a child who has AD/HD get frustrated, too. They may feel neglected as their parents or teachers try to cope with the hyperactive child. They may resent their brother or sister never finishing chores, or being pushed around by a classmate. They want to love their sibling and get along with their classmate, but sometimes it's so hard.

It's especially hard being the parent of a child who is full of un-controlled activity, leaves messes, throws tantrums, and doesn't lis-ten or follow instructions. Parents often feel powerless and at a loss. The usual methods of discipline, like reasoning and scolding, don't work with this child, because the child doesn't really choose to act in these ways. It's just that their self-control comes and goes. Out of sheer frustration, parents sometimes find themselves spanking, ridiculing, or screaming at the child, even though they know it's not appropri-ate. Their response leaves everyone more upset than before. Then they blame themselves for not being better parents. Once children are di-agnosed and receiving treatment, some of the emotional upset within the family may fade.

Medication can help to control some of the behavior problems that may have lead to family turmoil. But more often, there are other as-pects of the problem that medication can't touch. Even though AD/HD primarily affects a person's behavior, having the disorder has broad emotional repercussions. For some children, being scolded is the only attention they ever get. They have few experiences that build their sense of worth and competence. If they're hyperactive, they're often told they're bad and punished for being disruptive. If they are too dis-organized and unfocused to complete tasks, others may call them lazy. If they impulsively grab toys, butt in, or shove classmates, they may lose friends. And if they have a related conduct disorder, they may get in trouble at school or with the law. Facing the daily frustrations that can come with having AD/HD can make people fear that they are strange, abnormal, or stupid.

Often, the cycle of frustration, blame, and anger has gone on so long that it will take some time to undo. Both parents and their children may need special help to develop techniques for managing the pat-terns of behavior. In such cases, mental health professionals can coun-sel the child and the family, helping them to develop new skills, attitudes, and ways of relating to each other. In individual counsel-ing, the therapist helps children or adults with AD/HD learn to feel better about themselves. They learn to recognize that having a dis-ability does not reflect who they are as a person. The therapist can also help people with AD/HD identify and build on their strengths, cope with daily problems, and control their attention and aggression. In group counseling, people learn that they are not alone in their frus-tration and that others want to help. Sometimes only the individual with AD/HD needs counseling support. But in many cases, because the problem affects the family as well as the person with AD/HD, the entire family may need help. The therapist assists the family in finding better ways to handle the disruptive behaviors and promote change. If the child is young, most of the therapist's work is with the parents, teaching them techniques for coping with and improving their child's behavior.

Several intervention approaches are available and different therapists tend to prefer one approach or another. Knowing something about the various types of interventions makes it easier for families to choose a therapist that is right for their needs.

Psychotherapy works to help people with AD/HD to like and accept themselves despite their disorder. In psychotherapy, patients talk with the therapist about upsetting thoughts and feelings, explore self-defeating patterns of behavior, and learn alternative ways to handle their emotions. As they talk, the therapist tries to help them understand how they can change. However, people dealing with AD/HD usually want to gain control of their symptomatic behaviors more directly. If so, more direct kinds of intervention are needed.

Cognitive-behavioral therapy helps people work on immediate issues. Rather than helping people understand their feelings and actions, it supports them directly in changing their behavior. The support might be practical assistance, like helping Henry learn to think through tasks and organize his work. Or the support might be to encourage new behaviors by giving praise or rewards each time the person acts in the desired way. A cognitive-behavioral therapist might use such techniques to help a belligerent child like Mark learn to control his fighting, or an impulsive teenager like Lisa to think before she speaks.

Social skills training can also help children learn new behaviors. In social skills training, the therapist discusses and models appropriate behaviors like waiting for a turn, sharing toys, asking for help, or responding to teasing, then gives children a chance to practice. For example, a child might learn to read other people's facial expression and tone of voice, in order to respond more appropriately. Social skills training helped Lisa learn to join in group activities, make appropriate comments, and ask for help. A child like Mark might learn to see how his behavior affects others and develop new ways to respond when angry or pushed.

Support groups connect people who have common concerns. Many adults with AD/HD and parents of children with AD/HD find it useful to join a local or national support group. Many groups deal with issues of children's disorders, and even AD/HD specifically. Members of support groups share frustrations and successes, referrals to qualified specialists, and information about what works, as well as their hopes for themselves and their children. There is strength in numbers—and sharing experiences with others who have similar problems helps people know that they aren't alone.

Parenting skills training, offered by therapists or in special classes, gives parents tools and techniques for managing their child's behavior. One such technique is the use of time out when the child becomes too unruly or out of control. During time outs, the child is removed from the agitating situation and sits alone quietly for a short time to calm down. Parents may also be taught to give the child quality time each day, in which they share a pleasurable or relaxed activity. During this time together, the parent looks for opportunities to notice and point out what the child does well, and praise his or her strengths and abilities.

An effective way to modify a child's behavior is through a system of rewards and penalties. The parents (or teacher) identify a few desirable behaviors that they want to encourage in the child—such as asking for a toy instead of grabbing it, or completing a simple task. The child is told exactly what is expected in order to earn the reward. The child receives the reward when he performs the desired behavior and a mild penalty when he doesn't. A reward can be small, perhaps a token that can be exchanged for special privileges, but it should be something the child wants and is eager to earn. The penalty might be removal of a token or a brief time out. The goal, over time, is to help children learn to control their own behavior and to choose the more desired behavior. The technique works well with all children, although children with AD/HD may need more frequent rewards.

In addition, parents may learn to structure situations in ways that will allow their child to succeed. This may include allowing only one or two playmates at a time, so that their child doesn't get overstimulated. Or if their child has trouble completing tasks, they may learn to help the child divide a large task into small steps, then praise the child as each step is completed. Parents may also learn to use stress management methods, such as meditation, relaxation techniques, and exercise to increase their own tolerance for frustration, so that they can respond more calmly to their child's behavior.

Controversial Treatments

Understandably, parents who are eager to help their children want to explore every possible option. Many newly touted treatments sound reasonable. Many even come with glowing reports. A few are pure quackery. Some are even developed by reputable doctors or specialists—but when tested scientifically, cannot be proven to help.

Here are a few types of treatment that have not been scientifically shown to be effective in treating the majority of children or adults with AD/HD:

- biofeedback
- restricted diets
- allergy treatments
- medicines to correct problems in the inner ear
- megavitamins
- chiropractic adjustment and bone re-alignment
- treatment for yeast infection
- eye training
- special colored glasses

A few success stories can't substitute for scientific evidence. Until sound, scientific testing shows a treatment to be effective, families risk spending time, money, and hope on fads and false promises.

Sustaining Hope

Today, at age 14, Mark is doing much better in school. He channels his energy into sports and is a star player on the intramural football team. Although he still gets into fights now and then, a child psychologist is helping him learn to control his tantrums and frustration, and he is able to make and keep friends. His grandparents point to him with pride and say, "We knew he'd turn out just fine!"

Lisa is about to graduate from high school. She's better able to focus her attention and concentrate on her work, so that now her grades are quite good. Overcoming her depression and learning to like herself have also given her more confidence to develop friendships and try new things.

Lately, she has been working with the school guidance counselor to identify the right kind of job to look for after graduation. She hopes to find a career that will bypass her attention problems and make the best use of her assets and skills. She is more alert and focused and is considering trying college in a year or two. Her counselor reminds her that she's certainly smart enough.

These days, Henry is successful and happy in his job as a shoe salesman. The work allows him to move around throughout the day, and the appearance of new customers provides the variety he needs to help him stay focused. He recently completed a course in time management, and now keeps lists, organizes his work, and schedules his day. Now that he has harnessed his energy, his ability to think about several things at once allows him to be creative and productive.

He is proud that he and his wife have developed important parenting skills for working with their son, so that he, too, is doing better at home and at school. Henry is also pleased with his new ability to follow through on projects. In fact, he just finished making his son a beautiful wooden toy chest for his birthday.

Can AD/HD Be Outgrown or Cured?

Even though most people don't outgrow AD/HD, people do learn to adapt and live fulfilling lives. Mark, Lisa, and Henry are making good lives for themselves—not by being cured, but by developing their personal strengths. With effective combinations of medicine, new skills, and emotional support, people with AD/HD can develop ways to control their attention and minimize their disruptive behaviors. Like Henry, they may find that by structuring tasks and controlling their environment, they can achieve personal goals. Like Mark, they may learn to channel their excess energy into sports and other high energy activities. And like Lisa, they can identify career options that build on their strengths and abilities.

As they grow up, with appropriate help from parents and clinicians, children with AD/HD become better able to suppress their hyperactivity and to channel it into more socially acceptable behaviors, like physical exercise or fidgeting. And although we know that half of all children with AD/HD will still show signs of the problem into adulthood, we also know that the medications and therapy that help children also work for adults.

All people with AD/HD have natural talents and abilities that they can draw on to create fine lives and careers for themselves. In fact, many people with AD/HD even feel that their patterns of behavior give them unique, often unrecognized, advantages. People with AD/HD tend to be outgoing and ready for action. Because of their drive for excitement and stimulation, many become successful in business, sports, construction, and public speaking. Because of their ability to think about many things at once, many have won acclaim as artists and inventors. Many choose work that gives them freedom to move around and release excess energy. But some find ways to be effective in quieter, more sedentary careers. Sally, a computer programmer, found that she thinks best when she wears headphones to reduce distracting noises. Like Henry, some people strive to increase their organizational skills. Others who own their own business find it useful to hire support staff to provide day-to-day management.

What Hope Does Research Offer?

Although no immediate cure is in sight, a new understanding of AD/HD may be just over the horizon. Using a variety of research tools and methods, scientists are beginning to uncover new information on the role of the brain in AD/HD and effective treatments for the disorder Such research will ultimately result in improving the personal fulfillment and productivity of people with AD/HD.

For example, the use of new techniques like brain imaging to observe how the brain actually works is already providing new insights into the causes of AD/HD. Other research is seeking to identify conditions of pregnancy and early childhood that may cause or contribute to these differences in the brain. As the body of knowledge grows, scientists may someday learn how to prevent these differences or at least how to treat them.

NIMH and the U.S. Department of Education are cosponsoring a large national study—the first of its kind—to see which combinations of AD/HD treatment work best for different types of children. During this 5-year study, scientists at research clinics across the country will work together in gathering data to answer such questions as: Is combining stimulant medication with behavior modification more effective than either alone? Do boys and girls respond differently to treatment? How do family stresses, income, and environment affect the severity of AD/HD and long-term outcomes? How does needing medicine affect children's sense of competence, self-control, and self-esteem? As a result of such research, doctors and mental health specialists may someday know who benefits most from different types of treatment and be able to intervene more effectively.

NIMH grantees are also trying to determine if there are different varieties of attention deficit. With further study, researchers may find that AD/HD actually covers a number of different disorders, each with its own cluster of symptoms and treatment requirements. For example, scientists are exploring whether there are any critical differences between children with AD/HD who also have anxiety, depression, or conduct disorders and those who do not. Other researchers are studying slight physical differences that might distinguish one type of AD/HD from another. If clusters of differences can be found, scientists can begin to distinguish the treatment each type needs.

Other NIMH-sponsored research is examining the long-term outcome of AD/HD. How do children with AD/HD turn out, compared to brothers and sisters without the disorder? As adults, how do they handle their own children? Still other studies seek to better understand AD/HD in adults. Such studies give insights into what types of treatment or services make a difference in helping an AD/HD child grow into a caring parent and a well-functioning adult.

Animal studies are also adding to our knowledge of AD/HD in humans. Animal subjects make it possible to study some of the possible causes of AD/HD in ways that can't be studied in people. In addition, animal research allows the safety and effectiveness of experimental new drugs to be tested long before they can be given to humans. One NIH-sponsored team of scientists is studying dogs to learn how new stimulant drugs that are similar to Ritalin act on the brain. Piece by piece, through studies of humans and animals, scientists are beginning to understand the biological nature of attention disorders. New research is allowing us to better understand the inner workings of the brain as we continue to develop new medications and assess new forms of treatment.

As we learn more about what actually happens inside the brain, we approach a future where we can prevent certain brain and mental disorders, make valid diagnoses, and treat each effectively.

Chapter 2

Questions and Answers about AD/HD

What Is Attention Deficit Hyperactivity Disorder (AD/HD)?

AD/HD refers to a family of related chronic neurobiological disorders that interfere with an individual's capacity to regulate activity level (hyperactivity), inhibit behavior (impulsivity), and attend to tasks (inattention) in developmentally appropriate ways. The core symptoms of AD/HD include an inability to sustain attention and concentration, developmentally inappropriate levels of activity, distractibility, and impulsivity. Children with AD/HD have functional impairment across multiple settings including home, school, and peer relationships. AD/HD has also been shown to have long-term adverse effects on academic performance, vocational success, and social-emotional development. Children with AD/HD experience an inability to sit still and pay attention in class regardless of the negative consequences of such behavior. They experience peer rejection and engage in a broad array of disruptive behaviors. Their academic and social difficulties have far-reaching and long-term consequences. These children have higher injury rates. As they grow older, children with untreated AD/HD, in combination with conduct disorders, experience drug abuse, antisocial behavior, and injuries of all sorts. For many individuals, the impact of AD/HD continues into adulthood.

Excerpted from "Attention Deficit Hyperactivity Disorder (AD/HD)—Questions and Answers," National Institute of Mental Health (NIMH), 2000.

31

What Are the Symptoms of AD/HD?

Inattention. People who are inattentive have a hard time keeping their mind on one thing and may get bored with a task after only a few minutes. Focusing conscious, deliberate attention to organizing and completing routine tasks may be difficult.

Hyperactivity. People who are hyperactive always seem to be in motion. They can't sit still; they may dash around or talk incessantly. Sitting still through a lesson can be an impossible task. They may roam around the room, squirm in their seats, wiggle their feet, touch everything, or noisily tap a pencil. They may also feel intensely restless.

Impulsivity. People who are overly impulsive, seem unable to curb their immediate reactions or think before they act. As a result, they may blurt out answers to questions or inappropriate comments, or run into the street without looking. Their impulsivity may make it hard for them to wait for things they want or to take their turn in games. They may grab a toy from another child or hit when they are upset.

How Is AD/HD Diagnosed?

The diagnosis of AD/HD can be made reliably using well-tested diagnostic interview methods. Diagnosis is based on history and observable behaviors in the child's usual settings. Ideally, a health care practitioner making a diagnosis should include input from parents and teachers. The key elements include a thorough history covering the presenting symptoms, differential diagnosis, possible coexisting conditions, as well as medical, developmental, school, psychosocial, and family histories. It is helpful to determine what precipitated the request for evaluation and what approaches had been used in the past. As of yet, there is no independent test for AD/HD. This is not unique to AD/HD, but applies as well to most psychiatric disorders, including other disabling disorders such as schizophrenia and autism.

How Many Children Are Diagnosed with AD/HD?

AD/HD is the most commonly diagnosed disorder of childhood, estimated to affect 3 to 5 percent of school-age children, and occurring three times more often in boys than in girls. On average, about one child in every classroom in the United States needs help for this disorder.

Aren't There Various Types of AD/HD?

According to *DSM-IV*, the fourth and most recent edition of the *DSM* (short for the *Diagnostic and Statistical Manual of Mental Disorders*), while most individuals have symptoms of both inattention and hyperactivity-impulsivity, there are some individuals in whom one or another pattern is predominant (for at least the past 6 months).

How Are Schools Involved in Diagnosing, Assessing, and Treating AD/HD?

Physicians and parents should be aware that schools are federally mandated to perform an appropriate evaluation if a child is suspected of having a disability that impairs academic functioning. This policy was recently strengthened by regulations implementing the 1997 re-authorization of the Individuals with Disabilities Act (IDEA), which guarantees appropriate services and a public education to children with disabilities from ages 3 to 21. For the first time, IDEA specifically lists AD/HD as a qualifying condition for special education services. If the assessment performed by the school is inadequate or inappropriate, parents may request that an independent evaluation be conducted at the school's expense. Furthermore, some children with AD/HD qualify for special education services within the public schools, under the category of Other Health Impaired. In these cases, the special education teacher, school psychologist, school administrators, classroom teachers, along with parents, must assess the child's strengths and weaknesses and design an Individualized Education Program (IEP). These special education services for children with AD/HD are available though IDEA.

Is AD/HD Inherited?

Research shows that AD/HD tends to run in families, so there are likely to be genetic influences. Children who have AD/HD usually have at least one close relative who also has AD/HD. And at least one-third of all fathers who had AD/HD in their youth have children with AD/HD. Even more convincing of a possible genetic link is that when one twin of an identical twin pair has the disorder, the other is likely to have it too.

Is AD/HD on the Increase? If So, Why?

No one knows for sure whether the prevalence of AD/HD per se has risen, but it is very clear that the number of children identified with the disorder who obtain treatment has risen over the past decade. Some of this increased identification and increased treatment seeking is due in part to greater media interest, heightened consumer awareness, and the availability of effective treatments. A similar pattern is now being observed in other countries. Whether the frequency of the disorder itself has risen remains unknown, and needs to be studied.

Can AD/HD Be Seen in Brain Scans of Children with the Disorder?

Neuroimaging research has shown that the brains of children with AD/HD differ fairly consistently from those of children without the disorder in that several brain regions and structures (pre-frontal cortex, striatum, basal ganglia, and cerebellum) tend to be smaller. Overall brain size is generally 5% smaller in affected children than children without AD/HD. While this average difference is observed consistently, it is too small to be useful in making the diagnosis of AD/HD in a particular individual. In addition, there appears to be a link between a person's ability to pay continued attention and measures that reflect brain activity. In people with AD/HD, the brain areas that control attention appear to be less active, suggesting that a lower level of activity in some parts of the brain may be related to difficulties sustaining attention.

Can a Preschool Child Be Diagnosed with AD/HD?

The diagnosis of AD/HD in the preschool child is possible, but can be difficult and should be made cautiously by experts well trained in childhood neurobehavioral disorders. Developmental problems, especially language delays, and adjustment problems can sometimes imitate AD/HD. Treatment should focus on placement in a structured preschool with parent training and support. Stimulants can reduce oppositional behavior and improve mother-child interactions, but they are usually reserved for severe cases or when a child is unresponsive to environmental or behavioral interventions.

What Is the Impact of AD/HD on Children and Their Families?

Life can be hard for children with AD/HD. They're the ones who are so often in trouble at school, can't finish a game, and have trouble making friends. They may spend agonizing hours each night struggling to keep their mind on their homework, then forget to bring it to school. It is not easy coping with these frustrations day after day for children or their families. Family conflict can increase. In addition, problems with peers and friendships are often present in children with AD/HD. In adolescence, these children are at increased risk for motor vehicle accidents, tobacco use, early pregnancy, and lower educational attainment. When a child receives a diagnosis of AD/HD, parents need to think carefully about treatment choices. And when they pursue treatment for their children, families face high out-of-pocket expenses because treatment for AD/HD and other mental illnesses is often not covered by insurance policies. School programs to help children with problems often connected to AD/HD (social skills and behavior training) are not available in many schools. In addition, not all children with AD/HD qualify for special education services. All of this leads to children who do not receive proper and adequate treatment. To overcome these barriers, parents may want to look for school-based programs that have a team approach involving parents, teachers, school psychologists, other mental health specialists, and physicians.

Aren't There Nutritional Treatments for AD/HD?

Many parents have exhausted nutritional approaches, such as eliminating sugar from the diet, before they seek medical attention. However, there are no well-established nutritional interventions that have been consistently demonstrated to be efficacious for assisting the great majority of children with AD/HD. A small body of research has suggested that some children may benefit from these interventions, but delaying the implementation of well-established, effective interventions while engaged in the search for unknown, generally unproven allergens, is likely to be harmful for many children.

What Are Behavioral Treatments?

There are various forms of behavioral interventions used for children with AD/HD, including psychotherapy, cognitive-behavioral therapy, social skills training, support groups, and parent and educator skills training. An example of very intensive behavior therapy was used in the NIMH Multimodal Treatment Study of Children with AD/HD (MTA), which involved the child's teacher, the family, and participation in an all-day, 8-week summer camp. The consulting therapist worked with teachers to develop behavior management strategies that address behavioral problems interfering with class-room behavior and academic performance. A trained classroom aide worked with the child for 12 weeks in his or her classroom, to provide support and reinforcement for appropriate, on-task behavior. Parents met with the therapist alone and in small groups to learn approaches for handling problems at home and school. The summer day camp was aimed at improving social behavior, academic work, and sports skills.

How Often Are Stimulant Prescriptions Used?

Data from 1995 show that physicians treating children and adolescents wrote six million prescriptions for stimulant medications—methylphenidate (Ritalin) and dextroamphetamine (Dexedrine). Of all the drugs used to treat psychiatric disorders in children, stimulant medications are the most thoroughly studied.

Isn't Stimulant Use on the Increase?

Stimulant use in the United States has increased substantially over the last 25 years. A recent study saw a 2.5-fold increase in methylphenidate between 1990 and 1995. This increase appears to be largely related to an increased duration of treatment, and more girls, adolescents, adults, and inattentive individuals (in addition to those individuals with both hyperactivity and inattentiveness/attention deficit) receiving treatment.

Are There Differences in Stimulant Use Across Racial and Ethnic Groups?

There are significant differences in access to mental health services between children of different racial groups; and, consequently, there are differences in medication use. In particular, African American children are much less likely than Caucasian children to receive psychotropic medications, including stimulants, for treatment of mental disorders.

Why Are Stimulants Used When the Problem Is Overactivity?

The answer to this question is not well established, but one theory suggests that AD/HD is related to difficulties in inhibiting responses to internal and external stimuli. Evidence to date suggests that those areas of the brain thought to be involved in planning, foresight, weighing of alternative responses, and inhibiting actions when alternative solutions might be considered, are underaroused in persons with AD/HD. Stimulant medication may work on these same areas of the brain, increasing neural activity to more normal levels. More research is needed, however, to firmly establish the mechanisms of action of the stimulants.

Wasn't There a Large Conference Held at NIH on AD/HD Recently?

In 1998, the NIH held a two-day Consensus Conference on AD/HD, bringing together national and international experts, as well as representatives from the public. The Consensus statement is now available at http://odp.od.nih.gov/consensus/cons/110/110_statement.htm.

What Are the Future Research Directions for AD/HD?

Continued research on AD/HD is needed from many perspectives. The societal impact of AD/HD needs to be determined. Studies in this regard include (1) strategies for implementing effective medication management or combination therapies in different schools and pediatric healthcare systems; (2) the nature and severity of the impact on adults with AD/HD beyond the age of 20, as well as their families; and (3) determination of the use of mental health services related to diagnosis and care of persons with AD/HD. Additional studies are needed to improve communication across educational and health care settings to ensure more systematized treatment strategies. Basic research is also needed to better define the behavioral and cognitive components that underpin AD/HD, not just in children with AD/HD, but also in unaffected individuals. This research should include (1) studies on cognitive development, cognitive and attentional processing, impulse control, and attention/inattention; (2) studies of prevention/early intervention strategies that target known risk factors that may lead to later AD/HD; and (3) brain imaging studies before the initiation of medication and following the individual through young adulthood and middle age. Finally, further research should be conducted on the comorbid (coexisting) conditions present in both childhood and adult AD/HD, and treatment implications.

Chapter 3

Distinguishing AD/HD from Other Conditions

Chapter Contents

Section 3.1

AD/HD and Other Conditions

"Distinguishing AD/HD from Other Conditions," by Kathy Bishop, a medical writer in Ann Arbor, Michigan, © 2002 Omnigraphics, Inc.

In the last few years, attention deficit/hyperactivity disorder (AD/HD) has received a lot of attention in the media. As a result, parents, teachers, and even daycare providers have become more aware of AD/HD. Just because a child is not doing well in school, however, does not mean that the problem is AD/HD. Many of the symptoms that first cause a parent or teacher to consider AD/HD are also signs of other problems. Any child suspected of having AD/HD should be evaluated by an appropriate physician.

Many parents may feel embarrassed by having a child who is diagnosed with AD/HD. They may feel as if it is somehow their fault. Others may feel relieved knowing that the child has a real problem and is not just a troublemaker or a bad student. All parents should remember that AD/HD, and the other problems discussed here, have known treatments—but treatment must begin with an accurate diagnosis.

It is important to work with your child's doctor in order to decide whether a diagnosis of AD/HD is right for your child. You may want to provide reports from school, a journal of your child's behavior at home, and a list of any medicines that the child is taking. Give this information to your doctor and express all of your concerns. These details will help your doctor make a correct diagnosis.

Attention Deficit Disorder, or Just a Normal Kid?

A child who has trouble sitting still in class or who does not behave well in the classroom will often prompt a phone call home. Often, since AD/HD symptoms occur in more than one situation, the problem has already been noticed. Kids who do fine at home, but have problems only at school may have difficulties other than AD/HD. The American Academy of Pediatrics (AAP) now recommends that any child between the ages of 6-12 who does not pay attention well, is hyperactive or impulsive, is not doing as well as other children in school, or has other behavior problems should be tested for AD/HD.

A doctor will take information from parents and teachers and will also check the child for other conditions. Possibilities include other disorders that look like AD/HD but are actually something else and require other treatments, or other conditions that are coexisting—this means that the child has AD/HD but another condition is also present and must be treated.

Might Something Else Be Going on?

All kids have times when they are hyperactive, talk too much, don't listen, or seem to not be paying attention. Once you have decided that your child's behavior seems excessive or unusual for his or her age, a number of things can be done to figure out what is happening. Your doctor will want to know when the symptoms started so that they can be compared to how a normal child the same age should behave. Many other conditions share some of the same symptoms as AD/HD. For some, simple diagnostic tests can be used. Others may require evaluation by a specialist, such as a mental health expert. Since there is no single test for AD/HD, diagnosis often involves ruling out other things.

Lead Poisoning: A child who has lead poisoning may have a short attention span, hyperactivity, problems with reading and learning, and hearing loss. A child with these problems may act like a child with AD/HD. If you think that your child may have lead poisoning, make sure you tell your doctor since a simple blood test can detect it.

Learning Disabilities or Giftedness: The symptoms that commonly lead a teacher to ask that a child be tested for AD/HD are the inability to sit still in a classroom, difficulty paying attention, being easily distracted, and bothering other children. These symptoms may also be noticed in a child with a learning disability whose frustration with trying to learn results in acting out at school. At the same time, a child who is intellectually gifted may seem inattentive in class. Because the child is not challenged by schoolwork and is bored, he or she can fall into patterns of daydreaming and distraction which can be confused with the signs of AD/HD. Appropriate testing makes it possible for a parent or teacher to know the difference between a child with AD/HD and a child who either has a learning disability or who is gifted.

Hearing or Vision Loss: Hearing and vision screening may also be needed because the inability to hear a teacher or see the chalkboard may cause a child to act poorly in school.

Reaction to Medication: Some medicines, including many that are sold over the counter can cause a child to be jittery and unable to pay attention. These include some common cold medications. Other medicines may cause sleeping problems that will lead to AD/HD-like symptoms during the day. Sleeping problems may cause a child to seem disorganized and lack attention to detail in schoolwork, or be irritable and unable to concentrate.

Hypothyroidism and Anemia: Children who have a condition called hypothyroidism, meaning that the thyroid gland is not working right, may have mood swings, be depressed, or have visual problems which can look a lot like AD/HD. Anemia, a condition of having too little iron in the blood, can result in memory loss and mental confusion, which can frustrate a child and cause him to act poorly—much like a child with AD/HD.

Tic Disorders: Tic disorders, including Tourette's syndrome, may cause a child to act in an erratic way that can be confused with AD/HD. Certain seizure disorders and some cases of mental retardation may also be similar. If you are concerned about one of these conditions it is very important to bring it up with your doctor.

Mental Illness: There are many mental illnesses that can occur during childhood with symptoms similar to the signs of AD/HD. It is important to let your doctor know if your child has recently been under stress or suffered a traumatic event. A child with an adjustment disorder may respond to a stressful situation by becoming depressed, anxious, angry, aggressive, or by having temper tantrums. Even if nothing stressful has happened, it is possible that another mental illness, such as an affective disorder (like depression), a personality disorder, or obsessive-compulsive disorder is causing a child's symptoms. Your doctor may suggest that your child see a mental health professional in order to rule out a mental illness.

Common Coexisting Conditions

Oppositional Defiant and Conduct Disorders: The most common mental problems that occur along with AD/HD are called oppositional defiant and conduct disorders. The AAP estimates that as many as 35% of children who have AD/HD also have one of these types of disorders. Although they may also occur without AD/HD being present, AD/HD is often initially suspected.

Children with conduct disorders do things that violate the rights of other people or that are not socially acceptable. These actions repeat over time and are things that are not usual for a child's age. A child with a conduct disorder will be a rule breaker and may destroy property that does not belong to him.

Oppositional defiant disorder is a less severe condition in which a child is hostile toward parents or teachers, may annoy other people on purpose, and loses his temper easily. Sometimes a person with oppositional defiant disorder will have symptoms that later become more serious and are then diagnosed as a conduct disorder. Children with conduct disorders have more problems when they grow up than those who have AD/HD alone. Treating the disorder may help avoid this, and so it is important that both AD/HD and any other disorder be correctly diagnosed.

Because these problems occur in so many children with AD/HD additional information about them is provided at the end of this chapter.

Mood Disorders: Mood disorders (also called affective disorders), such as depression, are found in about 18% children with AD/HD. Because it often runs in families, your doctor may ask you about other members of your family who may have had problems with depression. Diagnosing depression is important because different medications will be used for a child who has AD/HD and depression. A child who is depressed may not be hyperactive but may have other problems with listening, paying attention, not caring about details, and being disorganized. A child who is sad for two weeks or more, who is withdrawing from social situations, or who is having trouble eating or sleeping should be checked for depression. This screening may be done by a family physician, pediatrician, or mental health specialist. Other mood disorders, including bipolar disorder, may also occur with AD/HD. A bipolar child may have the symptoms of depression but may also have times when he is hyperactive with extremely high energy, much like a child with AD/HD.

Anxiety Disorders: About 25% of children with AD/HD also have anxiety disorders. These children feel worried or afraid. The feelings are so serious that it becomes difficult for the child to live a normal life. Often the feelings will result in physical symptoms including a faster pulse, sweating, or stomach problems like nausea or diarrhea. Anxiety disorders can be treated with counseling and/or drug therapy.

Learning Disabilities: Specific learning disabilities may also result in many of the behaviors observed at school that cause a teacher to wonder if a child has AD/HD. While learning disabilities such as dyslexia may be mistaken for AD/HD, they also may occur along with AD/HD. Learning disabilities make it hard for a child to master specific skills like math or reading. While AD/HD may be treated in order to control the behavioral issues a child faces, the learning disability must also be treated so that the child can succeed in school.

Section 3.2

More Information on Conduct Disorders

From "Oppositional Defiant Disorder (ODD) versus Conduct Disorder," by Kathi Colton. © 2001 Kathi Colton; Ms. Colton is the owner of the website *Teens with Problems* (www.teenswithproblems.com). Reprinted with permission.

According to *DSM-IV* (*Diagnostic and Statistical Manual of Mental Disorders, 4th Edition*) criteria, conduct disorder may be diagnosed when a child seriously misbehaves with aggressive or nonaggressive behaviors against people, animals or property that may be characterized as belligerent, destructive, threatening, physically cruel, deceitful, disobedient, or dishonest. This may include stealing, intentional injury, and forced sexual activity. Keep in mind that this behavior disorder consists of a pattern of severe, repetitive acting-out behavior and not of an isolated incident here and there.

As stated, conduct disorder is a repetitive and persistent pattern of behavior in which the basic rights of others, or major rules and values of society are violated, as shown by the presence of three (or more) of the following behavior patterns in the past 12 months, with at least one behavior pattern present in the past six months.

- Aggression to people and animals:
    1. Often bullies, threatens, or intimidates others.
    2. Often initiates physical fights.
    3. Has used a weapon that can cause serious physical harm to others (for example, a bat, brick, broken bottle, knife, gun).
    4. Has been physically cruel to people.

5. Has been physically cruel to animals.
6. Has stolen while confronting a victim (for example, mugging, purse snatching, extortion, armed robbery.
7. Has forced someone into sexual activity.

- Destruction of property:
  1. Has deliberately engaged in fire setting with the intention of causing serious damage.
  2. Has deliberately destroyed others' property (other than by fire setting).

- Deceitfulness or theft:
  1. Has broken into someone else's house, building, or car.
  2. Often lies to obtain goods or favors or to avoid obligations (in other words, cons others).
  3. Has stolen items of nontrivial value without confronting a victim (for example, shoplifting, but without breaking and entering; forgery).

- Serious violations of rules:
  1. Often stays out at night despite parental prohibitions, beginning before age 13 years.
  2. Has run away from home overnight at least twice while living in parental or parental surrogate home (or once without returning for a lengthy period).
  3. Is often truant from school, beginning before age 13 years.

According to *DSM-IV*, in order to diagnosis conduct disorder in a teen, the disturbance in behavior must be causing significant problems in that person's life, including at school, with friends and family, and on the job. In other words, if a child gets into serious trouble one time, learns from the experience and never does it again, he or she probably does not have a conduct disorder. Conduct disorder may be diagnosed in an individual 18 years or older if that individual displays some of the previously listed but does not appear to have behaviors normally found in Antisocial Personality Disorder.

According to *Merck Manual*, the onset of conduct disorder is usually in late childhood or early adolescence. Conduct disorder appears to be much more common in boys than girls. Children with conduct disorder seem to have an inability to correctly read other people, and instead will misunderstand the intentions of others, many times believing that people are threatening them or putting them down, when this is not really the case. They tend to react to these supposed threats or put-downs in an aggressive manner with little show of feeling or remorse. They do not tolerate frustration well. They also tend to generally behave in a reckless manner, without regard for normal safety issues.

Kids with conduct disorder frequently will threaten suicide, and these threats should generally be taken seriously. Boys with conduct disorder will be more inclined to fight, steal and participate in acts of vandalism, such as fire setting. Girls with conduct disorder are more likely to lie, run away and be involved in severe sexual acting-out behavior, including prostitution. Both boys and girls with conduct disorder are at an extremely high risk of substance abuse along with severe difficulties getting along in school.

What Are the Signs of Oppositional Defiant Disorder (ODD)?

According to the *DSM-IV*, if a child's problem behaviors do not meet the criteria for Conduct Disorder, but involve a pattern of defiant, angry, antagonistic, hostile, irritable, or vindictive behavior, Oppositional Defiant Disorder may be diagnosed. These children may blame others for their problems.

Oppositional Defiant Disorder is a pattern of negativistic, hostile, and defiant behavior lasting at least six months, during which four (or more) of the following are present:

1. Often loses temper.
2. Often argues with adults.
3. Often actively defies or refuses to comply with adults' requests or rules.
4. Often deliberately annoys people.
5. Often blames others for his or her mistakes or misbehavior.
6. Is often touchy or easily annoyed by others.
7. Is often angry and resentful.
8. Is often spiteful or vindictive.

It is important to note that a counselor or therapist will consider a diagnosis of oppositional defiant disorder only if the behavior occurs more frequently than is typically observed in individuals of comparable age and developmental level. In other words, as teens are growing and learning, they will sometimes do some very ill-advised things that can cause them problems, both legal and in school. However, if this behavior does not repeat itself and is a one-time event, then a behavior disorder is probably not present.

The disturbance in behavior must be causing significant problems in school, in relationships with family and friends, and in the workplace. ODD will not be diagnosed if the behaviors are suspected to be occurring exclusively during the course of another psychotic or mood disorder, such as bipolar disorder.

Kids with oppositional defiant disorder will show some of the same behaviors as those listed above for conduct disorder, including being very negative, angry and defiant. However, with ODD, one does not generally see the mean behavior that is present in conduct disorder, such as cruelty to animals.

How Does the Therapist Find a Diagnosis for My Teen?

As you can see from the previously listed, there is a large overlap between conduct disorder and oppositional defiant disorder, with similarities in both disorders that include defiance, rebellion against authority, school problems, disobedience, anger and resentment, and bullying of brothers and sisters. In order to differentiate between the two, one of the things a therapist will generally look at is how a teen treats animals. Is he or she mean or cruel to the family pets or kind to them? Another area that is looked at is whether or not there have been legal problems, what those legal problems were, and if they are recurring or one-time events. Many young teens experiment with shoplifting and end up getting caught, but this does not mean they have either a conduct disorder or ODD. However, if they keep doing it and are picked up several times, then it is probably safe to assume that there is a more serious behavior problem going on. Setting fires and stealing behaviors, such as breaking into cars and stealing stereos, are more serious offenses that would generally tend to indicate a conduct disorder rather than oppositional defiant disorder.

To further complicate the process of making a diagnosis, some research is now beginning to show that conduct disorder may be a component of childhood bipolar disorder and there is a possibility that the behaviors that are attributed to conduct disorder or ODD are perhaps motivated by a mood disorder. Bipolar disorder, in simplest terms, is a chemical imbalance in the brain that causes major mood swings, from elation to severe depression, which can many times be helped greatly with the right medication. Other research shows that teens with attention deficit hyperactivity disorder (AD/HD) can present in a very similar way as conduct disorder and ODD, and may very well go hand in hand with both oppositional defiant disorder and conduct disorder. Therefore, both bipolar disorder and AD/HD are processes that the therapist must take into consideration when attempting to diagnose a teen who is displaying the behaviors listed above.

According to *Merck Manual*, more than half of teens with conduct disorder quit exhibiting these behaviors in early adulthood, but about one third of the cases persist, developing into antisocial personality disorder or other mood or anxiety disorders. Children with conduct disorder tend to have a higher than expected incidence of medical and psychiatric illness at follow-up.

Treatment of Conduct Disorder and ODD

Treatment of all medical, neurological and psychiatric conditions by the appropriate caregivers can improve self-esteem and self-control. These kids will sometimes respond favorably to a very structured approach with clearly stated rules and immediate consequences for breaking rules. A home rules contract, which is set up with the help of the therapist and enforced uniformly by all caregivers, can clarify rules and consequences and provide structure for the teen. However, in some cases, only separation from the current environment with external discipline and consistent behavior management and modification offer hope for success.

In the event that problems have become severe enough to require more intensive behavior modification in a residential setting, the World Wide Association of Specialty Programs six-level behavior modification programs can offer hope to parents who are dealing with teens diagnosed with either conduct disorder or oppositional defiant disorder.

For more information on the World Wide Association of Specialty Programs contact:

World Wide Association of Specialty Programs
231 North Mall Drive, Suite T-101
St. George, Utah 84790
Tel: 435-656-2313
Teen Help: 800-840-5704
Website: http://www.wwasp.com

Chapter 4

Is AD/HD Considered a Learning Disability?

Attention disorders, with or without hyperactivity, are not considered learning disabilities in themselves. However, because attention problems can seriously interfere with school performance, they often accompany academic skills disorders.

Nearly 4 million school-age children have learning disabilities. Of these, at least 20 percent have a type of disorder that leaves them unable to focus their attention.

Some children and adults who have attention disorders appear to daydream excessively. And once you get their attention, they're often easily distracted. Susan, for example, tends to mentally drift off into a world of her own. Children like Susan may have a number of learning difficulties. If, like Susan, they are quiet and don't cause problems, their problems may go unnoticed. They may be passed along from grade to grade, without getting the special assistance they need.

In a large proportion of affected children—mostly boys—the attention deficit is accompanied by hyperactivity. Dennis is an example of a person with attention deficit hyperactivity disorder—AD/HD. They act impulsively, running into traffic or toppling desks. Like young Dennis, who jumped on the sofa to exhaustion, hyperactive children can't sit still. They blurt out answers and interrupt. In games, they can't wait their turn. These children's problems are usually hard to miss. Because of their constant motion and explosive energy, hyperactive children often get into trouble with parents, teachers, and peers.

Excerpted from "Learning Disabilities," National Institute of Mental Health (NIMH), NIH Pub. No. 93-3611, updated 1999.

By adolescence, physical hyperactivity usually subsides into fidgeting and restlessness. But the problems with attention and concentration often continue into adulthood. At work, adults with AD/HD often have trouble organizing tasks or completing their work. They don't seem to listen to or follow directions. Their work may be messy and appear careless.

What Is a Learning Disability?

Unlike other disabilities, such as paralysis or blindness, a learning disability (LD) is a hidden handicap. A learning disability doesn't disfigure or leave visible signs that would invite others to be understanding or offer support.

LD is a disorder that affects people's ability to either interpret what they see and hear or to link information from different parts of the brain. These limitations can show up in many ways—as specific difficulties with spoken and written language, coordination, self-control, or attention. Such difficulties extend to schoolwork and can impede learning to read or write, or to do math.

Learning disabilities can be lifelong conditions that, in some cases, affect many parts of a person's life: school or work, daily routines, family life, and sometimes even friendships and play. In some people, many overlapping learning disabilities may be apparent. Other people may have a single, isolated learning problem that has little impact on other areas of their lives.

What Are the Types of Learning Disabilities?

Learning disability is not a diagnosis in the same sense as chickenpox or mumps. Chickenpox and mumps imply a single, known cause with a predictable set of symptoms. Rather, LD is a broad term that covers a pool of possible causes, symptoms, treatments, and outcomes. Partly because learning disabilities can show up in so many forms, it is difficult to diagnose or to pinpoint the causes. And no one knows of a pill or remedy that will cure them.

Not all learning problems are necessarily learning disabilities. Many children are simply slower in developing certain skills. Because children show natural differences in their rate of development, sometimes what seems to be a learning disability may simply be a delay in maturation. To be diagnosed as a learning disability, specific criteria must be met.

The criteria and characteristics for diagnosing learning disabilities appear in a reference book called the *DSM* (short for the *Diagnostic and Statistical Manual of Mental Disorders*). The *DSM* diagnosis is commonly used when applying for health insurance coverage of diagnostic and treatment services.

Learning disabilities can be divided into three broad categories:

- Developmental speech and language disorders

- Academic skills disorders

- Other, a catch-all that includes certain coordination disorders and learning handicaps not covered by the other terms

Each of these categories includes a number of more specific disorders.

Developmental Speech and Language Disorders

Speech and language problems are often the earliest indicators of a learning disability. People with developmental speech and language disorders have difficulty producing speech sounds, using spoken language to communicate, or understanding what other people say. Depending on the problem, the specific diagnosis may be:

- Developmental articulation disorder

- Developmental expressive language disorder

- Developmental receptive language disorder

Developmental Articulation Disorder—Children with this disorder may have trouble controlling their rate of speech. Or they may lag behind playmates in learning to make speech sounds. For example, Wallace at age 6 still said "wabbit" instead of "rabbit" and "thwim" for "swim." Developmental articulation disorders are common. They appear in at least 10 percent of children younger than age 8. Fortunately, articulation disorders can often be outgrown or successfully treated with speech therapy.

Developmental Expressive Language Disorder—Some children with language impairments have problems expressing themselves in speech. Their disorder is called, therefore, a developmental expressive language disorder. Susan, who often calls objects by the wrong names, has an expressive language disorder. Of course, an expressive language disorder can take other forms. A 4-year-old who speaks only in two-word phrases and a 6-year-old who can't answer simple questions also have an expressive language disability.

Developmental Receptive Language Disorder—Some people have trouble understanding certain aspects of speech. It's as if their brains are set to a different frequency and the reception is poor. There's the toddler who doesn't respond to his name, a preschooler who hands you a bell when you asked for a ball, or the worker who consistently can't follow simple directions. Their hearing is fine, but they can't make sense of certain sounds, words, or sentences they hear. They may even seem inattentive. These people have a receptive language disorder. Because using and understanding speech are strongly related, many people with receptive language disorders also have an expressive language disability.

Of course, in preschoolers, some misuse of sounds, words, or grammar is a normal part of learning to speak. It's only when these problems persist that there is any cause for concern.

Academic Skills Disorders

Students with academic skills disorders are often years behind their classmates in developing reading, writing, or arithmetic skills. The diagnoses in this category include:

- Developmental reading disorder

- Developmental writing disorder

- Developmental arithmetic disorder

Developmental Reading Disorder—This type of disorder, also known as dyslexia, is quite widespread. In fact, reading disabilities affect 2 to 8 percent of elementary school children.

When you think of what is involved in the three R's—reading, 'riting, and 'rithmetic—it's astounding that most of us do learn them. Consider that to read, you must simultaneously:

- Focus attention on the printed marks and control eye movements across the page

- Recognize the sounds associated with letters

- Understand words and grammar

- Build ideas and images

- Compare new ideas to what you already know

- Store ideas in memory

Such mental juggling requires a rich, intact network of nerve cells that connect the brain's centers of vision, language, and memory.

A person can have problems in any of the tasks involved in reading. However, scientists found that a significant number of people with dyslexia share an inability to distinguish or separate the sounds in spoken words. Dennis, for example, can't identify the word "bat" by sounding out the individual letters, b-a-t. Other children with dyslexia may have trouble with rhyming games, such as rhyming "cat" with "bat." Yet scientists have found these skills fundamental to learning to read. Fortunately, remedial reading specialists have developed techniques that can help many children with dyslexia acquire these skills.

However, there is more to reading than recognizing words. If the brain is unable to form images or relate new ideas to those stored in memory, the reader can't understand or remember the new concepts. So other types of reading disabilities can appear in the upper grades when the focus of reading shifts from word identification to comprehension.

Developmental Writing Disorder—Writing, too, involves several brain areas and functions. The brain networks for vocabulary, grammar, hand movement, and memory must all be in good working order. So a developmental writing disorder may result from problems in any of these areas. For example, Dennis, who was unable to distinguish the sequence of sounds in a word, had problems with spelling. A child with a writing disability, particularly an expressive language disorder, might be unable to compose complete, grammatical sentences.

Developmental Arithmetic Disorder—If you doubt that arithmetic is a complex process, think of the steps you take to solve this simple problem: 25 divided by 3 equals?

Arithmetic involves recognizing numbers and symbols, memorizing facts such as the multiplication table, aligning numbers, and understanding abstract concepts like place value and fractions. Any of these may be difficult for children with developmental arithmetic disorders. Problems with numbers or basic concepts are likely to show up early. Disabilities that appear in the later grades are more often tied to problems in reasoning.

Many aspects of speaking, listening, reading, writing, and arithmetic overlap and build on the same brain capabilities. So it's not surprising that people can be diagnosed as having more than one area of learning disability. For example, the ability to understand language underlies learning to speak. Therefore, any disorder that hinders the ability to understand language will also interfere with the development of speech, which in turn hinders learning to read and write. A single gap in the brain's operation can disrupt many types of activity.

Other Learning Disabilities

The *DSM* also lists additional categories, such as motor skills disorders and specific developmental disorders not otherwise specified. These diagnoses include delays in acquiring language, academic, and motor skills that can affect the ability to learn, but do not meet the criteria for a specific learning disability. Also included are coordination disorders that can lead to poor penmanship, as well as certain spelling and memory disorders.

Chapter 5

Ways of Thinking about AD/HD

At times it seems as though AD/HD has burst onto the scene as a major concern in the lives of a multitude of children and the adults who love and work with them. According to Dr. Dan Amen of The Amen Clinic in Fairfield, California, AD/HD is the most common learning problem among children and adolescents, affecting more than 17 million Americans—a neurological problem that, if left unaddressed, has serious learning, social, and emotional consequences. Though commonly regarded as a diagnosis attached to children and adolescents, AD/HD also occurs in adults.

As sometimes happens with such issues, confusion exists around causes and treatment. Clearly we all don't have to speak in one voice— indeed different opinions and experiences can lead to a useful and productive discussion—but too many voices can create frustration and lack of direction for families and teachers. There are things that do work with AD/HD and things that can bring relief to those struggling with the disruption this disorder can bring into their lives.

A few basic facts about AD/HD. A diagnosis of AD/HD is not a diagnosis for chaos. It does signal certain challenges to be faced. Strange as it may seem, brain studies reveal that the individual with AD/HD

From "Ways of Thinking about AD/HD," by Joyce Sousa, MA/LCPC. This article originally appeared in the June 1998 issue of *NPIN Parent News*, published monthly by the ERIC Clearinghouse on Elementary and Early Childhood Education, University of Illinois at Urbana-Champaign, Children's Research Center, 51 Gerty Drive, Champaign, IL 61820-7469, and funded by the Office of Educational Research and Improvement, U.S. Department of Education.

experiences a decrease in brain activity in the frontal lobes in response to intellectual exercise. The more this individual tries to concentrate, the worse it gets. To compensate or correct this uncomfortable state of mind, the individual seeks stimulation. This can be in the form of humming, increased activity level, or causing turmoil. Others repeatedly get upset with AD/HD children even though there seems to be no positive outcome for this behavior. A common fallacy is that children with AD/HD outgrow this disorder. This is not true. Though the hyperactivity may lessen as a component for most individuals, impulsivity, distractibility, and short attention span remain into adulthood. Imagine, since there is a strong hereditary factor in AD/HD, how difficult it would be for an adult with these symptoms to parent an AD/HD child. Additional symptoms of adult AD/HD are poor organization, procrastination, and trouble listening to directions.

These adults' lives are often cluttered with missed appointments, lost items, anger, and lack of stability in employment, as well as financial difficulties. More serious problems are often present such as substance abuse and frequent traffic violations. A major difficulty is that this reads like a list of irresponsible behaviors, and we think of these behaviors as willful activities. Irresponsible behavior certainly can coexist with AD/HD. It may indeed develop quite easily if inappropriate structure and inappropriate demands lead to excuse making and lack of follow-through. Those working and living with individuals diagnosed with AD/HD will be able to hold these individuals accountable with more confidence and consistency when expectations are in line with capabilities. It is particularly important to have expectations and accountability; the expectations need to be appropriate, and the consequences consistent.

Treatment

Medication can be a helpful part of the treatment and ought to be explored. Different medications, different doses, and different administration schedules are worth experimenting with until the most effective combination is found. But medication, if used, is only a part of the treatment. Another important component of treatment is providing structure. To help understand this, we can frame it in the following manner. We would never think of taking our children to school, dropping them off, and leaving them to spend six to eight hours in an unstructured setting.

What we have come to think of as appropriate structure to help a child without AD/HD manage his/her time and activities and promote optimal learning and social development needs to be adjusted for children with AD/HD. We can apply the same principle but in smaller increments of time and with more frequent adult direction. If a 5-year-old needs more structure than a 7-year-old who needs more than a 12-year-old, an AD/HD child needs this even more.

Structure

Imagining a continuum of the amount of structure needed to promote self-efficacy helps us to be more effective in our response. Instead, we tend to frame the problems of AD/HD children as deviant. We create another category. It is important to recognize this because it affects how we think about our response and the help we design. Much as we would not expect a 6-year-old to handle constructively an entire day undirected, let alone punish him/her for not doing so, a youngster with AD/HD may need help getting productively through an hour. Again, much as we would not expect an 8-year-old to follow through a series of successive steps to achieve a distant goal, children with AD/HD need larger tasks broken down into smaller units in order to make their way through complicated procedures. A history report on Abraham Lincoln may seem a completely overwhelming undertaking for an AD/HD child. But given a series of successive small steps, this youngster is better able to manage the project successfully.

If we understand this as an expectable need—filling different structural requirements—we can more easily do our part to help. Our expectations will be more appropriate and accountability can then be a meaningful part of the learning process of the AD/HD child, as it is for all children.

Chapter 6

Myths about AD/HD

Myth #1: AD/HD is a phantom disorder.

FACT: The existence of a neurobiological disorder is not an issue to be decided by the media through public debate, but rather as a matter of scientific research. Scientific studies spanning 95 years summarized in the professional writings of Dr. Russell Barkley, Dr. Sam Goldstein, and others have consistently identified a group of individuals who have trouble with concentration, impulse control, and in some cases, hyperactivity. Although the name given to this group of individuals, our understanding of them, and the estimated prevalence of this group has changed a number of times over the past six decades, the symptoms have consistently been found to cluster together. Currently called attention deficit hyperactivity disorder (AD/HD), this syndrome has been recognized as a disability by the courts, the United States Department of Education, the Office for Civil Rights, the United States Congress, the National Institutes of Health, and all major professional medical, psychiatric, psychological, and educational associations.

From "Myths about ADD/AD/HD," by Becky Booth, Wilma Fellman, LPC, Judy Greenbaum, Ph.D., Terry Matlen, ACSW, Geraldine Markel, Ph.D., Howard Morris, Arthur L. Robin, Ph.D., Angela Tzelepis, Ph.D., © 1996 National Attention Deficit Disorder Association; cited January 2002; reprinted with permission.

Myth #2: Ritalin is like cocaine, and the failure to give youngsters drug holidays from Ritalin causes them to develop psychosis.

FACT: Methylphenidate (Ritalin) is a medically prescribed stimulant medication that is chemically different from cocaine. The therapeutic use of methylphenidate does not cause addiction or dependence, and does not lead to psychosis. Some children have such severe AD/HD symptoms that it can be dangerous for them to have a medication holiday—for example a child who is so hyper and impulsive he'll run into traffic without stopping to look first. Hallucinations are an extremely rare side-effect of methylphenidate, and their occurrence has nothing to do with the presence or absence of medication holidays. Individuals with AD/HD who are properly treated with stimulant medication such as Ritalin have a lower risk of developing problems with alcohol and other drugs than the general population. More importantly, fifty years of research has repeatedly shown that children, adolescents, and adults with AD/HD safely benefit from treatment with methylphenidate.

Myth #3: No study has ever demonstrated that taking stimulant medications can cause any lasting behavioral or educational benefit to AD/HD children.

FACT: Research has repeatedly shown that children, adolescents, and adults with AD/HD benefit from therapeutic treatment with stimulant medications, which has been used safely and studied for more than 50 years. For example, The *New York Times* reviewed a recent study from Sweden showing positive long-term effects of stimulant medication therapy on children with AD/HD.

Myth #4: AD/HD kids are learning to make excuses, rather than take responsibility for their actions.

FACT: Therapists, educators, and physicians routinely teach children that AD/HD is a challenge, not an excuse. Medication corrects their underlying chemical imbalance, giving them a fair chance of facing the challenges of growing up to become productive citizens. Accommodations for the disabled, as mandated by federal and state laws, are not ways of excusing them from meeting society's responsibilities, but rather make it possible for them to compete on a leveled playing field.

Myth #5: AD/HD is basically due to bad parenting and lack of discipline, and all that AD/HD children really need is old-fashioned discipline, not any of these phony therapies.

FACT: There are still some parent-bashers around who believe the century-old anachronism that child misbehavior is always a moral problem of the bad child. Under this model, the treatment has been to "beat the Devil out of the child." Fortunately, most of us are more enlightened today. A body of family interaction research conducted by Dr. Russell Barkley and others has unequivocally demonstrated that simply providing more discipline without any other interventions worsens rather than improves the behavior of children with AD/HD. One can't make a paraplegic walk by applying discipline. Similarly, one can't make a child with a biologically-based lack of self-control act better by simply applying discipline alone.

Myth #6: Ritalin is unsafe, causing serious weight loss, mood swings, Tourette's syndrome, and sudden, unexplained deaths.

FACT: Research has repeatedly shown that children, adolescents, and adults with AD/HD benefit from treatment with Ritalin (also known as methylphenidate), which has been safely used for approximately 50 years. There are no published cases of deaths from overdoses of Ritalin; if you take too much Ritalin, you will feel terrible and act strange for a few hours, but you will not die. This cannot be said about many other medications. The unexplained deaths cited in some articles are from a combination of Ritalin and other drugs, not from Ritalin alone. Further investigation of those cases has revealed that most of the children had unusual medical problems which contributed to their deaths. It is true that many children experience appetite loss, and some moodiness or rebound effect when Ritalin wears off. A very small number of children may show some temporary tics, but these do not become permanent. Ritalin does not permanently alter growth, and usually does not result in weight loss. Ritalin does not cause Tourette's syndrome, rather many youngsters with Tourette's also have AD/HD. In some cases, Ritalin even leads to an improvement of the tics in children who have AD/HD and Tourette's.

Myth #7: Teachers around the country routinely push pills on any students who are even a little inattentive or overactive.

FACT: Teachers are well-meaning individuals who have the best interests of their students in mind. When they see students who are struggling to pay attention and concentrate, it is their responsibility to bring this to parents' attention, so parents can take appropriate action. The majority of teachers do not simply push pills—they provide information so that parents can seek out appropriate diagnostic help. We do agree with the position that teachers should not diagnose AD/HD. However, being on the front lines with children, they collect information, raise the suspicion of AD/HD, and bring the information to the attention of parents, who then need to have a full evaluation conducted outside the school. The symptoms of AD/HD must be present in school and at home before a diagnosis is made; teachers do not have access to sufficient information about the child's functioning to make a diagnosis of AD/HD or for that matter to make any kind of medical diagnosis.

Myth #8: Efforts by teachers to help children who have attentional problems can make more of a difference than medications such as Ritalin.

FACT: It would be nice if this were true, but recent scientific evidence from the multi-modal treatment trials sponsored by the National Institute of Mental Health suggests it is a myth. In these studies, stimulant medication alone was compared to stimulant medication plus a multi-modal psychological and educational treatment, as treatments for children with AD/HD. The scientists found that the multi-modal treatment plus the medication was not much better than the medication alone. Teachers and therapists need to continue to do everything they can to help individuals with AD/HD, but we need to realize that if we don't also alter the biological factors that affect AD/HD, we won't see much change.

Myth #9: It is not possible to accurately diagnose ADD or AD/HD in children or adults.

FACT: Although scientists have not yet developed a single medical test for diagnosing AD/HD, clear-cut clinical diagnostic criteria have been developed, researched, and refined over several decades. The current generally accepted diagnostic criteria for AD/HD are listed in the *Diagnostic and Statistical Manual of Mental Disorders* (*DSM-IV*) published by the American Psychiatric Association (1995). Using these criteria and multiple methods to collect comprehensive information from multiple informants, AD/HD can be reliably diagnosed in children and adults.

Myth #10: Children outgrow ADD or AD/HD.

FACT: AD/HD is not found just in children. We have learned from a number of excellent follow-up studies conducted over the past few decades that AD/HD often lasts a lifetime. Over 70% of children diagnosed as having AD/HD will continue to manifest the full clinical syndrome in adolescence, and 15-50% will continue to manifest the full clinical syndrome in adulthood. If untreated, individuals with AD/HD may develop a variety of secondary problems as they move through life, including depression, anxiety, substance abuse, academic failure, vocational problems, marital discord, and emotional distress. If properly treated, most individuals with AD/HD live productive lives and cope reasonably well with their symptoms.

Myth #11: Methylphenidate prescriptions in the U.S. have increased 600%.

FACT: The production quotas for methylphenidate increased 6-fold; however that DEA (Drug Enforcement Administration) production quota is a gross estimate based on a number of factors, including FDA (Food and Drug Administration) estimates of need, drug inventories at hand, exports, and industry sales expectations. One cannot conclude that a 6-fold increase in production quotas translates to a 6-fold increase in the use of methylphenidate among U.S. children any more than one should conclude that Americans eat 6 times more bread because U.S. wheat production increased 6-fold even though much of the grain is stored for future use and export to countries that have no wheat production. Further, of the approximately 3.5 million children who meet the criteria for AD/HD, only about 50% of them are diagnosed and have stimulant medication included in their treatment plan. The estimated number of children taking methylphenidate for AD/HD suggested in some media stories fails to note that methylphenidate is also prescribed for adults who have AD/HD, people with narcolepsy, and geriatric patients who receive considerable benefit from it for certain conditions associated with old age such as memory functioning.

Chapter 7

Research Update on AD/HD

A great deal of research on AD/HD is published every month in the professional journals in medicine, psychology, and education. It would be impossible to summarize all of this research. Instead, a small number of significant and interesting studies are highlight in this chapter.

What Causes AD/HD?

More and more evidence from recent research is pointing to the fact that AD/HD is passed on through heredity. Dr. Russell Barkley recently wrote a succinct, highly readable summary of research on genetics and AD/HD. For example, in this article, he mentioned how molecular genetic researchers in five different studies have discovered a link between a particular gene called the DRD4 repeater gene and AD/HD. This is the same gene that has previously been associated with the personality trait of high novelty seeking. This gene is not thought to be involved in all cases of AD/HD, but in a significant number. Of course, scientists are investigating many other genes too, but any consistent association of particular genes with AD/HD helps us better understand what causes AD/HD.

Dr. Barkley also summarized the status of twin studies. Identical twins have been found to have higher concordance rates for AD/HD than fraternal twins. By concordance, we mean the chances that if

From "Research Update on ADHD," by Arthur L. Robin, Ph.D. © 1998 National Attention Deficit Disorder Association; reprinted with permission.

one twin has AD/HD, the other twin will also have it. In one study, the concordance rate was 81% for identical twins versus 29% for fraternal twins. In another study, it was 67% for identical twins and 0% for fraternal twins. These twin studies suggest that up to 80% of the variance in the trait of hyperactivity/impulsivity is now thought to be genetically based.

Controlled Study of the Effectiveness of Adderall

Until now, there has been very little research on the effectiveness of Adderall. Dr. Swanson and his colleagues recently published a randomized, double-blind, cross-over study of the effectiveness of Adderall in 30 children with AD/HD attending a specially designed laboratory classroom. The researchers compared the effectiveness of 5, 10, 15, and 20 mg. of Adderall to the best dose of Ritalin which was known to have helped each child before the child entered the study. A placebo or pill without any active ingredients was also included. The children's behavior and academic performance was observed throughout the school day. Each child received each dose of Adderall, Ritalin, and placebo in a specially established order.

All of the doses of Adderall were superior to the placebo. Ritalin was also superior to the placebo. Adderall generally lasted longer than Ritalin, and higher doses of Adderall lasted longer than lower doses of Adderall. These effects were obtained both in terms of the children's behavior and their academic performance. Hopefully, there will soon be more such studies on Adderall, including some done with adults. One notable finding was that higher doses of Adderall gave a longer lasting effect. Until now, at least with Ritalin, it has commonly been thought that higher doses give a more powerful effect, but not necessarily a longer lasting effect. Apparently, this is different with Adderall than with Ritalin. Of course, this study must be replicated and extended to definitively accept this conclusion.

New Research on Women and AD/HD

Two recent studies have given us some new information on how AD/HD impacts women at various stages of life.

Gender Differences in Cognitive Abilities and Self-Ratings. Arcia and Conners (1998) examined gender differences in intellectual ability, neuropsychological performance and self-ratings of AD/HD symptoms and other behavioral and emotional problems with 360 AD/HD patients. The sample included 280 males and 80 females, ages 5 to 60. The Wechsler Intelligence Tests were used to measure IQ, and the Conners' Continuous Performance Test and the Rey-Osterrieth Complex Figure Test were used to measure neuropsychological functioning. The Rey-Osterrieth Complex Figure Test is a task that requires the subject to copy a complex design and later reproduce it from memory; it taps ability to plan, organize, and assemble complex material and is a sensitive measure of the kinds of difficulties experienced by many people with AD/HD. For the younger children, parents and teachers completed ratings scales of their AD/HD symptoms and general functioning on the Conners' Parent and Teacher Rating Scales. For the adolescents and the adults, they rated themselves on AD/HD symptoms and general functioning on standardized rating scales.

Arcia and Conners (1998) found that there were no differences between males and females at any age on the IQ tests, the Conners' Continuous Performance Test, or the Rey-Osterrieth Complex Figure Test. Thus, on objective measures of intellectual ability and neuropsychological functioning, males and females were similar. For the children, there were no differences between males and females on either parent or teacher rating scales. However, for the adolescents and the adults, there were significant differences between males and females on the self-ratings. Compared to the males, female adolescents and adults with AD/HD rated themselves as having fewer assets, more problems of concentration, more problems of restlessness, more problems dealing with anger, less self-confidence, more emotional problems with feelings such as anxiety and depression, and more conflicts with their families.

It was indeed interesting that despite the fact that objectively speaking, males and females with AD/HD looked similar on cognitive and neuropsychological measure at any age, by adolescence and adulthood, the females perceived themselves to be having more problems. They perceived themselves to be having more problems not only with AD/HD symptoms such as concentration and restlessness, but also with associated factors such as anger, self-confidence, feelings, and family relations. This finding is consistent with the clinical impression of many therapists that AD/HD may sometimes create a greater burden for women than for men, although there are certainly other interpretations of the data that are possible.

In another recent study, Rucklidge & Kaplan (1998) investigated the psychological functioning of 51 women diagnosed as having AD/HD compared to 51 not fulfilling criteria for AD/HD. The women in both groups averaged 41 years of age. The investigators used a variety of interview and self-report measures to compare the AD/HD and non-AD/HD women on psychiatric history, depression, anxiety, life stresses, coping styles, and self-esteem. Women with AD/HD reported having had more depressive episodes in their lives, lower self-esteem, more feelings of anxiety, higher levels of stress, and more frequent involvement in psychotherapy than women without AD/HD. The AD/HD group also engaged in less task-oriented coping and more emotional coping than the AD/HD group, and had a more external locus of control than the non-AD/HD group (e.g. felt they had less control over their lives). This study clearly provides further documentation for the negative impacts of AD/HD on women.

Presenting Symptoms and Subtypes of AD/HD in Adults

What percentage of adults with AD/HD fall into each of the major subtypes, e.g. Inattentive, Hyperactive/ Impulsive, or Combined subtypes? Which AD/HD symptoms are most common in adults? Are comorbidities for other psychiatric conditions more common in one subtype of AD/HD than another? These were some of the questions which Millstein, Wilens, Biederman, and Spencer recently addressed. Using a meticulous recruitment and screening/diagnostic process involving structured psychiatric interviews, these investigators examined the functioning of 149 adults clinically referred and diagnosed as having AD/HD. The sample included 88 males and 61 females, and had a mean age of 37 years. They found that 56% of the adults had the combined subtype, 37% had the inattentive subtype, and only 2% had the hyperactive/impulsive subtype.

They analyzed which AD/HD symptoms were most common in adulthood. Results indicated that the inattentive symptoms were most commonly reported, particularly difficulty sustaining attention, shifting activities frequently, and difficulty following through on tasks. Hyperactive and impulsive symptoms were less common, but nonetheless the majority of the adults reported long-standing difficulties with fidgeting, interrupting, speaking out of turn, and impatience. Hyperactive/impulsive symptoms were reported to have decreased more from childhood to adulthood than inattentive symptoms.

Comorbidity—the presence of a coexisting condition—was very common. Only 3% had no comorbidity, 11% had a lifetime history of one comorbid condition, 12% had two, 18% had three, and 56% had four or more psychiatric comorbidities. Adults with the combined subtype tended to have more comorbid psychiatric conditions than those with the inattentive or hyperactive/impulsive subtype, particularly oppositional, bipolar, and substance use disorders. Men had higher rates of conduct disorder, antisocial disorder, alcohol and drug dependence, and stuttering than women; women had higher rates than men of depression, bulimia nervosa, and simple phobias.

This study reinforces previous research in children showing that the combined subtype of AD/HD is the most common, and the hyperactive/ impulsive subtype is the least common. It also reinforces previous findings that the inattentive symptoms persist more than the hyperactive/impulsive symptoms into adulthood, and provides valuable information about the types of comorbidities present in adults with AD/HD.

Chapter 8

Drug and Alcohol Use during Pregnancy Linked to AD/HD in Children

Alcohol and tobacco use during pregnancy have both been associated with a number of adverse effects on the growth, cognitive development, and behavior of the exposed child. Understanding the effects of prenatal tobacco exposure allows researchers to identify those characteristics that are uniquely related to tobacco and those that are affected by alcohol exposure. This research, along with studies on the effects of alcohol use during pregnancy, has implications for preventing various types of substance use during pregnancy and for treating children affected by prenatal substance use.

Women who smoke during pregnancy are also likely to drink alcohol. In one survey, conducted as part of the Maternal Health Practices and Child Development (MHPCD) project in Pittsburgh, Pennsylvania, 76 percent of adult women who reported smoking during their first trimester of pregnancy said that they also drank alcohol during that period.

Among pregnant teenagers surveyed, 61 percent of those who smoked during the first trimester also drank alcohol. In addition, tobacco

---

This chapter includes excerpts from "The Effects of Tobacco Use During and After Pregnancy on Exposed Children, Relevance of Findings for Alcohol Research," by Marie D. Cornelius, Ph.D., and Nancy L. Day, Ph.D., from *Alcohol Research & Health,* National Institute on Alcohol Abuse and Alcoholism (NIAAA), Volume 24, Number 4, 2000, and excerpts from "Drinking Moderately and Pregnancy," by Joseph L. Jacobson, Ph.D., and Sandra W. Jacobson, Ph.D., from *Alcohol Research & Health,* National Institute on Alcohol Abuse and Alcoholism (NIAAA), Volume 23, Number 1, 1999.

and alcohol use are both prevalent among women who use illicit drugs during pregnancy. In the National Pregnancy and Health Survey, 74 percent of women who used illicit drugs during pregnancy also reported either smoking, drinking, or both. The use of either one of these drugs is, in itself, a risk factor for poorer pregnancy outcome.

Although alcohol and tobacco are frequently used together during pregnancy, researchers studying the negative effects of prenatal exposure to tobacco and alcohol have generally examined the effects of each drug separately. Therefore, it is difficult to discuss the effects of the combined use of the two drugs.

Effects of Tobacco Use during Pregnancy

Smoking during pregnancy is more prevalent among Caucasian women compared with African-American or Hispanic women. Caucasian women also smoke at higher levels than do women of other ethnicities. Women who smoke during pregnancy are less likely to be married, have less education, have lower incomes, and attend fewer prenatal visits compared with women who do not smoke during pregnancy. Compared with alcohol, marijuana, and other illicit drug use, tobacco use is less likely to decline as the pregnancy progresses. In the National Pregnancy and Health Study, approximately two-thirds of the women who smoked prior to their pregnancy continued smoking into the last trimester.

In contrast, only one-fourth of the women who used alcohol prior to conception continued to drink into the third trimester. Women who smoke during pregnancy also continue smoking after the pregnancy. Therefore, children born to women who use tobacco during pregnancy are likely to continue to be exposed to tobacco after birth. This environmental, or passive, exposure may also affect the children's development.

Effects on Activity, Attention, and Impulsivity

Researchers have also reported associations between prenatal tobacco exposure and increased activity, inattention, and impulsivity. Kristjansson and colleagues found that prenatal tobacco exposure predicted impulsivity and increased overall activity among 4- to 7-year-olds after controlling for prenatal exposure to other drugs and postnatal exposure to second-hand smoke. In addition, Fried and colleagues reported a significant relationship between prenatal tobacco exposure and impulsivity among 6-year-olds in the same cohort.

Milberger and colleagues found a positive relationship between maternal smoking during pregnancy and an increased risk of attention deficit hyperactivity disorder (AD/HD) in exposed children between the ages of 6 and 17, although the study did not control for current maternal smoking or prenatal exposure to other substances. In the MHPCD study of adult mothers, prenatal tobacco exposure significantly predicted increased errors of commission on the Continuous Performance Test among 6-year-olds. However, the mothers' current tobacco use correlated so highly with the prenatal exposure levels that these exposures could not be separated. Eskenazi and Trupin did not find a relationship between prenatal tobacco use and activity.

When the children of the adult mothers in the MHPCD study were assessed at age 10, prenatal tobacco exposure predicted deficits on neuropsychological tests that measured planning ability and fine motor coordination.

Effects on Cognitive Function

Laboratory research with animals has shown that nicotine affects the Central Nervous System (CNS) at exposure levels below those at which growth changes are evident. For example, animal studies have shown associations between fetal nicotine exposure and increased locomotor activity in male rat pups.

In the literature on humans, prenatal tobacco exposure has also been linked to CNS effects, including cognitive and neurobehavioral outcomes, although the reports are inconsistent. At birth, prenatal tobacco exposure has been associated with poorer auditory orientation and autonomic regulation and increased tremors and startles. In a recent race-matched study of cocaine-exposed and non-cocaine-exposed infants, neurological exams showed that prenatal tobacco exposure was significantly related to muscle tone abnormalities when controlling for other variables, including prenatal cocaine and ethanol exposure, head circumference, and prenatal care. The authors concluded that maternal cigarette smoking, rather than cocaine exposure, might be the major predictor of tone abnormalities.

Studies have also reported adverse effects of prenatal tobacco exposure on cognitive and behavioral development in older children. In one study, cognitive functioning at age 3 was higher among the children of mothers who quit smoking during pregnancy than among children whose mothers smoked throughout pregnancy. Poor language development and lower cognitive scores have also been reported in 2-, 3-, and 4-year-old children prenatally exposed to tobacco. When those children were 9 to 12 years old, prenatal tobacco exposure was negatively associated with language and reading abilities.

Other researchers have argued that initially significant associations between prenatal tobacco exposure and cognitive development were explained better by differences in social class and the home environment. For example, after controlling for socioeconomic and environmental differences, Eskenazi and Trupin failed to find consistent relationships between prenatal tobacco exposure and performance on the Raven Colored Matrices Test, a measure of nonverbal reasoning, or the Peabody Picture Vocabulary Test (PPVT). However, in the MHPCD study of adult mothers, prenatal tobacco exposure predicted deficits in visual memory and verbal learning scores on the Wide Range Assessment of Memory and Learning test (WRAML), and these associations remained after consideration of other factors, including socioeconomic status, maternal psychological status, home environment, other prenatal substance exposures, and current maternal tobacco and other substance use.

Behavioral and Psychological Effects

Behavioral and psychological problems have also been linked to prenatal tobacco exposure. Orlebeke and colleagues reported a significant effect of prenatal tobacco exposure on externalizing behaviors, including oppositional, aggressive, and overactive behaviors in 3-year-olds. This study did not control for other prenatal substance exposures or the mothers' current smoking habits. Weitzman and colleagues found that women who smoked both during and after pregnancy rated their children as having more behavior problems, but the researchers found no effects on children who were only exposed during pregnancy.

Brook and colleagues found that mothers who smoked during pregnancy were significantly more likely to have toddlers who displayed negativity than did mothers who only smoked after delivery. This relationship was maintained after controlling for a number of psychosocial risk factors, including the mother's distress, socioeconomic status, and perinatal risk factors. In the adult cohort of the MHPCD project, 3-year-olds who were exposed prenatally to tobacco were significantly more likely to display oppositional behavior, immaturity, and aggressive behavior, according to the mothers' reports. These relationships persisted after controlling for socioeconomic status, current home environment, maternal psychological status, current maternal tobacco use, and other prenatal substance exposures.

The behavior problems observed in toddlers prenatally exposed to tobacco persist through the adolescent and adult years. Fergusson and colleagues followed a birth cohort through age 12 and reported that prenatal tobacco exposure was significantly related to childhood behavior problems, whereas current maternal smoking was not. At ages 16 to 18, children in that cohort who were exposed to prenatal smoking had higher rates of conduct disorder, substance use, and depression than did nonexposed children. Wakschlag and colleagues also reported a significant relationship between prenatal tobacco exposure and conduct disorder in a clinical sample; however, this study did not control for current exposure. In addition, maternal smoking during pregnancy predicted persistent criminal outcomes in adult male offspring in a Danish prospective study.

In another prospective study in Finland, maternal smoking during pregnancy was significantly associated with an increase in violent offenses among the adult male offspring. A few studies have evaluated the relationships between prenatal substance exposure and subsequent substance use in the offspring. Animal researchers have noted that changes resulting from prenatal nicotine exposure might affect susceptibility to later tobacco use. In a retrospective study of humans, Kandel and colleagues reported a fourfold increased risk of tobacco use among female offspring who were exposed to tobacco prenatally.

In a later report, Griesler and colleagues showed that maternal smoking during pregnancy was significantly associated with higher levels of child behavior problems and that these behavior problems increased the likelihood of smoking among daughters between the ages of 9 and 17. The association between prenatal tobacco exposure and early tobacco experimentation was also found in the MHPCD prospective study of adult women and their offspring. In this study, 10-year-old children exposed to tobacco at the level of at least one half pack per day during gestation had a 5.5-fold increased risk for early tobacco experimentation, controlling for prenatal exposure to other substances and their mothers' current smoking habits.

Effects on Infant Growth

Maternal smoking during pregnancy has long been considered an important risk factor for low birth weight (LBW). This association was first reported in 1957 and has been proven in numerous subsequent studies. Birth weight decreases in direct proportion to the number of cigarettes smoked, and children of smokers are 150 to 250 grams lighter than are the children of nonsmokers. The reduction in infant weight is not attributable to earlier gestation, because infants of smokers exhibit growth retardation at all gestational ages.

In a recent study of pregnant teenagers, more than one-half of whom were smokers, prenatal tobacco exposure was significantly related to reduced birth weight, birth length, head circumference, and chest circumference. These reductions were even more pronounced than those found in a similar cohort of the children of adult women. For example, in the study of adult mothers and their children, prenatal tobacco use was significantly associated with a reduction in birth weight of 158 grams per pack per day. In the children of teenage mothers, prenatal tobacco exposure was significantly associated with a reduction in birth weight of 202 grams per pack per day. The increased problems associated with young maternal age and poor fetal outcomes, coupled with the high prevalence of smoking among pregnant teenagers, magnify the risks to children of pregnant teenagers who smoke.

Two key ingredients of cigarette smoke that are known to affect fetal growth are carbon monoxide and nicotine. Carbon monoxide causes fetal hypoxia, a reduction in the amount of oxygen available to the fetus, whereas nicotine can lead to a decrease in the flow of oxygen and other nutrients across the placenta by constricting uterine arteries. In addition, nicotine itself can cross the placenta to affect the fetal cardiovascular and central nervous systems (CNS). Other constituents of tobacco smoke (e.g., cadmium and toluene) have also been shown to cause fetal growth retardation.

Summary and Conclusions

Smoking during pregnancy has been associated significantly with a number of adverse effects on the growth, cognitive development, and behavior of the exposed child. However, because women who smoke during pregnancy are also likely to use alcohol or other drugs, researchers must account for these confounding factors in order to identify accurately the specific and unique role of tobacco exposure. In addition, even nonsmoking mothers can expose their children through environmental tobacco exposure. Compared with alcohol and other drug use, tobacco use is less likely to decline during pregnancy, and women who smoke during pregnancy are more likely to continue to smoke after delivery. This means that children who are prenatally exposed to tobacco are at higher risk for continued exposure to environmental tobacco smoke from the mother and from other household smokers.

Drinking Moderately and Pregnancy— Effects on Child Development

Children exposed to moderate levels of alcohol during pregnancy show growth deficits and intellectual and behavioral problems similar to, although less severe than, those found in children with fetal alcohol syndrome. Research has begun to examine the extent to which these problems affect the child's ability to function on a day-to-day basis at school and with peers. Findings indicate that moderate drinking has much more impact on child development when the mother consumes several drinks in a single day than when she drinks the same quantity in doses of one to two drinks per day over several days.

Moderate drinking during pregnancy is associated with developmental problems in childhood that resemble but are less severe than the growth deficiencies and intellectual and behavioral impairment found among children with fetal alcohol syndrome (FAS). Children with FAS grow more slowly than do other children both before and after birth, exhibit intellectual and social problems, and display a distinctive pattern of abnormal facial features. Intellectual and behavioral impairment are the most disabling characteristics of FAS. About one-half of all FAS patients are mentally retarded (i.e., they have an IQ below 70), and virtually all FAS patients exhibit serious attention and behavioral problems.

Several studies have found that children exposed to alcohol during pregnancy at lower levels than FAS children experience moderate intellectual and behavioral deficits that resemble those of FAS children but on a less severe level. Most of the mothers of children in these studies drank an average of 7 to 14 drinks per week, a range generally considered as moderate drinking. Although the deficits associated with full-blown FAS are devastating, the more subtle developmental problems associated with lower levels of prenatal alcohol exposure are far more prevalent among children than FAS.

Behavioral Function

In addition to the intellectual and attention deficits found among non-FAS alcohol-exposed children, researchers also have documented behavior problems that resemble but are less severe than those found among FAS children. The socialization deficits associated with FAS include poor interpersonal skills and an inability to conform to social conventions. Streissguth has described FAS patients as being unaware of the consequences of [their] behavior, especially the

77

social consequences, showing poor judgment in whom to trust, and unable to take a hint [i.e., needing strong clear commands].

Relatively limited information is available regarding behavioral effects in alcohol-exposed non-FAS children. Using the Achenbach Child Behavior Checklist—Teacher's Report Form (TRF), Brown and colleagues found poorer social competence and more aggressive and destructive behavior in children whose mothers drank throughout their pregnancies than in children whose mothers had stopped drinking in mid-pregnancy or abstained during pregnancy, independent of current maternal drinking patterns. In another study, prenatal alcohol exposure was associated with higher teacher ratings in three of the eight TRF problem areas—social, attention, and aggression—and greater inattention and impulsivity on the DuPaul-Barkley Attention Deficit Hyperactivity Disorder (AD/HD) Scale, after controlling for potential confounding factors such as maternal smoking during pregnancy, quality of parenting, and current caregiver drinking. Analyses showed that the social, aggression, and impulsivity problems were not merely by-products of the children's attention deficits, indicating that alcohol directly affects diverse aspects of central nervous system function. A high proportion of children had problems in the borderline or clinical range. For example, 33 percent of the children prenatally exposed to moderate or heavy levels of alcohol exhibited aggressive behavior problems of this magnitude, compared with only 4 to 5 percent of the general population.

One study found that at age 14, children with higher levels of prenatal alcohol exposure were more likely to have negative feelings about themselves; to be aggressive and delinquent; and to use alcohol, tobacco, and other drugs.

Intellectual Function

Unlike children with FAS, who frequently have reduced IQ scores, non-FAS alcohol-exposed children do not necessarily demonstrate IQ deficits. For example, one study failed to find an overall IQ deficit among non-FAS alcohol-exposed children but found that they exhibited poorer arithmetic, reading, and spelling skills than did non-alcohol-exposed children.

Researchers have documented arithmetic and attention deficits both in FAS children and in at least three groups of children with ARND (alcohol-related neurodevelopmental disorder)—(1) a group of predominantly white, middle-class children in Seattle who were prenatally exposed to moderate amounts of alcohol, (2) a group of economically disadvantaged African-American children in Detroit whose mothers drank moderately during pregnancy, and (3) a group of disadvantaged African-American children in Atlanta who were prenatally exposed to moderate-to-heavy amounts of alcohol.

To measure attention deficits, researchers commonly use tests for the four attention components identified by Mirsky and colleagues. Sustained attention refers to the child's ability to maintain focused concentration and alertness over time. Focused attention is a measure of the length of time the child maintains attention in the presence of distractions.

Executive function involves the child's ability to coordinate, plan, and execute appropriate responses and modify his or her behavior in response to feedback. Working memory is a measure of the child's ability to mentally manipulate the information presented and to link this information with other information retrieved from memory. Although research has documented low levels of sustained attention, focused attention, and executive function in ARND children, these children's most consistent deficits are in working memory.

Effects on Children's Day-to-Day Function

The effects of moderate prenatal alcohol exposure on children's intellectual performance and behavior have been established. When examining the results of psychological tests, however, children with ARND often appear to have relatively subtle impairments (i.e., their average test scores are no more than a few points below normal). Although the average effect may be small, researchers have recently begun to examine whether the effects of moderate drinking are severe enough in certain children to affect their ability to manage on a day-to-day basis at school, home, and with peers.

Growth

Although growth deficits are not a hallmark of ARND, consistent evidence indicates modest growth retardation in alcohol-exposed non-FAS infants before birth, and several studies have reported an association between prenatal alcohol exposure and slower-than-normal growth during the first 6 to 8 months after birth. Moreover, deficits in height and head circumference have been documented in alcohol exposed non-FAS children through age 6. This slower growth pattern contrasts with the traditional finding that infants who weigh less at birth because of maternal smoking during pregnancy grow faster and tend to catch up during their first 5 to 6 months.

Conclusions

Several studies have found that moderate prenatal alcohol exposure has statistically significant effects on children's cognitive and behavioral development. Using the IOM (Institute of Medicine)-proposed terminology, many of these children would be diagnosed as having ARND. ARND differs from FAS, however, in that FAS is characterized by reduced IQ scores and more severe socialization problems.

Nevertheless, evaluations of the specific domains in which deficits occur reveal important parallels between FAS and ARND. In the cognitive domain, arithmetic, attention, and working memory are most severely and consistently affected in both disorders. In the behavioral domain, both disorders are marked by increased impulsivity, aggression, and social problems. Researchers are only beginning to address the importance of these deficits for the day-to-day functioning of the ARND child. The aforementioned data suggest that although some non-FAS alcohol exposed children are only minimally affected by prenatal alcohol exposure, other more susceptible children are impaired to a degree likely to interfere with their ability to function normally.

Detailed information about the functional significance of each of the deficits found among ARND children is needed to fully understand the implications of prenatal alcohol exposure for child development. More attention also should be devoted to determining the specific drinking levels and patterns associated with functionally significant developmental impairment. Research has documented functionally significant deficits in infants whose mothers drank, on average, five or more drinks per occasion once or twice per week.

Although considered excessive for a pregnant woman, this level of drinking falls short of the rate usually associated with having a serious drinking problem. Given the marked individual differences in alcohol metabolism and fetal vulnerability, five drinks per occasion may be too high a threshold for many women. Functional deficits may occur in some children who are repeatedly exposed prenatally to only three or four drinks per occasion, especially if the alcohol is consumed on an empty stomach. In evaluating the risk associated with exposure to environmental and food contaminants, a safety margin is usually incorporated to allow for individual differences in sensitivity.

Chapter 9

Successful People with AD/HD

Did you know that many successful and famous people grew up with AD/HD and/or learning disabilities (LD)? Whoopi Goldberg, Charles Schwab, and Greg Louganis, to name a few, are all inspirations. They show us how people with learning differences can use their strengths to become highly successful in their field.

Following is a list of famous people with LD and AD/HD. You may want to use this information for a special research project or report that your child is doing for school. Go through the names, pick a few who share your child's interests and talents, and learn about them together. Talk to your child about these successful people to help him understand that he's not alone with his struggles. Knowing that AD/HD doesn't prevent people from achieving their goals in life will foster hope for the future. You and your child will realize that he, too, can succeed in learning and life and even become a role model for others.

Artists

- *Chuck Close* is one of the most celebrated contemporary artists whose work is exhibited at museums of modern art around the country.

From "Successful People with LD and AD/HD," by Jodie Dawson, Ph.D. © 2001 Schwab Learning. Reprinted with permission. For more information, visit www.schwablearning.org.

- *Robert Rauchenberg* is a multi-media artist who has had significant influence in the world of modern art and has even been called the Picasso of the 21st Century.

- *Robert Toth*, acclaimed artist, has his paintings, sculptures and bronzes on display in museums throughout the world, including the Smithsonian's National Portrait Gallery in Washington, D.C.

Athletes

- *Bruce Jenner*, 1976 gold medalist in the Olympic decathlon, is described as the World's Greatest Athlete.

- *Greg Louganis* received an Olympic gold medal in diving in the 1984 and 1988 games and advocates for AIDS awareness.

- *Neil Smith*, NFL professional football player, is defensive end for the San Diego Chargers.

- *Jackie Stewart* is a race car driving champion who has been inducted into the Grand Prix Hall of Fame.

- *Stan Wattles* is an up-and-coming race car driver in the Indy Racing League.

Business Leaders

- *Stephen Bacque* is a renowned entrepreneur who has shown success and expertise in many areas, including international and small business growth.

- *Richard Branson* is an enormously successful entrepreneur and founder of 150 enterprises that carry the Virgin name, such as Virgin Airlines.

- *John T. Chambers*, CEO of multi-billion dollar Internet management company, Cisco Systems, has revolutionized the technology industry and is recognized as one of the most fascinating business leaders of our times.

- *Paul Orfalea* is the founder and chairperson of Kinko's, an international, billion-dollar copy service company.

- *Charles Schwab* is the founder, chairperson, and CEO of the Charles Schwab Corporation, the largest brokerage firm in the

U.S. In 1987, he and his wife, Helen O'Neill Schwab, established Schwab Learning, a foundation dedicated to increasing awareness about learning differences. He continues to be an active voice in the world of LD.

- *Donald Winkler*, CEO of Ford Motor Credit, has inspired businesses to overcome obstacles to success. He actively supports individuals with LD.

Community Concerns

- *Erin Brockovich*, inspiration for the movie of the same name, now serves as Director of Environmental Research at the law offices of Masry & Vititoe.

Entertainers

- *Cher*, an Academy Award-winning actress, is also well-known for her pop music and 1970s hit TV variety show.

- *Danny Glover*, acclaimed actor of theatre and film, has used his celebrity status to advance many community programs and worthy causes, such as AIDS awareness in South Africa and the advancement of minority youth.

- *Whoopi Goldberg*, born Caryn Johnson, is an actress and comedian who has used her stardom to raise money to eliminate homelessness.

- *Woody Harrelson*, actor, rose to fame as Woody on TV's hit series, "Cheers." His movie career includes many starring roles and an Academy Award nomination.

- *Jay Leno* is a popular comedian and late-night talk show host.

- *Edward James Olmos* is a celebrated actor, entrepreneur, and activist who supports and advocates for Latino culture in the U.S.

- *Lindsay Wagner*, most famous for her role as the Bionic Woman in the hit 1970s TV series, has dedicated much of her time to raising awareness about learning differences.

- *Henry Winkler*, also known as "The Fonz" from the hit TV series Happy Days, is a producer, Yale graduate, and children's advocate.

Explorers

- *Ann Bancroft*, an honoree in the National Women's Hall of Fame, was the first woman to travel to the North Pole and lead an all-woman dog-sled team to the South Pole. She started her own nonprofit foundation that supports girls and women as leaders.

Musicians

- *Harry Belafonte* is a famous African-American singer, actor, entertainer and political activist who, even into his 70's, uses his position as a celebrity to promote human rights worldwide.

- *Jon Finn* is active in the music business as a musician, songwriter, and engineer/producer. Since 1988 he has been the most in-demand rock guitar teacher at Berklee College of Music in Boston.

- *Jewel* is a young pop-music sensation who recently wrote an autobiography of her life growing up in Alaska.

Politicians

- *Nelson Rockefeller* served as governor of New York for 12 years and as Vice President of the United States under Gerald Ford.

Scientists

- *Dr. John (Jack) Horner* is a famous paleontologist, or dinosaur expert, who advised Steven Spielberg on films such as "Jurassic Park" and "The Lost World."

Writers

- *Stephen J. Cannell* is a successful novelist and an Emmy Award-winning TV writer and producer who has created or co-created over 40 different shows.

- *Fannie Flagg* is a writer and actor who is most famous for her novel "Fried Green Tomatoes" which was later produced as a movie.

- *John Irving* is a novelist and screenplay writer of "World According to Garp," "Hotel New Hampshire," and "Cider House Rules," a movie that recently won acclaim and award nominations.

Part Two

Diagnosis and Treatment

Chapter 10

Diagnosis and Treatment of AD/HD: An Overview

Introduction

Attention deficit hyperactivity disorder (AD/HD) is the most commonly diagnosed behavioral disorder of childhood, estimated to affect 3 to 5 percent of school-age children.

Despite the progress in the assessment, diagnosis, and treatment of children and adults with AD/HD, the disorder has remained controversial. The diverse and conflicting opinions about AD/HD have resulted in confusion for families, care providers, educators, and policymakers. The controversy raises questions concerning the literal existence of the disorder, whether it can be reliably diagnosed, and, if treated, what interventions are the most effective.

One of the major controversies regarding AD/HD concerns the use of psychostimulants to treat the condition. Psychostimulants, including amphetamine, methylphenidate, and pemoline, are by far the most widely researched and commonly prescribed treatments for AD/HD. Because psychostimulants are more readily available and are being prescribed more frequently, concerns have intensified over their potential overuse and abuse.

Excerpted from "Diagnosis and Treatment of Attention Deficit Hyperactivity Disorder," National Institutes of Health (NIH), Consensus Development Conference Statement, November 1998.

What Is the Scientific Evidence to Support AD/HD As a Disorder?

The diagnosis of AD/HD can be made reliably using well-tested diagnostic interview methods. However, as of yet, there is no independent valid test for AD/HD. Although research has suggested a central nervous system basis for AD/HD, further research is necessary to firmly establish AD/HD as a brain disorder. This is not unique to AD/HD, but applies as well to most psychiatric disorders, including disabling diseases such as schizophrenia. Evidence supporting the validity of AD/HD includes the long-term developmental course of AD/HD over time, cross-national studies revealing similar risk factors, familial aggregation of AD/HD (which may be genetic or environmental), and heritability.

Additional efforts to validate the disorder are needed: careful description of the cases, use of specific diagnostic criteria, repeated follow-up studies, family studies (including twin and adoption studies), epidemiologic studies, and long-term treatment studies. To the maximum extent possible, such studies should include various controls, including normal subjects and those with other clinical disorders. Such studies may provide suggestions about subgrouping of patients that will turn out to be associated with different outcomes, responses to different treatment, and varying patterns of familial characteristics and illnesses.

Certain issues about the diagnosis of AD/HD have been raised that indicate the need for further research to validate diagnostic methods.

1. Clinicians who diagnose this disorder have been criticized for merely taking a percentage of the normal population who have the most evidence of inattention and continuous activity and labeling them as having a disease. In fact, it is unclear whether the signs of AD/HD represent a bimodal distribution in the population or one end of a continuum of characteristics. This is not unique to AD/HD as other medical diagnoses, such as essential hypertension and hyperlipidemia, are continuous in the general population, yet the utility of diagnosis and treatment have been proven. Nevertheless, related problems of diagnosis include differentiating AD/HD from other behavioral problems and determining the appropriate boundary between the normal population and those with AD/HD.

2. AD/HD often does not present as an isolated disorder, and comorbidities (coexisting conditions) may complicate research

studies, which may account for some of the inconsistencies in research findings.

3.   Although the prevalence of AD/HD in the United States has been estimated at about 3 to 5 percent, a wider range of prevalence has been reported across studies. The reported rate in some other countries is much lower. This indicates a need for a more thorough study of AD/HD in different populations and better definition of the disorder.

4.   All formal diagnostic criteria for AD/HD were designed for diagnosing young children and have not been adjusted for older children and adults. Therefore, appropriate revision of these criteria to aid in the diagnosis of these individuals is encouraged.

In summary, there is validity in the diagnosis of AD/HD as a disorder with broadly accepted symptoms and behavioral characteristics that define the disorder.

What Is the Impact of AD/HD on Individuals, Families, and Society?

Children with AD/HD experience an inability to sit still and pay attention in class regardless of the negative consequences of such behavior. They experience peer rejection and engage in a broad array of disruptive behaviors. Their academic and social difficulties have far-reaching and long-term consequences. These children have higher injury rates. As they grow older, children with untreated AD/HD in combination with conduct disorders experience drug abuse, antisocial behavior, and injuries of all sorts. For many individuals, the impact of AD/HD continues into adulthood.

Families who have children with AD/HD, as with other behavioral disorders and chronic diseases, experience increased levels of parental frustration, marital discord, and divorce. In addition, the direct costs of medical care for children and youth with AD/HD are substantial. These costs represent a serious burden for many families because they frequently are not covered by health insurance.

In the larger world, these individuals consume a disproportionate share of resources and attention from the health care system, criminal justice system, schools, and other social service agencies. Methodological problems preclude precise estimates of the cost of AD/HD to society. However, these costs are large. Moreover, AD/HD, often in conjunction with coexisting conduct disorders, contributes to societal problems such as violent crime and teenage pregnancy.

Families of children impaired by the symptoms of AD/HD are in a very difficult position. The painful decision-making process to determine appropriate treatment for these children is often made substantially worse by the media war between those who overstate the benefits of treatment and those who overstate the dangers of treatment.

What Are the Effective Treatments for AD/HD?

A wide variety of treatments have been used for AD/HD including, but not limited to, various psychotropic medications, psychosocial treatment, dietary management, herbal and homeopathic treatments, biofeedback, meditation, and perceptual stimulation/training. Of these treatment strategies, stimulant medications and psychosocial interventions have been the major foci of research. Studies on the efficacy of medication and psychosocial treatments for AD/HD have focused primarily on a condition equivalent to *DSM-IV* (short for the *Diagnostic and Statistical Manual of Mental Disorders, 4ᵗʰ Edition*) combined type, meeting criteria for Inattention and Hyperactivity/Impulsivity. Until recently, most randomized clinical trials have been short term, up to approximately 3 months. Overall, these studies support the efficacy of stimulants and psychosocial treatments for AD/HD and the superiority of stimulants relative to psychosocial treatments. However, there are no long-term studies testing stimulants or psychosocial treatments lasting several years. There is no information on the long-term outcomes of medication-treated AD/HD individuals in terms of educational and occupational achievements, involvement with the police, or other areas of social functioning.

Short-term trials of stimulants have supported the efficacy of methylphenidate (MPH) dextroamphetamine and pemoline in children with AD/HD. Few, if any, differences have been found among these stimulants on average. However, MPH is the most studied and the most often used of the stimulants. These short-term trials have found beneficial effects on the defining symptoms of AD/HD and associated aggressiveness as long as medication is taken. However, stimulant treatments may not normalize the entire range of behavior problems, and children under treatment may still manifest a higher level of some behavior problems than normal children. Of concern are the consistent findings that despite the improvement in core symptoms, there is little improvement in academic achievement or social skills.

Several short-term studies of antidepressants show that desipramine produces improvements over placebo in parent and teacher ratings of AD/HD symptoms. Results from studies examining the efficacy of imipramine are inconsistent. Although a number of other psychotropic medications have been used to treat AD/HD, the extant outcome data from these studies do not allow for conclusions regarding their efficacy.

Psychosocial treatment of AD/HD has included a number of behavioral strategies such as contingency management (e.g., point/token reward systems, timeout, response cost) that typically is conducted in the classroom, parent training (where the parent is taught child management skills), clinical behavior therapy (parent, teacher, or both are taught to use contingency management procedures), and cognitive-behavioral treatment (e.g., self-monitoring, verbal self-instruction, problem-solving strategies, self-reinforcement). Cognitive-behavioral treatment has not been found to yield beneficial effects in children with AD/HD. In contrast, clinical behavior therapy, parent training, and contingency management have produced beneficial effects. Intensive direct interventions in children with AD/HD have produced improvements in key areas of functioning. However, no randomized control trials have been conducted on some of these intensive interventions alone or in combination with medication. Studies that compared stimulants with psychosocial treatment consistently reported greater efficacy of stimulants.

Combined medication and behavioral treatment added little advantage overall, over medication alone, but combined treatment did result in more improved social skills, and parents and teachers judged this treatment more favorably. Both systematically applied medication (monitored regularly) and combined treatment were superior to routine community care, which often involved the use of stimulants. An important potential advantage for behavioral treatment is the possibility of improving functioning with reduced dose of stimulants. This possibility was not tested.

There is a long history of a number of other interventions for AD/HD. These include dietary replacement, exclusion, or supplementation; various vitamin, mineral, or herbal regimens; biofeedback; perceptual stimulation; and a host of others. Although these interventions have generated considerable interest and there are some controlled and uncontrolled studies using various strategies, the state of the empirical evidence regarding these interventions is uneven, ranging from no data to well-controlled trials. Some of the dietary elimination strategies showed intriguing results suggesting the need for future research.

The current state of the empirical literature regarding the treatment of AD/HD is such that at least five important questions cannot be answered. First, it cannot be determined if the combination of stimulants and psychosocial treatments can improve functioning with reduced dose of stimulants. Second, there are no data on the treatment of AD/HD, Inattentive type, which might include a high percentage of girls. Third, there are no conclusive data on treatment in adolescents and adults with AD/HD. Fourth, there is no information on the effects of long-term treatment (treatment lasting more than 1 year), which is indicated in this persistent disorder. Finally, given the evidence about the cognitive problems associated with AD/HD, such as deficiencies in working memory and language processing deficits, and the demonstrated ineffectiveness of current treatments in enhancing academic achievement, there is a need for application and development of methods targeted to these weaknesses.

What Are the Existing Diagnostic and Treatment Practices, and What Are the Barriers to Appropriate Identification, Evaluation, and Intervention?

The American Academy of Child and Adolescent Psychiatry has published practice parameters for the assessment and treatment of AD/HD. The American Academy of Pediatrics has formed a subcommittee to establish parameters for pediatricians. Primary care and developmental pediatricians, family practitioners, (child) neurologists, psychologists, and psychiatrists are the providers responsible for assessment, diagnosis, and treatment of most children with AD/HD. There is wide variation among types of practitioners with respect to frequency of diagnosis of AD/HD. Data indicate that family practitioners diagnose more quickly and prescribe medication more frequently than psychiatrists or pediatricians. This may be due in part to the limited time spent making the diagnosis. Some practitioners invalidly use response to medication as a diagnostic criterion, and primary care practitioners are less likely to recognize comorbid (coexisting) disorders. The quickness with which some practitioners prescribe medications may decrease the likelihood that more educationally relevant interventions will be sought.

Diagnoses may be made in an inconsistent manner with children sometimes being overdiagnosed and sometimes underdiagnosed. However, this does not affect the validity of the diagnosis when appropriate guidelines are used. Some practitioners do not use structured parent questionnaires, rating scales, or teacher or school input. Pediatricians, family practitioners, and psychiatrists tend to rely on parent rather than teacher input. There appears to be a disconnect between developmental or educational (school-based) assessments and health-related (medical practice-based) services. There is often poor communication between diagnosticians and those who implement and monitor treatment in schools. In addition, follow-up may be inadequate and fragmented. This is particularly important to ensure monitoring and early detection of any adverse effect of therapy. School-based clinics with a team approach that includes parents, teachers, school psychologists, and other mental health specialists may be a means to remove these barriers and improve access to assessment and treatment. Ideally, primary care practitioners with adequate time for consultation with such school teams should be able to make an appropriate assessment and diagnosis, but they should also be able to refer to mental health and other specialists when deemed necessary.

What Are the Barriers to Appropriate Identification, Evaluation, and Intervention?

Studies identify a number of barriers to appropriate identification, evaluation, and treatment. Barriers to identification and evaluation arise when central screening programs limit access to mental health services. The lack of insurance coverage for psychiatric or psychological evaluations, behavior modification programs, school consultation, parent management training, and other specialized programs presents a major barrier to accurate classification, diagnosis, and management of AD/HD. Substantial cost barriers exist in that diagnosis results in out-of-pocket costs to families for services not covered by managed care or other health insurance. Mental health benefits are carved out of many policies offered to families, and thus access to treatment other than medication might be severely limited. Parity for mental health conditions in insurance plans is essential.

Another cost implication lies in the fact that there is no funded special education category specifically for AD/HD, which leaves these students underserved, and there is currently no tracking or monitoring of children with AD/HD who are served outside of special education. This results in educational and mental health service sources disputing responsibility for coverage of special educational services. Barriers exist in relationship to gender, race, socioeconomic factors, and geographical distribution of physicians who identify and evaluate patients with AD/HD.

Other important barriers include those perceived by patients, families, and clinicians. These include lack of information, concerns about risks of medications, loss of parental rights, fear of professionals, social stigma, negative pressures from families and friends against seeking treatment, and jeopardizing jobs and military service. For health care providers, the lack of specialists and difficulties obtaining insurance coverage present significant obstacles to care.

Conclusions

Attention deficit hyperactivity disorder or AD/HD is a commonly diagnosed behavioral disorder of childhood that represents a major public health problem. Children with AD/HD usually have pronounced difficulties and impairments resulting from the disorder across multiple settings. They can also experience long-term adverse effects on academic performance, vocational success, and social-emotional development.

Despite progress in the assessment, diagnosis, and treatment of AD/HD, this disorder and its treatment have remained controversial in many public and private sectors. The major controversy regarding AD/HD continues to be the use of psychostimulants both for short-term and long-term treatment.

Although an independent diagnostic test for AD/HD does not exist, evidence supporting the validity of the disorder can be found. Further research will need to be conducted with respect to the dimensional aspects of AD/HD, as well as the comorbid (coexisting) conditions present in both childhood and adult AD/HD. Therefore, an important research need is the investigation of standardized age- and gender-specific diagnostic criteria.

The impact of AD/HD on individuals, families, schools, and society is profound and necessitates immediate attention. A considerable share of resources from the health care system and various social service agencies is currently devoted to individuals with AD/HD. Often the services are delivered in a nonintegrated manner. Resource allocation based on better cost data leading to integrated care models needs to be developed for individuals with AD/HD.

Effective treatments for AD/HD have been evaluated primarily for the short term (approximately 3 months). These studies have included randomized clinical trials that have established the efficacy of stimulants and psychosocial treatments for alleviating the symptoms of AD/HD and associated aggressiveness and have indicated that stimulants are more effective than psychosocial therapies in treating these symptoms.

Lack of consistent improvement beyond the core symptoms leads to the need for treatment strategies that utilize combined approaches. At the present time, there is a scarcity of data providing information on long-term treatment beyond 14 months. Although trials combining drugs and behavioral modalities are under way, conclusive recommendations concerning treatment for the long term cannot be made easily.

The risks of treatment, particularly the use of stimulant medication, are of considerable interest. Substantial evidence exists of wide variations in the use of psychostimulants across communities and physicians, suggesting no consensus among practitioners regarding which AD/HD patients should be treated with psychostimulants. As measured by attention/activity indices, patients with varying levels and types of problems (and even possibly unaffected individuals) may benefit from stimulant therapy. However, there is no evidence regarding the appropriate AD/HD diagnostic threshold above which the benefits of psychostimulant therapy outweigh the risks.

Existing diagnostic and treatment practices, in combination with the potential risks associated with medication, point to the need for improved awareness by the health service sector concerning an appropriate assessment, treatment, and follow-up. A more consistent set of diagnostic procedures and practice guidelines is of utmost importance. Current barriers to evaluation and intervention exist across the health and education sectors. The cost barriers and lack of coverage preventing the appropriate diagnosis and treatment of AD/HD and the lack of integration with educational services represent considerable long-term cost for society. The lack of information and education about accessibility and affordability of services must be remedied.

Finally, after years of clinical research and experience with AD/HD, our knowledge about the cause or causes of AD/HD remains speculative. Consequently, we have no strategies for the prevention of AD/HD.

Chapter 11

The National Institute of Mental Health's "Multimodal Treatment Study"

Attention deficit hyperactivity disorder (AD/HD) is the most commonly diagnosed disorder of children, estimated to effect 3-5% of school age children. On average, at least one child in every classroom in the United States needs help for the disorder. The core symptoms of AD/HD include an inability to sustain attention and concentration, developmentally inappropriate levels of activity, distractibility and impulsivity.

"AD/HD is a major public health problem of great interest to many parents, teachers, health care providers, and researchers. Up-to-date information concerning the safety and efficacy of treatments over a significant period of time is critical," said Steven E. Hyman, M.D., Director of NIMH. In this landmark study, the first major clinical trial to look at childhood mental illness and the largest NIMH clinical trial to date, the NIMH and the Department of Education tested the leading treatments for AD/HD for long-term efficacy at multiple research sites in the U.S. and Canada.

Including nearly 600 elementary school children, ages 7-9, the MTA study[1] randomly assigned them to one of four treatment programs: (1) medication management alone; (2) behavioral treatment alone; (3) a

Excerpted from "Collaborative Study Finds Effective Treatments for Attention Deficit Hyperactivity Disorder," by Clarissa Wittenberg and Marilyn Weeks, National Institute of Mental Health (NIMH), December 1999; and text following the heading "What Is the Multimodal Treatment Study of Children with AD/HD?" is from "Research on Treatment for Attention Deficit Hyperactivity Disorder (AD/HD): The Multimodal Treatment Study—Questions and Answers," National Institutes of Mental Health (NIMH), 2000.

combination of both; or (4) routine community care. "All children tended to improve over the course of the study, but they differed in the relative amount of improvement," said Peter Jensen, M.D., one of the primary NIMH collaborators for the study and Senior Advisor to the Director of the NIMH, on assignment to Columbia University. "Nonetheless, determining what treatment will be most effective for a particular child is an important question that needs to be answered by each family in consultation with their health care professional."

The MTA study has demonstrated, on average, that carefully monitored medication management with monthly follow-up, and input from teachers, is more effective than intensive behavioral treatment for AD/HD. The combination of medication management and intensive behavioral treatments was also significantly superior to psychosocial treatments alone in reducing AD/HD symptoms. For some outcomes that are important in the daily functioning of these children (e.g., academic performance, familial relations), the combination of behavioral therapy and medication was necessary to produce improvements, and families and teachers reported somewhat higher levels of consumer satisfaction for those treatments that included the behavioral therapy components. Furthermore, the combination program allowed children to be treated over the course of the study with somewhat lower doses of medication.

The study also found substantial differences between the study-provided medication treatments and those provided in the community, differences mostly related to the quality and intensity of the medication management treatment. During the first month of treatment, special care was taken to find an optimal dose of medication for each child receiving the MTA medication treatment. After this period, the MTA prescribing therapist met with the family for monthly, one-half hour visits with the parent and the child, to assess any concerns that the family might have regarding the medication or the child's AD/HD-related difficulties. In addition, the MTA physicians sought input from the teacher on a monthly basis, and used this information to make any necessary adjustments in the child's treatment. If the child was experiencing any difficulties, the MTA physician was encouraged to consider adjustments in the child's medication. In comparison, the community-treatment physician generally saw the children face-to-face only 1-2 times per year, and for shorter periods of time each visit. Furthermore, they did not have any interaction with the teachers, and generally prescribed lower doses of stimulant medication.

"As the first major randomized treatment study, one of the most important results is that these same findings were replicated across

6 sites, located at diverse but representative geographical areas in this country and in Canada, despite substantial differences among sites in their samples' socio-demographic characteristics. This means that the study's overall results are probably applicable and generalizable for the many and diverse children and families in need of treatment services for AD/HD," said Laurence Greenhill, M.D., a research psychiatrist at Columbia University, one of the research sites.

What Is the Multimodal Treatment Study of Children with AD/HD?

The Multimodal Treatment Study of Children with AD/HD—MTA for short—brought together 18 nationally recognized authorities in AD/HD at 6 different university medical centers and hospitals to evaluate the leading treatments for AD/HD, including various forms of behavior therapy and medications. The study has included nearly 600 elementary school children, ages 7-9, randomly assigned to one of four treatment modes: (1) medication alone; (2) psychosocial/behavioral treatment alone; (3) a combination of both; or (4) routine community care.

Why Is This Study Important?

AD/HD is a major public health problem of great interest to many parents, teachers, and health care providers. Up-to-date information concerning the long-term safety and comparative effectiveness of its treatments is urgently needed. While previous studies have examined the safety and compared the effectiveness of the two major forms of treatment, medication and behavior therapy, these studies generally have been limited to periods up to 4 months. The MTA study demonstrates for the first time the safety and relative effectiveness of these two treatments (including a behavioral therapy only group), alone and in combination, for a time period up to 14 months, and compares these treatments to routine community care. The children involved in the study will be tracked into adolescence to document and evaluate long-term outcomes.

What Are the Major Findings of This Study So Far?

The MTA results published in December 1999 indicate that long-term combination treatments as well as medication-management alone are both significantly superior to intensive behavioral treatments and routine community treatments in reducing AD/HD symptoms. The study also shows that these differential benefits extend as long as 14 months. In other areas of functioning (specifically anxiety symptoms, academic performance, oppositionality, parent-child relations, and social skills), the combined treatment approach was consistently superior to routine community care, whereas the single treatments (medication-only or behavioral treatment only) were not. In addition to the advantages provided by the combined treatment for several outcomes, this form of treatment allowed children to be successfully treated over the course of the study with somewhat lower doses of medication, compared to the medication-only group. These same findings were replicated across all six research sites, despite substantial differences among sites in their samples' sociodemographic characteristics. Therefore, the study's overall results appear to be applicable and generalizable to a wide range of children and families in need of treatment services for AD/HD.

Given the Effectiveness of Medication Management, What Is the Role and Need for Behavioral Therapy?

As noted in the National Institutes of Health (NIH) AD/HD Consensus Conference in November 1998, several decades of research have amply demonstrated that behavioral therapies are quite effective. What the MTA study has demonstrated is that on average, carefully monitored medication management with monthly follow-up is more effective than intensive behavioral treatment for AD/HD symptoms, for periods lasting as long as 14 months. All children tended to improve over the course of the study, but they differed in the relative amount of improvement, with the carefully done medication management approaches generally showing the greatest improvement. Nonetheless, children's responses varied enormously, and some children clearly did very well in each of the treatment groups. For some outcomes that are important in the daily functioning of these children (e.g., academic performance, familial relations), the combination of behavioral therapy and medication was necessary to produce improvements better than community care. Of note, families and teachers reported somewhat higher levels of consumer satisfaction for those treatments that included the behavioral therapy components. Therefore, medication alone is not necessarily the best treatment for every child, and families often need to pursue other treatments, either alone or in combination with medication.

Which Treatment Is Right for My Child?

This is a critical question that must be answered by each family in consultation with their health care professional. For children with AD/HD, no single treatment is the answer for every child; a number of factors appear to be involved in determining which treatments are best for which children. For example, even if a particular treatment might be effective in a given instance, the child may have unacceptable side effects or other life circumstances that might prevent that particular treatment from being used. Furthermore, findings indicate that children with other accompanying problems, such as co-occurring anxiety or high levels of family stressors, may do best with approaches that combine both treatment components, (i.e., medication management and intensive behavioral therapy). In developing suitable treatments for AD/HD, each child's needs, personal and medical history, research findings, and other relevant factors need to be carefully considered.

Why Do Many Social Skills Improve with Medication?

This question highlights one of the surprise findings of the study: although it has long been generally assumed that the development of new abilities in children with AD/HD (e.g., social skills, enhanced cooperation with parents) often requires the explicit teaching of such skills, the MTA study findings suggest that many children can often acquire these abilities when given the opportunity. Children treated with effective medication management (either alone or in combination with intensive behavioral therapy) manifested substantially greater improvements in social skills and peer relations than children in the community comparison group after 14 months. This important finding indicates that symptoms of AD/HD may interfere with their learning of specific social skills. It appears that medication management may benefit many children in areas not previously well known to be salient medication targets, in part by diminishing symptoms that had previously interfered with the child's social development.

Why Were the MTA Medication Treatments More Effective Than Community Treatments That Also Usually Included Medication?

There were substantial differences between the study-provided medication treatments and those provided in the community, differences mostly related to the quality and intensity of the medication management treatment. During the first month of treatment, special care was taken to find an optimal dose of medication for each child receiving the MTA medication treatment. After this period, these children were seen monthly for one-half hour at each visit. During the treatment visits, the MTA prescribing therapist spoke with the parent, met with the child, and sought to determine any concerns that the family might have regarding the medication or the child's AD/HD-related difficulties. If the child was experiencing any difficulties, the MTA physician was encouraged to consider adjustments in the child's medication (rather than taking a wait and see approach). The goal was always to obtain such substantial benefit that there was no room for improvement compared with the functioning of children not suffering from AD/HD. Close supervision also fostered early detection and response to any problematic side effects from medication, a process that may have facilitated efforts to help children remain on effective treatment. In addition, the MTA physicians sought input from the teacher on a monthly basis, and used this information to make any necessary adjustments in the child's treatment. While the physicians in the MTA medication-only group did not provide behavioral therapy, they did advise the parents when necessary concerning any problems the child may have been experiencing, and provided reading materials and additional information as requested. Physicians delivering the MTA medication treatments generally used 3 doses per day and somewhat higher doses of stimulant medications. In comparison, the community-treatment physician generally saw the children face-to-face only 1-2 times per year, and for shorter periods of time each visit. Furthermore, they did not have any interaction with the teachers, and prescribed lower doses and twice-daily stimulant medication.

How Were Children Selected for This Study?

In all instances, the child's parents contacted the investigators to learn more about the study, after first hearing about it through local pediatricians, other health care providers, elementary school teachers, or radio/newspaper announcements. Children and parents were then carefully interviewed to learn more about the nature of the child's symptoms, and rule out the presence of other conditions or factors that may have given rise to the child's difficulties. In addition, extensive historical information was gathered and diagnostic interviews were conducted to establish whether or not the child exhibited the long-standing pattern of symptoms characteristic of AD/HD across home, school, and peer settings. If children met full criteria for AD/HD and study entry (and many did not), informed parental consent with child assent and school permission were received; the children and families then were eligible for study entry and randomization. Children who had behavior problems but not AD/HD were not eligible for study participation.

Where Is This Study Taking Place?

Research sites include:

- New York State Psychiatric Institute at Columbia University, New York, NY

- Mount Sinai Medical Center, New York, NY

- Duke University Medical Center, Durham, NC

- University of Pittsburgh, Pittsburgh, PA

- Long Island Jewish Medical Center, New Hyde Park, NY

- Montreal Children's Hospital, Montreal, Canada

- University of California at Berkeley, CA

- University of California at Irvine, CA

Note

1. MTA study: The full name of this study is the "Multimodal Treatment Study of Children with AD/HD."

Chapter 12

Guiding Principles in Diagnosis and Treatment of AD/HD

Over the past two decades there has been an explosion of diagnosis, treatment and research regarding attention deficit hyperactivity disorder (AD/HD), sometimes referred to as attention deficit disorder (ADD). As clinicians and researchers have gained more experience working with AD/HD, it has become clearer that its impact on life is far greater than we had ever appreciated. AD/HD cannot only interfere with learning and behavior control in childhood, but, as a critical neurobehavioral condition, it can profoundly compromise functioning in multiple areas throughout the life span. Research and clinical experience suggest that AD/HD difficulties can lead to significant educational, occupational, and family dysfunction and can be a significant contributor to a variety of health, social, and economic problems.

AD/HD is a common disorder. The *Diagnostic and Statistical Manual of the American Psychiatric Association, Fourth Edition (DSM-IV)*, estimates that AD/HD is found in 3%-5% of school-age children. A recent review of thirteen community studies of the prevalence of AD/HD indicated that between 1.7% and 16% of children have AD/HD, depending on the populations and the diagnostic methods. As more and more is written and broadcast about AD/HD, increasing numbers of adults and parents wonder whether AD/HD might be underlying the problems they or their children are experiencing.

From "Guiding Principles for the Diagnosis and Treatment of Attention Deficit Hyperactivity Disorder." © 2000 National Attention Deficit Disorder Association; reprinted with permission.

Most parents first turn to their family physician, pediatrician, or a mental health professional for help. The care they receive varies greatly, ranging from a brief office visit that ends with a prescription for medication to a thorough evaluation cooperatively conducted by members of several disciplines. Often, AD/HD is incorrectly diagnosed when it is not present and under diagnosed when it is present; AD/HD is both incorrectly treated and under treated.

One of the most critical steps in properly addressing the significant influence AD/HD has on contemporary society is to establish a standard of care for its diagnosis and treatment. While gaps exist in the knowledge about the precise cause of AD/HD and controversy abounds about aspects of its diagnosis and treatment, research, and clinical experience over the past few decades have been sufficient to begin to identify certain principles regarding the evaluation and treatment of AD/HD.

This chapter seeks to define the essential elements of diagnosis and treatment necessary for producing a high quality of care. The guiding principles listed in this chapter should not be viewed as a diagnostic tool or a therapeutic cookbook. Rather, they represent an organizational framework guiding consumers in navigating the healthcare maze and focusing on our understanding of the essential ingredients of diagnosis and treatment. In addition, they will greatly benefit the work of health care providers, educators, and clinicians, as well as the policy making decisions of health insurance companies, governmental agencies, educational administrators and corporate executives whose actions can have a profound effect on the lives of individuals with AD/HD.

These guiding principles represent a synthesis of lay and professional literature, the experiences of clinicians, and conversations with thousands of patients and families. They should serve as a step towards identifying the essential components of assessment and treatment of AD/HD.

The Guiding Principles in Diagnosis and Treatment of AD/HD

1. Evaluate and Treat the Whole Person

A comprehensive diagnostic protocol for AD/HD provides a description of the whole person. That is, it should seek to identify how a person's AD/HD symptoms interact and contribute to his or her physical and mental functioning, as well as his or her personality. Each person is unique, with unique strengths and weaknesses. Making a diagnosis based solely on plugging attentional symptoms into a diagnostic checklist, for example, is inadequate. After considering the complete person, the role of AD/HD, if present, can be placed in its proper context. The success of treatment is dependent upon understanding and managing AD/HD within the context of an understanding of the whole person.

2. AD/HD Should Be Suspected but Not Presumed

AD/HD is a common problem and may be suspected as a contributing factor whenever a child or an adult experiences problems in learning, self-control, addiction, independent functioning, social interaction, or health maintenance. AD/HD symptoms present across a wide spectrum—from extremely mild to extremely severe. The appropriate diagnosis of AD/HD can help clarify the presence of other physical, learning, and emotional disorders, or may be present in combination with any number of these. The professional will need to identify and address potentially coexisting conditions. These may include:

- Depressive and Bipolar Disorders
- Anxiety Disorders
- Chemical and Behavioral Addictions—drugs, alcohol, disordered eating, gambling, sexual addictions, etc.
- Oppositional Defiant Disorder and Conduct Disorders
- Learning Disorders—including receptive and expressive language problems, reading and written language
- Psychotic Disorders and Pervasive Developmental Disorders
- Obsessive/Compulsive Disorders
- Personality Disorders
- Tic Disorders
- Hypo and Hyperthyroidism—and other hormonal disorders, such as PMS and menopause
- Sleep Disturbances
- Chromosomal Anomalies and other Developmental Syndromes
- Brain Trauma
- Dementia
- Autism
- Asperger's Syndrome

3. AD/HD May Present Across the Life Span

AD/HD is the result of biological differences in the parts of the brain associated with paying attention, impulse control, and activity level. While AD/HD is biologically-based and usually present from birth, symptoms may not become problematic until the individual begins to struggle trying to meet life's expectations. As a result, AD/HD can present clinically anywhere along the life span and in any life domain.

Even though the symptoms of AD/HD may not impair an individual until later in life, some of these symptoms must be present since childhood to make a positive diagnosis. Thus, an early history of AD/HD symptoms is essential in making a diagnosis of AD/HD in an adult. The evaluator should look for evidence of a childhood onset of AD/HD symptoms through third party interviews, transcripts, report cards, teacher comments, medical records, past psycho educational testing, and other archival data.

AD/HD often negatively affects a person's educational achievements. Lack of school success can contribute to a myriad of economic, social and life adjustment problems throughout a person's life. Educational functioning should be reviewed carefully. In children, adolescents, or adult students, a review of educational functioning should include administration of intelligence and achievement tests. However, it should be noted that success in the educational arena is not by itself a reason to rule out the diagnosis of AD/HD.

4. A Comprehensive Assessment Is Necessary for An Accurate Diagnosis

AD/HD is complex and influences all aspects of a person's life. It can co-exist with and/or mimic a variety of health, emotional, learning, cognitive, and language problems. An appropriate, comprehensive evaluation for AD/HD includes a medical, educational, and behavioral history, evidence of normal vision and hearing, recognition of systemic illness, and a developmental survey. The diagnosis of AD/HD should never be made based exclusively on rating scales, questionnaires, or tests. The evaluation should be designed to answer three basic questions: (1) Are a sufficient number of AD/HD symptoms present and causing impairment, at the present time in the person's life; (2) Have these symptoms been present since childhood; and (3) Is there any alternative explanation for the presence of these AD/HD symptoms? A thorough clinical interview reviewing the individual's current and past functioning is the central method for answering these three questions.

5. The Evaluation and Treatment of AD/HD Should Be Conducted by a Qualified Professional

A qualified professional may be from any one of the following disciplines and would have the appropriate license to practice this discipline: psychiatrist, neurologist, pediatrician, internist, family physician, other qualified physician, psychologist, social worker, professional counselor, and psychiatric nurse. A qualified professional not only has a license to practice but has training and experience in the differential diagnosis and treatment of AD/HD, and the full range of metabolic and psychiatric disorders.

6. Response to Medication Should Not be Used As the Basis to Diagnose AD/HD

There are a number of reasons why an individual's response to a stimulant or other medication is not a valid indication of the presence of AD/HD. First, stimulant medications do not work only for people with AD/HD; individuals with other disorders and without any disorders may respond positively to them, though rarely dramatically. Second, failure to respond to medication may be the result of an incorrect dose or that the person's body is not responsive to that drug, rather than because the person does not have the diagnosis of AD/HD. Third, a positive response to medication may be the result of a placebo effect rather than a true indication of the presence of AD/HD. Fourth, the use of medication as a diagnostic tool may lead the physician to prematurely conclude the diagnostic process without considering disorders that coexist with AD/HD and jointly interfere with the individual's functioning.

7. Diagnosis Should Be Based Primarily Upon the DSM-IV AD/HD Criteria

In order to promote standardization, the diagnosis of AD/HD should be based upon the prevailing professional criteria for the diagnosis of mental conditions. At the present time, the prevailing criteria are the *Diagnostic and Statistical Manual of the American Psychiatric Association, Fourth Edition*, known as *DSM-IV*. A number of professionals have justifiably criticized the *DSM-IV* AD/HD criteria, noting several problems. In particular, they are not adjusted for age, making them too stringent in their published form for diagnosis of adults, e.g., adults will be under diagnosed. Minor adjustments have been suggested in the professional literature, but nonetheless, it is strongly recommended that diagnosis be based primarily upon these criteria.

8. Diagnosis and Treatment of AD/HD Should Involve Others Familiar with the Person Undergoing the Evaluation

Proper diagnosis and treatment of AD/HD should involve others when available, such as parents, spouses, teachers, and when appropriate, employers. These individuals can corroborate and provide information and can be enormously helpful in the diagnostic and treatment process. When guided to better understand and accept AD/HD, they can also become positive supports for the person with AD/HD.

9. Treatment Should Often Involve More Than One Discipline Working Cooperatively

Since there is currently no way to cure AD/HD, the goal of treatment is to improve the individual's ability to cope with it. Coping successfully with AD/HD often requires a combination of treatments provided by specialists from different disciplines. The physician prescribes stimulant or other types of medication. The mental health professional and/or the coach provides supportive counseling for the individual with AD/HD and the family, teaches the individual compensatory strategies for home, school, and workplace, and provides training in behavior management. The educator helps to remediate school-based problems, and often provides feedback to the parents and the physician about the effectiveness of medication. Members of different disciplines should communicate with each other coordinating their efforts to help the individual cope most effectively with AD/HD.

10. Stimulant Medications Are the Benchmark of Treatment for Most AD/HD Patients

For many individuals with AD/HD, medication is the cornerstone of an effective overall treatment regimen. Research has repeatedly indicated that stimulant medication ameliorates the symptoms of AD/HD and sets the stage for the individual to benefit synergistically from behavioral, psychological, educational, and coaching interventions. The use of medication, however, should not be undertaken until a comprehensive evaluation has been completed and the diagnosis firmly established. In addition, a physical examination should be performed to assure that the patient is in good health and there are no other medical conditions that would account for the diagnosis. It is also imperative that the patient or the patient's parents thoroughly understand how to monitor the effectiveness of the medication or medications and that all potential side effects be explained.

Since AD/HD is a pervasive problem that affects the quality of life through the lifespan, the majority of individuals diagnosed with AD/HD, both children and adult patients, deserve the benefits of effective medication morning, noon, and night, every day of life. This would include school days, work days, holidays, vacation, and all school breaks, unless there is a compelling reason to do otherwise.

11. Practitioners Should Become Familiar with Current Research and Diagnostic Tools

It is the responsibility of each professional involved in the evaluation and management of AD/HD to continually integrate the most up to date understanding of AD/HD into his/her repertoire of clinical skills. The improved understanding of the cause, diagnosis, and treatment of AD/HD which comes from a review of the current literature will improve the quality of care. Professionals should become familiar with updated diagnostic tools and treatment methods, as well as standards for a comprehensive assessment.

Chapter 13

Medication Management of Children and Adults with AD/HD

Chapter Contents

Section 13.1

Medication in the Management AD/HD

All individuals with attention deficit disorder (AD/HD) experience chronic problems with inattention or hyperactivity-impulsivity to a greater degree than the average person. It is a life span disorder, affecting both children and adults.

Children with AD/HD comprise approximately three to five percent of the school age population. While it has long been thought that boys with AD/HD outnumber girls by approximately three-to-one, recent research shows that the actual numbers may be nearly equal.

AD/HD can be a major problem for adults as well. It is conservatively estimated that two to four percent of adults are affected by AD/HD. In the past, clinicians believed that children outgrew AD/HD before or during adolescence. In part, this belief was due to the fact that researchers and clinicians focused on hyperactivity as the major symptom of AD/HD. We now understand that the major symptoms of AD/HD are primarily inattention and impulsivity, not hyperactivity. Impulsivity and inability to focus attention may continue into adulthood, while hyperactivity can decrease with age.

"AD/HD is one of the best-researched disorders in psychiatry, and the overall data on its validity are far more compelling than for most mental disorders and even many medical conditions" (*Scientific Affairs*, American Medical Association, June 1997, "Diagnosis and Treatment of Attention-Deficit Hyperactivity Disorder in School-Age Children"). Multiple studies have been conducted to discover the cause of the disorder. While there may be other causes of AD/HD, research has certainly indicated that at least three separate yet interactive brain regions have been associated with the condition. AD/HD tends to run in families. More than 20 genetic studies have supported the tendency for inheritability. Also, at least two genes have been reliably documented as being associated with the disorder.

Undoubtedly, a number of genes will likely be identified in the near future as AD/HD is a complex trait and complex traits are typically the result of multiple interacting genes. This information provides increasing support for the concept that AD/HD is largely a neurologically based condition. Without early identification and appropriate treatment, AD/HD can have serious consequences that include school failure and drop out, depression, conduct disorder, failed relationships, underachievement in the workplace, and substance abuse.

Diagnosis of AD/HD

Determining if a child has AD/HD is a multifaceted process. Many biological and psychological problems can contribute to symptoms similar to those exhibited by children with AD/HD. For example, anxiety, depression and certain types of learning disabilities may cause similar symptoms.

There is no single test to diagnose AD/HD. Therefore, a comprehensive evaluation is necessary to establish a diagnosis, rule out other causes and determine the presence or absence of co-existing conditions. Such an evaluation requires time and effort and should include a clinical assessment of the individual's academic, social and emotional functioning and developmental level. A careful history should be taken from the parents, teachers and the child, when appropriate. Checklists for rating AD/HD symptoms and ruling out other disabilities are often used by clinicians.

There are several types of professionals who can diagnose AD/HD, including school psychologists, private psychologists, clinical social workers, nurse practitioners, neurologists, psychiatrists, pediatricians and other medical doctors. Regardless of who does the evaluation, the use of the *Diagnostic and Statistical Manual IV* criteria is necessary. A medical exam by a physician is important and should include a thorough physical examination, including assessment of hearing and vision, to rule out other medical problems that may be causing symptoms similar to AD/HD. In rare cases, persons with AD/HD also may have a thyroid dysfunction. Only medical doctors can prescribe medication if it is needed. Diagnosing AD/HD in an adult requires an evaluation of childhood, academic and behavioral history as well as examining current symptoms.

Treatment for AD/HD

Getting appropriate treatment for AD/HD is very important. There may be very serious negative consequences for persons with AD/HD who do not receive adequate treatment. These consequences can include low self-esteem, social and academic failure, substance abuse, and a possible increase in the risk of later antisocial and criminal behavior. Treating AD/HD in children requires medical, educational, behavioral and psychological interventions. This comprehensive approach to treatment is called multimodal and includes:

- Parent training
- Behavioral intervention strategies
- An appropriate educational program
- Education regarding AD/HD
- Individual and family counseling
- Medication when required

Behavior interventions are a major component for children who have AD/HD. Important strategies include being consistent and using positive reinforcement and teaching problem solving, communication and self-advocacy skills. Children, especially teenagers, should be actively involved as respected members of the school planning and treatment teams. Treatment plans should be tailored to the specific needs of each individual and family. School success may require a range of interventions. Many children with AD/HD can be taught in the regular classroom with minor adjustments to the environment. Some children will require additional assistance using special education services.

This service may be provided within the regular education classroom or may require a special placement outside of the regular classroom that fits the child's unique learning needs. A major research study done by the National Institute of Mental Health (MTA Cooperative Group 1999), called the Multimodal Treatment study was conducted with 579 children with AD/HD (combined type) who received one of four possible treatments for over a 14-month period. The results of this landmark study showed that children in the group treated with medication that was carefully-managed and individually tailored, including intensive behavioral management, plus the treatment group that only received closely monitored medical management, had much greater improvement in their AD/HD symptoms then the groups that received intensive behavior treatment alone or community care.

Treatment for adults with AD/HD also needs to be tailored to the needs of the individual patient. Education is the first strategy for intervention. Initially, most adults with AD/HD have little understanding of their disability. Accurate diagnosis helps adults with AD/HD understand that their educational, vocational and/or personal difficulties may be related to a disability, not to some personal failure or irremediable personality flaw. Many adults have co-existing medical conditions to which they are genetically susceptible, that may require additional medical treatment in order for the adult to achieve maximal improvement. These co-existing disorders may include depression, manic/depressive (bipolar) disorder, anxiety, panic and obsessive-compulsive disorders, Tourette's syndrome, substance abuse, migraine headaches, irritable bowel syndrome and thyroid dysfunction.

Adults benefit from learning to structure their environment to improve time management skills. These involve consistent use of an appointment book, a personal computer or tape recorder. Other strategies include making a daily list of tasks, posting schedules and appointments throughout the home or office, and setting up a self-reward program. Short-term psychotherapy can help an adult with AD/HD identify how his or her disability might be associated with a history of sub-par performance and difficulties in personal relationships. Longer-term psychiatric therapies, which may involve treatment with medication, can help address any mood swings that may exist, stabilize relationships and alleviate any guilt or discouragement.

The Role of Medication

For most children and adults with AD/HD, medication is an integral part of treatment. Medication is not used to control behavior. Medication is used to improve the symptoms of AD/HD so that the individual can function more effectively. Research shows that children and adults who take medication for the symptoms of AD/HD attribute their successes to themselves, not to the medication.

Psychostimulant compounds are the most widely used medications for the management of AD/HD-related symptoms. Psychostimulant medications were first administered to children with behavior and learning problems in 1937. It is believed that psychostimulant medications change the levels of important transmitter chemicals in the brain. These neurotransmitters help the different nerve cells to communicate among themselves. Between 70-80 percent of children with AD/HD respond positively to these medications. Attention span, impulsivity and on-task behavior improve, especially in structured environments. Some children also demonstrate improvements in frustration tolerance, compliance and even handwriting. Relationships with parents, peers and teachers may also improve. Psychostimulant medication can also be effective in adults who have AD/HD. The reaction to these medications can be similar to that experienced by children with AD/HD—a decrease in impulsivity and an increase in attention. Many adults with AD/HD treated with psychostimulant medication report that they are able to bring more control and organization to their lives.

Common psychostimulant medications used in the treatment of AD/HD include methylphenidate (Ritalin), mixed salts of a single-entity amphetamine product (Adderall) and dextroamphetamine (Dexedrine, Dextrostat). Methylphenidate and amphetamine are available as both short and long acting preparations, whereas mixed amphetamine salts are generally short-acting at low doses and longer acting at higher doses.

Short-acting preparations generally last approximately 4 hours; long-acting preparations are more variable in duration—with some preparations lasting 6-8 hours, and newer preparations lasting 10-12 hours. Of course, there can be wide individual variation that cannot be predicted, and will only become evident once the medication is tried.

The specific dose of medicine must be determined for each individual. However, there are no consistent relationships between height, age and clinical response to a medication. A medication trial is often used to determine the most beneficial dosage. The trial usually begins with a low dose that is gradually increased until clinical benefits are achieved. It is common for the dosage to be raised several times during the trial. The patient is monitored both on and off the medication. For children, observations are collected from parents and teachers, even coaches and tutors. Parent and teacher rating scales are often used. In the case of an adult, the patient and significant family members share their impressions with the treatment team. Hundreds of studies on thousands of children have been conducted regarding the effects of psychostimulant medications, making them among the most studied medications in history. Unfortunately, there are no long-term studies on the use of psychostimulant medications. Each family must weigh the pros and cons of choosing medication as part of the treatment plan for AD/HD.

Possible Side Effects of Medications for AD/HD

Most immediate side effects related to these medications are mild and typically short-term. The most common side effects are reduction in appetite and difficulty sleeping. Some children experience stimulant rebound—a negative mood or an increase in activity when medication is losing its effect. This tends to occur in younger children, and is usually seen just as the child arrives home from school. If the child continues to exhibit signs of rebound after about two weeks, consult your doctor. These side effects are usually managed by changing the dose and the scheduling for short-acting medications, or by changing to a prolonged-release formulation. Headache and stomachache are occasionally seen; these often disappear with time or, if necessary, a dose reduction. There may be an initial, slight effect on height and weight gain, but studies suggest that ultimate height and weight is rarely affected.

Parents often report that medication that had previously worked during childhood no longer works once the child reaches adolescence. This is not a time to give up on medical management if it was needed in past years. If this should occur with your child, discuss your observations and concerns with your medical doctor. Some studies suggest that children with AD/HD reach puberty later than their peers. However, for any child who seems to be lagging behind his or her peers, height and weight should be closely monitored.

A relatively uncommon side effect of psychostimulant medications may be the unmasking of latent tics—the medical term for involuntary motor movements, such as eye blinking, shrugging and clearing of the throat. Psychostimulant medications can facilitate the emergence of a tic disorder in susceptible individuals. Often, but not always, the tic will disappear when the medication is stopped. For many youth, vocal tics (throat clearing, sniffing, or coughing beyond what is normal) or motor tics (blinking, facial grimacing, shrugging, head-turning) will occur as a time-limited phenomenon concurrent with AD/HD. The medications may bring them to notice earlier, or make them more prominent than they would be without medication, but they often eventually go away, even while the individual is still on medication.

Tourette's syndrome is a chronic tic disorder that involves vocal and motor tics. Some experts estimate that seven percent of children with AD/HD have tics or Tourette's syndrome, which is often mild, but can have social impact in the rare—but severe form, while 60 percent of children with Tourette's have AD/HD. Recent research suggests that the development of Tourette's syndrome in children with AD/HD is not related to psychostimulant medication. However, a cautious approach to treatment is recommended when there is a family history of tics or of Tourette's syndrome. In these cases, consideration can also be given to treatment with non-stimulant medications as an alternative.

Medications initially developed as antidepressants are used less frequently for AD/HD than stimulant medications, but have been shown to be effective. Those antidepressants that have active effects on the neurotransmitters—norepinephrine and dopamine (the tricyclic classes, and novel medications like bupropion) can have an effect on AD/HD. They are used when contraindications to psychostimulant medications exist, when psychostimulant medications have been ineffective, or when unacceptable side effects have resulted. Antidepressants that affect just the serotonin system (the serotonin selective reuptake inhibitors, or SSRIs, e.g. Prozac, Paxil, Zoloft) have not been shown effective for treating primary symptoms of AD/HD but may be effective against co-existing conditions. Clonidine and Guanfacine (Catapres and Tenex) are sometimes prescribed to reduce excessive hyperactivity or severe insomnia in children with AD/HD, though these medications have not been shown to be effective for alleviating inattention problems Ultimately, the success of an individual with AD/HD depends on a collaborative effort between the patient and a committed team of caregivers. These medications provide an opportunity for the complete multimodal treatment program to be effective and can maximize the effects of other interventions.

Taken alone, however, medication is often not enough to help.

Frequently Asked Questions

How long does it take to achieve a therapeutic dose of medication?

The effects of psychostimulant medications are usually noticeable within 30 to 60 minutes. However, it often takes a few weeks to determine the proper dosage and medication schedule for each individual.

As a child grows, or if an adult changes weight, will the dosage need to be changed?

Not necessarily. Many adolescents and adults continue to respond well to the same doses of psychostimulant medication. However, many others will require higher doses. On the other hand, some children may respond well initially to a low dose of medication and then require a modest dose increase after a few weeks or months once a honeymoon period has passed.

Will my child need to take medication forever, even into adulthood?

Not necessarily. AD/HD is a chronic condition. Its severity and developmental course are quite variable. Up to 67 percent of children with AD/HD continue to exhibit symptoms into adulthood.[1] For these adults, continuing effective treatment modalities, including medication, can be helpful.

Should medication only be taken when the child is in school, or only when the adult is at work?

This should be decided with the doctor and the therapeutic team. Children can often benefit from medication outside of school because it can help them succeed in social settings, peer relations, home environment and with homework. Medication can be of help to children who participate in activities that require sustained attention, such as musical programs, debate or public speaking activities, and organized sports. For adults, the improved organizational and time management skills at home, as well as reduced irritability, are often beneficial for the family unit. As always, the benefits and potential side effects of medications should be considered carefully. Many individuals and families find that consistent use of medication leads to the best long-term results.

What about individuals who do not respond to medication, either psychostimulants or antidepressants?

In general, two or three different stimulant medications should be tried before determining that this group of medications is not helpful. Similarly, several different anti-depressant medications can also be tried. Most individuals will respond positively to one of these medication regimens. But some individuals, because of the severity of their disability or the presence of other conditions, will not respond. And some individuals will exhibit adverse side effects. In such cases, the entire treatment team—family, medical doctor, mental health professional and educator—must work together to develop an effective intervention plan. Other medications such as clonidine may be helpful, and occasionally, combinations of medication may be needed.

When all medication appears to be ineffective, consideration needs to be given to whether the diagnosis of AD/HD is accurate, whether other conditions are affecting functioning, whether appropriate criteria for improvement have been established, and whether objective and accurate feedback is being provided regarding medication efficacy.

Are children who take psychostimulant medications more likely to have substance abuse problems later in life?

No. Although there is potential for abuse when misused, in those being treated appropriately, psychostimulant medications do not cause addictions to develop. Several studies that have followed children with AD/HD for 10 years or more support the conclusion that the clinical use of these medications does not increase the risk of later substance abuse. In fact, emotional difficulties, including substance abuse, are more likely to occur when a child with AD/HD is not treated. Unfortunately, research does show that children who demonstrate conduct disorders (delinquent behaviors) by age 10, and who are smoking cigarettes by age 12, are at higher risk for substance abuse in the teenage years, possibly persisting into mid-life. Therefore, it is important to recognize this subgroup early and get them involved in an effective multimodal therapeutic program.

Overview of Medications Often Used in the Treatment of AD/HD

This information is provided for educational purposes only. Discuss the specifics of any medication with your physician. The names used are the generic (chemical) names of the compounds, with common brand names made by different pharmaceutical companies. It should be noted that a number of new medications for the treatment of AD/HD are currently being researched and should be available in the near future.

Methylphenidate (Ritalin, Methylin, or generic methylphenidate)

- *Form:* Short-acting tablets administered by mouth. Methylphenidate 5 mg, 10 mg, 20 mg.

- *Dosage:* Very individual. Usually between 2.5-20 mg per dose. Effective dose does not necessarily correlate with age, body weight or severity of AD/HD symptoms. Usually the physician prescribes a small starting dose and then gradually increases to find the most effective dose that will not produce excessive adverse effects.

- *Duration of Action:* Rapid-acting methylphenidate starts to work in 15-20 minutes and lasts about 3.5-4 hours. Because of its relatively short action, methylphenidate is discontinued every night and started again in the morning.

- *Possible Side Effects:* Moderate appetite suppression, mild sleep disturbances, transient weight loss, and irritability. Rebound effect can occur—anger and frustration—when the effect of medication dissipates. When the dosage is too high, motor tics may be unmasked, and depression and lethargy may occur. These are managed by lowering the dose. Tics will usually disappear if the dose is lowered.

122

Longer-Acting Methylphenidate

To avoid the need for taking short-acting methylphenidate three to four times daily, several new long-acting delivery systems have been developed. Each of the six systems described delivers the same medicine used in short-acting methylphenidate tablets, but does so in a way designed to give extended coverage so a child can get through a school day without having to take pills at school. Many adults find longer acting preparations more convenient because they do not have to interrupt their workday to take medication for AD/HD as often as would be needed for short-acting tablets. Possible side effects are the same as methylphenidate.

- *Methylphenidate SR 20* (methylphenidate sustained release) (Ritalin) is a long-acting tablet administered by mouth with a duration of action of approximately 6-8 hours. The dosage is prescribed on an individualized basis. Form: 20 mg tablets.

- *Ritalin 20-SR*, the earliest form of extended-release methylphenidate uses a wax-matrix to deliver two doses from one pill. Each of these 20-SR tablets releases about 10 mg of methylphenidate within about one hour after ingestion and then releases another 10 mg about 3.5 hours later. It is intended to last 6-8 hours. Clinicians report that this preparation works well for some individuals, but is unsatisfactory for many others because it may release too quickly or unevenly. Form: 20 mg tablet.

- *Metadate ER*, is similar to the Ritalin 20-SR tablet. Form: 10 mg, 20 mg tablet.

- *Methylin ER*, is similar to the Metadate ER tablet. Form: 10 mg, 20 mg tablet.

- *Metadate CD*, a new extended-release capsule, was approved by the FDA in April 2001. This capsule contains many tiny beads containing methylphenidate. Beads have various types of coatings so they can release 30% of the methylphenidate dose immediately and then continue to release methylphenidate over an extended period of time designed to cover a school day. These capsules should not be chewed; they should only be opened at the direction of a physician. Form: 20 mg capsule.

- *Concerta*, a new osmotic release system for methylphenidate was approved by the FDA in September 2000. This capsule contains three chambers, two filled with different concentrations of methylphenidate and one with a polymer substance that expands when a liquid contacts it; there is a laser-drilled hole in one end. An initial dose of methylphenidate is released from the outer coating soon after the capsule is ingested. Gradually, the medication in the two internal chambers is pushed out as the polymer substance expands, piston-like, in response to liquids absorbed from the digestive tract. Concerta is reported to be effective for about 10-12 hours from ingestion, though individuals may vary on this. Concerta capsules should not be opened or chewed. Form: 18 mg, 36 mg, 54 mg capsules (Each 18 mg is equivalent to about 5 mg of short-acting methylphenidate given three times over the day.)

Mixed Salts of a Single-Entity Amphetamine Product (Adderall)

- *Form:* Double-scored tablets administered by mouth. 5 mg, 7 mg, 10 mg, 12 mg, 15 mg, 20 mg, 30 mg.

- *Dosage:* Very individual.

- *Duration of Action:* Variable. Depending on dose, can last from 3.5-8 hours.

- *Possible Side Effects:* Same as methylphenidate.

Dextroamphetamine (Dexedrine, Dextrostat)

- *Form:* Short-acting tablets administered by mouth. Dextroamphetamine tablets 5 mg, 10 mg.

- *Dosage:* Very individual. Average: 2.5-10 mg.

- *Duration of Action:* Rapid onset of action, 20-30 minutes. Lasts about 4-5 hours.

- *Possible Side Effects:* Same as methylphenidate.

Dextroamphetamine Spansules (Dexedrine)

- *Form:* Long-acting, administered by mouth. Dextroamphetamine spansules. 5 mg, 10 mg, 15 mg. Each spansule releases about one-half of its face-value dose in about 1 hour and then releases the balance about 3.5 hours later. Thus, a 5 mg spansule actually releases the equivalent of 2.5 mg initially and 2.5 mg later. It does not provide the equivalent of 5 mg throughout the duration of its action.

- *Dosage:* Very individual. Average: 5-20 mg.

- *Duration of Action:* Very individual. Usually lasts 6-8 hours, but individual reaction may vary from several hours to the whole day.

- *Possible Side Effects:* Same as methylphenidate.

Pemoline (Cylert)

Note: Not a first choice for the management of AD/HD symptoms due to potential for very serious liver damage.

- *Form:* Long-acting tablets administered by mouth. Pemoline 18.75 mg, 37.5 mg, 75 mg.

- *Dosage:* Very individual.

- *Duration of Action:* Slow onset of action. Generally lasts 8-10 hours.

- *Possible Side Effects:* Same as methylphenidate. Effect on liver functioning of concern, but significant complications are extremely rare. There is no evidence that monitoring liver functions has predictive value with regard to averting complications.; nonetheless, very frequent lab testing is recommended.

Imipramine and Desipramine (Tofranil and Norpramin)

- *Form:* Tablets administered by mouth. 10 mg, 25 mg, 50 mg, and 100 mg.

- *Dosage:* Very individual.

- *Duration of Action:* Variable. Often has 24-hour effect.

- *Effect:* Lower doses may improve AD/HD symptoms within several days, but may take 1-3 weeks for full effect. Higher doses may improve depressive symptoms and mood swings.

- *Possible Side Effects:* Nervousness, sleep problems, fatigue, stomach upset, dizziness, dry mouth, accelerated heart rate. May affect conduction time of the heart, leading to irregular heart rate. In rare cases, may affect blood count. Should not be abruptly discontinued.

Bupropion (Wellbutrin)

- *Form:* Tablets 75 mg and 100 mg; extended release as 100 mg and 150 mg.

- *Dosage:* Very individual.

- *Duration of Action:* About 4-6 hours in short-acting form; 6-8 hours in long-acting form.

- *Effect:* Improves symptoms of AD/HD and can affect depressive moods.

- *Possible Side Effects:* Difficulty sleeping, headache.

Clonidine (Catapres)

- *Form:* Clonidine is available in patches applied to back of shoulder or tablets administered by mouth—0.1 mg, 0.2 mg, and 0.3 mg.

- *Dosage:* Very individual. The clonidine patch is available in three strengths.

- *Duration of Action:* Patches last 5-6 days. Tablets last 4-6 hours.

- *Effect:* Often will improve excessive hyperactivity or insomnia associated with AD/HD, but has not been demonstrated effective for improving inattention symptoms. May decrease facial and vocal tics in Tourette's syndrome. Often has positive side effect on oppositional defiant behavior and may be beneficial for management of excessive anger.

- *Possible Side Effects:* Major side effect is fatigue, though this will usually disappear over time. Other side effects may include dizziness, dry mouth, increased activity, irritability, and/or behavior problems. Physician should be consulted prior to discontinuation of medication to prevent rebound hypertension or other effects.

Guanfacine (Tenex)

- *Form:* Tenex is available in 1 mg tablets taken by mouth.

- *Dosage:* Very individual.

- *Duration of Action:* Guanfacine lasts 6-8 hours.

- *Effect:* Often will improve excessive hyperactivity or insomnia associated with AD/HD, but has not been demonstrated effective for improving inattention symptoms. May decrease facial and vocal tics in Tourette's syndrome. Often has positive side effect on oppositional defiant behavior and may be beneficial for management of excessive anger.

- *Possible Side Effects:* Major side effect is fatigue, though this will usually disappear over time. Other side effects may include dizziness, dry mouth, increased activity, irritability, and/or behavior problems. Physician should be consulted prior to discontinuation of medication to prevent rebound hypertension or other effects.

Section 13.2

An Update on Medications Used in the Treatment of Attention Deficit Disorder

From "An Update On Medications Used in the Treatment of Attention Deficit Disorder," by John Ratey, M.D. This article originally appeared in the Winter 1999 issue of *Focus,* the newsletter of the National ADDA, © 1998 National Attention Deficit Disorder Association; reprinted with permission.

The use of medication to treat adults with attention deficit disorder is a happy intersection of neuroscience and availability of a drug to fit the supposed problem. To the best of our knowledge the major problem in the attention system in the brain of the person who has the diagnosis of AD/HD, or of ADD without the H, is a difference in their dopamine system. Current research shows that there may be as many as 13 different genes that vary from the so-called normal genes that are involved in making up what we call the attention deficits. These genes, which are called alleles as they are alternatives to the most common variety of gene, are mainly involved with the dopamine system. This is reflected in the fact that there is not enough dopamine around to support the system to work in a consistent and predictable manner.

Thus the treatment for AD/HD/ADD rests on the drugs we know as those which effect the dopamine system: the antidepressants, the stimulants, and precursors that may boost the effectiveness of dopamine. While most neuroscientists and neuroscience wannabes are hesitant to reduce anything to a simple equation or catch phrase we might be on fairly firm ground in saying that attention problems may be seen as a dopamine deficiency. Thus the job of medication is to correct this deficit and its associated problems like anxiety, depressed and demoralized moods, overactive startle response, and the many problems with aggression and addictions.

The use of stimulant medications is still the easiest and most accurate route and the one that has proven to be the most efficacious for the greatest number of people with the diagnosis of AD/HD. Contrary to popular wisdom and media perception, they are among the safest drugs. For instance, the only longitudinal studies to date on adolescents show that rather than being a stepping stone to addiction, the one robust finding is that those AD/HD adolescents who took Ritalin were less likely to have a substance abuse problem at the end of their teens and early twenties. For the adult population this is also true. Most of the patients who are treated with stimulants do very well and have little need to escalate the dose once the proper level has been established. In fact, given the pain that monthly prescriptions are for both physician and patient, most adult patients use less and less stimulant as time goes on rather than any creep upwards in dose which some fear may be the quick step to problems with addictions.

The stimulants are usually the first choice because they have a positive effect almost 90% of the time and have fewer side effects than any of the antidepressants. We are still confined to using three types of stimulants: methylphenidate or Ritalin, amphetamine and its brothers and sisters known to most as Dexedrine or Adderall, and pemoline or Cylert. All these medications act by effecting the levels of dopamine at the synapse. Some release dopamine directly, Ritalin and Dexedrine act also to block the reuptake mechanism, and they also act to block some of the metabolic enzymes that hang around the synapse to gobble up loose dopamine.

Pemoline (Cylert) is a long acting medication that takes a while to get to its therapeutic action and thus it does not have an immediate effect like Ritalin or Dexedrine. It also has a saga attached to its use of reported deaths due to liver failure. While the circumstances and the real incidences of the number versus the chance effect is yet to be fully detailed, as of yet it is considered controversial as a first line treatment and recommended only as a second line treatment by the FDA. Abbot Pharmaceuticals, the company that produces Cylert, has not been aggressive in countering the complaints and perception of the risk so that its use has dropped off and Cylert probably will continue to be a second line choice. It is unfortunate as this is truly the only all-day stimulant we have available. Clinical experience shows that the longer the drug acts, the better and the closer it is to producing a normalized attention span, a predictable state of consciousness, and a stable inner core to interact with the environment.

When treating patients, the longer the medication works the better. One of the most important therapeutic actions is to try and produce consistency in brain functions. We try to help them achieve a stable mood and attention function so that they begin to realistically anticipate that each day will be like the next. The argument that the shorter acting compounds offer more control over the attention system seems ludicrous since for most patients the most troubling aspect of using stimulants is the second or third dose, which they often forget. One of the major problems in the ADDer is the ability to remember and plan—so that the need to take another pill at a certain time, and to be aware of the decreasing effectiveness of the medication as it wears off, is a huge problem. Secondly, the up and down effect of the shorter acting agents can add to the disruptive inner state that the patient has dealt with all of his or her life. The shorter acting stimulants thus present problems with not getting to an important goal and benefit of any treatment—stability and predictability of attention, mood, and behavior.

Ritalin for all the media coverage has been the most used by most physicians but I see it as the second line drug, because of its short action and because in my experience it has more side effects than Dexedrine or Adderall. It seems to effect the body more than amphetamine and gives people more muscle discomfort, tenseness and the hibbey gibbeys. Its one advantage that is certainly intangible is that for some it has more of a motivational edge, driving people to do their work with a bit more intensity. But like many other aspects of medicine this is a double-edged sword and can lead some to complain of robotic effects, lack of flexibility, workaholic tendencies and the like.

Ritalin lasts from 1 1/2 to 3 hours in most people, and the SR preparation is no bargain in that it only seems to last another hour or so. Furthermore the idea that people are getting 20 mg of the slow release preparation is troubling as Paul Wender M.D. long ago studied the slow release form and found that this 20 mg pill only gave the equivalence of 7.5 mg of the quick release preparation. The amphetamine compounds are longer acting, usually lasting anywhere from an hour to two hours longer. The longer acting preparations like Dexedrine spansules and Adderall definitely seem to work upwards of 4-6 hours for most patients. But as with any drugs that effect the brain, there is no cookbook as the variety in absorption, distribution, and metabolism system in each individual makes it impossible to predict how each person will handle a given drug. Then you have the fact that the target organ here is the brain, arguably the most complicated structure in the universe and vastly different from one person to another. Therefore, despite our need to reduce and control symptoms we have to accept the fact that dosage, effectiveness, and side effects will vary greatly. The amphetamine preparations have less side effects, and their long acting preparations are definitely the real item. The difference between Adderall and Dexedrine spansules in most patients is minimal. However, there are some who have a much better response on Adderall than on long acting Dexedrine. The reverse is also true but to a much lesser extent.

It is preferable to use the antidepressants with patients as they have the 24 hour action that is so critical. The problem is that they work less well and in a smaller percentage of patients than the more popular stimulant medications. First there are the tricyclics—they have been around for more than 30 years and have proved to be invaluable and relatively safe as a treatment for ADD and related problems. The use of low doses of desipramine (10-40 mg/day) in many adult patients has very low toxicity and is effective in about 30% of patients. Joseph Biederman M.D. and colleagues have written much about the use of desipramine, nortriptyline, and imipramine in adults and children and have found them to be effective about 50% of the time, though they use higher doses approaching what is recommended as treatment for depression (150-200 mg/day).

There is controversy over the use of desipramine in children as to its side effect on the heart's conduction system. There are a number of reports of sudden death from cardiac arrhythmia in children using desipramine. The irritant effect on the heart conduction pathway is reduced after adolescence. As in the case of Cylert, if one uses statistics to look at the actual numbers of untoward incidences of dire problems one would conclude that these drugs are not the cause of the problem. However the availability of decent alternatives seems to make the fears carry more weight and make the tricyclics second line treatments in children, and for Cylert second line treatment in adults as well. These drugs effect the norepinephrine and the dopamine system in the brain so again they act to counter the suspected dopamine deficit.

Wellbutrin (bupropion) came out as a hoped for wonder drug that was touted as the replacement for Ritalin. It blocks the reuptake of dopamine and should be an effective alternative to the stimulants. It is long acting, now there is a slow-release preparation, and it is was claimed to have fewer side effects than the tricyclics. Unfortunately, the effectiveness that we find in the clinical setting is not as happy as we had predicted and hoped for. It works well in about 50% of cases but has many more side effects than any of the previously mentioned choices. For use as an antidepressant, Wellbutrin typically is used in doses of 300-450 mg/day. To treat ADD the dose varies greatly and I have found that the new slow-release preparation marketed for smoking cessation (another dopamine problem) has fewer side effects and may be easier for patients to use, though effectiveness is still very variable.

Both of these antidepressants can be used with the stimulants and synergistically they may help overcome side effects and deficiencies of each of the agents if used separately. For instance, many people experience the rebound effect of Ritalin and Dexedrine whereby the person notices a huge return and worsening of their symptoms as the stimulant is wearing off and being metabolized out of the system. The addition of an antidepressant which acts throughout the day may help cushion this rebound effect. In like manner, the targeted use of the stimulant while the person is on the antidepressant sharpens the attention and focusing when it is necessary.

The newer antidepressant Effexor, which is used in low doses, 1/2 of a 37.5 mg pill twice daily, is useful for some patients. Higher doses often lead to unnecessary side effects, and there is a problem for some in withdrawal of the drug when the trial is finished. Remeron, the new antidepressant on the block, is again mainly a dopamine and norepinephrine acting agent. A problem with Remeron is that most people cannot wake up easily if they take the medicine. Without a doubt this is the best sleeping agent I have ever used over the years but the dose has to be low, low, low.

In summary, we have a number of medications, which are proven effective in the treatment of attention deficit disorders. There are newer medications being developed and undergoing clinical testing, including a long acting 10-hour formulation of methylphenidate. We should always keep in mind the huge variability between individuals as to how they respond to a particular medication, dosage, or drug interaction. We should also keep in mind that medication management of AD/HD is a crucial part of a comprehensive treatment plan, but may not be enough in itself for most ADDers. Medication should be accompanied in most cases by education, behavioral therapies which address developing better coping skills, and ADD coaching.

Suggested Reading

Barkley, R. (1998). *Attention Deficit Hyperactivity Disorders: A Handbook for Diagnosis and Treatment*. New York: Guilford Press.

Brown, T.E. (Ed) (2000) *Attention Deficit Disorders and Comorbidities in Children, Adolescents and Adults*. Washington: American Psychiatric Press.

Goldman, L.S., M. Genel, et al. (1998) "Diagnosis and Treatment of Attention-Deficit/Hyperactivity Disorder in Children and Adolescents." *Journal of the American Medical Association*, 279 (14) 1100-1107.

Greenhill, L.L., Halperin, J.M., Abikoff, H. (1999) "Stimulant Medications," *Journal of the American Academy of Child and Adolescent Psychiatr*, 38 (5) 503-512.

Goldstein, M. Goldstein (1998) *Managing Attention Deficit Hyperactivity Disorder in Children: A Guide for Practitioners — Second Edition*. New York: John Wiley & Sons.

MTA Cooperative Group (1999) "A 14-Month Randomized Clinical Trial of Treatment Strategies for Attention-Deficit/Hyperactivity Disorder." *Archives of General Psychiatry*. 56:12.

MTA Cooperative Group (1999). Moderators and Mediators of Treatment Response for Children With Attention-Deficit/Hyperactivity Disorder. *Archives of General Psychiatry*. 56:1088-1096.

Pliszka, S.R., C.L. Carlson & J.M. Swanson (1999) *AD/HD with Comorbid Disorders*. New York: Guilford Press.

Robin, Arthur L. (1998) *AD/HD in Adolescents: Diagnosis and Treatment*. New York: Guilford Press.

Spencer, T., J. Biederman, et al. (1996) "Pharmacotherapy of Attention-Deficit Disorder Across the Life Cycle" *Journal of the American Academy of Child & Adolescent Psychiatry*, 35 (4) 409-432.

Weiss, M, L.T. Hechtman, et al., (1999) *AD/HD in Adulthood: A Guide to Current Theory, Diagnosis and Treatment*. Baltimore: Johns Hopkins University Press.

Wilens, Timothy (1999) *Straight Talk About Psychiatric Medications for Kids*. New York: Guilford Press.

Reference

1. Barkley, RA, Fischer, M., Fletcher, K., & Smallish, L., (2001). Young adult outcome of hyperactive children as a function of severity of childhood conduct problems, I: Psychiatric status and mental health treatment. Submitted for publication.

Chapter 14

Stimulant Medicines and Children: Ritalin, Wellbutrin, and Other AD/HD Drugs

Sometimes the treatment regime for AD/HD includes stimulant medications that suppress impulsive, disruptive behavior. Medication is often recommended in severe cases where children have received so much negative feedback, they have poor self-esteem and problems in school and at home. Statistics show that 70 to 80 percent of hyperactive youngsters react favorably to treatment medications such as dextroamphetamine (Dexedrine), pemoline (Cylert), and methylphenidate (Ritalin). At the NIH day hospital program, they have been studying a whole host of medications in an effort to find alternative drugs. There are other stimulant medications on the market, but none has been found to be as safe and effective as the three commonly used.

In a pioneering study conducted at the Clinical Center in the 1970s, a single one-time dose of dextroamphetamine was given to normal children to determine if stimulant medication affected them differently than AD/HD children. We found no difference in the two groups. This is a relief to some parents and scientists who once thought

This chapter includes text from "Stimulant Medicines and Children," Department of Health and Human Services (DHHS), Publication Number 94-3501, cited January 2001. Beginning with the heading "Adderall," the information in this chapter is excerpted from "Medication Treatment," found on the Internet site, AD/HD Living Guide, at http://www.adhdliving guide.com, © 2000 Clinical Tools, Inc., reprinted with permission. Additional information about the ADHD Living Guide is included at the end of this chapter.

that medical stimulants slow hyperactive children down below normal levels.

Experts agree that these medications should be used in moderation. In the past, however, some parents were only administering medication during school hours, which often led to good behavior at school and terrible, disruptive behavior at home. The consistent use of medications throughout the day to improve not only behavior, but also self-esteem, is recommended.

Stimulant Research

Debunking the theory that stimulant medications contribute to drug use, a study found that children treated with stimulants are not likely to have a chemical dependency later in life. In yet another study, NIH researchers hoping to find a biological indicator for the disorder, discovered that hyperactive children have less of a breakdown compound of norepinephrine called MHPG. Scientists thought stimulant medication would normalize levels of MHPG, but in fact, it further decreased it.

Foods and AD/HD

In other research, we have been unable to prove that stimulants improve academic achievement in hyperactive children, although several studies indicate otherwise. Researchers have found that children's behaviors generally do not worsen when certain food additives are consumed.

By injecting deoxyglucose (a form of sugar) intravenously into the bloodstream as well as very small amounts of radioactivity, it is possible to make a photograph of the brain and measure brain metabolism. This procedure can be performed on adults and teens with minimal risk, but is not recommended for young children.

Adderall

Adderall (mixed salts of a single-entity amphetamine product) typically improves attention span, increases the ability to follow directions and decreases distractibility among children ages three and older. Adderall may also decrease impulsivity, stubbornness, and aggression. Adderall is convenient for patients, parents, and caregivers because it is effective for most patients when taken once or twice a day. Since it is a different mixture of amphetamine isomers, Adderall may help some individuals when other medications (such as Ritalin) have not proven effective.

When Will My Medication Start to Work?

The effects of Adderall can be felt after a few doses or even after the first dose. Often it takes additional time to achieve the full effect. This may require changes in dosing. Most people can achieve maximum benefit in 3 to 4 weeks.

Are There Any Drug Interactions?

Taking more than one medication at a time may cause a negative or harmful reaction. However, never discontinue the use of any medication unless permission is given by your doctor. Be sure to tell your doctor if you are taking any other medications, including over-the-counter medications like aspirin, herbal remedies, and vitamins.

Any Other Important Information?

If you are pregnant, plan to become pregnant, or breastfeeding, discuss the potential risks of this or any medication with your doctor. Stimulant medications such as Adderall have the potential of being abused; use caution when prescribing or taking this medication.

What Are the Side Effects?

Remember that only some people will experience side effects—and that no one experiences side effects in exactly the same way. If you experience any side effects, contact your doctor or clinician right away and continue taking your medication. The following list may not contain all of the side effects associated with this medication.

- Most common side effects:
  loss of appetite & weight loss, insomnia, headache

- Infrequent side effects:
  dry mouth, nausea

- Rare side effects/risks:
  tics, dizziness, irritability, stomach pain, increased heart rate, hallucinations

Are There Any Drug Interactions?

Remember, always follow your physician's recommendations on how to take your medication. Continue taking your medication as prescribed and consult your physician. Also, if you are taking any herbal remedies, vitamins, and/or over-the-counter medications, be sure to tell your physician.

Possible Drug Interactions

Do not take with MAO Inhibitors; serious, even fatal, interactions can occur. Do not take Adderall if you have taken a MAO Inhibitor in the past 14 days; at least 14 days must pass before you can take Adderall. Acidifying agents such as guanethidine, reserpine, and fruit juices can lower absorption of Adderall. Alkalinizing agents such as Diamox (acetazolamide) increase absorption of amphetamines. Tricyclic antidepressants may increase their levels when taken with Adderall. Thorazine (chlorpromazine), lithium, and Haldol (haloperidol) can blunt the effects of Adderall. Adderall increases the effects of norepinephrine.

What's Different about Adderall XR?

Adderall XR has the same chemical makeup as normal Adderall, but the capsule it is packaged in releases the doses over time. Specifically, it gives two doses: one immediately and the other after a few hours.

Research has shown that Adderall XR works as effectively as normal Adderall, but without the need for a mid-day dose (when a child would be at school). Clinical trials only explored the effects of the drug for three weeks, so doctors are encouraged to monitor their patients if they take Adderall XR for more than three weeks.

Since Adderall XR and Adderall have the same chemical makeup, their side effects are the same. However, it should always be noted that different people experience different side effects from the same drug. Consult your physician for more details.

Catapres (Clonidine)

Catapres (clonidine) is an alternative to stimulants for treating AD/HD. It seems to work best in decreasing hyperactivity, but does not always improve distractibility (as stimulants do). Some physicians have found benefits in using this medication with children who have AD/HD and conduct problems.

When Will My Medication Start to Work?

It may take two or three weeks before you begin to feel better. It may take longer to feel the full therapeutic effects of Catapres due to use, dosage, and other factors.

Any Other Important Information?

If you are pregnant, plan to become pregnant, or breastfeeding, discuss the potential risks of this or any medication with your doctor.

Catapres (clonidine) is also used to prevent migraine headaches, improve outcome in head injury patients, aid menopausal hot flashes and treat severe menstrual cramps, help lessen alcohol or narcotic drug withdrawal, has a role in abnormal heart rhythms, and may have a role in limiting the size of heart damage after a heart attack.

Avoid excess salt. Ask your physician about the proper amount of salt you should have in your diet.

Do not stop this drug suddenly; possible serious, even fatal, withdrawal symptoms can occur.

Hot weather or fever can reduce blood pressure significantly; in these instances, the current Catapres (clonidine) dosage may need to altered.

Side Effect Information

Remember that only some people will experience side effects — and that no one experiences side effects in exactly the same way. If you experience any side effects, contact your doctor or clinician right away and continue taking your medication. The following list may not contain all the side effects associated with this medication.

- Most common side effects:
    constipation, dizziness, drowsiness, dry eyes, dry mouth, decreased heart rate

- Infrequent side effects:
    headache, fatigue, burning eyes, anxiety, sleep disorders (nightmare or vivid dreaming), skin rash, hives, swelling, itching, sexual dysfunctions (decreased libido, impotence)

- Rare side effects/risks:
    hallucinations, depression, psychosis, heart rhythm disorders, urination at night, nausea

Are There Any Drug Interactions?

Remember, always follow your physician's recommendations on how to take your medication. Also, if you are taking any herbal remedies, vitamins, and/or over-the-counter medications, be sure to tell your physician. Following are some, but not necessarily all, the possible drug interactions.

Catapres (clonidine) may decrease the effects of Sinemet (levodopa), causing an increase in parkinsonism symptoms. Inderal/Lopressor etc. (beta-adrenergic-blocking drugs) may increase rebound high blood pressure if Catapres is discontinued before the other drug. Narcan/Talwin NX (naloxone) may blunt the effects of Catapres. NSAIDs (nonsteroidal anti-inflammatory drugs such as acetaminophen) may blunt the blood-pressure lowering effects of Catapres. Calan (verapamil) when taken with Catapres may cause heart problems. TCA antidepressants may decrease the effects of Catapres (clonidine). Use Alcohol with caution; excessive drowsiness and reduction of blood pressure can occur.

Cylert (Pemoline)

You may feel better after taking Cylert for just a few days, although it takes about three to four weeks to feel the full effects. Cylert will work better for some people than others, depending on dosage and individual differences.

Any Other Important Information?

If you are pregnant, plan to become pregnant, or breastfeeding, discuss the potential risks of this or any medication with your doctor.

Stimulant medications such as Cylert (pemoline) have the potential of being abused; use caution when prescribing or taking this medication.

Side Effect Information

Remember that only some people will experience side effects—and that no one experiences side effects in exactly the same way. If you experience any side effects, contact your doctor or clinician right away and continue taking your medication. The following list may not contain all the side effects associated with this medication.

- Most common side effects:
    agitation/irritability, insomnia

- Infrequent side effects:
    dry mouth, headache, nausea, weight loss

- Rare side effects/risks:
    hallucinations, liver irritation/toxicity, increased heart rate,
    tics, Tourette's syndrome

Are There Any Drug Interactions?

Remember, always follow your physician's recommendations on how to take your medication. Continue taking your medication as prescribed and consult your physician. Also, if you are taking any herbal remedies, vitamins, and/or over-the-counter medications, be sure to tell your physician.

Cylert (pemoline) should not be taken with antiepileptic drugs such as Tegretol or drugs that affect the CNS (central nervous system) such as Ritalin (methylphenidate) due to possible adverse reactions.

Dexedrine (Dextroamphetamine)

You may feel better after taking Dexedrine for just a few days, although it takes about three to four weeks to feel the full effects. Dexedrine will work better for some people than others, depending on dosage and individual differences.

Any Other Important Information?

If you are pregnant, plan to become pregnant, or breastfeeding, discuss the potential risks of this or any medication with your doctor. Stimulant medications such as Dexedrine (dextroamphetamine) have the potential of being abused; use caution when prescribing or taking this medication.

Side Effect Information

Remember that only some people will experience side effects—and that no one experiences side effects in exactly the same way. If you experience any side effects, contact your doctor or clinician right away and continue taking your medication. The following list may not contain all of the side effects associated with this medication.

- Most common side effects:
  agitation/irritability, insomnia

- Infrequent side effects:
  dry mouth, headache, nausea, weight loss

- Rare side effects/risks:
  hallucinations, liver irritation/toxicity, increased heart rate,
  tics, Tourette's syndrome, sexual difficulties (impotence,
  changes in libido)

Are There Any Drug Interactions?

Remember, always follow your physician's recommendations on how
to take your medication. If you are taking any herbal remedies, vitamins,
and/or over-the-counter medications, be sure to tell your physician.

Do not take with MAO Inhibitors; serious, even fatal, interactions can
occur. Do not take Dexedrine (dextroamphetamine) if you have taken a
MAO Inhibitor in the past 14 days; at least 14 days must pass before
you can take Dexedrine (dextroamphetamine). Acidifying agents such as
guanethidine, reserpine, and fruit juices can lower absorption of
Dexedrine. Alkalinizing agents such as Diamox (acetazolamide) increase
absorption of amphetamines. Tricyclic antidepressants may increase
their levels when taken with Dexedrine. Thorazine (chlorpromazine),
lithium, and Haldol (haloperidol) can blunt the effects of Dexedrine (dextroamphetamine). Dexedrine increases the effects norepinephrine.

Dextroamphetamine Sulfate (DextroStat)

When Will My Medication Start to Work?

It may be three to four weeks before you begin to feel the effects of
DextroStat. However, some effects may occur only after a few days
or even sooner. It may take longer in some individuals due to dosage,
symptoms, and other factors.

Any Other Important Information?

If you are pregnant, plan to become pregnant, or breastfeeding, discuss the potential risks of this or any medication with your doctor.

Stimulant medications such as DextroStat (dextroamphetamine
sulfate) have the potential of being abused; use caution when prescribing or taking this medication.

Side Effect Information

Remember that only some people will experience side effects—and that no one experiences side effects in exactly the same way. If you experience any side effects, contact your doctor or clinician right away and continue taking your medication. The following list may not contain all the side effects associated with this medication.

- More common side effects:
    loss of appetite/weight loss, insomnia, headache

- Less common side effects:
    dry mouth, nausea

- Rare side effects/risks:
    tics, dizziness, irritability, stomach pain, increased heart rate, hallucinations

Are There Any Drug Interactions?

Remember, always follow your physician's recommendations on how to take your medication. If you are taking any herbal remedies, vitamins, and/or over-the-counter medications, be sure to tell your physician.

Do not take with MAO Inhibitors; serious, even fatal, interactions can occur. Do not take DextroStat if you have taken a MAO Inhibitor in the past 14 days; at least 14 days must pass before you can take DextroStat. Acidifying agents such as guanethidine, reserpine, and fruit juices can lower absorption of DextroStat. Alkalinizing agents such as Diamox (acetazolamide) increase absorption of amphetamines. Tricyclic antidepressants may increase their levels when taken with DextroStat. Thorazine (chlorpromazine), lithium, and Haldol (haloperidol) can blunt the effects of DextroStat.

Metadate CD

When Will My Medication Start to Work?

Metadate CD capsule is taken orally and has an initial peak plasma level after 1.5 hours. Due to its biphasic design, the drug has a second peak at 4.5 hours.

Any Other Important Information?

Metadate CD uses Eurand's Diffucaps technology to help it release the pill contents in a biphasic design. This system allows 30% of the drug to be released immediately and then the other 70% to be released during the course of the day.

The drug has been approved by the FDA for use in patients of 6 years of age or older. Patients with the following conditions should be cautious:

- history of seizures
- hypertension/cardiovascular disease
- glaucoma
- motor tics
- family history of Tourette's
- history of psychosis
- drug dependence/alcoholism

Patients who also have marked anxiety, tension, or agitation should also be cautioned.

Side Effect Information

Remember that only some people will experience side effects—and that no one experiences side effects in exactly the same way. If you experience any side effects, contact your doctor or clinician right away and continue taking your medication. The following list may not contain all the side effects associated with this medication.

- Most Common Side Effects:
  headache, loss of appetite, abdominal pain, insomnia
- Infrequent Side Effects
  no data
- Rare Side Effects
  no data

Are There Drug Interactions?

Remember, always follow your physician's recommendations on how to take your medication. If you are taking any herbal remedies, vitamins, and/or over-the-counter medications, be sure to tell your physician.

Metadate CD should not be taken within 14 days of taking MAO inhibitors. Patients who are taking the following drugs should be cautioned:

- anti-coagulants
- anti-convulsants
- anti-depressants: tricyclics and SSRIs

Ritalin—Methylphenidate

Methylphenidate is a medication prescribed for individuals (usually children) who have an abnormally high level of activity or attention-deficit hyperactivity disorder (AD/HD). According to the National Institute of Mental Health, about 3 to 5 percent of the general population has the disorder, which is characterized by agitated behavior and an inability to focus on tasks. Methylphenidate also is occasionally prescribed for treating narcolepsy.

Health Effects

Methylphenidate is a central nervous system (CNS) stimulant. It has effects similar to, but more potent than, caffeine and less potent than amphetamines. It has a notably calming effect on hyperactive children and a focusing effect on those with AD/HD.

Recent research at Brookhaven National Laboratory may begin to explain how methylphenidate helps people with AD/HD. The researchers used positron emission tomography (PET—a noninvasive brain scan) to confirm that administering normal therapeutic doses of methylphenidate to healthy, adult men increased their dopamine levels. The researchers speculate that methylphenidate amplifies the release of dopamine, a neurotransmitter, thereby improving attention and focus in individuals who have dopamine signals that are weak, such as individuals with AD/HD.

When taken as prescribed, methylphenidate is a valuable medicine. Research shows that people with AD/HD do not become addicted to stimulant medications when taken in the form prescribed and at treatment dosages. Another study found that AD/HD boys treated with stimulants such as methylphenidate are significantly less likely to abuse drugs and alcohol when they are older than are non-treated AD/HD boys.

Because of its stimulant properties, however, in recent years there have been reports of abuse of methylphenidate by people for whom it is not a medication. Some individuals abuse it for its stimulant effects: appetite suppression, wakefulness, increased focus/attentiveness, and euphoria. When abused, the tablets are either taken orally or crushed

143

and snorted. Some abusers dissolve the tablets in water and inject the mixture—complications can arise from this because insoluble fillers in the tablets can block small blood vessels.

Trends in Ritalin Abuse

At their June 2000 meeting, members of NIDA's Community Epidemiology Work Group (CEWG) shared the following information.

The abuse of methylphenidate has been reported in Baltimore, mostly among middle and high schools students; Boston, especially among middle and upper-middle class communities; Detroit; Minneapolis/St. Paul; Phoenix; and Texas.

When abused, methylphenidate tablets are often used orally or crushed and used intranasally.

In 1999, 165 methylphenidate-related poison calls were made in Detroit; 419 were reported in Texas, with 114 of those involving intentional misuse or abuse.

On Chicago's South Side, some users inject methylphenidate (this is referred to as west coast). Also, some mix it with heroin (a speedball) or in combination with both cocaine and heroin for a more potent effect.

Because stimulant medicines such as methylphenidate do have potential for abuse, the U.S. Drug Enforcement Administration (DEA) has placed stringent, Schedule II controls on their manufacture, distribution, and prescription. For example, DEA requires special licenses for these activities, and prescription refills are not allowed. States may impose further regulations, such as limiting the number of dosage units per prescription.

Stimulants

The term stimulants is a broad term used to describe a type of medication that is used to treat AD/HD. The individual types of stimulants have been discussed previously in this chapter.

Of all the medications used, stimulants most effectively treat the symptoms of AD/HD. In fact, up to 80% of people who try stimulants for AD/HD find relief from their symptoms, usually in just a few days. However, since stimulants have a high potential for abuse, they should be prescribed with close supervision by a healthcare professional.

Common stimulants include:

- Adderall (mixed salts of a single-entity amphetamine product)

- Cylert (magnesium pemoline)

- Dexedrine (dextroamphetamine)
- DextroStat (dextroamphetamine sulfate)
- Ritalin (methylphenidate)

Stimulants are sometimes used to treat depression, especially among people who experience unpleasant side effects from standard antidepressants such as TCAs and MAOIs. Stimulants are also used to treat narcolepsy, a sleep disorder characterized by sudden and unpredictable sleep attacks.

Tenex

Tenex (guanfacine) is an alternative to stimulants for treating AD/HD. It seems to work best in decreasing hyperactivity, but does not always improve distractibility (as stimulants do). Some physicians have found benefits in using this medication with children who have AD/HD and conduct problems.

When Will My Medication Start to Work?

This medication should be taken for at least four to six weeks to determine the therapeutic effects on lowering high blood pressure and other indications. Tenex (guanfacine) may not show peak beneficial effects until 12 weeks. It may take longer to feel the full therapeutic effects of Catapres due to indication, dosage, and other factors.

Any Other Important Information?

If you are pregnant, plan to become pregnant, or breastfeeding, discuss the potential risks of this or any medication with your doctor. Tenex (guanfacine) is also used to treat heroin withdrawal, useful in problem pregnancies, and may help in treating some sleep disorders. Hot environments, fever, and heavy exercise can cause fluctuations in blood pressure. Ask your physician for guidance in these instances.

Do not stop this medication suddenly; serious withdrawal symptoms can occur.

Side Effect Information

Remember that only some people will experience side effects—and that no one experiences side effects in exactly the same way. If you experience any side effects, contact your doctor or clinician right away and continue taking your medication. The following list may not contain all the side effects associated with this medication.

- Most common side effects:
    drowsiness, dry mouth, constipation, mild lowering of blood pressure on standing (orthostatic hypotension)

- Infrequent side effects:
    skin problems (skin rash, itching), headache, dizziness, fatigue, insomnia, indigestion, nausea, diarrhea, slow heartbeat

- Rare side effects/risks:
    amnesia, liver toxicity, edema or leg cramp, rebound high blood pressure (if stopped abruptly), sexual problems (decreased libido, impotence)

Are There any Drug Interactions?

Remember, always follow your physician's recommendations on how to take your medication. Also, if you are taking any herbal remedies, vitamins, and/or over-the-counter medications, be sure to tell your physician. Following are some, but not all, the possible drug interactions.

Tenex (guanfacine) taken with Elavil (amitriptyline) and other tricyclic antidepressants may cause decreased effectiveness in lowering blood pressure. Phenobarbital can also blunt the therapeutic effects of Tenex(guanfacine).

Avoid excessive salt; consult your doctor about safe amounts of salt in your diet. Use alcohol with caution; it can cause excessive drowsiness and reduction of blood pressure when taken with Tenex (guanfacine).

Wellbutrin

Bupropion Hydrochloride is also prescribed to help people quit smoking. In this version, it is called Zyban. Zyban and Wellbutrin are the same exact medication, Bupropion Hydrochloride, but are marketed differently. The doses used are different also because Wellbutrin is used to treat depression and AD/HD, and Zyban is used for smoking cessation.

This medication works by increasing the levels of the neurotransmitters dopamine and norepinephrine in the brain, thereby relieving the symptoms of depression.

When Will My Medication Start to Work?

Usually, you should start feeling the effects of Wellbutrin within one to four weeks. It may take longer to experience the full effects of Wellbutrin, which depends on dosage and varies from person to person.

Any Other Important Information?

If you are pregnant, plan to become pregnant, or breastfeeding, discuss the potential risks of this or any medication with your doctor. If you take Wellbutrin, you may be more vulnerable to seizures if your dosage is too high, have suffered brain damage, or have had seizures before. In recent studies, 28% of patients exhibited weight loss of 5 lb. or more. Caution should be taken if weight loss is a major factor in your depressive illness.

Also, many patients experience a period of increased restlessness, especially when first taking the drug. This may take the form of agitation, insomnia, and anxiety.

What Are the Side Effects?

Remember that only some people will experience side effects—and that no one experiences side effects in exactly the same way. If you experience any side effects, contact your doctor or clinician right away and continue taking your medication. The following list may not contain all the side effects associated with this medication.

- Most common side effect:
    weight loss, insomnia, nervousness, fever, headache, chills, seizures, constipation, rash, blurred vision, excitement, loss of appetite.

- Infrequent side effects:
    agitation, constipation, dry mouth, nausea, increased libido, skin problems, tremors, nightmares, excessive sweating

- Rare side effects/risks:
    hypomania, fainting, seizures, tinnitus, white blood cell decrease

Are There Any Drug Interactions?

Remember, always follow your physician's recommendations on how to take your medication. Also, if you are taking any herbal remedies, vitamins, and/or over-the-counter medications, be sure to tell your physician.

Avoid excessive use of alcohol; it can increase the risk of seizures. Do not use Wellbutrin and marijuana; there have been cases of induced psychotic behavior. Adverse interactions have been found with other medications such as MAO inhibitors, Levodopa, major tranquilizers such as Thorazine, other antidepressants, Tagamet, Tegretol, and phenobarbital.

About ADHD Living Guide

The ADHD Living Guide project, which includes information for kids, teens, parents, physicians, and teachers, is produced by Clinical Tools, Inc. under contract with the Agency for Healthcare Research and Quality. Clinical Tools, Inc. is a physician-owned, multimedia company with offices in Chapel Hill, NC and Pittsburgh, PA. The company is dedicated to producing interactive health education materials for both professionals and the general public.

Visit the ADHD Living Guide online at www.adhdlivingguide.com. To learn more about Clinical Tools, Inc. or to view information about project administrators and consultants, visit www.clinicaltools.com.

Chapter 15

Long-Term Effects of Stimulant Medications on the Brain

Stimulant medications (i.e., methylphenidate, d-amphetamine, other amphetamines, and pemoline) are commonly used in the treatment of children with attention deficit hyperactivity disorder (AD/HD). Their efficacy is well established, being supported by many controlled studies. AD/HD usually manifests itself in the first 7 years of life and runs a chronic course. Stimulants suppress the symptoms of AD/HD but do not cure the disorder. As a result, children with AD/HD are often treated with stimulants for many years. There has been a major increase in the use of stimulants in the treatment of AD/HD during the last decade.

Stimulants are usually well tolerated when used to treat AD/HD and devoid of acute severe toxicity. Decrease of appetite and sleep disturbance are among the most common side effects. A transient slowing of weight and height growth has been reported for prepubertal children who received continuous treatment with stimulants, but ultimate height does not seem to be affected. However, controlled studies of the long-term safety of these drugs beyond 2 years are not available. Such data are especially important given the major developmental changes that children undergo while being treated with stimulants.

Excerpted from "Long-Term Effects of Stimulant Medications on the Brain: Possible Relevance to the Treatment of AD/HD," National Institute of Mental Health (NIMH), 1999; and "Boys Treated with Ritalin, Other Stimulants Significantly Less Likely to Abuse Drugs Later," National Institute on Drug Abuse (NIDA), 1999.

One major concern is that long-term stimulant administration in children may alter the way the brain reacts to further exposure to stimulants or other drugs with potential for abuse. Stimulants are known to induce behavioral sensitization in animals, but this has been shown only at much higher doses than those used in clinical practice. Subjects with AD/HD are at higher risk for conduct problems, including substance abuse. Thus far, an association between therapeutic use of stimulants and substance abuse has not been proven, within the limitations of the currently available follow-up studies.

A more general concern is that chronic exposure to stimulants during development may change the way the brain reacts to a variety of environmental challenges, including stressful events and pharmacological agents. Although there is no evidence from the available data that this is the case in humans, the extensive, sustained use of stimulants for the treatment of children with AD/HD adds significance to these issues.

From an effectiveness point of view, it is similarly unknown whether successful treatment of AD/HD symptoms in childhood results in a better prognosis regarding such outcomes as incidence of psychopathology, involvement with substance of abuse, antisocial behavior, rate of accidents, educational achievement, social adjustment, and occupational status.

Boys Treated with Ritalin and the Relationship to Substance Abuse Later in Life

In an August 2, 1999, news release, the National Institute on Drug Abuse (NIDA) reported the findings of a study conducted jointly with the National Institute of Mental Health (NIMH). The study compared the susceptibility to substance use disorder among three groups of boys: 56 boys with attention deficit hyperactivity disorder (AD/HD) who had been treated with stimulants for an average of 4 years, 19 boys with AD/HD who had not been treated with stimulants, and 137 boys without AD/HD. AD/HD, the NIDA news release explained, is characterized by difficulties in paying attention, in keeping still, and in suppressing impulsive behaviors. It is usually treated with stimulants, such as methylphenidate (Ritalin) or dextroamphetamine (Dexedrine, Adderall) because these drugs reduce the behavioral and attentional problems connected to AD/HD.

All boys in the study were at least 15 years old when they were evaluated for substance abuse involving alcohol, marijuana, hallucinogens, stimulants, or cocaine. Results of the study showed that 75%

of the nonmedicated AD/HD boys had at least one substance use disorder, compared to 25% of the medicated AD/HD boys and 18% of the boys without AD/HD.

The study researchers at Massachusetts General Hospital, Harvard School of Public Health, and Harvard Medical School calculated that treating AD/HD with medication (stimulants were used in over 90% of the cases) was associated with an 84% reduction in risk of developing a substance use disorder. The researchers will continue to study this entire group of boys in a follow-up study funded by the NIDA.

NIDA Director Alan Leshner says, "while some clinicians have expressed concern about giving stimulants to children with AD/HD because they fear it might increase the risk that these children will abuse stimulants and other drugs when they get older, this study seems to show the opposite. Treating the underlying disorder, even if with stimulants," says Leshner, "significantly reduces the probability they will use drugs later on."

Chapter 16

Homeopathy as an Alternative to Ritalin

The epidemic proportions of the ADD diagnosis are gaining widespread attention from parents, educators, physicians, and other healthcare providers. Many people are seriously questioning the possibility of over diagnosis. This issue was raised in an informative cover article in *Newsweek* magazine. "AD/HD has become America's No. 1 childhood psychiatric disorder. Since 1990, Dr. Daniel Safer of Johns Hopkins University School of Medicine calculates, the number of kids taking Ritalin has grown two and a half times. Among today's 38 million children at the ages of five to fourteen, he reports, 1.3 million take it regularly. Sales of the drug last year alone topped $350 million. This is, beyond question, an American phenomenon. The rate of Ritalin use in the United States is at least five times higher than in the rest of the world, according to federal studies." The article continues, "For all the success they've had in treating AD/HD, many doctors are convinced that Ritalin is over prescribed."

We have seen a number of children who were high-spirited, extremely imaginative, and so precocious that their parents were unable to keep up with their ceaseless questions and insatiable intellectual

This text is reprinted from "An Alternative to Ritalin: Homeopathy as a Highly Effective Treatment for ADD," in *Ritalin-Free Kids: Safe and Effective Homeopathic Medicine for ADD and Other Behavioral and Learning Problems* (2nd Edition) by Judyth Reichenberg-Ullman, N.D., M.S.W., and Robert Ullman, N.D. (Prima Publishing 2000), © Judyth Reichenberg-Ullman and Robert Ullman; reprinted with permission. Complete information about the authors is included at the end of this chapter.

appetites. We have also met children who were overamped, but performed just fine in school. Many of these children have been diagnosed with ADD, even though we feel they fall more into the category of unusual, remarkable, or gifted children. Some youngsters are the victims of rigid, overly strict teachers whose highly structured classroom environments simply do not pace their temperaments and learning styles. Or they have excessively rule-bound parents who do not extend to their children the freedom that they need to thrive and expand their creative talents.

We have also seen a large number of children whose behaviors are very disruptive and disturbing through no fault of teachers. No one can expect a teacher in a classroom of forty active children to cope happily with the statistical average of 10 percent (four children) in her class with ADD. The amount of extra attention, discipline, and time just trying to keep these children and those around them safe is more than many teachers can handle.

Can we, however, lump all of these children together under one diagnostic category? Can a child who lashes out at his family, peers, and teachers in a violent, destructive manner and has no interest in his schoolwork fit into the same diagnostic group as a sweet, gregarious child who simply cannot pay attention in class? Conventional medicine would say that, based on their scores on standardized ADD tests, both children could indeed have ADD. Homeopathy would say that these are two distinct children whose problems and temperaments are as different as night and day. A homeopath would prescribe very different medicines for the two children, rather than giving them both stimulants.

Table 16.1. The Pros of Homeopathic Treatment of ADD

Treats the whole person at the root of the problem

Considered safe, without the side effects of Ritalin and other medications

Uses natural, nontoxic medicines

Treats each person as an individual

Heals physical as well as mental and emotional symptoms

Lasts for months or years rather than hours

Is inexpensive

Is cost-effective

And what about the many conditions that mimic ADD, such as dyslexia and other learning disabilities, vision and auditory problems, epilepsy, developmental disorders, hypothyroidism, hyperthyroidism, hypoglycemia, food allergies, lead poisoning, caffeinism, anxiety, depression, and obsessive compulsive disorder, just to name a few? It is essential to understand and differentiate each individual child, not only from the viewpoint of psychological testing, but also to comprehend deeply the physical symptoms, experience, feelings, beliefs, and motivations of each child.

Unlike many other syndromes there is no physical examination or laboratory test that definitely confirms the diagnosis of ADD. While some psychologists and educators use the Conners' Rating Scales, others, including physicians, often base the diagnosis on the subjective reports of parents and teachers. The inconsistency of diagnostic criteria and apparent over diagnosing in this country has led many to question the diagnosis of ADD. Some educational experts acknowledge that "The position that AD/HD is not a proven syndrome has many advocates, physicians as well as educators. However, whether or not a syndrome exists, it is clear that many children have difficulty in school because of an inability to attend to tasks. The ideal would be to describe each child's strengths and weaknesses and offer an individualized program." We would like to take this a step further: Offer an individualized medicine as well as a learning program tailored to the needs of the individual child.

The Homeopathic Approach to ADD

Homeopaths are able to treat ADD effectively in many cases by bringing the individual into balance. Homeopaths treat people with ADD, not the ADD itself. For a homeopath, what needs to be treated is the specific pattern of symptoms which an individual presents. Only the one homeopathic medicine that specifically matches the unique symptoms of the individual will allow the person to live in a functional way.

Homeopaths always take the whole person into account. If the chief complaint of the person were his inability to sit still, difficulty concentrating, or other symptoms of ADD, these behaviors would certainly be taken into account, but in combination with all the person's other symptoms. The homeopath would note anything unusual about that person. That might include a history of scarlet fever during childhood, a strong fear of birds, recurrent dreams of falling out of bed at night and no one coming to the rescue, or a craving for persimmons.

The homeopath sincerely seeks to understand the uniqueness of the patient.

Why Choose Homeopathy Over Conventional Medicine for ADD?

The most common reason patients choose homeopathic treatment is the positive results they have heard from others with similar problems or because they have been referred by another physician or practitioner who is familiar with homeopathic treatment of ADD.

The patient or parents have read about homeopathy, and the philosophy and approach make more sense to them than conventional medicine.

Many adults and parents choose homeopathic treatment because it is safe, nontoxic, and effective.

Conventional medications for ADD act very briefly. A dose of Ritalin, for example, lasts only about four hours. One dose of the correct homeopathic medicine usually lasts at least four to six months.

Homeopathic medicines often result in growth spurts in children and never suppress a child's normal development. Nor do they cause such side effects as tics, appetite suppression, and insomnia.

Homeopathic medicines are very inexpensive. The only significant cost of homeopathic treatment is office visits. Once the person has responded well to the homeopathic medicine, appointments are infrequent.

Homeopathy treats the whole person. Not only do learning and behavioral problems improve, so do most or all of the other physical, mental, and emotional complaints of the person. Conventional medication for ADD works only on specific learning and behavioral problems. Sally Smith, a parent of an ADD child formerly on Ritalin, describes this phenomenon by holding up a ruler and pointing to the one-inch mark: "Ritalin makes you available to learn. You and your parents and teachers have to work on all the rest."

Homeopathy will not make a child depressed or dull. Parents sometimes complain that, although stimulant and antidepressant medications have eliminated some of the more severe problem behaviors, their children's spirits seem dampened and they do not seem like their former selves.

Homeopathic medicines are generally given infrequently and over limited periods of time. Conventional medications put only a temporary lid on ADD symptoms. Doctors often recommend that these medications be taken for the rest of the patient's life.

What Can I and My Family Expect from Homeopathic Treatment?

Homeopaths have high expectations for their patients. We generally do not consider a homeopathic medicine effective for a patient unless the person's symptoms are at least 50 percent (usually 70 percent or more) improved and this improvement lasts for a year or more. This requires that the patient stay with homeopathic treatment for at least a year. The homeopath keeps a careful record of all of the symptoms and characteristics that were elicited during each interview. As treatment progresses, these symptoms should get better and better. An improvement can usually be noticed within one month, and often within days or weeks.

A patient can expect his energy and overall sense of well being to improve as well as an improvement in most or all of his mental, emotional, and physical complaints. This means, as you will see over and over that not only does attention and behavior improve, but also headaches, growing pains, constipation, nail biting, and other symptoms improve after the homeopathic medication has been prescribed.

Can Homeopathic and Conventional Medicines Be Used Together?

This is one of the most common questions we are asked by adults or parents of children who have been diagnosed with ADD. This is ultimately a decision between the patient and the prescribing physician. A general guideline is to assess whether the prescription medication is effective. In cases where the patient sees no improvement from the medication that has already been prescribed, the prescribing physician and patient generally agree to stop the medication and to try homeopathy instead.

In other cases, the medication is working but the side effects are disturbing. With still other patients, the prescription medication is having a positive effect, but the patient or parents do not like the idea of staying on medication and seek a more natural alternative. In these situations, the patient or parents may inform the prescribing physician that they wish to discontinue the medication long enough to try an alternative.

Another category of patients feels that their symptoms of ADD are so severe that they dare not discontinue their medications until they have found another therapy that is effective. In such a case, many homeopaths will prescribe the homeopathic medication in addition to the prescription drugs the person is already taking. As the homeopathic medicine works and the patient improves, the patient can work with his physician to taper off the prescription medication. This process requires knowledge and experience and is another compelling reason to seek an experienced homeopath.

What If My Doctor Does Not Believe in Homeopathy?

From the time that homeopathic medicine was first brought to this country in the early 1800s, there have been many skeptics among medical doctors. Homeopathic philosophy is very different from what is taught in conventional medical schools. When homeopathy is mentioned in a medical history class, it is generally dismissed as an aberration of the past.

With the growing interest in homeopathic medicine and with the disillusionment about the side effects and short-term benefits of much of modern medical treatment, a growing number of conventional doctors are opening their minds to homeopathy. Some medical doctors are incorporating homeopathy into their conventional practices or referring to other homeopathic practitioners. In our practice, we receive many referrals from medical doctors and osteopaths. Many conventionally trained physicians and other licensed healthcare practitioners have studied homeopathy in the courses that we teach through the International Foundation for Homeopathy. Many physicians, although they may know nothing about homeopathy, encourage their patients, especially children, to use any therapies that are of real benefit to that person rather than, or in combination with, conventional medicines.

If your physician or your child's physician is adamantly opposed to you trying homeopathy and it is your choice to do so, you can try to educate him or her about homeopathic treatment of ADD or you can find a physician who is more supportive of your freedom of choice. Homeopathic practitioners are generally happy to educate conventional physicians about homeopathic philosophy and treatment. Even a skeptical person may be convinced of the possible benefits of homeopathy if he or she reads case studies, attends a homeopathic case conference, or sees the results of successful homeopathic treatment.

Using Homeopathy Along with Other Therapies

Homeopathic medicine is very compatible with many other treatment modalities. Family and individual counseling is often much more effective and proceeds more quickly when one or more family members are under homeopathic treatment. When the whole person is in balance, his mind is generally clearer and he is much more able to move forward in his life.

Therapies such as chiropractic, craniosacral, auditory integration, psychotherapy, and biofeedback are fine to pursue along with homeopathy. Once the correct homeopathic medicine has been given, many patients find that they no longer need to follow strict allergy rotation diets, receive desensitization injections, take megadoses of numerous vitamins and minerals, and use other therapies aimed at treating individual symptoms. It is very understandable that individuals with ADD want to try anything that has the possibility of helping them, but using too many therapies, conventional or alternative, at the same time can make it very difficult to discern what effect each specific therapy is having. When a person receives the correct homeopathic medicine, she knows it. She feels an improvement in energy, physical ailments, concentration, attitude, and creativity. Once she feels so much better, she generally no longer needs lots of other therapies.

Are There Any Things I Can't Do During Homeopathic Treatment?

There are certain substances and exposures that consistently interfere with homeopathic treatment. Most practitioners will advise you to avoid the following substances: coffee, eucalyptus, camphor, menthol, recreational drugs, and electric blankets. You will be asked to avoid using topical medications such as topical steroids, antibiotics, antifungals, and to use oral antibiotics and cortisone products only after consulting your homeopath, except in cases of emergency. Acupuncture, although a treatment of tremendous value, is not recommended during homeopathic treatment. Nor are other treatments, which are prescribed in order to remove specific symptoms without treating the whole person.

Can Homeopathy Help Me or My Child?

Most people are potential candidates for homeopathic treatment As with any treatment, you must make a commitment to follow the recommendations of your homeopath. You must be willing to follow these guidelines:

1. You should stay with homeopathic treatment for a minimum of six months to one year before seeking out other therapies.

2. You, as a patient or a parent or family member, need to provide thorough and honest information to the homeopath. The better the homeopath understands the patient, the more likely the best medicine can be found and a lasting cure can result.

3. You need to inform the homeopath of any medications that you or your child is taking. Once there has been improvement with homeopathic treatment, prescription medications for ADD are generally unnecessary. A growing number of conventional physicians are encouraging parents to seek alternative treatment for ADD in hopes that the children will not need to be medicated throughout childhood and sometimes throughout much of their lives.

4. There are a small number of substances and influences, such as coffee and recreational drugs, which are likely to interfere with homeopathic treatment and which you will need to avoid. Homeopathic practitioners will make their own recommendations regarding this matter.

5. You need to come for scheduled appointments and to inform the homeopath of any significant changes in your health during the course of homeopathic treatment. Homeopathic follow-up appointments are generally every six weeks to three months. Once you are doing well, follow-ups are generally scheduled less frequently.

The Limitations of Homeopathic Treatment

Homeopathic treatment is not for everyone. The following are factors that prevent a person from being a good candidate for homeopathic treatment:

1. There are some children, particularly teenagers, who are so opposed to anything their parents recommend that they will sabotage homeopathic treatment, either by refusing to go to appointments or take the medicines or by intentionally using substances that interfere with homeopathic treatment. Similarly, both parents need to be convinced that homeopathy is a valid treatment or willing to try it for at least six months.

2. Some people have such severe behavioral problems that they need to be in an institution, such as a jail or drug or alcohol

treatment center, rather than outpatient treatment. We are aware of only one such institutional program, which offered homeopathy as part of a research study and hope others will in the near future.

3. Individuals who are unwilling to avoid those substances which interfere with homeopathic treatment, such as coffee or recreational drugs, are not good candidates for homeopathy.

4. Homeopathic medicines may not act as quickly initially as prescription drugs, though the positive effects last much longer. This requires patience and a willingness to stick with the treatment process.

Why Not Treat Yourself or Your Family?

There are many classes available on prescribing homeopathic medicines for acute illnesses such as colds, flus, and minor infections. We encourage you to take these classes, to read more about acute prescribing, to buy a homeopathic home kit, and to try homeopathic medicines on yourself and your family for minor illnesses. If the person treated does not improve in a day or two, be sure to consult your homeopathic or conventional physician.

There are over 2,000 homeopathic medicines. It takes years of homeopathic study and practice to make the fine distinctions about when to prescribe which medicine. Although homeopathic medicines do not have long lists of side effects like many conventional medicines, it is also possible to experience a reaction to the medicine. In any chronic condition, whether physical, mental, or emotional, do not treat yourself or your child. Find an experienced homeopathic practitioner. If you were considering brain surgery, you would not read a book or two, buy a set of scalpels, and start cutting. Homeopathy is just as complicated an art as neurosurgery. Just because homeopathic medicines are widely available does not mean they are easy to use. Please do not experiment on yourself or your family members for ADD. Find an expert.

How Can I Find a Homeopath?

A growing number of health care practitioners, including medical doctors (M.D.), naturopathic physicians (N.D.), osteopathic physicians (D.O.), chiropractors (D.C.), family nurse practitioners (F.N.P.), physicians' assistants (P.A.), acupuncturists (L.A., C.A., or O.M.D.), and veterinarians (D.V.M.), practice homeopathic medicine. Most homeopaths have a family practice. We know of no experienced homeopaths in the United States who focus solely on patients with ADD. Since a homeopath always treats the whole person, such specialization is not necessary to find good treatment. What is most important is to find a practitioner who specializes in classical homeopathy, who spends at least an hour with each new patient, prescribes one homeopathic medicine at a time based on a detailed interview rather than a machine, and waits at least five weeks before assessing the progress of the patient. If at all possible, find a homeopath who is board certified. It is not always possible to find a homeopath in your immediate area, or even your state. You will be likely to find much better results, even if you need to travel or do your homeopathic consultations by telephone, than to go to someone in your area who knows some homeopathy, but is not experienced and does not specialize in homeopathy.

About the Authors

Judyth Reichenberg-Ullman, N.D., M.S.W. and Robert Ullman, N.D. are licensed naturopathic physicians and board-certified diplomats of the Homeopathic Academy of Naturopathic Physicians. In addition to *Ritalin-Free Kids*, Drs. Reichenberg-Ullman and Ullman are co-authors of numerous books including *Homeopathic Self-Care* (1997), *The Patient's Guide to Homeopathic Medicine* 1995), *Prozac-Free* (1999), and *Rage-Free Kids* (1999). Dr. Reichenberg-Ullman is the author of *Whole Woman Homeopathy* (2000).

The doctors practice at The Northwest Center for Homeopathic Medicine in Edmonds and Langely, Washington. For more information about Drs. Reichenberg-Ullman and Ullman, contact The Northwest Center for Homeopathic Medicine, 131 Third Avenue North, Edmonds, WA 98020, 425-774-5599, or visit their website at www.healthyhomeopathy.com.

Chapter 17

What Is AD/HD Coaching?

The idea of hiring a coach to improve one's performance in the worlds of work, athletics or the arts is certainly not new. But what about hiring a coach to help your overall performance and ability to live a balanced and fulfilling life? The field of personal and professional coaching aims to do just that.

A partnership with a personal coach will provide you with structure, support and feedback so you can take action toward the realization of your vision and goals in life. Through this process of personal discovery, you will build a greater level of awareness and responsibility to make lasting changes in your life. Even though personal coaching is still young as a profession, it has given rise to many specialty areas of coaching, including the coaching of individuals with attention deficit disorder.

ADD coaching is a supportive, practical, concrete process in which you and the coach work together to identify and pursue your goals. The primary purpose of coaching is to help the individual with ADD develop the structures necessary to function effectively and to teach practical approaches to the challenges of daily life.

What Is the Role of the Coach?

The coach provides encouragement, recommendations, feedback, and practical techniques such as reminders, questions, and calendar

From "What Is ADD Coaching?" by Nancy Ratey, Ed.M. © 1998 National Attention Deficit Disorder Association; reprinted with permission.

monitoring. Strategies are developed to address issues of time management, eliminating clutter in one's home or office, and becoming more effective in one's personal and professional life. ADD coaching is not psychotherapy. Coaches are not licensed therapists, nor do coaches make any representation of such.

What Is the Role of the Client?

Coaching is a process that happens over time. Since it is a client-driven service, for coaching to be successful you must possess a strong desire for personal growth and improvement. Coaching focuses on your being in action towards self-edification, self-improvement, creating life balance, and reaching goals.

How Does ADD Coaching Work?

Regular meetings and check-ins are an essential part of the coaching process. These sessions can be done in person, by telephone, by fax or by e-mail, whichever is preferable to you. However, before coaching begins, you and the coach will need to have an in-depth, one to two-hour initial meeting to develop the step-by-step plans needed to achieve goals. You might also arrange periodic progress reviews as part of the on-going coaching process.

Programming, structuring and guided-self exploration are the core elements of the ADD coaching process. By customizing the coaching service to meet your needs through programming, you are able to develop a user-friendly partnership to motivate and steer you forward. Structuring improves your focus and attention so you are able to channel your abilities to function at your best and achieve goals. The non-judgmental questions of guided self-exploration assist you to analyze the situation at hand and work toward an achievable resolution.

How Does Coaching Help You Take Charge of Your Brain?

Coaching helps you learn about your brain and its deficits in order to demystify it. If you understand the strengths and weaknesses of your brain, you can develop strategies to sustain attention and maintain motivation to reach your goals. The concrete, practical strategies and tools explored through coaching transform an "I can't" attitude into "Yes, I can!" The brain can learn! There is hope for making positive, lasting changes in your life.

About the Author

Nancy A. Ratey, Ed.M., ABDA (D), has been active locally and nationally in the disability arena. She serves on the National ADDA Board of Directors, consults to businesses and educational institutions, and runs a full coaching practice in Wellesley, MA. Nancy may be reached at e-mail address: nancy@nancyratey.com.

Chapter 18

Mutual Life Coaching

Mutual Life Coaching is creating a partnership in which each person provides support for the other.

Recently I received correspondence about the concept of mutual life coaching for adult ADD. According to the writer, this works in much the same way as the Buddy System in 12 step programs, allowing each person to guide and help the other through difficult times. It does require that each member of the team have a commitment to improving their own life, as well as guiding another. The shared experiences can provide support and feedback for both partners.

The partnership must have trust and each partner must feel secure within the relationship. This is not a professional relationship, where one person is paying for the services of another, but an opportunity for two people with ADD to come together. As a team, they build a relationship on trust and mutual respect, allowing the person to work through situations on their own, by being there to give advice when asked, give support whenever needed, provide feedback on actions and share successes, no matter how big or small. In order for this to be successful, guidelines must be set in the beginning to outline the relationship, what each person desires to gain, how the support will be offered, and the roles each person is to play. Confidentiality, avoiding unasked questions and not interfering with another person's situation are of utmost importance to allow both partners to feel secure in the relationship.

The following is the result of further correspondence to help understand the concept of mutual life coaching. The individual wishes to remain anonymous—we will call him "John."

John's Background and ADD Diagnosis

Early in my scientific career I had instinctively done a number of tricks to make myself productive. I teamed up with others, who helped me finish papers on subjects that my ideas had started. I committed myself to high-profile articles with ironclad deadlines—that forced me into crash completion of work. Otherwise, my high creativity and wide interests combined with poor work habits and low self-esteem created compulsive distractibility. I had extreme difficulty in finishing products and experienced increasing memory lapses. A string of mental health clinics, psychiatrists and psychologists found no Alzheimer's or deterioration, which I had feared, but gave me various diagnoses including bipolar disorder, for which treatments—mainly medication—didn't work.

Eventually I was diagnosed with ADD by a highly competent psychiatrist. It was a huge relief to know what was causing my problems. Once defined—it was obvious. But counseling and various medication cocktails of Ritalin/Dexedrine with antidepressants provided only minor help. By now things were so serious that I had gotten demoted. I was humiliated and my depression made my effectiveness and distractibility even worse. Guilt regarding unfulfilled tasks and responsibilities put a sort of repelling electric fence around them.

Once a rising star for my creative breakthroughs in earth science research, the demotion sank me into greater depression. I realized once-a-week therapy would never be enough.

The First Step—Reaching Out to Others

Having experience with Al Anon, the companion 12-Step program to Alcoholics Anonymous, I knew about 90 meetings in 90 days and the importance of that kind of intense contact for people in trouble. In desperation I started an ADD support group with others.

In the early 90's Dr. Edward Hallowell and Dr. John Ratey came out with their best-selling book on Attention Deficit Disorder, *Driven to Distraction*. A year or two later Dr. Hallowell released a videotape, "ADD from A to Z" (1997). This tape announced a life coach approach toward helping adults with ADD/ADHD.

We bought Ned Hallowell's video, and advertised a showing open to the public at our regular meeting. Only in this way could I even marshal enough discipline to watch it all the way through.

What Is Mutual Life Coaching?

An ADD Coach is trained and paid and can provide brief daily contact with an ADD client. This allows for more frequent support than possible in standard therapy. Our group decided to try the life coaching—with a twist. I teamed up with another meeting member to try mutual life coaching. After a difficult start, I achieved the first breakthrough in following a task list in my life. Other breakthroughs followed. I got hope and my depression lifted.

How Did You Start?

I started my mutual life coaching with a young health care professional man. According to Dr. Hallowell's guidelines we would contact each other once a day by phone and exchange HOPE messages: HOPE was an acronym for Hello, Objectives, Plan, and Encouragement. We were to give three objectives—no more. It wasn't good enough to say "I'm going to complete my report today." We had to provide a plausible plan of how we would tackle the target. Finally, we gave each other Encouragement—no phony backslapping. We provided no advice but might occasionally ask a pointed question or share some technique that had worked for us.

Did You See Improvement?

My buddy was initially way ahead of me. For the first 4-6 weeks— yes, it's true—in daily contacts I could hardly complete a single one of my tasks unless they were phony or trivial. Putting them on the list made my crazy mind deviously procrastinate them day after day. Finally I become worried that my life coach would dump me. I couldn't cheat—12-step program experience steered me away from that. Finally, I managed to complete one task. That breakthrough was critical. Over weeks and months I was able to increase my success ratio. I began to go beyond one day and try to build bigger tasks that would have to be broken down and worked on for longer periods.

My work improved markedly, and I picked up confidence. Meanwhile, things took a downturn for my friend. He had a young family and an extremely busy life making ends meet. He had scheduled a professional qualifying exam and failed it. Now he realized he hadn't put advance preparation at a high enough priority level—and he mobilized his Life Coach Objectives to work on that—it was extremely difficult to make time for studying, and it appeared that only a life coach could have provided frequent enough support and reminders to sustain his effort. He passed the second time around.

Do You Still Use Mutual Life Coaching?

My partner quit life coaching. I found a new partner. After a year or so I moved to my present location with major increases in responsibilities and new initiatives under my leadership. My new partner also was shaky in his job but went past me like a rocket with the help of a Life Coach. We e-mailed each other daily. I am shortly going to ask to get my old rating back. But let me admit it—I'm still in the soup. This time, however, it's because I have taken on too many projects, some of a scope I would have never had the courage to undertake in the past. To cope with this new crisis I am now taking professional time management counseling. The bottom line that has been burned into my consciousness is that I can't make it by myself, but I can if I am willing to accept help.

Chapter 19

Unproven Treatments for AD/HD

In the past decade, there has been a tremendous upsurge of scientific and public interest in attention deficit/hyperactivity disorder (AD/HD). This interest is reflected not only in the number of scientific articles, but in the explosion of books and articles for parents and teachers. Great strides have been made in understanding and managing this disorder. Children with AD/HD who would have gone unrecognized and untreated only a few short years ago are now being helped, sometimes with dramatic results.

There are still many questions to be answered concerning the developmental course, outcome and treatment of AD/HD. Although there are a number of effective treatments, they are not equally effective for all children with AD/HD. Among the most effective methods to date are the judicious use of medication and behavior management. Cognitive self-control programs, when applied carefully and consistently, can also be helpful. Results of the landmark NIMH-sponsored MTA study showed that children in the group treated with medication that was carefully-managed and individually tailored, including intensive behavioral management, plus the treatment group that only received closely monitored medical management, had much greater improvement

From "Assessing Complementary and/or Controversial Interventions," this article originally appeared as "CHADD Fact Sheet No. 6," Spring 2000, © CHADD; reprinted with permission. For more information write to CHADD at 8181 Professional Place, Suite 201, Landover, MD 20875, or visit CHADD at their website at www.chadd.org.

in their AD/HD symptoms then the groups that received intensive behavior treatment alone or community care.

In an effort to seek effective help for AD/HD, however, many people turn to treatments which claim to be useful, but which have not been shown to be truly effective in accord with standards held by the scientific community.

How Are Treatments Evaluated?

Treatments may be evaluated in one of two ways:

1. standard scientific procedure or

2. limited case studies or testimonials.

The scientific approach involves testing a treatment in carefully controlled conditions, with enough subjects to allow researchers to be comfortable with the strength of their findings. These studies are repeated a number of times by various research teams before arriving at a conclusion that a particular treatment alleviates a particular problem.

Good scientific studies go through a peer review before they are published in a scientific journal. Peer review is the analysis of research by a group of professionals with expertise in a specific scientific or medical field. Findings are not considered substantive until additional studies have been conducted to reaffirm (or refute) the findings.

In the second method of evaluation, conclusions are drawn from a limited sample size and are often based solely on testimonials from doctors or patients. A treatment that is evaluated only in this manner is not necessarily a harmful or ineffective treatment. However, when standard scientific evaluation is lacking, it does raise questions about the effectiveness and safety of a treatment.

How Do I Assess Alternative Treatments?

Alternative treatment approaches are usually publicized in books or journals which do not require independent review of the material by recognized experts in the field. Often, in fact, the advocate of a particular treatment approach publishes the work himself. Measurement techniques and statistical means of evaluation are scant at best, and often single-case studies are offered as proof of the effectiveness of the treatment.

Questions to Ask Alternative Health Care Providers

Have clinical trials been conducted regarding your approach? Do you have information regarding the results? Can the public obtain information about your alternative approach from the National Center for Complementary and Alternative Medicine Clearinghouse at the National Institutes of Health? (The NCCAM develops and disseminates fact sheets, information packages and publications to assist the public in understanding NIH research in the areas of complementary and alternative medicines.) The office can be reached toll free at (888) 644-6226 or through their web site: http://ncaam.nih.gov/. Is there a national organization of practitioners? Are there state licensing and accreditation requirements for practitioners of this treatment? Is your alternative treatment reimbursed by health insurance?

Checklist for Spotting Unproven Remedies

This list has been adapted from *Unproven Remedies*, Arthritis Foundation, 1987.

Is it likely to work for me?

Suspect an unproven remedy if it claims it will work for everyone with AD/HD and other health problems; uses only case histories or testimonials as proof; cites only one study as proof; cites a study without a control (comparison) group.

How safe is it?

Suspect an unproven remedy if it comes without directions for proper use; does not list contents; has no information or warnings about side effects; is described as harmless or natural. Remember, most medication is developed from natural sources.

How is it promoted?

Suspect an unproven remedy if it claims it's based on a secret formula; claims that it will work immediately and permanently for everyone with AD/HD; is described as astonishing, miraculous, or an amazing breakthrough; claims it cures AD/HD; is available from only one source; is promoted only through infomercials, self-promoting books, or by mail order; claims that treatment is being suppressed or unfairly attacked by the medical establishment.

How Do I Evaluate Media Reports?

Develop a healthy skepticism and be sure to watch for red flags when evaluating media reports of medical advances. When evaluating reports of health care options, consider the following questions.

What is the source of the information?

Good sources of information: medical schools, government agencies (such as the National Institutes of Health and the National Institute of Mental Health), professional medical associations, and national disorder/ disease-specific organizations (such as CHADD). Information from studies in reputable peer-reviewed medical journals is more credible than popular media reports.

Who is the authority?

The affiliations and relevant credentials of experts should be provided, although initials behind a name do not always mean that the person is an authority. Reputable medical journals now require researchers to reveal possible conflicts of interest—such as when a researcher conducting a study also owns a company marketing the treatment being studied.

Is the finding preliminary or confirmed?

Unfortunately, a preliminary finding is often reported in the media as a breakthrough result. An interesting preliminary finding is a more realistic appraisal of what often appears in headlines as an exciting new breakthrough. You should track results over time and seek out the original source, such as a professional scientific publication, to get a fuller understanding of the research findings.

Tips for Negotiating the World Wide Web

The good news is that the Internet is becoming an excellent source of medical information. The bad news is that with its low cost and global entry, the web is also home to a great deal of dubious health information. In addition to the tips cited earlier, web-surfing requires special considerations.

Know Where You Are

Part of the address tells you what kind of domain owns the host computer (e.g., .edu = university, .com = company, .org = non-profit organization, .gov = government agency).

To obtain a second opinion regarding information on the web, you can pick a key phrase or name and run it through a search engine to find other discussions of the topic, or talk to your health care professional.

Forewarned Is Forearmed

Get into the habit of actively seeking out information about AD/HD and every prescribed medication and intervention that is proposed for you or your child. If you use alternative medicines, don't forget that they, too, are drugs. To prevent harmful interactions with prescribed medications, inform your health care provider of any alternative medication used.

Controversial Treatments for AD/HD

Dietary Intervention

Over the years, proponents of the Feingold Diet have made many dramatic claims. They state that the diet—which promotes the elimination of most additives from food—will improve most (if not all) children's learning and attention problems. They claim that the diet will lead to improvements in school, and report a deterioration in learning and behavior when the diet is not followed.

In the past 15 years, dozens of well-controlled studies published in peer-reviewed journals have consistently failed to find support for the Feingold Diet. While a few studies have reported some limited success with this approach, at best this suggests that there may be a very small group of children who are responsive to additive-free diets.

A large number of studies have also examined the relationship between sugar and hyperactive behavior, but most of them are difficult to interpret. A few well-designed studies have found that sugar does have some effect on behavior, but this effect is very small and only a small percentage of those with AD/HD seem to be vulnerable. At this time, it has not been shown that dietary intervention offers significant help to children with learning and attention problems.

Megavitamins and Mineral Supplements

The use of very high doses of vitamins and minerals to treat AD/HD is based on the theory that some people have a genetic abnormality which results in increased requirements for vitamins and minerals. The theory postulates that when these higher-than-normal requirements are not met, various forms of illness result, including AD/HD.

Although vitamins are virtually synonymous with health, there is a complete lack of supporting scientific evidence for this treatment. There are no well-controlled studies supporting these claims, and of those studies in which proper controls were applied, none reported positive results. Both the American Psychiatric Association and the American Academy of Pediatrics have concluded that the use of megavitamins to treat behavioral and learning problems is not justified.

Anti-Motion Sickness Medication

Advocates of this theory believe that there is a relationship between AD/HD and problems with coordination and balance, attributed to problems in the inner-ear system (which plays a major role in balance and coordination). Advocates of this approach recommend a mixed array of medications including anti-motion sickness medication. They claim a success rate in excess of 90 percent in a group of 100 children with AD/HD children but—these results were not published and cannot be verified.

This approach is not consistent in any way with what is currently known about AD/HD, and is not supported by research findings. Anatomically and physiologically, there is no reason to believe that the inner-ear system is involved in attention and impulse control in other than marginal ways.

Candida Yeast

Candida is a type of yeast which lives in the human body. Normally, yeast growth is kept in check by a strong immune system and by friendly bacteria, but when the immune system is weakened or friendly bacteria are killed by antibiotics, candida can overgrow. Advocates of this model believe that toxins produced by the yeast overgrowth weaken the immune system and make the body susceptible to AD/HD and other psychiatric disorders. They tout the use of antifungal medication and a low-sugar or elimination diet as treatment.

There is no evidence from controlled studies to support this theory, and it is not consistent with what is currently known about the causes of AD/HD.

EEG Biofeedback

Proponents of this approach believe that children with AD/HD can be trained to increase the type of brain-wave activity associated with sustained attention and to decrease the type of activity associated with daydreaming and distraction.

While the theory underlying EEG biofeedback as a treatment for AD/HD is consistent with what is known about low levels of arousal in frontal brain areas in individuals with AD/HD, its effectiveness is not demonstrated at this time. Several studies have produced impressive results, but these studies are seriously flawed by the use of small numbers of children with ambiguous diagnoses, and the lack of appropriate control groups. This is an expensive, unproven approach, and parents are advised to proceed with caution.

Applied Kinesiology

Advocates of this approach—also known as the Neural Organization Technique—believe that learning disabilities are caused by the misalignment of two specific bones in the skull which creates unequal pressure on different areas of the brain, leading to brain malfunction. This misalignment is also said to create ocular lock, an eye-movement malfunction which contributes to reading problems. Treatment consists of restoring the cranial bones to the proper position through specific bodily manipulations.

This theory is not consistent with either current knowledge of the cause of learning disabilities nor knowledge of human anatomy, as even standard medical textbooks state that cranial bones do not move. No research has been done to support the effectiveness of this form of treatment. It has no place in the treatment of children with learning-disabilities.

Optometric Vision Training

Advocates of this approach believe that visual problems—such as faulty eye movements, sensitivity of the eyes to certain light frequencies and focus problems—cause reading disorders. Treatment programs vary widely, but may include eye exercises, educational and perceptual training, biofeedback, nutritional counseling and family therapy.

Scientific studies of this approach are few in number and flawed in design. In 1972, a joint statement highly critical of this optometric approach was issued by the American Academy of Pediatrics, the American Academy of Ophthalmology and Otolaryngology, and the American Association of Ophthalmology. In the absence of supporting evidence for its effectiveness, this approach should not be employed in the treatment of AD/HD. Parents are advised to proceed with caution.

Suggested Reading

Ingersoll, B. (1993). ADD and LD—Realities, Myths and Controversial Treatments. New York, New York: Doubleday Publishing Group.

Zametkin, A. Current Concepts: Problems in the Management of Attention-Deficit Hyperactivity Disorder. *The New England Journal of Medicine*, 340: 40 - 46.

Chapter 20

Vision Therapy: Is It an Effective Treatment for AD/HD?

Children with undetected vision problems are sometimes inaccurately diagnosed as having ADD (attention deficit disorder) or AD/HD (attention deficit hyperactivity disorder, attention deficit hyperactive disorder, ADD/AD/HD, ADD-AD/HD, AD(H)D or LD/ADD, LD. In the last two decades, the diagnoses of attention deficit disorder or attention deficit hyperactivity disorder have become very popular (some would say epidemic). Before labeling a child as having attention deficit disorder or attention deficit hyperactivity disorder, it would be wise to evaluate them for developmental problems such as problems with visual development, motor development and/or auditory development.

Can discipline and behavior problems in the classroom (such as those associated with attention deficit disorder) be related to problems with visual development?

It is the feeling of most authorities on the subject that there is a very positive correlation between the two kinds of problems. Furthermore, it is felt that a cause and effect relationship exists between visual problems and school behavior problems.

From "Comments on Attention Deficit Disorder (or Attention Deficit Hyperactivity Disorder) and Vision Therapy," by Donald J. Getz, O.D., F.C.O.V.D., F.A.A.O., © 2000 Donald J. Getz; reprinted with permission. And from "Position Statement on Optometric Vision Therapy," an undated document produced by the American Optometric Association, © American Optometric Association, cited January 2002; reprinted with permission.

When vision is difficult and requires greater effort than normal, the child will usually exhibit an avoidance reaction to near point work, and thus will appear not to be trying or daydreaming.

The child with an undetected visual problem is often accused of having a short attention span and is often told he could do better if he tried harder. However, the child soon learns that no matter how hard he tries, success is not possible. Consequently, he soon gives up academically and must find other ways to occupy his time. Unfortunately, most of his alternatives are not socially acceptable in a large classroom.

Human nature also dictates that what the child does not do well, he would rather not do. Therefore, he will look for things which he can do well and these, also, might be socially unacceptable in the classroom.

The answer does not lie in stricter discipline and regimentation of these children, but rather in making a stronger attempt to detect and correct the underlying visual problems with the proper lenses and/or vision therapy.

What are the clues that I should look for in a child that might indicate a possible need for vision therapy?

Besides the more obvious clues of blurred vision, discomfort, double vision, words running together, etc., I feel a deeper probe in the history might elicit some of the following signs:

1. Reversals when reading (i.e., "was" for "saw", "on" for "no", etc.)

2. Reversals when writing (b for d, p for q, etc.)

3. Transposition of letters and numbers (12 for 21, etc.)

4. Loss of place when reading, line to line and word to word.

5. Use of finger to maintain place

6. Holding book too close

7. Distorted posture when reading or writing

8. Omitting small words

9. Confusing small words

10. Short attention span

11. Daydreaming in class

12. Poor handwriting

13. Clumsiness on playground or at home

In addition to the specific items mentioned, I believe the single most important clue is performance that is not up to potential. Any child whose verbal ability surpasses his ability to learn visually should be suspected of a vision problem.

Additional signposts, which alert me to a possible vision problem, are statements from parents and teachers such as "he is lazy," "he does not try," "he could do better if he exerted more effort," and other such statements. It is obvious that various kinds of vision problems could cause these types of observations.

It is vital that a complete case history be obtained so that any vision problems uncovered can be related directly to both the child and the parental observations. A vision problem standing alone can only be of academic interest. But if that problem can be related to observable behavior, then it takes on significance and can, in turn, be related to lowered academic performance.

What are the vision skills necessary for classroom achievement which can be provided through vision therapy?

It has been estimated that 75 to 90 percent of all learning in the classroom comes to the student either wholly or partially via the visual pathways. There are numerous learned skills that the child must develop in order to achieve in the classroom. The most obvious skill is that the child must already have learned to coordinate his two eyes together. If he has difficulty in this area, he might perceive overlapping images or—if he is not perceiving in this manner—he is using an abnormal amount of effort to overcome the coordination problem, thus reducing performance.

In addition, he must have learned accurate, smooth versional eye movements and quick, accurate saccadic movements so that he can point his eyes where he will with a minimum of effort. Focusing ability must be adequately developed so that it can be maintained over extended periods of time. Also, accommodative flexibility must be present so that attention can be shifted quickly, smoothly and effortlessly from book to chalkboard and back to book. Form perception must be developed so that he can make the many fine discriminations necessary to distinguish one letter from another and one word from another. Span of perception must be wide enough so that he can read in terms of ideas rather than letter-by-letter or word-by-word. The left-to-right directionality pattern must be firmly established so that eye movements are carried out in the conventional direction for the English language. Visualization is one of the most important visual skills, and it is vital for reading, spelling, and particularly, abstract thinking.

In brief, these are some of the visual skills needed for success in school. But I would like to emphasize that since all of these skills are learned, it is possible to train them to a more highly skilled degree.

What is the importance of directionality and laterality and how can be these functions be trained?

The left to right direction pattern of the English language is a convention of our culture. As you know, some languages are read right to left and some are read in a vertical top to bottom direction. This left to right directionality must become a habit, unconsciously used as a movement pattern in large movements, in small activities and in eye movements.

Many reading problems are rooted in the failure to develop a good habitual movement pattern and most poor readers have faulty movement patterns. These directionality problems can be uncovered by observing the direction of his pencil strokes by observing the pattern in which the child arranges his work, and by observations during his oral reading. A child with directionality problems often reverses words and may attack words from the right end rather than the left. With regard to laterality, it is important that a child be aware of his own right and left sides, because this is a vital prerequisite of projecting left and right out into space. A child lacking in firm laterality often reverses words when reading and writes letters and numbers in a backwards direction.

In teaching a child the difference between left and right, it is important to first make him aware that he has a left and right side and these must be teamed together in order to achieve bilaterality. This can be accomplished with such activities as balance boards, walking rails, trampolines, etc. Then it becomes important that a child be able to label right and left on himself and then later out in space. This can be accomplished with such activities as making angels in the snow, playing Simon says, jump board activities with right and left directions, eye fixations, catching with right and left hands, doll and stick figure play, etc.

In developing the left to right pattern, the training is first started with large muscle, wide scan activities such as connecting dots on a chalkboard, and making various right to left as well as left to right patterns on a chalkboard. Thus, he learns the difference between the movement patterns. This graduates to small muscle, small scan activities with paper and pencil. Both of these are accompanied by eye movement training since the eyes are used to direct all of these activities. Visual tracking procedures are then used to reinforce the skill so that the end result is good laterality and firmly entrenched left to right direction patterns.

What is meant by the statement: "Vision is learned?"

A child learns a visual skill or ability just as he learns to walk and to talk. Unfortunately, he doesn't have the opportunity to mimic his parents and siblings as he does in learning to walk and to talk. By the same token, a parent cannot observe how his child's visual skills are developing as he can in observing his child learning to walk and talk. We can watch the child learn to roll over, lift his head, sit up, crawl, creep, stand, walk, etc., but learning to see is a process that goes on, generally, without assistance or even informed awareness. The child who is learning vision:

- must learn his own center,

- must learn to team the two halves of his body,

- must learn where he is in relation to other visually observable stimuli,

- must learn to move against gravity and to operate in a gravitationally controlled environment.

It is possible that some parents restrain their children in limiting the full range of activity through the restricting use of playpens and walkers. By so doing, they prevent adequate range of movement and the normal development patterns found necessary during this period through crawling and creeping activities. Later, children are given scooters and wagons which they invariably learn to push with a particular foot and leg. This contributes to shortening the leg on that side and hence a change takes place in the pelvic height that distorts the body balance.

Children who don't creep long enough or who are restricted in the physical exploration of their environment, frequently head into life with a physically produced disability. This may handicap them throughout life and never show in the usual routine physical or eye examination. From a developmental viewpoint, a child must first learn to team the two halves of his body together before he can team his two eyes together. Also, from a developmental standpoint, a child must first learn to control his large gross muscles before he can control the fine muscles of his eyes. Consequently, when we find a problem in bilaterality, we find a problem in binocularity and visual perception. Therefore, apparatus such as balance boards, walk rails, jump boards and such activities as crawling and creeping constitute an integral part of a developmental visual training practice.

What are the postural distortions associated with visual problems?

We are aware of the more obvious postural distortions that can be observed in many patients. When a patient tilts his head laterally, we frequently find astigmatism at an oblique axis. Likewise, when we see a patient with his head inclined backwards leading with his chin, we frequently discover that he is a myope (has myopia or near-sightedness). When a patient has his head rotated to one side, he may well be found to be an anisometrope.

If a child does not possess good binocularity, or if he cannot maintain binocularity over a period of time, he will attempt to make compensations so that he doesn't have to use the two eyes together. The easiest way to do this is to adjust his posture so that one eye is taken out of the act. One way to accomplish this is by rotating the head so that one eye is blocked by the bridge of the nose; another way is by putting the head down so that one eye is covered by an arm. Still another way is by holding a hand over one eye, or by bring the head down so that one hand covers an eye. All of these compensations can produce postural warps which, if continued for some time, can cause other problems.

A child who has difficulty in binocularity usually becomes a head mover rather than an eye mover. He will move his head as he looks at successive words with a reluctant stress on head, neck and shoulder muscles. There are also environmental conditions that can create visual and postural problems. In an experiment with over 6,000 children conducted at the University of Texas, it was found that the minimum of stress occurs when the reading or writing material is parallel to the plane of the face.

In some of today's so-called modern classrooms, most reading and writing materials are placed on a flat desk. In order to achieve the parallel, minimum stress position, the child must bend over. This often brings his eyes within just three to four inches of his task. The focusing and converging effort for this close distance is at least five times greater than that required for a usual working distance and this increased effort usually lowers performance. Therefore, it becomes important that we realize the direct interrelationship that exists between vision and posture.

Is there a relationship between faulty eye teaming and poor reading?

I feel that there is an absolute direct relationship between the child's ability to team his two eyes together and his ability to learn to read successfully. A child is born with two eyes, but he must learn to team those eyes together. Most children learn to do this quite well, but there are others who do not adequately develop this skill.

There has been some controversy over the definition of exophoria. Some define exophoria as a tendency of the eyes to deviate outwards. Others define exophoria as that visual situation where the eyes converge beyond the plane of regard for accommodation.

Regardless of the definition for exophoria, the same situation exists during the act of reading. The visual demand while reading is for the eyes to point inward at the printed page. Since the relaxed posture for the exophore is for the eyes to go outward, it means that he must use an excessive amount of energy and effort just to keep the eyes pointing at the reading distance. Many university studies have shown that the greater the amount of effort involved in the reading process, the lower the comprehension and thus the lower the performance.

Eye movement photography show that when the saccadic eye movements are made during the act of reading, and each time fixation is broken as the child moves from word to word, an exophore's eyes will move outward and then move in to regain fixation. Consequently, the eyes will often regain binocularity two or three words over rather than on the next word. Therefore, it is not uncommon for him to make up the intervening words to make the sentence make sense. Typically, then, we have a reader who substitutes little words, confuses little words, and doesn't understand what he is reading.

Human nature being what it is, the child would rather not do anything that is difficult to do. Thus, we observe an avoidance reaction in which the child would rather look out the window or talk to his neighbor than have to concentrate on the difficult visual task of reading. He often is labeled as having a short attention span, not trying, having a behavioral problem, or being just plain dumb. We often observe this type of child who gives up and develops a strong dislike for school. It is possible that there is nothing else wrong with him other than an undetected visual problem.

An exophoric child often will make compensations in an attempt to minimize the effect of the problems. It usually is helpful for him to use his finger when reading to prevent the loss of place associated with a break in fixation. Unfortunately, too many educators have been taught not to let a child use his finger when reading. Fortunately, however, modern educational training teaches that when a child uses his finger, he is displaying to the teacher that he has a visual problem in teaming the two eyes together and that he is unable to read successfully without the finger.

Children will also distort their posture in an attempt to eliminate one eye during the act of reading. Many will cover one eye with a hand, or put their head down on their arm so that one eye is covered. Others will rotate their arm so that one eye is covered. Others will rotate their heads in such a manner so that the bridge of their nose will act as a shield between one eye and the printed page. Therefore, the observation of these postural distortions should alert the observer to the possibility of the existence of an eye teaming problem.

What is the relationship between crossed dominancy and academic failure?

This is a question which has generated a great deal of controversy. There are some authorities who have claimed that cross dominancy is the leading cause of all reading failures. There are still other authorities who claim that there is zero relationship between cross dominancy and reading failures. This controversy, however, has had the beneficial effect of pointing out the relationship of visual skills to academic success.

A large part of the controversy has been created by a failure to define terms, especially what is meant by the dominant eye. Various tests have been designed to determine the so-called dominant eye. Many of these tests merely determine which is the dominant eye for sighting. The dominant eye for sighting may or may not be the same eye which is dominant during the process of reading. It is even less likely to be the same eye if the sighting tests are done at a distant object rather than an object located at the reading distance and position of the particular child.

Most of the studies that I have read show that a larger proportion of cross dominant children exist in a population of under-achieving children than in a normal population. I feel, however, that a mistake has been made in drawing a cause-effect conclusion from this information. It has been assumed by many that the cross dominancy was the cause of the reading problem. It is felt by most authorities in optometry today that the cross dominancy is not the cause of the reading problem but, rather, just another symptom of the neurological disorganization which is at the root of the reading problem.

Most children who are cross dominant display a right to left visual direction pattern. It is this directionality problem which, I feel, has the more direct relationship to the reading problem. Therefore, vision therapy, which is directed towards establishment of a firmly established left to right direction pattern will produce more positive results in a shorter length of time.

Will children grow out of perceptual motor problems?

The answer to that question is frequently, yes, but whether or not a child will grow out of perceptual-motor problems must be related to the environmental demands on and opportunities open to the child. Most of the perceptual-motor skills which are prerequisite for academic success are skills which are developmental in nature. In other words, they are learned skills. Since children learn at different rates, it can be assumed that these skills will be mastered at different chronological ages. The problem to the child is created by the culturally imposed task of being required to learn to read at a definite chronological age. Some children are ready to learn to read at this age and others are not.

The child who has not developed the necessary perceptual motor skills may eventually develop these skills if left to his own devices. However, at the time he develops the skills, he might be hopelessly behind the rest of his class. It is also possible that he may never be exposed to the cultural experiences which would lead to the natural development of the perceptual-motor skills in question, in which case, unless he received therapy to develop these skills, he has no way of growing out of the problem. In addition, he might develop such negative attitudes towards education, based on his personal failures, that his natural desire to learn might be nullified.

It is the goal of optometric vision therapy to provide the child with these necessary perceptual-motor skills at the time he most needs them so that he will be able to meet the demands of the culture at the time that they are imposed on him.

The American Optometric Association's Position on Vision Therapy

The American Optometric Association (AOA) affirms its long-standing position that optometric vision therapy is effective in the treatment of physiological neuromuscular and perceptual dysfunctions of the vision system.

The ability to learn in school, achieve on the job, and enjoy sports and recreation depends upon efficient vision. Optometric vision therapy assists individuals in developing visual abilities and efficiency most suited to their needs and enables those individuals to achieve maximal levels of visual performance. Optometric vision therapy can help individuals achieve and maintain good vision throughout life.

Vision and Learning

Many children who experience academic difficulty may have a treatable visual dysfunction in addition to their primary reading or learning dysfunction.

1. Vision problems can interfere with the ability to perform in the classroom or can impair the ability to read with comfort and efficiency. These treatable conditions include focusing deficiencies, eye muscle imbalances, motor fusion deficiencies and refractive errors.

2. Although optometrists do not teach reading, optometric vision therapy programs are used to treat contributory vision problems thus enabling the individual to take better advantage of his/her educational opportunities.

3. Management of the learning disabled and/or dyslexic child or adult should be multidisciplinary. Since it is important to deal with any defect or problem that may be causal or contributory, evaluation of a learning disabled individual should include a thorough optometric analysis of the vision system. Interdisciplinary communication and involvement are essential in helping an individual overcome a learning problem.

Research

Extensive research related to strabismus and amblyopia, accommodative and non-strabismic binocular dysfunction, vision development and learning-related vision problems is conducted at the schools and colleges of optometry and other clinical and research settings. These scientific studies support the effectiveness and value of optometric vision therapy in the treatment of vision dysfunctions.

Summary

Evaluation of individuals with learning difficulties (i.e., attention deficit disorder, AD/HD, dyslexia, etc.) should include a thorough optometric analysis as part of a multidisciplinary approach. The American Optometric Association continues to support quality optometric care, education and research in the area of vision therapy.

Part Three

Help for Parents and Teachers

Chapter 21

Guidelines for Parenting Your Attention-Different Child

Parents with a child having the diagnosis of attention deficit hyperactivity disorder (AD/HD) will recognize some or all of these behaviors. Their child may: have a hot, quick, temper, jump to oppose authority, throw fits when he hears the word "no," have a problem remembering rules and sequences, behave impulsively and inappropriately, and have difficulty making friends.

Research has established that upwards of 5 per cent of all children (more boys than girls) show some or all of these behaviors. Some kids also suffer from obsessive thoughts and compulsions like hand washing, depression, rage, or may be given to taking dangerous risks.

The good news, which is overlooked by many involved with these kids, is that they also have special gifts. They tend to be highly purposeful, creative, have a splendid capacity for argument, and have a powerful sense of personal justice. This is why I call them attention-different. They are most certainly not deficit in intellectual capacity or redeeming qualities. Their positive characteristics will serve them well in adulthood but we have to get them through childhood first. It is mainly the context of the modern classroom, with its requirement for high volume route learning that makes them appear deficit for they do not learn well in this setting.

From "Guidelines for Parenting Your Attention Different Child," by George T. Lynn, M.A., L.M.H.C., © 1997 George Lynn. Reprinted with permission. Complete information about George Lynn is included at the end of this chapter.

Stimulus Overload Causes the ADD Child's Problems

ADD kids do not behave the way they do out of deliberate spite. Though all children will naturally challenge their parents, the most persistent problems of ADD children have another cause. They are set off by the stress the child feels because he is so open to stimulation. ADD children are biochemically less able to screen out stimulation from all their senses and from their minds and emotions. The child feels overwhelmed by impressions from what he sees, smells, hears, feels, or thinks. Or he may be overcome by the sensation of pressure that results in hyperactivity or pressured speech.

Awash in so much stimulation, the child can not sort out any one thing to focus on—he has too much of a good thing. This makes learning very difficult and prevents him from getting the satisfaction, the pleasure, of really taking things in. Writer Thom Hartmann suggests that the child who is so numbed, experiences the inability to feel alive. This causes a lot of stress. To attempt to soothe this restlessness, a child may go into the wild search pattern of hyperactivity. Or he may deliberately provoke others to react to him. Or he may take dangerous risks, following fire, knives, and all the forbidden things as far as they will take him. The child seeks a sense of stimulus satisfaction from this activity.

Another child may feel so overwhelmed that he withdraws into depression, dreaminess, or is given to rage when disturbed. He is trying so hard to hold on to a sense of who he is and what he is doing that interruption is perceived as excruciating. This child is seeking a sense of stimulus safety. The first step to helping yourself and your child is to get an understanding of what function problematic behavior serves for him. You must determine if his behavior is an attempt to gain stimulus satisfaction or stimulus safety and go from there. To do this, observe your child's reactions and keep a log in which you record his behavior and mood changes.

Simply get into the habit of watching him. Observe him especially closely for signs that he is having a problem by noting situations in which he does not pay attention and therefore cannot remember details of the situation. Note when he has problems. The time of day he misfires will tell you a lot about how to reduce his stress by adjusting what is happening around him.

Enter Into a Consultancy Relationship with Him

I like the consultant model of helping your child. If he wants your help, offer it but do so only on his request. Your objective must be to make your child more self-supporting and less in need of your help.

Ask him what he is experiencing when he is having a problem, and assist him in articulating his feelings to you. If, for example, he starts screaming at you when you require him to finish a particular project, ask "Are you mad at me because I didn't give you enough time to finish or because you have to go back to the beginning when I interrupted you?"

Ask him why he does certain things. One bright nine-year-old I've worked with in counseling told me that he aggravates his teacher to see her face turn red. This is a clue to me that he is experiencing a lack of stimulus satisfaction due to stimulus flooding in the crowded classroom. Another child ventured the comment that this was a way to get the teacher's attention, because his interpersonal skills were so poor he couldn't get it any other way.

Some Key Problem Management Skills for ADD Children

Our basic challenge as parents is to bring out our child's special strengths while staying firm and consistent Here are some ways to do this:

1. Create positive alternative choices based on your child's purposes and encourage him to make a choice.

Example: If you want him to finish a project, say "Would you like ten minutes or fifteen to finish your project?" or; If you want him to get his homework done, say "When would you like to complete your homework: after school or after dinner so that you can have your friend over?"

This kind of language structure, which hands choices to the child, gives him some control enabling him to shift gears at his own pace so as to avoid the distress of feeling jerked from one activity to another.

2. Use positive statements to move him toward positive outcomes.

Do not say: "Don't talk to me in that tone of voice." *Say:* "I'll be glad to discuss this when respect is shone."

Do not say: "Stop arguing with me." *Say:* "I'll be glad to discuss this as soon as the arguing stops."

Do not say: "Pay attention." *Say:* "I'll start again as soon as I know that you are with me."

Keeping your language positive keeps his attitude positive. Remember, he is very open to your tone. Treat him the way you want him to respond and you will notice the difference in his behavior immediately.

3. In problem situations use reminder language to overcome short term memory problems.

Example: To get him to move out of contact when he is yelling or poking others say "When you can show me that you have control of your body by stopping your swearing and poking and get to your room, we can talk about what you want."

4. Give him lots of up-front warnings for transition. The feeling of being lost, out-of-control, anxious, and overwhelmed by stimulation can come when the ADD child is required to pull focus from one activity and put it on another. These transition times need to be managed carefully.

Examples: If you want him in bed by 8:30 school nights, remind him at 8:15 "You need to brush your teeth and be in bed in the next fifteen minutes so that I can read to you." Or to help him learn to get his stuff together to get out the door in the morning, teach him a rhyme such as "Two, four, six, eight, get backpack, lunch, homework, and wait," some attention-different children have a keen ear for music and can carry a tune splendidly. Or to help him do chores around the house, post a list of required steps on the fridge for him to follow.

5. Keep your cool. Know your stress triggers and have another adult available to support you if possible. Attention-different kids react best to matter-of-fact communications. When you show anger, they will react quickly, in an oppositional manner. An ugly battle can result. Because they are so open to stimulation, they can catch a mood from you and give it back to you with equal force.

6. Help him work through obsessions and compulsions by making it okay to talk about them. These tend to get worse when the child is tired. Experiment with creative methods to ease the stress of obsessions using visualizations of peace and completion to relax him. Medication and behavior therapy have also been shown to be very effective for the elimination

of compulsive behavior. Don't pry—ask "Is there anything I can do to help?"

7. Attend to physical factors. Research has shown that mental performance is improved by a good diet and exercise. This is especially true in the case of ADD children. Make sure that his diet is well balanced and watch out for a carbohydrate craving that may signal the presence of an addiction to refined carbs that many ADD children have and that can make behavior worse. Help him get frequent aerobic style exercise that is not too strenuous. Physical exercise is a great way to let off the pressure that causes hyperactivity. Team sports may be difficult for attention-different kids so encourage solo exercise such as rope jumping, running for points, or bicycling.

When all is said and done, you can't take care of your child unless you are taking care of yourself so don't bash yourself for not being a perfect parent. Give yourself credit. Yours is one of the most difficult, stressful, jobs in the world. Your child is lucky to have you in his life. Know that some of the most successful people in the world are attention-different and that with persistence and love you will help your child grow to be an interesting and happy person who achieves his full potential.

About the Author

George Lynn, M.A., L.M.H.C. is a psychotherapist in Bellevue, Washington who has pioneered the use of counseling approaches for people with neuropsychiatric diagnoses such as ADD, Bipolar Disorder, Tourette's Syndrome, and Asperger's Syndrome. He is the author of *Survival Strategies for Parenting Your ADD Child* (Underwood books, 1996) and *Survival Strategies for Parenting Children with Bipolar Disorder* (Jessica Kingsley Publishers, 2000). Additional information about George Lynn's books is available on his website at www.childspirit.com.

Chapter 22

AD/HD—Advice for Parents and Families

When parents have a child with any type of problem, it is not unusual for the parents to feel guilty or blame themselves. Parenting education and support has been shown to be very helpful for families with an AD/HD child and its value cannot be overemphasized. However, as scientists and medical professionals learn more about the possible causes of this condition, there is growing evidence that parents likely had little control over the cause of AD/HD.

As researchers continue to look at the causes of AD/HD, continued advances will likely be made so that the diagnosis will not be confused with other unrelated conditions.

How Will This Affect Our Family and Our Other Children?

The impact that the AD/HD child may have on the family will vary greatly depending on the extent that the child is affected, the family culture, and other siblings. If the family culture and the parents place a high value on activities and athletic prowess, then it is likely that a very active child will be admired and given appropriate outlets for

Excerpted from "AD/HD: What Does It Mean for Parents and Families When Their Child is Diagnosed with This Condition?" by Anne S. Robertson, from *Parent News*, May 1998, National Parent Information Network (NPIN). And "How Can Parents Encourage Responsible Behavior?" U.S. Department of Education, 1993; cited January 2002. Despite the older date of this document, those seeking advice for encouraging responsible behavior in their children will find this information helpful.

physical activity. The same may be true of an intensely emotional child in a family that values dramatics and the arts. However, it may be very difficult for a highly active or intense child if the family culture is more sedate or less vocal. In a situation where the child's behavior is significantly different than family expectations, it is easy when problems arise for the AD/HD child to become the family scapegoat. Understanding how the family culture can change to positively impact the child's temperament is an important goal of parenting education.

Also, any parent with more than one child knows that children within the same family can have vastly different personalities. Under the illusion of fairness, parents often feel that siblings should be treated identically, have the same rules, and aspire to similar expectations. There is evidence to suggest that parents shouldn't be quite as concerned about equal treatment since children do understand, and think it is all right, when parents treat them differently. Learning to understand and respect the different strengths in your children, and encouraging their individual development, will likely help the siblings respect and accept each other.

How Can Parents Encourage Responsible Behavior?

Especially when they are young, children learn best about responsibility in concrete situations. What they do and what they witness have lasting effects. Most of the activities described in this chapter are for you and your child.

We are always teaching our children something by our words and our actions. They learn from seeing. They learn from hearing. They learn from overhearing. They learn from us, from each other, from other adults, and by themselves.

All of us acquire habits by doing things over and over again, whether in learning to play a musical instrument, to pick up after ourselves, to play games and sports, or to share with others. The best way to encourage our children to become responsible is to act as responsibly as we can in their presence. We must genuinely try to be the sort of people we hope they will try to become. We can show them by our words and by our actions that we respect others. We can show them our compassion and concern when others are suffering. They need to see our own self-control, courage, and honesty. They need to learn that we treat ourselves, as well as others, with respect, and that we always try to do our best. As they grow older, they should have the chance to learn why we live as we do.

As our children watch us daily, as we talk to them, encouraging their questions and trying to answer them thoughtfully, they begin to understand us—and we begin to understand them. Understanding each other well is the best way to teach our children respect for our ideals of good character.

Using Literature and Stories

Children learn about responsibility through many activities, including reading stories. They learn by identifying with individual characters or because the message from a favorite story strikes a particular chord. Children can be touched deeply by good literature, and they may ask to have things read to them again and again.

Children can learn all sorts of lessons from stories. They might learn about courage by reading about David standing up to Goliath. Or they might learn the value of persistence and effort from *The Little Engine That Could*.

When they are older, reading can help prepare children for the realities and responsibilities of adulthood. It is usually better for children to read a good book about such things as war, oppression, suicide, or deadly disease before seeing these things up close.

When our children grow up they often remember stories that were told to them by family members when they were young. When we tell stories to our children, we should remember old favorites of ours, like *The Three Little Pigs*, not leaving out a single time the wolf says, "I'll huff, and I'll Puff, and I'll blow your house in!"

Developing Judgment and Thoughtfulness

Judgment on ethical issues is a practical matter. Children develop their capacity for judging what is a responsible act, just as they come to appreciate the meaning of responsibility, through practice. Especially when they are young, children need to see moral questions in terms that are meaningful to them.

We can also help our children develop good judgment by talking through complicated situations with them. One way is to help them understand the long-term consequences of different choices. If they tell us about a story they have read, we might ask them to imagine what the result might have been if a favorite character had acted differently.

Sometimes, it can be difficult to know the difference between acting bravely and acting recklessly or how to balance duties when they conflict. As parents, we can help by making it clear, through what we do as well as what we say, that it is important in such situations to think carefully and honestly about what should be done, as well as to keep in mind how others will be affected by what we do.

Your child's ability to reason about different issues, including ethical ones, will improve as your child matures. Just as reasoning can lead to a more thoughtful understanding of responsibility, or what actions to take in complicated situations, it may also become easier to rationalize selfish or reckless behavior. But if you have helped your young child develop strong habits of considering the welfare of others, honesty, courage, and admiration for worthy accomplishments, your child will have a solid foundation on which to build.

Chapter 23

Fatherhood and AD/HD

Fathers of children with AD/HD have a special calling—to stand with their children during times of emotional or behavioral difficulties, to give their children hope and courage, and to provide opportunities so that their children might define themselves by their strengths rather than their weaknesses. To do this, it helps to appreciate the experiences and struggles these children face each day and to create a positive environment within the family to allow them to overcome these difficulties.

Understanding Mutual Frustration

As a father, it may be helpful to keep in mind that when you are frustrated with your child's behavior, your child is also feeling the same level of frustration. At such a moment, your son may be momentarily frozen in time, like a deer caught in headlights. His natural desire to please and conform is overshadowed by his emotional state. With each demand for him to "snap out of it" or indication that he is a disappointment, the pain sinks deeper and the headlights get brighter.

"Fatherhood and AD/HD," by Patrick J. Kilcarr, Ph.D. and Patricia O. Quinn, M.D., from *Attention!* Magazine, Volume 4, Number 2, Fall 1997, © 1997 CHADD. For more information write to CHADD at 8181 Professional Place, Suite 201, Landover, MD 20875, or visit CHADD at their website at www.chadd.org.

Fathers can change this downward spiral by attending to positive behaviors, and either ignoring or calmly dealing with the negative behaviors. This approach creates a major shift in the way a child will see himself and the world. Training yourself to ignore impulsive or inappropriate behavior requires an understanding of what your child can and can't control. If you continue to reinforce positive movements toward success, that is how your child will begin to define himself— as a success.

Creating a Self-Disciplined Child

What is the connection between disciplining a child and a child's learning self-discipline? There is a direct link between the way children are disciplined and the degree to which they assume responsibility for their own actions and behaviors.

Disciplining a child, especially a child with AD/HD, is complicated by our own emotional response to what we consider misbehaving or other social improprieties. The more emotionally consumed we become by our children's behavior, the more likely we are to utilize ineffective or inappropriate disciplining strategies, such as hitting, screaming, threatening, bullying, or withdrawing love and attention. When we lead with our emotions, the outcome is usually less then desirable, and often regrettable.

How we choose to discipline our children is one of the most fundamental aspects of raising a child with AD/HD. As noted by one father:

> "I used to be a lot stricter with him. I'd treat him like a 'normal' kid, meaning that I really didn't take into account that he had difficulty processing information or following rules. I would keep harping on him and trying to make him act like any other kid his age. I've come to learn that is not him, that he is not like many of his friends. In some ways he is more in control. I attribute that to the work we have been doing to create more consistency in our home, and definitely to reduce getting too emotionally attached to the issue. It is not that he doesn't want to do things, it is just that he can't always do it the way others expect or want."

An essential aspect of learning how to discipline your child effectively is understanding what he or she is personally capable of doing and when he/she is most able to do it. A child with AD/HD needs his father to lean on during times when he cannot hold it together himself. If you are angry, upset, or out of control as a result of your child's behavior, you cannot provide the type of emotional support and discipline necessary to resolve the problem.

A child with AD/HD needing his father's support is much like a person with a broken foot needing a crutch. He will not need to use the crutch permanently; however, in order to feel comfortable with going about his daily duties, he needs the broken foot and the crutch to work together to minimize discomfort. As the child with AD/HD matures, he will need his father less for support, and more as an important sounding board and resource.

Practicing Calm Discipline

The practice of remaining calm with our children who have AD/HD and establishing effective methods of discipline are fraternal twins. Remaining calm and consistently disciplining inappropriate behavior results in a child who understands and takes responsibility for his or her own actions and behaviors.

The father of a nine-year-old boy gives us a clear example of this:

"I don't think the way I deal with Marty now at all resembles the way I used to treat him. I used to think he was just a spoiled little kid who wouldn't stop until he got his way. If he didn't get his way, he would say stuff like, 'I hate you' or mumble derogatory comments under his breath. I would literally chase him up the stairs and around the house just so I could scream in his face. I think after he was diagnosed with AD/HD and we put him on medication, I believed he was going to stop a lot of the behavior that would drive me and my wife nuts. At that time, I didn't realize that a change in him hinged on a change in us—especially in me, because my wife was much more tolerant and forgiving of his behavior. The fact that he was on medication and still acting out made me even angrier.

"I didn't know how to make him act like he was supposed to. Even though my wife said I should look at how I reacted to Pete, it had very little effect on how I treated him. Believe it or not, things began to change for me after I read an article on disciplining your child. It was my wife's magazine, and one morning I was flipping through it and saw the article. After reading it, I was shocked at how I basically did everything to ensure that Pete did not develop self-control and self-discipline. The screaming and punishment tactics I used made him feel even more helpless and out of control.

"Shortly after this, I read another article about AD/HD. It helped me understand what is going on inside of Pete's mind and body. I suppose I became more sensitive to what he was going through. I began doing more reading about how to help him when he was out of control. I rarely yell anymore. I let him know what is expected of him and what needs to happen in order for him to do what he wants. I think my not yelling and being on an even keel with him has had a huge impact on him. I see him as being much more responsible and listening much better.

"This was the gist of the article: Don't get excited about what your child does, be clear about expectations, be clear about family rules, and be clear about what the family limits are regarding certain behaviors and choices. The most counterproductive thing you can do is scream or hit the kid. This definitely makes the kid shrink from taking responsibility for what he did."

The Parenting Paradox

When a dad becomes accepting of his child's behavior, a paradox occurs: the problematic behavior diminishes in frequency, intensity, and duration. We are not suggesting that you accept the inappropriate behavior, but rather that you accept your child for who he or she is and for what he or she can and cannot do at that point in time. This does not mean that AD/HD is or can be used as an excuse for acting out or engaging in disrespectful behaviors. We can and must hold our children accountable for their behavior while still maintaining a position of love and support. One father described how changing his attitude toward his son changed the relationship:

"When Paul is off his medication and his emotions are swirling all around, if I say something that irritates him, which isn't hard to do, he'll immediately say something like 'shut up' or 'get out of my face.' It took me a while to accept the fact that that is his impulsive side showing. At that moment he really can't control what he is saying. When he is on medication, that type of response is very rare. I also respond to it very differently now, so he doesn't hang on to the negative feeling. I can tell he wants to say or do something different, but this surge happens and he blurts out this stuff. Since my attitude has changed, the more negative impulsive responses happen far less frequently."

The following is a wonderful example of how even the most difficult AD/HD temperament can respond positively to sound parental
structure and ongoing support:

"I have seen Quint use many of the techniques and strategies
that my wife and I have used with him over the years. If he is
getting too aggressive or angry, he pulls himself temporarily out
of the situation to cool down, focus, and figure out what exactly
is going on and how he is contributing to the problem. We are
starting to see the results of years of working with him, modeling for him, and standing by him. When he was first diagnosed
at age four, he was aggressive, agitated, and difficult to control.
Now at age eight, he still has his down moments, but it is nothing compared to what it was. I see Quint as a happy and self-
confident young boy. Because he was so disruptive at an early
age, it would have been easy to be angry and disapproving of
him a lot. But with guidance, talking with other parents, and
professional help, Quint is, and is going to be, fine. Each day he
learns to cope with AD/HD more effectively."

Parenting calls us to a level of responsibility unparalleled in any
other area of our lives. Our children are more than an extension of
us; they represent all the possibilities and potential the world has to
offer. They have the opportunity to exceed our expectations and to
excel in unimaginable directions. We place enormous responsibility
on our children to succeed, make good choices, establish sound values,
and be good citizens. We often expect them to capitalize on opportunities we failed to, or were unable to, and to construct a magnificent
staircase carrying them to their—and, by extension, our—individual
success. We want them to heal our historical wounds. In reality, however, our children must battle the same battles we fought, feel the
same disappointments we felt, and learn the way we did to make sense
out of an unpredictable world.

However, your child does not have to face the world entirely alone;
he has you as a guiding force. While our children may offer us an opportunity to heal, what they definitely offer us is the chance to live
honestly, demonstrate integrity, model forgiveness, and show compassion. We can give our children the things, emotional and physical, we
did not get. As many parents have learned over the ages, it is much
easier to provide physical comforts than the emotional comfort we may
not have received ourselves. Fathers, especially, must push against
both gender and social stereotypes in order to provide their children,

and especially their sons with AD/HD, with the level of emotional sustenance they need.

Raising a Resilient Child

Children with AD/HD are incredibly resilient, resourceful, and determined. Even in the face of disappointed parents and disillusioned teachers, these kids try to hang on and do better next time. Children who do not receive the support, empathy, and care that they need will eventually break under the weight of years of negative criticism and failed attempts at improvement. One father described his son's desire to fit in and do well:

> "I know Bret wants to control himself and fit in. I can just tell. But once things start going bad for him, he becomes more frustrated and has an even harder time. He doesn't give up, though. I know he is trying to pull things back on track. And he knows I am supporting him in doing his best at the moment. I sometimes think of myself as his emotional airbag. I know the way I deal with him makes him feel safer and better able to get things back together. I want him to walk away from a bad episode knowing that he is OK, and that he can handle his frustration rather than it handling him."

The following can be seen as a metaphor for personal resiliency and emotional fortitude:

> One day a mule fell into a dry well. There was no way to lift the mule out, so the farmer directed his boys to bury the mule in the well. But the mule refused to be buried. As the boys would throw dirt on the mule, it would simply trample the dirt. Very soon, enough had been thrown into the well that the mule walked out.

That which was intended to bury the mule was the very means by which it rose. This story speaks as much to the experience of parents of children with AD/HD as it does to that of the children themselves. As parents, we sometimes feel like we are being buried alive by all the problems caused by AD/HD. It is not that our children intend to smother us; rather, the symptoms emerging from the AD/HD are themselves suffocating to both the parent and the child.

Like the mule, a surprising number of children with AD/HD refuse to be emotionally buried by negative feedback, parental disapproval, isolation, and academic difficulty. Somehow these children walk into their adult lives making significant contributions to their communities and chosen vocations. It is believed that these children often had at least one person who unconditionally believed in them and supported the competent and capable side of their personality. It is amazing what one person, especially a father, can do to ensure a child's success.

In conclusion, children with disabilities, whether emotional or physical, can open overcome sizable odds if they believe a parent believes in them. Like a chameleon who takes on the color of its environment as a form of protection against danger, children with AD/HD often take on the attitudes and beliefs of their parents. Children often define themselves by how they are defined. If they perceive that they are considered "bad," a "waste of time," "worthless," or only tolerated, they will begin living out this belief by seeking out negative experiences. On the other hand, when a child feels loved, even when he doesn't feel particularly loving, he feels a sense of redemption and hope. The following shows that a shift in a father's heart and understanding of his son's AD/HD is a catalyst toward reducing tension and increasing his son's overall sense of self worth:

> "Before Chris was diagnosed and medicated, I would go ballistic on him if he disobeyed, talked back, or caused problems. I became so aggravated that I just would lose it. This in turn would send him even deeper into a bad attitude or defiance. The louder he got, the louder I got, and so forth.

> "There was a tremendous amount of stress and tension in the house. Now, since I have learned more about AD/HD and realize my previous way of dealing with Chris was, at best, ineffective, I now deal with him in a different way. If he starts spiraling out of control, I reduce my negativity and greet his intensity with a calm manner and reason. The change in his behavior in response to this is remarkable. There is very little tension in the house, and if he does something really inappropriate, I will calmly send him to timeout. The whole way of dealing with him now is different and productive, especially when he feels overwhelmed by his emotions."

This chapter is based on a book written by Drs. Kilcarr and Quinn, recently published by Brunner/Mazel, Inc. titled *Voices from Fatherhood: Fathers, Sons and AD/HD*. This book examines the inner thoughts, experiences, and feelings of over 100 fathers who have sons with AD/HD. This is a book written especially for fathers who have sons with attention deficit/hyperactivity disorder and don't know how to interact with them. It is filled with quotes from fathers describing their observations about the impact of an AD/HD son on their marriage, their families, and themselves. This is a book that everyone— fathers, mothers, educators, and mental health professionals—will find useful in helping to understand the dynamics of healthy father-son relationships.

About the Authors

Patrick J. Kilcarr, Ph.D. is Director of the Center for Substance Abuse Prevention and the Georgetown Outdoor Leadership School at Georgetown University, Washington, D.C. He has presented numerous seminars on AD/HD, including Working with Children and ADD, and The Impact of AD/HD on the Child and the Family. Two of his sons have AD/HD.

Patricia O. Quinn, M.D., is a developmental pediatrician practicing in the Washington, D.C. area. She specializes in child development and psychopharmacology, and works extensively in the areas of ADD, learning disabilities, and mental retardation. She gives workshops and has published widely in these fields. She is also the author of *Attention Deficit Disorder*, *ADD and the College Student*, and *Adolescents and ADD*; coauthor of *Putting on the Brakes* and *The "Putting on the Brakes" Activity Book*; and co-editor of *BRAKES: The Interactive Newsletter for Kids with ADD*.

Chapter 24

How Food Affects the Brain

Editor's Note

The possibility of a relationship between that of sugar in a child's diet and attention deficit/hyperactivity disorder is controversial. Many studies have failed to demonstrate a connection; however, other studies have produced results that can be interpreted in varying ways.

This chapter explaining how food choices affect brain activity includes text from the point of view that sees a direct link between sugar and hyperactivity symptoms. It is offered to provide readers with information about how proponents of this theory explain the data. Others provide alternate explanations. For example: The National Institute of Mental Health claims, "The restricted diet only seemed to help about 5 percent of children with AD/HD, mostly either young children or children with food allergies;" and, CHADD (Children and Adults with Attention Deficit/Hyperactivity Disorder) states, "At this time, it has not been shown that dietary intervention offers significant help to children with learning and attention problems."

This text is excerpted from *The ADD Nutrition Solution*, by Marcia Zimmerman, C.N., © 1999, reprinted with permission of Henry Holt & Company, Inc. To obtain *The ADD Nutrition Solution,* which includes Ms. Zimmerman's 30-day nutrition plan for decreasing AD/HD symptoms, go to www.henryholt.com. Additional information about Marcia Zimmerman is included at the end of this chapter.

Why Sugar Is Poison for AD/HD

Many parents are convinced that sugar increases their child's hyperactivity and consequently they restrict its use. Other parents report just the opposite—their child is calmed down by eating sugar, in essence it provides therapy for the hyperactivity. Numerous studies have attempted to resolve the sugar issue, but none have found a clear connection between sugar and hyperactive behavior. What is the real story?

About twenty five-years ago, Dr. Benjamin Feingold warned that sugar aggravates hyperactivity. Since that time the idea has been repeatedly challenged by other investigators, but the truth is that nothing can be worse for people with AD/HD than eating sugar. Investigators have been looking for proof that sugar will increase hyperactivity in most AD/HD children most of the time. They have failed to illustrate this point, because sugar's effects can be altered by whatever else the child has eaten either before or after the sugar test. They also failed to consider the broad range of response between individuals to the amount of sugar that can be eaten before it affects behavior. Even the time of day sugar is eaten can make a big difference in its effects, and that was seldom taken into consideration. Finally, hyperactivity was selected as the only measurable effect of sugar when, in fact, sugar goes beyond influencing our energy level—it also has a profound effect on brain function.

New sophisticated brain-imaging tests, like positron emission tomography (PET) scans, have confirmed what Dr. Feingold and others have maintained for years: that hyperactivity is an adverse response to sugar. Now we know that it is not the only adverse effect.

Pet Scans Reveal the Evidence

Such a study was conducted by N. L. Girardi, School of Medicine, Yale University, and colleagues and published in the *Journal of Pediatric Research* in October 1995. The study compared, by means of PET scans, the differences in response between AD/HD and non-AD/HD children fed a glucose-rich meal. Glucose is a simple sugar that the brain needs to function; we normally get glucose from dietary sugars and other carbohydrates. Seventeen children with AD/HD and eleven without it were given a glucose beverage before eating breakfast that contained approximately eight times the amount of sugar required by the brain in a single hour. That's about the amount of sugar you would consume if you ate a large sweet roll, a large glass of orange juice, and a cup of coffee with two rounded teaspoons of sugar. Both groups of children exhibited an expected jump in blood glucose levels within the first half hour.

Hormonal Control of Blood Sugar

Let me digress for a moment to explain briefly what this means. The increase of blood glucose in these children was countered by a rapid rise in blood insulin levels, which was expected. Insulin's role is to move glucose from the circulating system into our cells, where it will be stored as a sugar complex called glycogen. Storage enables our cells to scoop up extra glucose and save it for later energy needs. Not all cells have this capacity for glycogen storage, however, and your brain cells are ones that do not. Your liver, muscles, and fatty tissues can all make glycogen, and they get the lion's share of glucose. The brain gets what little glucose it can immediately use, and even this meager amount can be severely restricted if insulin levels are high. Your body guards against the ensuing deficits in brain glucose in an interesting way, however.

Within three hours of eating a sugary meal, blood glucose levels drop back to normal or slightly below. This decrease in glucose triggers another important event that affects brain chemistry. The adrenal glands, two tiny organs on top of the kidneys, produce the fight or flight hormones epinephrine and norepinephrine. These hormones step up glucose entry into the brain, which offsets the effects of insulin.

In both groups of children, glucose and insulin levels dropped within three hours, as expected, but what Girardi and his colleagues found when they checked epinephrine and norepinephrine levels was startling. The AD/HD children showed an amazing 50 percent lower rise in these counterbalancing hormones as compared to their non-AD/HD counterparts. The AD/HD children were less able to counteract the stressful effects on their brains of the high sugar meal. Since norepinephrine is a neurotransmitter that increases alertness and the flow of information between brain cells, these findings were of major importance.

Results of Girardi's Trial

A battery of tests measuring attention and learning ability were given to both groups of children a little more than three hours after their sugary meal. The AD/HD children scored significantly lower than the non-AD/HD children, which was not surprising and confirmed norepinephrine's role in offsetting insulin's slowing of brain function.

The investigators also noted that many of the AD/HD children had a marked increase in physical activity as their blood sugar levels plummeted. The researchers interpreted this as indicating they were using rapid movement, which increases levels of norepinephrine, to jump start their brains. Physical activity prompts the adrenal glands to pump out their hormones, which include norepinephrine.

Might hyperactivity then be considered the child's natural response to low levels of norepinephrine and glucose in the brain? I suspect, from my many years of working with AD/HD children and the evidence I have gathered from clinical trials, that this may in fact be the cause of some children's hyperactive behavior. If a child eats a sugary food on an empty stomach, the chances of it causing hyperactivity increase. Not all AD/HD children will react this way, but it explains why many do.

Risk Taking: A Symptom of Hyperactivity

I have interviewed many parents who report that their AD/HD child is a risk taker, and this behavior has often been reported by others working in the field. This is another way a child can naturally elevate norepinephrine, and we see this behavior even in very young children. They climb all over the place and can seriously injure themselves trying to master skills for which they are ill equipped. The observations of Girardi and his associates help explain why risky behavior is considered by many experts to be a form of hyperactivity. What happens to AD/HD children as they mature? Do their bodies outgrow the inability to handle sugar properly?

To answer these questions a research team investigated how glucose utilization differs in the brains of teens with AD/HD as compared to those without the condition. Monique Ernst and colleagues, from the National Institute of Mental Health (NIMH) Laboratory of Cerebral Metabolism, tested 20 fourteen-year-old girls with AD/HD against 19 normal girls. Each girl was given a high-glucose drink and then tested for response to auditory signals.

AD/HD Girls and Brain Glucose

PET scans were again used to trace brain areas of high glucose concentration, indicating increased processing of information. The AD/HD girls had 15 percent lower glucose utilization over the entire cerebral cortex of the brain than did the girls without AD/HD.

Paradoxically, a similar test of boys revealed no differences in glucose metabolism between the two groups. This was a somewhat surprising finding, but may explain the tendency of some boys to outgrow hyperactivity, but not attention deficits. If, indeed, hyperactivity is an expression of the AD/HD brain's inability to get glucose into processing centers, the normal glucose metabolism found in these AD/HD boys suggests they may have outgrown one of the major causes of their childhood hyperactive behavior. Because they are attributed primarily to faulty neurotransmission, attention deficits can remain throughout life, although glucose metabolism plays a major role as well.

This study highlights the importance of gaining a better understanding of the differences in glucose metabolism between girls with AD/HD and those who do not have it, and between AD/HD girls and AD/HD boys. Teenage boys are much more expressive in their hyperactive behavior. They have been the subject of more research and are diagnosed with AD/HD four times more often than girls. The alarming thing is that girls seem less likely to outgrow impulsivity and hyperactivity. They express it differently, as short temper, fidgetiness, extreme procrastination, anxiety, and even depression. The future outcome of these conditions in girls might be better predicted if more studies on brain glucose metabolism were done. Do errors in sugar metabolism persist into adulthood?

Brain Glucose Metabolism in AD/HD Adults

Alan Zametkin, M.D., another research psychiatrist from NTMH, published results of a trial in the *New England Journal of Medicine* in 1990 that answers this question. Dr. Zametkin found that adults with AD/HD continue to metabolize glucose abnormally—at a rate 8 percent lower than that of non-AD/HD adults. More importantly, glucose metabolism was lowest in the prefrontal part of the brain, the section that regulates behavior, impulsivity, and attention—the very faculties impaired in AD/HD. Although the frontal cortex was most affected, other specific regions of the brain were also affected. Abnormal glucose metabolism in the AD/HD brain appears to be a lifelong condition—at least in the group tested by Dr. Zametkin. Clearly, this avenue of impaired brain metabolism needs to be further investigated.

The adult men and women in Dr. Zametkin's study had a history of hyperactivity as children, and each had at least one child with the condition. A strong case can be made for faulty glucose metabolism as the genetic link that causes AD/HD to run in families. The findings in these three studies are highly significant in that glucose is the brain's energy source—vital for its functioning—and if the brain does not process glucose properly, energy deficits follow and communication between neurons becomes garbled. AD/HD individuals have described the feeling inside their brains as having all the TV channels on at the same time with the volume turned up. Stimulant medications beam messages over the gap between neurons, thus bypassing blocked channels and casing the static. While medication clarifies the signals between neurons, bringing quick relief to many, it does nothing to improve the underlying problems, one of which is faulty sugar metabolism.

We can overcome these errors in brain glucose metabolism by priming the receptors to efficiently send and gather information. Although sugar consumption by AD/HD individuals, regardless of their age, must be avoided, it is especially important for AD/HD children.

Brain Nutrient Requirements in Children

Amazingly, until the age of two, a small child's brain is using around 80 percent of the total calories he or she eats every day. By the time the child goes to school, his brain is utilizing up to 50 percent of his caloric intake. In addition, the greater size of the child's brain in proportion to the rest of the body demands a different ratio of protein to carbohydrate in the diet. We can apply this information to all our children, but especially those with AD/HD. What is glucose, and why is it so important to the brain?

Glucose is a simple sugar produced when we digest carbohydrates. Every cell in your body uses glucose to provide energy for cellular processes such as absorbing nutrients, getting rid of wastes, processing information, making proteins, and reproducing and repairing itself. Enzymes within the cell split the glucose molecule into smaller pieces. Energy that had been keeping the molecule intact is released and transferred to tiny storage units called ATP (adenosine triphosphate). All cells make ATP and use it as an energy bank upon which they can draw at any time.

Cells band together in functional groups called tissues to produce the products we need to live. For example, groups of cells making up respiratory membranes produce mucus that traps air so that we can breathe and that holds dust and other particles until they can be discharged. Other tissues like those in the pancreas produce the hormone insulin that regulates sugar metabolism in your entire body. Neurons, or brain cells, carry on many of the same activities as other cells, but unlike others, neurons churn out information twenty-four hours a day, every day of your life. Glucose is the only fuel your brain can use for this activity, and the demand for it is great. While other body cells can convert fats and proteins into glucose when extra fuel is needed, the brain cannot. Any disruption in the utilization or distribution of glucose in the brain—the control center of the body—will ultimately affect all body systems.

As we have seen, those with AD/HD appear to have a disruption in glucose metabolism in the frontal region of the brain. How, then, does eating sugar, the source of glucose, cause such a problem for those with AD/HD?

How Sugar Sabotages Brain Function

Sugar can provide the necessary glucose to increase brain efficiency, and many of those with AD/HD do crave sugar. Yet, eating sugar actually lowers brain glucose, rather than raising it as might be expected. That's because our bodies still haven't adapted to a high consumption of refined carbohydrates like sugar. Only during the past two or three hundred years have we eaten sugar or sugary foods, yet today many forms of sugar have found their way into most of the processed foods we eat.

Over the course of human existence glucose has been provided by the slow release of sugar from complex carbohydrates, and this delayed insulin response. Our bodies are well adapted to handling a slower and more controlled release of glucose. Consequently, the body interprets a rapid rise in blood glucose from eating sugary foods as stressful and potentially life threatening. Let's look at what occurs.

When sugar enters our circulation after a meal high in carbohydrates, it triggers an output of the pancreatic hormone insulin into the bloodstream. Insulin insures that glucose gets into all cells and out of the bloodstream. The liver processes glucose and prepares it for storage. Some glucose from a meal will enter muscle tissues that also store it. Remember that glucose is a fuel, and the body provides it first to the largest soft tissues. If we engage in physical activities that demand muscular action, we need a back-up in case of energy depletion, and our liver provides this.

Everything we eat and drink passes through the liver, which determines how each substance should be processed, even if it is harmful and should be destroyed. As a result of this process, the brain

217

receives glucose that is released by the liver, but how much it gets depends on the amount of protein that is eaten along with the carbohydrates. A high-sugar meal with very little protein, such as a sweet roll and orange juice for breakfast, will have a different effect than one containing concentrated proteins like those from animal sources, legumes, or a complete protein combination such as oatmeal and soy milk.

Moreover, the effects of breakfast are even more pronounced on brain function than other meals, because we haven't eaten for several hours when we come to breakfast. Therefore, a mixed protein and complex carbohydrate breakfast is very important for those with AD/HD. For this reason, leftovers from dinner, which are often higher in protein, make excellent breakfasts. During the post digestive process, insulin is rapidly diverting glucose away from the brain. This effect is most pronounced when the meal contains little protein. We experience this as tiredness after a high carbohydrate meal. The higher the sugar composition of the meal, the more likely we are to become tired. Two processes are at work here.

First, the brain compensates for lowered glucose levels by activating norepinephrine, which halts the flow of glucose away from the brain. Norepinephrine, a brain chemical that increases alertness and concentration, comes from protein foods and is readily available when the meal contains protein. If it does not, sufficient norepinephrine may not be available and we become less alert.

Second, insulin selects specific amino acids digested from protein for uptake in the liver and muscles and, in doing so, shifts the balance between brain chemicals. Another of these brain chemicals, serotonin, makes us sleepy and increases in concentration in the brain as norepinephrine is declining, which shifts brain activity from alert to sleepy. Ultimately a vicious cycle is set up as the brain demands more glucose: we eat more sugar, then insulin kicks in, further lowering glucose levels. The AD/HD sufferer who chooses sugar may calm his brain down, an effect of serotonin, but he will also decrease his attention span and increase his mood swings—even depression. For some people, hyperactivity is a natural response to the lower glucose levels, as we have seen. Their bodies try to raise norepinephrine levels through movement, and the muscles have been well primed by insulin, which has moved extra glucose and amino acids into storage in these tissues. In the meantime, the brain struggles to maintain communication between neurons, but the messages become unclear and confusing, making it impossible for a person experiencing this dynamic to concentrate. Another event now takes place in the brain as it builds up glucose deficits.

Glucose Effects on Neurotransmitters

A sugary meal causes a rise in glucose storage outside the brain and a shift in neurotransmitters, the chemical messengers that regulate the flow of information between neurons. In a tiny space between neurons, called the synapse, more than forty neurotransmitters are at work. The four most important in our discussion of AD/HD are norepinephrine and dopamine, also called catecholamines, which speed up the rate at which one neuron signals another; acetylcholine, which amplifies the signal being sent; and serotonin, which slows it down. By means of these four and the other neurotransmitters in the synapse, the brain controls the speed, intensity, and selectivity of messages being communicated.

Glucose metabolism in the brain dramatically affects the balance between the catecholamines and serotonin. High levels can slow down brain function as serotonin rises, but uneven distribution of energy from glucose also reduces brain activity as neurons struggle to process information. Thus, when you already have a genetic error of metabolism—as it is now believed a significant number of AD/HD individuals do—consuming more sugar is a sure way to exaggerate the brain's malfunction. We must achieve a good balance between complex carbohydrates, proteins, and fats to restore optimum brain function.

Carbohydrates provide fuel for our bodies, especially the brain, which cannot break down either fats or proteins. In overcoming AD/HD, therefore, we must carefully plan the type of carbohydrates we eat and when we eat them. Let's distinguish between the various types of carbohydrates.

Types of Carbohydrates

Simple sugars come into the diet from two sources, either those found naturally in fruit, fruit juices, dried fruit, fruit concentrates, and syrups, or those synthetically produced from corn, sugar beets, or sugarcane. Natural syrups include honey, maple, molasses, rice bran, and sorghum. All simple sugars, regardless of source, raise blood glucose levels quickly, and your body responds with a rapid production of insulin.

Foods that contain simple sugars are processed foods, such as candy, ice cream, jam, jellies, and condiments like ketchup and steak sauce. We rarely eat a teaspoon of sugar straight, although we add it liberally to beverages like coffee and iced tea. Over time this adds up. It is estimated that the average American eats 120 pounds of sugar each year. Most of the sugar comes from the processed foods and condiments that we consume, perhaps without realizing we are doing so. These sugary foods are wreaking havoc on our health but are especially deadly for AD/HD sufferers.

Natural sugars are considered more acceptable because they come from foods, rather than being synthesized, and are accompanied by other nutrients in the food that assist their assimilation. However, sugar-sensitive bodies do not tolerate these natural sugars any better than those from highly processed foods. AD/HD individuals with yeast (Candida) overgrowth stemming from overuse of antibiotics will have to eliminate even natural sugars until they can reestablish normal intestinal flora.

As you observe the response you or your child has to natural sugars, you can decide if these foods must be eliminated from your diet as well. Many individuals with AD/HD have a marked inability to process sugars, and they experience severe drops in blood glucose levels two to three hours after eating that leave them shaky, dizzy, weak, and confused. This condition is known as hypoglycemia and requires extra vigilance in carbohydrate intake.

The best type of carbohydrates to eat are complex carbohydrates, which slowly release glucose into the system, slowing down the release of insulin and thereby preventing its action in diverting brain glucose. A complex carbohydrate is composed of starches—large molecules of several sugars combined—and fiber. Grains, beans, pasta, and vegetables all contain complex carbohydrates. Complex carbohydrates provide needed glucose without causing a rapid release of insulin and upsetting brain chemistry. Simple carbohydrates, in contrast, consist of sugars like glucose, sucrose, (table sugar), lactose (milk sugar), fructose, or corn syrup.

Whole grains contain the outer layer and inner germ of the grain as well as the starchy core. They also contain protein, essential fatty acids, vitamins, and minerals needed to digest and metabolize the grain. These are more desirable than refined carbohydrates because they come naturally with these essential nutrients.

Refining whole grains strips the outer layers, the bran, the germ, and most of the protein, fatty acids, vitamins, and minerals. To partly compensate for these losses, some of the B vitamins and one or two minerals are added back to enriched flours and cereal grains. Chromium is one of the trace minerals that is not added back, and it is a necessary element for your body to shuttle glucose into cells. Chromium makes insulin more efficient, thereby reducing the amount it takes to get glucose into your body cells.

We have seen that there are two sides to the carbohydrate picture. On the one hand, they provide necessary energy for your body, but on the other hand, they can disrupt brain function. We have also seen that the best choice for meeting these energy requirements is to choose complex carbohydrates from whole grains rather than anything made from refined flours or simple sugars. The next step is to choose the best time of day to eat carbohydrates in order to most benefit brain function.

When Children Should Eat Carbohydrates

Several investigations have been made into the effects of meal composition on school performance. According to Bonnie Spring, Ph.D., a researcher in the department of psychology at Texas Tech University, in Lubbock, Texas, the most significant effects were seen after breakfast. Children who ate a high-carbohydrate breakfast scored more poorly on tests of attention than children who had no breakfast at all! Those who had eaten a high-protein breakfast did much better than those who either ate no breakfast or ate one rich in carbohydrates.

Moreover, the children who ate a high-carbohydrate breakfast were affected quickly, within thirty minutes after they ate. The effect lasted for four hours. In other words, if your child eats a high-carbohydrate breakfast without a balance of protein, his mind may be under siege all morning. If he then eats a high-carbohydrate or sugary lunch, the effect can last the entire school day. In the clinical trials, the effects seen after a high-carbohydrate lunch were not as dramatic as those seen after a high carbohydrate breakfast. Yet carbohydrates, which raise serotonin levels, can have a dramatic impact on brain function in children.

How Carbohydrates Affect Adults

Similar tests run on adults failed to find such a clear-cut response to carbohydrates, although many adults have learned to mix and match proteins and carbohydrates for clearer thinking and smoother energy response. In an adult study reviewed by Bonnie Spring, Ph.D., and published in *Nutrition and the Brain*, carbohydrate-rich meals produced significantly greater sleepiness 2 hours after being consumed than did protein-rich meals. Many adults reported calming effects from eating carbohydrates, presumably because serotonin levels were raised. One research team noted that women will change carbohydrate and protein choices depending on their menstrual cycle. Carbohydrates that raise serotonin levels are preferred just prior to menstruation.

Nevertheless, the reported glucose impairment in the frontal lobes of AD/HD adults can seriously affect mental performance, since the frontal lobe handles mental representations involved in cognition, ideas, and abstractions. If sugar metabolism is disturbed in those with AD/HD, how is it affected by artificial sweeteners? Are they a healthy, helpful option?

Aspartame—Sweet Promises

I was enthusiastic at first when the sweetener aspartame, registered under the trade names NutraSweet and Equal, was introduced in the early 1980s. It was expected there would be few if any side effects caused by aspartame, since it is made from the amino acids phenylalanine and aspartic acid, which your body needs. Phenylalanine is an essential amino acid, one that must be supplied daily because your body can't manufacture it. It is the precursor of two of the major neurotransmitters, namely norepinephrine and dopamine. The amino acid aspartic acid is also an important excitatory neurotransmitter, although the body can manufacture it.

A tasteless sweetener with no calories, which could be safely used by those who react to sugar, seemed too good to be true...and it was. Shortly after its introduction into foods, the Centers for Disease Control published the results of a 1983 study they conducted on consumer-based complaints associated with food products containing aspartame. Complaints involved upsets to the central nervous and digestive systems and gynecological problems.

Reported central nervous system symptoms included mood changes, insomnia, and seizures. Gastrointestinal complaints included abdominal pain, nausea, and diarrhea. Irregular menses was the single gynecological complaint reported. To illustrate how severe these symptoms can be, here is a case reported in the scientific literature. It involved a teenage girl who discovered her sensitivity to NutraSweet. She was extremely popular, athletic, and had excellent grades, but like many teenage girls she became obsessed with her weight. So she decided to switch to diet beverages sweetened with NutraSweet. At first she consumed one or two per day, but she quickly increased her intake to several each day because she enjoyed the high they gave her.

After a few weeks of drinking several diet beverages a day, her behavior began to change dramatically. She was less agile, became moody, and had difficulty sustaining her grade point average. Her friends noticed that she became irritable, short tempered, and argumentative. During the summer break, she went away to cheerleader camp for a week. No diet drinks were available. After an initial two days of feeling lethargic and having headaches, she began to feel better. By the end of the week she felt better than she had in months, and her friends noticed a complete reversal of her symptoms. Upon her return home, she sampled a diet beverage and immediately became depressed and lethargic. Suspecting a reaction to the Nutra-Sweet, she withdrew diet beverages for a few days and then tried them again, with the same results. Now she was certain of her sensitivity to aspartame, and she has avoided it ever since. How, then, does NutraSweet affect the brain?

William Pardridge, M.D., of the UCLA Department of Medicine, explained its effects in a paper entitled "Potential Effects of the Dipeptide Sweetener Aspartame on the Brain," published in *Nutrition and the Brain, Volume 7.* As we have seen, aspartame consists of the amino acids aspartic acid and phenylalanine. Because of the protective blood brain barrier, the entry of aspartic acid is slowed down and its effects appear to be minimal.

However, phenylalanine readily crosses the blood brain barrier and is converted within the neurons into the excitatory neurotransmitters norepinephrine and dopamine. If the blood is delivering more phenylalanine than other amino acids to the brain, the natural balance of neurotransmitters is upset. The neurotransmitters that are crowded out are the calming and stabilizing ones, serotonin and dopamine. As a result, symptoms that occur may include insomnia, short attention span, hyperactivity, behavioral changes, hormone changes, decreased agility, and seizures in those with a family history of this condition. No wonder the teenage girl described in the medical literature had these symptoms. She consumed as many as eight aspartame-laden drinks per day!

According to Dr. Pardridge, levels of phenylalanine high enough to push the upper limits of safety can occur if your child drinks a quart (four standard cans) or more per day of beverages containing NutraSweet. If your child is eating snacks containing NutraSweet or Equal, these may contribute even more of these potentially harmful ingredients to his diet.

In addition to the neurotransmitters, NutraSweet contains methanol, which must be metabolized by the liver in the same manner as ethanol, the alcohol found in wine, beer, and spirits. For adults consuming diet mixers with alcoholic drinks, the methanol in the mixer adds additional work for the liver. Methanol, sometimes called wood alcohol, is produced in small amounts by bacteria in the digestive system. Normally the amount produced is not harmful, but if enough additional methanol is ingested, the potential for toxicity, especially in children, is considerably increased.

Incredibly, in twenty years of testing, the developers of NutraSweet never checked to see what effects this chemical might have on the brain. Yet it was approved for use by the FDA before this was known, and they have approved several other artificial sweeteners that can detrimentally affect brain function as well.

Acesulfame K: Use Approval Expanded

Acesulfame K (acesulfame potassium), sold under the name Sunett, is an artificial sweetener two hundred times sweeter than sucrose or table sugar. Sunett is used in foods, beverages, tabletop sweeteners, pharmaceuticals, dietary supplements, including protein powders and nutrition bars, and cosmetics requiring a sweet taste. Sunett is extremely stable, making it suitable also for baked or frozen products. It isn't as fluffy as sugar and recipes using it must be revised, but otherwise it seems like a chemist's dream come true. Even though Sunett is sweeter than sugar, it contains no calories!

Like aspartame, saccharin, cyclamates, and other artificial sweeteners, Sunett is not metabolized as sugar. In fact, it's not metabolized at all, but passes unchanged from the body. While the tongue perceives it as intensely sweet, the digestive system doesn't recognize it and therefore cannot break it down.

Sunett was approved for dietary use in the late 1980s, just a few years after aspartame. However, most of us were not aware of its existence — why? If Sunett is used as the exclusive sweetening agent, it leaves an unpleasant bitter aftertaste on the tongue but it could still be used to substantially reduce the amount of sugar needed in sweetened foods, which would cut calories and make it a winner in the diet food category. However, there are questions about whether Sunett is safe, when consumed even in moderate amounts, and this limits its broad acceptance by the food industry.

The significant danger for those with AD/HD, however, is that Sunett stimulates insulin release even though it isn't metabolized by the body. The sweetness perceived in the mouth sends a powerful message to the pancreas to release insulin because a sugar meal is on the way! We can try to fool the body, but if insulin is released, the accompanying dampening effects on neurotransmitters occur.

Sucralose: Another Promise of Sweetness That Doesn't Deliver

The FDA approved another new sweetener, called sucralose, in May 1998. Splenda, the Canadian name, has been in use in Canada since 1991. This sweetener can be added to baked goods and foods that are to be heated to high temperatures. Thus, it has the potential of inclusion in even more foods than NutraSweet, which breaks down when it is heated. Sucralose has been approved for addition into all baked goods, baking mixes, nonalcoholic beverages, chewing gum, coffee and tea products, confections and frostings, fat and oils, frozen dairy desserts and mixes, fruit and water ices, gelatins, puddings and fillings, jams and jellies, milk products, processed fruits and fruit juices, sugar substitutes, sweet sauces, toppings, syrups, and as a tabletop sweetener.

Sucralose was originally produced in England in 1976 by two chemists who found that ordinary table sugar could be combined with chlorine gas to produce a complex chemical that the tongue detected as sweet with an intensity six hundred times that of sugar. It turns out that beyond its sweet promise, sucralose is so artificial, the body cannot recognize it and passes it up for absorption as a nutrient. However, it still goes to the liver, which must figure out what to do with it.

Since it can't be broken down, the liver treats sucralose as a xenobiotic or foreign chemical, one that must be detoxified by protective enzymes in the liver. The ultimate toxicity of sucralose rests on how difficult it is for these enzymes to get rid of it and what kind of by-products will be produced as a result. Experience has taught us that the potential toxicity of a chemical depends on whatever else the liver has had to process. The more toxic food, chemicals, inhalants, and drugs (prescription or OTC) the liver is confronted with, the greater the potential for toxic effects of artificial ingredients like sucralose.

It's tempting to think you can eat all the sweet-tasting foods you want and not have any calories to count. But the reason it sounds too good to be true is that—to date—it is. This new sweetener may have the potential for doing even more harm than aspartame or acesulfame K. The good news is that sucralose is less likely to promote cavities than sugar, because the bacteria in the mouth that cause dental caries cannot utilize it either. Sucralose also does not have the unpleasant aftertaste of acesulfame K. Although sucralose offers no substantial advantage over xylitol and sorbitol—the sweeteners commonly found in toothpastes—in cavity prevention, whereas the latter are metabolized because they are normally found in the body, sucralose is not. Therefore, sucralose may be an excellent addition to mouthwash, toothpaste, and other oral hygiene products that should taste good but never be swallowed.

Artificial Indigestible Ingredients: Presumed Innocent?

Alpha-amylase inhibitors or starch blockers were popular in the mid 1980s because they blocked the digestion of carbohydrates, promising that you could eat as much pasta as you wanted without any calories. Americans rushed to try the newest weight-control gimmick, but so many people complained about stomachaches and other gastrointestinal upsets that the fad died before long.

Chitin from shellfish is another material that is not digested, but traps and removes dietary fats on its way through our digestive systems. This material toughens the shells of crustaceans like crabs, shrimp, and lobsters. The processed material, known by trade names such as Chitosan, traps fats before they can pass through the intestinal wall, thus preventing their absorption in the digestive system. Unfortunately, chitin can cause irritation to the digestive system and indiscriminately remove good as well as bad fats; it is therefore not used much at all.

Olestra—More Trouble

And now we have olestra, marketed under the name Olean and manufactured by Procter & Gamble. Olestra is a conglomerate of many sugar molecules tightly bound to fatty acids. This sugar/fat polymer is so big it cannot pass intact through the intestinal wall, and so complex, that digestive enzymes cannot split the molecule into smaller, more absorbable units. Your tongue will pick up the creaminess of fat and this causes a pleasant taste sensation, but like acesulfame K, sucralose, and chitin, olestra goes right through you...and drags along some important nutrients in the process that should be left for your body to absorb.

Olestra traps fat-soluble vitamins like vitamin A, vitamin D, vitamin E, and the antioxidant carotenes that are waiting for passage into circulation during the digestive process. The FDA was worried about the problem this could cause, especially for children, but not worried enough to withhold approval of the material for use in snack foods. The FDA approval was conditional upon Procter & Gamble advising its customers to fortify all foods containing olestra with vitamins A, D, and E. However, no label warning is required to advise consumers of the anti-vitamin activity of olestra. Besides robbing the body of nutrients, olestra also interferes with metabolism of essential fatty acids and fat-soluble antioxidants such as beta-carotene, lycopene, lutein, and zeaxanthin. Incredibly, the reported response of the FDA, when confronted with this reality, was that fatty acids and carotenoids haven't been established as vitamins and therefore are of less concern.

Olestra was test-marketed in several U.S. cities. Snack items containing olestra were made freely available to citizens in a city in Iowa, and the initial response was very favorable. In a few hours, however, many local citizens who had sampled several of the snacks suddenly suffered distressing bouts of diarrhea. One could only hope similar episodes occur frequently enough to limit use of this product! Obviously, I do not recommend this product to anyone, let alone those with AD/HD. I do not recommend buying products with any of these artificial ingredients in them, because they disturb glucose and fatty acid metabolism, both of which are vital to brain function.

Effects of Proteins on the Brain

Proteins contain twenty or more amino acids, of which eight are considered essential, or must be eaten daily, and two as semi-essential for adults but essential for children. Amino acids are the basic units of growth, building muscles, organs, and other tissues of our bodies. They are also essential for brain function.

When we eat proteins, more norepinephrine and dopamine are available than serotonin. That's because tyrosine and phenylalanine, which yield dopamine and norepinephrine, are more plentiful in proteins than tryptophan, one of the eight essential amino acids, which Yields serotonin. These three amino acids compete for delivery to the brain, and tryptophan, being less concentrated, loses out. Even when high-tryptophan-containing foods such as dairy products or turkey are eaten, tyrosine and phenylalanine still have the advantage.

Recall for a moment what I said earlier, that tryptophan will be picked up and concentrated best when carbohydrate foods are eaten along with proteins. We can think of proteins as fuel for thought and carbobydrates as good for promoting drowsiness.

Amino acids also function in many ways that are just as important to brain function as neurotransmitters. They make up the enzymes that regulate neurotransmitters. Without these enzymes, neurons could not receive, process, interpret, and output vital information. Any amino acid or small protein that has an effect on the transmission of information between neurons is called a neurotransmitter.

Other Neurotransmitters: Effects

Overcoming AD/HD, especially in children, necessitates consumption of a high percentage (30 percent of daily calories) of good, high-quality proteins such as fish, poultry, lamb, pork, and beef, as well as organically grown vegetables, legumes such as soybeans and peas, and whole grains. Allergies and food sensitivities must be considered when we discuss proteins because they can also play a major role in symptoms of AD/HD. These symptoms also interfere with good digestion and impede the effective delivery of amino acids into the system. According to Jon Pangborn, Ph.D., who has reviewed thousands of laboratory tests on individuals with AD/HD, poor protein digestion is a common factor in those suffering from food allergies. When proteins are improperly digested, large peptide units pass into the system and trigger an immune response. Not only that, if proteins are not properly digested, they cannot yield the amino acids needed for neurotransmitters. They may even yield toxic byproducts that can slow down mental processing and further compromise the immune system. Therefore, it is necessary to address this potential problem by using digestive enzymes that ensure efficient delivery of the needed amino acids to the brain.

Acetylcholine (AC) is the neurotransmitter associated with memory and efficient cognition. Choline, the main constituent of acetylcholine, is also a component of phosphatidyl choline or PC. PC is one of four phosphatides that act like Velcro on the surface of neurons and other cells in your body. They grab messages that are being transferred between neurons and are the attachments for the essential fatty acids.

Both dietary and supplemental choline must be available to become well absorbed and utilized in the manufacture of both acetylcholine and PC if our thought processes are to flow quickly and smoothly. Disruption of acetylcholine activity has not been demonstrated in AD/HD, although it has been in memory disorders. Of importance in AD/HD is the role choline plays as PC and its stress-rebound ability. PC is the base attachment of arachidonic acid, the second most important fatty acid in the brain.

Acetylcholine is classified as a cholinergic neurotransmitter—one that is opposite in action from the catecholamines. AC amplifies messages being sent across the synapse, while the catecholamines speed the rate of transmission. We experience a shift between these neurotransmitters as quick thinking and responsiveness (catecholamines) and contemplation (acetylcholine). We need a balance of both. During stressful periods, we selectively drive our neurons with catecholamines. Catecholamine activity keeps us sharp, but we usually experience less depth to our thoughts. Our bodies need to recoup with periods of selecting acetylcholine to restore mental balance.

Can we increase the yield of acetylcholine by dietary change? The answer is yes, and the use of soy foods increases the amount of choline available to the brain. The foods that contain large amounts of choline are liver, oatmeal, soy foods, cauliflower, kale, and cabbage.

It is important to note that acetylcholine, phosphatidyl choline, and the other important phosphatide, phosphatidyl serine, are all present in significant levels in human breast milk. Nature has supplied the perfect balance of phosphatides and fatty acids needed for development of the baby's brain. These building blocks for a healthy brain are very important to the developing child. This is just another reason why mothers should breast-feed their children if possible.

Fats, Fatty Acids, and AD/HD

We have been repeatedly warned about the dangers of a high-fat diet; it is believed to contribute to the major chronic diseases of our day, and rightly so. However, the message has gotten confused. Americans have also confused cholesterol with fat, often considering them as one and the same. However, as medical experts have learned more about the role of cholesterol in heart disease, they have modified their stand. Now we know that the kind of cholesterol present, low-density lipoproteins (LDL) or high-density lipoproteins (HDL), is as important as total cholesterol. HDL is considered the good kind, while LDL is considered the bad one and an indicator of future cardiovascular disease. Furthermore, many of the processed fats we once thought were good for us are no longer considered so. The result is a vigorous debate over the most widely consumed spreads—butter and margarine. The medical community needs to clarify this message about fats.

Which ones are good for you? According to results obtained from the ongoing Boston Nurses Health Study, there is good reason to worry about the artificial fats found in margarine, fast foods, French fries, doughnuts, crackers, and commercial baked goods. In assessing the effects on eighty thousand nurses of the bad fats found in these foods, a crucial factor in the development of heart disease has been identified. Researchers now think the risk from consuming these fats is greater than that from smoking and high blood pressure. The result? Please pass the butter!

As for the current love affair we Americans have for fat-free, the creamy texture and taste we have come to love is now replaced in many processed foods by sugars of various forms. Actually when we eat them we wind up sabotaging our efforts to reduce fat accumulation in our bodies. When introduced to our systems in excess, these sugars are converted and stored—you guessed it—as fat! In addition, some of the weight gain that is occurring in this country's population since our awareness of the dangers of fats has come from people thinking of fat-free items as ones they can eat much more of than their fat-filled equivalent. This is just not true. We have made some beneficial changes to our diets over the last three years, but there still is a long way to go.

About Marcia Zimmerman

Marcia Zimmerman is a certified nutritionist, a lecturer, and a consultant to some of the country's leading nutrition and supplement companies. She has studied both Chinese and Ayurvedic medicine. Ms. Zimmerman is the author of *The ADD Nutrition Solution* (Henry Holt & Company, 1999), which contains a 30-day nutrition plan for decreasing AD/HD symptoms. She is also the author of *Eat Your Colors* (Henry Holt & Company 2001).

Chapter 25

Resolving Differences between Teachers and Parents

Disagreements over what is in the best interest of a child are inevitable between teachers and parents during the course of a child's education. Teachers and parents share responsibility for the education and socialization of children, and it is important that they be mindful of the impact of their interactions as a model of problem-solving behavior. It is necessary for both teachers and parents to be discreet and respectful in expressing their thoughts and feelings to each other, and to avoid involving children in their disagreements.

On the one hand, it is useful for teachers to keep in mind that, for parents, being their child's strongest advocate is intrinsic to the parenting role, regardless of what the teacher thinks may be best for the child. Teachers should be aware that some parents may be reluctant to express their concerns for fear of possible negative repercussions for their child's relationship with the teacher, or may lack knowledge of appropriate ways to express their concerns. On the other hand, it is helpful for parents to consider that some teachers may be anxious or fearful of encounters with parents. While it is up to teachers to set a respectful tone in their relations with parents, it is up to parents to express concerns directly to their child's teacher and to

Excerpted from "Resolving Differences between Teachers and Parents," by Lilian G. Katz, Amy Aidman, Debbie A. Reese, and Ann-Marie Clark, from *ERIC/EECE Newsletter*, Spring 1996, Volume 8, Number 1, published by the ERIC Clearinghouse on Elementary and Early Childhood Education, University of Illinois at Urbana-Champaign.

avoid destructive criticism of teachers and schools in front of their children.

Strategies for Teachers

There are several strategies teachers can use to establish a climate of open communication with parents.

Let parents know that they can contact their children's teachers. As early in the school year as possible, teachers can take opportunities to let parents know that they are eager to be informed directly should questions or concerns arise. Teachers can let parents know the best ways and times to reach them and have an appointment book ready at hand to set up meetings. In early fall, some teachers send home a newsletter containing their teaching philosophy, a discussion of class rules and teacher expectations, and a message encouraging parents to stay in touch which includes a phone number or an electronic mail address.

Invite parents to observe in the classroom. Teachers can invite parents to visit the class to monitor their child's perceptions of a situation and to see what teachers are trying to achieve with students as individuals and as a group.

Elicit expressions of parents' concerns and interests. Early in the school year, teachers can ask parents what their main concerns and goals are for their child. Brief questionnaires and interest surveys make good bases for meaningful discussions with parents as teachers are getting to know each child. It is also helpful for teachers to initiate contacts with parents as frequently as possible.

Know the school policy for addressing parent-teacher disagreements. It is a good idea for teachers to check school and school district policies about handling conflicts or disagreements with parents, and to follow the procedures outlined in the policies.

Involve parents in classroom activities. Teachers can let parents know how they can be helpful in general, and should use opportunities as they arise to solicit their help with specific activities.

Be discreet about discussing children and their families. It is important to resist the temptation to discuss children and their families in inappropriate public and social situations, or to discuss particular children with the parents of other children.

Strategies for Parents

When parents perceive that children are having difficulties at school, there are steps they can take to investigate and hopefully help to alleviate problems.

Listen to the child. Paying close attention to children's comments about what is going on at school is vital to staying aware of difficulties children are experiencing. Parents can solicit more information from their children. It is important to maintain a nonjudgmental attitude while listening to the child's side of a story, realizing that there may be aspects to the situation that are still unknown.

Decide if a call to the school is necessary. It is helpful for parents to decide whether the issue is serious enough to warrant contacting the school. A cooling off period may be appropriate before making this decision. Parents should keep in mind that the end of the day, when they are picking up their child, may not be the best time for a discussion involving strong feelings. With an older child, it may be useful to ask if he or she wants the parent to discuss a difficult issue with the teacher.

Talk directly with the teacher. Parents should contact the teacher directly in person or by phone. Sometimes the teacher is unaware of the child's difficulty. Sometimes a parent hears a report from the child that seems outlandish. Sometimes a child misunderstands a teacher's intentions, or the teacher is unaware of the child's confusion about a rule or an assignment. It is important to check the facts with the teacher before drawing conclusions or allocating blame. Direct contact with the teacher helps to define the problem accurately and to develop a solution. Failing a resolution of the problem, it may be necessary to contact other school personnel.

Avoid criticizing teachers in front of children. Criticizing teachers and schools in front of children may confuse them. Even very young children can pick up the worry, frustration, or disdain that parents may feel concerning their children's school experiences. In the case of the youngest children, it is not unusual for them to attribute heroic qualities to their teachers and overheard criticism may put a child in a bind over divided loyalties. In the case of older children, such criticism may foster rudeness or defiance to their teachers. Besides causing confusion, criticizing teachers in front of children is not conducive to solving the underlying problem.

Help children cope with disappointments and negative feelings about their school experiences. While it is inevitable that almost all children will encounter teachers whom they do not especially like, parents can help their children cope with their disappointments. It is highly unlikely, after all, that children will like all of their teachers. Parents are most likely to help their children by pointing out that throughout their lives they will have to work with people they may not especially like or enjoy. Parents can encourage their child to focus on what must be done, to concentrate on what can be learned, and to keep his or her sights on the larger goals of learning and strengthening the competencies essential for a productive and satisfying life in the future.

Model effective problem-solving behaviors. As children grow older, they are generally aware when their parents are upset about the teacher or a school-related incident. As parents discuss these incidents with their children, they provide an opportunity for their children to observe effective and appropriate ways to express frustration with the problems of life—in schools and other group settings. These are problems they are likely to face throughout life. Approaching these problems with good humor and respect for all the persons involved increases children's ability to cope with such situations throughout their lives.

Creating Family-Centered Child Care Programs

Family-centered child care is based on the premise that families are the center of children's lives. Programs that are family-centered reflect and respect the unique characteristics of all members of a child's family, including not only the child's mother and father but also all other significant adults who are involved in caring for the child. Historically, parent involvement in child care programs has been understood from a program perspective. In family-centered settings, however, parent involvement is understood from the families' perspective. From this viewpoint, families' goals and needs are the basis for program design and practice.

In February, 1996, the Child Care Bureau, Administration for Children and Families, Department of Health and Human Services convened a national leadership forum focusing on promoting family-centered child care. This forum provided an opportunity for approximately 150 participants to paint the picture of what family-centered programs should look like and to develop recommendations for making that picture a reality.

Family-Centered Child Care: What Does it Look Like?

Because family-centered child care is flexible by definition, it will look different in different settings. However, there are some common characteristics.

Family-centered child care supports the connections between children and their families. It recognizes that children draw their identities from the family. All family members are included and treated with respect and warmth. A basic belief in the value of families permeates program policies and practices. Such programs are welcoming and non-judgmental, and all staff are available to assist family members.

A family-centered program speaks the languages and respects the cultures of families in the program. Staff is drawn from the community the program serves. Efforts are made to build inclusiveness and to welcome all family members as partners in the program. Family-centered programs build on family strengths and collaborate closely with other service providers. Such programs recognize various stages of development in family members and attempt to work with them to meet their needs. There is a natural give-and-take in these programs that empowers parents to make contributions to the program in ways that are not pre-determined.

Family-centered child care supports and trains caregivers. It is important to provide training for staff on the basic principles of family-centered care. Capacity-building opportunities such as pre-service and in-service training, peer coaching, and mentoring are provided on a continuous basis. Program administrators set the tone and lead by example in their relationships with families and routinely reassess their communications with them. Joint training is also provided for staff and families.

Family-centered child care forges true partnerships with families. Unlike partnerships in traditional models, in which parents are in a passive role of being informed or educated, in this partnership, parents are in a creative role of establishing goals and making decisions. In family-centered programs, families know that their feedback will effect change.

What Are It's Guiding Principles?

The distinguishing characteristic of family-centered programs is that all policies and practices are based on an underlying set of principles regarding their relationships with families.

Families are the primary influence in the lives of their children. Families are the center of children's lives. Programs should create an environment which reflects the culture, strengths, and desires of families for their children.

It is not possible to accurately generalize about families. Professional caregivers take the time to get to know family members individually and to support them in their goals for their children.

Families have strengths. Families and child care professionals are partners who have the shared responsibility of doing the best for the children in their care. Child care professionals need to get to know families and build upon their strengths.

Families have something to offer child care providers. Traditionally, exchanges between parents and child care professionals have been viewed as a means of informing families about their child. However, in family-centered programs it is recognized that, while professionals bring information to parents about child development and about their experiences with many children, families provide information about the individual child, across time and in a variety of settings.

Contemporary families experience multiple demands. Employment, housing, health care, and transportation are some issues facing families, whose lack of contact with child care programs should not be mistaken for lack of concern for their child.

There are many ways for a family to be involved. It is important to provide a range of options for families to participate in this aspect of their child's life, and to allow families to choose the type and level of participation which suits them.

How Do We Get There?

Achieving family-centered child care calls for action on the part of families, program providers, communities, and policymakers. The following are steps toward encouraging family-centered child care.

Get the message out. Educate others on the importance of children and families and the role of high-quality programs in their lives.

Provide training for staff and families. Shifts in philosophy and attitude result from training and education of staff, families, and all those responsible for the achievement of family-centered child care.

Consider the cost of child care. Family-centered child care is not necessarily more expensive than other child care. However, when considering funding, programs must account for the true cost of care so barriers can be minimized and must support and follow up training with adequate resources.

Collaborate. A key practice in creating family-centered care is exceptional collaboration among providers. Policymakers should view child care as a hub for service delivery. Linkages must be forged at the community level among child care programs, mental health organizations, child care resource and referral agencies, and family support services.

Chapter 26

Individualized Education Program (IEP): What You Should Know

Chapter Contents

Section 26.1

IEP Team Members

By law, certain individuals must be involved in writing a child's Individualized Education Program (IEP). An IEP team member may fill more than one of the team positions if properly qualified and designated. For example, the school system representative may also be the person who can interpret the child's evaluation results.

These people must work together as a team to write the child's IEP. A meeting to write the IEP must be held within 30 calendar days of deciding that the child is eligible for special education and related services.

Each team member brings important information to the IEP meeting. Members share their information and work together to write the child's Individualized Education Program. Each person's information adds to the team's understanding of the child and what services the child needs.

Parents are key members of the IEP team. They know their child very well and can talk about their child's strengths and needs as well as their ideas for enhancing their child's education. They can offer insight into how their child learns, what his or her interests are, and other aspects of the child that only a parent can know. They can listen to what the other team members think their child needs to work on at school and share their suggestions. They can also report on whether the skills the child is learning at school are being used at home.

Teachers are vital participants in the IEP meeting as well. At least one of the child's regular education teachers must be on the IEP team if the child is (or may be) participating in the regular education environment. The regular education teacher has a great deal to share with the team. For example, he or she might talk about:

- the general curriculum in the regular classroom;

- the aids, services, or changes to the educational program that would help the child learn and achieve; and
- strategies to help the child with behavior, if behavior is an issue.

The regular education teacher may also discuss with the IEP team the supports for school staff that are needed so that the child can:

- advance toward his or her annual goals;
- be involved and progress in the general curriculum;
- participate in extracurricular and other activities; and
- be educated with other children, both with and without disabilities.

Supports for school staff may include professional development or more training. Professional development and training are important for teachers, administrators, bus drivers, cafeteria workers, and others who provide services for children with disabilities.

The child's special education teacher contributes important information and experience about how to educate children with disabilities. Because of his or her training in special education, this teacher can talk about such issues as:

- how to modify the general curriculum to help the child learn;
- the supplementary aids and services that the child may need to be successful in the regular classroom and elsewhere;
- how to modify testing so that the student can show what he or she has learned; and
- other aspects of individualizing instruction to meet the student's unique needs.

Beyond helping to write the IEP, the special educator has responsibility for working with the student to carry out the IEP. He or she may:

- work with the student in a resource room or special class devoted to students receiving special education services;
- team teach with the regular education teacher; and
- work with other school staff, particularly the regular education teacher, to provide expertise about addressing the child's unique needs.

Another important member of the IEP team is the individual who can interpret what the child's evaluation results mean in terms of designing appropriate instruction. The evaluation results are very useful in determining how the child is currently doing in school and what areas of need the child has. This IEP team member must be able to talk about the instructional implications of the child's evaluation results, which will help the team plan appropriate instruction to address the child's needs.

The individual representing the school system is also a valuable team member. This person knows a great deal about special education services and educating children with disabilities. He or she can talk about the necessary school resources. It is important that this individual have the authority to commit resources and be able to ensure that whatever services are set out in the IEP will actually be provided.

The IEP team may also include additional individuals with knowledge or special expertise about the child. The parent or the school system can invite these individuals to participate on the team. Parents, for example, may invite an advocate who knows the child, a professional with special expertise about the child and his or her disability, or others (such as a vocational educator who has been working with the child) who can talk about the child's strengths and/or needs. The school system may invite one or more individuals who can offer special expertise or knowledge about the child, such as a paraprofessional or related services professional. Because an important part of developing an IEP is considering a child's need for related services, related service professionals are often involved as IEP team members or participants. They share their special expertise about the child's needs and how their own professional services can address those needs.

Depending on the child's individual needs, some related service professionals attending the IEP meeting or otherwise helping to develop the IEP might include occupational or physical therapists, adaptive physical education providers, psychologists, or speech-language pathologists.

When an IEP is being developed for a student of transition age, representatives from transition service agencies can be important participants. Whenever the purpose of meeting is to consider needed transition services, the school must invite a representative of any other agency that is likely to be responsible for providing or paying for transition services. This individual can help the team plan any transition services the student needs. He or she can also commit the resources of the agency to pay for or provide needed transition services. If he or she does not attend the meeting, then the school must take alternative steps to obtain the agency's participation in the planning of the student's transition services.

And, last but not least, the student may also be a member of the IEP team. If transition service needs or transition services are going to be discussed at the meeting, the student must be invited to attend. More and more students are participating in and even leading their own IEP meetings. This allows them to have a strong voice in their own education and can teach them a great deal about self-advocacy and self-determination.

Section 26.2

Suggestions for IEP

An IEP is written specifically for your child, it provides strategies for helping your child to overcome their particular challenges. It is difficult for parents, especially those going through the process for the first time, to fully understand the IEP process without understanding the details of what is included.

Leaving the process to the school officials is one option, but this takes away from your understanding of your child and the needs they may have. Being able to objectively look at the progress your child has made, and what factors helped in that success will help you in determining what should be included. Looking objectively at the challenges your child faces and the area in which he struggles and brainstorming for a solution, will also help.

Although AD/HD affects each child a little differently, there are certain similarities that can also be found in many children. The questions and suggestions that follow are just a starting point. Ask yourself the questions and look at some of the suggestions and solutions that have been used by parents in the past. You can modify these, and add your own, so that walking into the IEP meeting, you will be prepared with a list of accommodations that can benefit your child.

1. Is your child easily distracted away from school lessons?

   - Seating in the front row of the classroom can help as the child is in close proximity to the teacher and may be more apt to pay attention.

   - Developing a signal between the teacher and the student, such as tapping on the desk, clearing her throat, walking past the student and touching him on the shoulder. Be sure both student and teacher understand the signal to be given and what it means.

   - Certain friends sitting close by may be more of a hindrance, you can include that certain friends never sit next to each other during class time.

2. Does your child freeze up during tests?

   - Oral tests can be given by a teacher in order to determine the knowledge of a subject.

   - Sometimes the other students in the class diligently working on the test can be a major distraction, and large source of worry to a child. Maybe allowing them to go to the resource room or the library to complete the test would help.

   - Allow the child to return during free periods or after school to complete the test. Do not allow lunch or recess to be taken away from a hyperactive child in order to complete work.

   - Continue with teacher/student signals, with a gentle reminder to get back on task.

   - Adapted testing. The teacher can reduce the length of a test, for example, instead of completing 10 math problems, would 4 problems show knowledge of the subject?

3. Does written seatwork come home incomplete, sloppy or just not done, causing lower grades than your child deserves?

   - If your child feels he cannot complete the work, can he go to the resource center or the library and work quietly by himself?

- Uncompleted seatwork is to be sent home so that the parent can oversee completion of it after school. No grades should be lowered for seatwork brought back the next day.

- Reduced seatwork. The teacher can reduce the amount of seatwork, so that a satisfactory practice session is accomplished.

4. Does your child lose homework, forget homework, and not hand in completed homework?

- Use signed assignment books—an assignment book that is signed by both the teacher and yourself. Before leaving school, the teacher can sign the book and make sure all homework is listed and let you know immediately of any missing assignments. You are therefore, sure, you know exactly what he has for homework and can sign once you see that it has been complete.

- Have a teacher (or your child if older and computers are available) email the assignment home so that a written account is available at home.

- Does your school have a homework line where you can call a recording a listen to the assignment for the day?

- Add extra time for homework, without a deduction in grading, maybe one to two days so that you can review and make sure everything is completed.

- Allow your child to carry a pocket tape recorder and record assignments as well as other notes that should be brought home, this cuts down on the amount of papers a student needs to keep track of during the day.

5. Is your child extremely disorganized, with papers falling out of all books and the desk or locker reminds you of the Bermuda Triangle?

- Extra help with organization. Children with AD/HD tend to be extremely disorganized with papers everywhere. The teacher can take a few minutes each day to make sure all assignments; tests, papers etc. are properly organized before the child heads for home.

- Some guidance counselors meet with a few students each week to teach organizational skills.

- Does your child have a free period during the day in which a mentor (either a teacher, counselor or older student) can work with him to organize schoolwork?

6. Do you receive reports that show missing assignments, even though everyone has taken extra precautions to make sure the work has been completed?

   - Determine what is considered late, if your IEP states that your child will have an extra day for homework, and then it is not missing until the extra day has gone by.

   - Set up a weekly schedule for you to be provided a list of any work not handed in during the week. Then make Tuesday the last day for any of the work to be handed in. (End of marking periods may be an exception to this).

   - Ask for a syllabus, copies of worksheets and extra copies of all textbooks that you can keep at home. Check the syllabus every day to make sure you have the needed papers for work to be completed.

7. Are you told about a major project the night before it is due?

   - Be sure that you are receiving not only reports of progress but upcoming events and dates, including tests, projects, and book reports.

8. Does your child come home from school each day with glowing reports that everything is fine, no problems, never gets in trouble?

   - Have weekly reports that cover not only schoolwork but also behavioral issues. Go to daily reports if necessary.

9. When your child is out sick for a few days does it seem that they just can't get back on track after returning?

   - On return to school, have the teacher sit with your child, providing a written list of all work that was missed; all needed supplies and worksheets in a complete packet. Have included a plan of action for when the work is to be completed.

- Set up a time frame for tests to be taken when missed, giving your child a few days to return to the routine of school before the test is taken.

10. Does your child fall behind in classes because he is too embarrassed to ask for extra help when needed?

   - Have the teacher set aside a few minutes each week to sit down you're your child to review the work for the week and ask questions to determine if your child needs some extra help in a specific area.

   - Keep communication with the teacher a two way street, providing the teacher with feedback once a week as to your perceptions of how your child is doing and what areas he continues to struggle with.

11. Does your child's work seem to fall during the afternoon because he forgets or is too embarrassed to go to the nurse to take medication?

   - The IEP can include that the teacher gently reminds the student to go at a specific time of the day.

I am sure that there are many more ideas that can be included, based on your child's own needs. But looking this list over should provide you with a starting point on the questions to ask yourself, your child and his teacher in recognizing the areas he can use extra help. Keep going and coming up with both challenges and solutions.

Section 26.3

10 Things You Should Do before Attending Your Child's IEP

Words of Wisdom:

1. Read last year's IEP—It's important to review what came out of last year's plan. Was it successful? Did the methods of instruction work? Did the measurement process used really tell you if progress was being made? Were the goals and objectives really functional for your child? Also try to think back to the actual meeting—what part of the discussion did you feel least prepared for? Remembering will help you prepare better this time around.

2. Update your advocacy notebook—Hopefully you have a single book that allows you to keep all of your child's information (evaluations, old IEPs, correspondence with school and service providers, etc.) organized and easily accessible. If there is new information from doctors, teachers, or related service providers that needs added to your book—take care of the filing now. You'll be glad to have the most current information if the issue comes up during the meeting.

3. Do your homework—is there any new information on your child's disability, have you heard about any promising new intervention strategies that caught your attention? Now is the time to check them out. Research them on the internet or contact a local resource person who can tell you more or provide you with information to review.

4. Come prepared to grow your team—If you've found anything interesting during your research, the IEP meeting is an excellent time to share this information. Rather than contacting everyone individually or relying on one person to pass on your information, you can share it with everyone at once. If the information describe an intervention strategy you would like used in this year's IEP then be sure to bring copies so everyone can look over the information at once during the meeting. Few professional team members are going to be willing to sign off on something they don't understand or feel comfortable with. By helping them learn, you maximize your chances of getting what you want. PEAK (the Colorado Parent Training and Information Center) offers an upbeat video with tips on how parents can really become active players in the IEP process.

5. Make your list—Once you're organized and your research is complete is time to make your list. What are the issues you feel really need to be addressed in your child's IEP? Remember other team members may want to add additional items during your discussion, but you don't want to be thinking afterwards, "Oh I really wanted to discuss X and forgot to bring it up." Right now, while you're calm and not under time pressure is the time to decide what the issues are from your perspective.

6. Prioritize—Because IEPs are a team process they, by their very nature, demand compromise. So once you've developed you list, you'll need to go back through and divide it into two categories.

    - the issues that are non-negotiable to me—they must be addressed for me to give my consent for this IEP and

    - the issues that I am concerned about, but I'm not sure how I want them addressed or what the critical components are. On these issues I'm willing to compromise or settle for minimal supports while we gather more information.

7. Decide who's coming with you—IEPs tend to be extremely anxiety provoking for parents. When you are experiencing a lot of emotion it is unlikely that you will be able to absorb all

the information being given to you. Having someone else there who can listen to the discussion and take notes, will free you up to participate in the discussion and focus on your own agenda.

8. What about taping the meeting—Recording IEP meetings can be a touchy issue for many school districts. However, if you cannot find anyone to come with you to the meeting you may want to consider tape recording it so that you can refer back to the discussion after you're home and calm. One caution, you will need to notify the school that you would like to tape record the meeting. Explain that it will be only for your reference and ask if there are any school guidelines or policies that you should be aware of regarding taping. Start this process as soon as you've been notified about the meeting as some school districts have time guidelines that the notice of recording must be given at least X amount of time before the meeting.

9. Determine your child's participation—If you see a future of self-advocacy for your child, then it is important to involve them in IEPs as early as possible. This will let them watch your advocacy skills and learn by imitation. It also give you the opportunity to get their input on what and how they would like to learn. If you aren't comfortable with your child attending the meeting, then consider how their presence can be felt by proxy. Two ways recommended by other parents are:

- Bring your child's picture and set it in the center of the table—this should effectively remind everyone at the table that the decisions made will impact the life of a real person and should not be arbitrary or for convenience sake.

- Bring your child's portfolio—originally developed to introduce new teachers to your child, the portfolio illustrates all that is unique and special about your child. This is a wonderful way to remind participants that everyone has strengths and special qualities to bring to the table of life.

10. Review your rights—Right before you attend a meeting filled with professionals is the perfect time to read again how the federal laws see your role as parent. It will reinforce your feeling of importance within the team and also ensure that no one

surprises you with any questionable tactics during the meeting. *Special Education Law* by Pete Wright is an exceptional resource for parents in this area.

If you have completed all 10 steps, you should be feeling pretty prepared, but if you still need some moral support here are 2 to consider:

- "The IEP Support and Discussion Group" at Yahoo.com.
- "The IEP Assistance and Consultation Service" at Ideal Lives, www.ideallives.com.

Now go into that conference room with confidence knowing that you are the ultimate expert on your child!

Chapter 27

Teaching Children with Attention Deficit/Hyperactivity Disorder

Establishing the proper learning environment for children with AD/HD is important to ensure their success in the classroom or learning situation. Following are suggestions for creating this proper environment.

- Seat students with ADD near the teacher's desk, but include them as part of the regular class seating.

- Place these students up front with their backs to the rest of the class to keep other students out of view.

- Students with ADD should be surrounded with good role models, preferably students whom they view as significant others. Encourage peer tutoring and cooperative/collaborative learning.

- Avoid distracting stimuli. Try not to place students with ADD near air conditioners, high traffic areas, heaters, or doors or windows.

- Children with ADD do not handle change well, so avoid transitions, physical relocation (monitor them closely on field trips), changes in schedule, and disruptions.

"Teaching Children with Attention Deficit Disorder," 1998 ERIC Clearinghouse on Disabilities and Gifted Education, Reston, VA, U.S. Department of Education. ERIC Identifier: ED423633. ERIC (Educational Resources Information Center) is a service of the U.S. Department of Education. Online databases are available at www.ed.gov/databases.

- Be creative! Produce a stimuli-reduced study area. Let all students have access to this area so the student with ADD will not feel different.

- Parents should set up appropriate study space at home, with set times and routines established for study, parental review of completed homework, and periodic notebook and/or book bag organization.

Giving Instructions to Students with ADD

- Maintain eye contact during verbal instruction.

- Make directions clear and concise. Be consistent with daily instructions.

- Simplify complex directions. Avoid multiple commands.

- Make sure students comprehend the instructions before beginning the task.

- Repeat instructions in a calm, positive manner, if needed.

- Help the students feel comfortable with seeking assistance (most children with ADD will not ask for help).

- Gradually reduce the amount of assistance, but keep in mind that these children will need more help for a longer period of time than the average child.

Require a daily assignment notebook if necessary:

- Make sure each student correctly writes down all assignments each day. If a student is not capable of this, the teacher should help him or her.

- Sign the notebook daily to signify completion of homework assignments. (Parents should also sign.)

- Use the notebook for daily communication with parents.

Giving Assignments

- Give out only one task at a time.

- Monitor frequently. Maintain a supportive attitude.

- Modify assignments as needed. Consult with special education personnel to determine specific strengths and weaknesses of each student. Develop an individualized education program.

- Make sure you are testing knowledge and not attention span.

- Give extra time for certain tasks. Students with ADD may work slowly. Do not penalize them for needed extra time.

- Keep in mind that children with ADD are easily frustrated. Stress, pressure, and fatigue can break down their self-control and lead to poor behavior.

Modifying Behavior and Enhancing Self-Esteem

Providing Supervision and Discipline:

- Remain calm, state the infraction of the rule, and avoid debating or arguing with the student.

- Have preestablished consequences for misbehavior.

- Administer consequences immediately, and monitor proper behavior frequently.

- Enforce classroom rules consistently.

- Make sure the discipline fits the crime, without harshness.

- Avoid ridicule and criticism. Remember, children with ADD have difficulty staying in control.

- Avoid publicly reminding students on medication to take their medicine.

Providing Encouragement:

- Reward more than you punish, in order to build self-esteem.

- Praise immediately any and all good behavior and performance.

- Change rewards if they are not effective in motivating behavioral change.

- Find ways to encourage the child.

- Teach the child to reward himself or herself. Encourage positive self-talk (e.g., "You did very well remaining in your seat today. How do you feel about that?"). This encourages the child to think positively about himself or herself.

Other Educational Recommendations

- Educational, psychological, and/or neurological testing to determine learning style and cognitive ability and to rule out any learning disabilities (common in about 30% of students with ADD).

- A private tutor and/or peer tutoring at school.

- A class that has a low student-teacher ratio.

- Social skills training and organizational skills training.

- Training in cognitive restructuring (positive self-talk, e.g., "I did that well.").

- Use of a word processor or computer for schoolwork.

- Individualized activities that are mildly competitive or noncompetitive such as bowling, walking, swimming, jogging, biking, karate. (Note: Children with ADD may do less well than their peers in team sports.)

- Involvement in social activities such as scouting, church groups, or other youth organizations that help develop social skills and self-esteem.

- Allow child with ADD to play with younger children if that is where they fit in. Many children with ADD have more in common with younger children than with their age-peers. They can still develop valuable social skills from interaction with younger children.

Chapter 28

How to Help Children Succeed in School

The involvement of parents or caregivers in the education of children, can be directly linked to their success in school. By taking an active part in the education of your child, you are showing them the importance of their education, and teaching by example. The following information will help you to help your child.

Show You Think Education and Homework Are Important

Children need to know that their parents and adults close to them think homework is important. If they know their parents care, children have a good reason to complete assignments and turn them in on time. There is a lot that you can do to show that you value education and homework.

"How To Help: Show You Think Education and Homework Are Important," and "The Basics," from *Helping Your Child with Homework*, a brochure produced in September 1995 by the U.S. Department of Education; and "Helping Your Child Improve in Test-Taking," and "Help Your Child Learn to Write Well," U.S. Department of Education, Office of Educational Research and Improvement, 1993; and "What Does it Mean to be Ready for School?" and undated document produced by the U.S. Department of Education; cited January 2002. Despite the older date of these documents, readers interested in helping their children succeed in school will find the information in this chapter useful.

Set a Regular Time

Finding a regular time for homework helps children finish assignments. The best schedule is one that works for your child and your family. What works well in one household may not work in another. Of course, a good schedule depends in part on your child's age, as well as individual needs. For instance, one youngster may work best in the afternoon after an hour of play, and another may be more efficient after dinner (although late at night, when children are tired, is seldom a good time).

Outside activities, such as sports or music lessons, may mean that you need a flexible schedule. Your child may study after school on some days and in the evening on others. If there isn't enough time to finish homework, your child may need to drop some outside activity. Homework must be a high priority.

You'll need to work with your elementary school child to develop a schedule. An older student can probably make up a schedule independently, although you'll want to make sure it's a good one. It may help to write out the schedule and put it in a place where you'll see it often, such as the refrigerator door.

Some families have a required amount of time that children must devote to homework or some other learning activity each school night (the length of time can vary depending upon the child's age). For instance, if your seventh-grader knows she's expected to spend an hour doing homework, reading, or visiting the library, she may be less likely to rush through assignments so that she can watch television. A required amount of time may also discourage her from forgetting to bring home assignments and help her adjust to a routine.

Pick a Place

A study area should have lots of light, supplies close by, and be fairly quiet. A study area doesn't have to be fancy. A desk in the bedroom is nice, but for many youngsters the kitchen table or a corner of the living room works just fine.

Your child may enjoy decorating a special study corner. A plant, a brightly colored container to hold pencils, and some favorite artwork taped to the walls can make study time more pleasant.

Remove Distractions

Turn off the television and discourage social telephone calls during homework time. (A call to a classmate about an assignment may, however, be helpful.)

Some youngsters work well with quiet background music, but loud noise from the stereo or radio is not okay. If you live in a small or noisy household, try having all family members take part in a quiet activity during homework time. You may need to take a noisy toddler outside or into another room to play. If distractions can't be avoided, your child may want to complete assignments in a nearby library.

Provide Supplies and Identify Resources

For starters, collect pencils, pens, erasers, writing paper, an assignment book, and a dictionary. Other things that might be helpful include glue, a stapler, paper clips, maps, a calculator, a pencil sharpener, tape, scissors, a ruler, index cards, a thesaurus, and an almanac. Keep these items together in one place if possible. If you can't provide your child with needed supplies, check with the teacher, school guidance counselor, or principal about possible sources of assistance.

For books and other information resources, check with the school library or local public library. Some libraries have homework centers designed especially to assist children with school assignments (there may even be tutors and other kinds of individual assistance).

These days many schools have computers in classrooms, and many households have personal computers. However, you don't have to have a computer in your home in order for your child to complete homework assignments successfully.

You may want to ask the teacher to explain school policy about the use of computers—or typewriters or any special equipment—for homework. Certainly, computers can be a great learning tool and helpful for some assignments. They can be used for word processing and on-line reference resources, as well as educational programs and games to sharpen skills. Some schools may offer after-school programs where your child can use the school computers. And many public libraries make computers available to children.

Set a Good Example

Children are more likely to study if they see you reading, writing, and doing things that require thought and effort on your part. Talk with your child about what you're reading and writing even if it's something as simple as making the grocery list. Tell them about what you do at work. Encourage activities that support learning—for example, educational games, library visits, walks in the neighborhood, trips to the zoo or museums, and chores that teach a sense of responsibility.

Show an Interest

Make time to take your child to the library to check out materials needed for homework (and for fun too), and read with your child as often as you can. Talk about school and learning activities in family conversations. Ask your child what was discussed in class that day. If he doesn't have much to say, try another approach. For example, ask your child to read aloud a story he wrote or discuss the results of a science experiment.

Another good way to show your interest is to attend school activities, such as parent-teacher meetings, shows, and sports events. If you can, volunteer to help in the classroom or at special events. Getting to know some classmates and other parents not only shows you're interested but helps build a network of support for you and your child.

The Basics: Helping Your Child with Homework

Before discussing ways you can help your child with homework, it is important to discuss why teachers assign homework and how it benefits your child.

Why Do Teachers Assign Homework?

Teachers assign homework for many reasons. Homework can help children:

- review and practice what they've learned;
- get ready for the next day's class;
- learn to use resources, such as libraries, reference materials, and encyclopedias; and
- explore subjects more fully than time permits in the classroom.

Homework can also help children develop good habits and attitudes. It can:

- teach children to work independently;
- encourage self-discipline and responsibility (assignments provide some youngsters with their first chance to manage time and meet deadlines); and
- encourage a love of learning.

Homework can also bring parents and educators closer together. Parents who supervise homework and work with their children on assignments learn about their children's education and about the school. Homework is meant to be a positive experience and to encourage children to learn. Assignments should not be used as punishment.

Does Homework Help Children Learn?

Homework helps your child do better in school when assignments are meaningful, are completed successfully, and are returned with constructive comments from the teacher. An assignment should have a specific purpose, come with clear instructions, be fairly well matched to a student's abilities, and designed to help develop a student's knowledge and skills.

In the early elementary grades, homework can help children develop the habits and attitudes described earlier. From fourth through sixth grades, small amounts of homework, gradually increased each year, may support improved academic achievement. In seventh grade and beyond, students who complete more homework score better on standardized tests and earn better grades, on the average, than students who do less homework. The difference in test scores and grades between students who do more homework and those who do less increases as children move up through the grades.

What's the Right Amount of Homework?

Many educators believe that homework is most effective for the majority of children in first through third grades when it does not exceed 20 minutes each school day. From fourth through sixth grades, many educators recommend from 20 to 40 minutes a school day for most students. For students in seventh through ninth grades, generally, up to 2 hours a school day is thought to be suitable. Amounts that vary from these guidelines are fine for some students. Talk with your child's teacher if you are concerned about either too much or too little homework.

Help Your Child Improve in Test-Taking

American children must be ready to learn from the first day of school. And of course, preparing children for school is a historic responsibility of parents.

Test. It's a loaded word. Important...something to care about...something that can mean so much we get apprehensive thinking about it.

Tests are important, especially to school children. A test may measure a basic skill. It can affect a year's grade. Or, if it measures the ability to learn, it can affect a child's placement in school. So it's important to do well on tests. Besides, the ability to do well on tests can help throughout life in such things as getting a driver's license, trying out for sports, or getting a job. Without this ability, a person can be severely handicapped.

Your child can develop this ability. And you can help the child do it. Just try the simple techniques developed through Office of Educational Research and Improvement (OERI) research.

Why Test?

It's helpful for a child to understand why schools give tests and to know the different kinds of tests. Tests are yardsticks. Schools use them to measure, and then improve education. Some tell schools that they need to strengthen courses or change teaching techniques. Other tests compare students by schools, school districts, or cities. All tests determine how well your child is doing. And that's very important.

Most of the tests your child will take are teacher-made. That is, teachers design them. These tests are associated with the grades on report cards. They help measure a student's progress—telling the teacher and the student whether he or she is keeping up with the class, needs extra help, or, perhaps, is far ahead of other students.

Now and then your child will take standardized tests. These use the same standards to measure student performance across the country. Everyone takes the same test according to the same rules. This makes it possible to measure each student's performance against that of others. The group with whom a student's performance is compared is a norm group and consists of many students of the same age or grade who took the same test.

Ask the School

It could be useful for you to know the school's policies and practices on giving standardized tests and the use of test scores. Ask your child's teacher or guidance counselor about the kinds of tests your child will take during the year—and the schedule for testing.

One other thing: some schools give students practice in taking tests. This helps to make sure that they are familiar with directions and test format. Find out whether your child's school gives test-taking practice on a regular basis or will provide such practice if your child needs it.

Avoid Test Anxiety

It's good to be concerned about taking a test. It's not good to get test anxiety. This is excessive worry about doing well on a test and it can mean disaster for a student. Students who suffer from test anxiety tend to worry about success in school, especially doing well on tests. They worry about the future, and are extremely self-critical. Instead of feeling challenged by the prospect of success, they become afraid of failure. This makes them anxious about tests and their own abilities. Ultimately, they become so worked up that they feel incompetent about the subject matter or the test.

It does not help to tell the child to relax, to think about something else, or stop worrying. But there are ways to reduce test anxiety. Encourage your child to do these things:

- Space studying over days or weeks. (Real learning occurs through studying that takes place over a period of time.) Understand the information and relate it to what is already known. Review it more than once. (By doing this, the student should feel prepared at exam time.)

- Don't cram the night before—cramming increases anxiety, which interferes with clear thinking. Get a good night's sleep. Rest, exercise, and eating well are as important to test-taking as they are to other schoolwork.

- Read the directions carefully when the teacher hands out the test. If you don't understand them, ask the teacher to explain.

- Look quickly at the entire examination to see what types of questions are included (multiple choice, matching, true/ false, essay) and, if possible, the number of points for each. This will help you pace yourself.

- If you don't know the answer to a question, skip it and go on. Don't waste time worrying about it. Mark it so you can identify it as unanswered. If you have time at the end of the exam, return to the unanswered question(s).

Do's and Don'ts

You can be a great help to your children if you will observe these do's and don'ts about tests and testing:

- Don't be too anxious about a child's test scores. If you put too much emphasis on test scores, this can upset a child.

- Do encourage children. Praise them for the things they do well. If they feel good about themselves, they will do their best. Children who are afraid of failing are more likely to become anxious when taking tests and more likely to make mistakes.

- Don't judge a child on the basis of a single test score. Test scores are not perfect measures of what a child can do. There are many other things that might influence a test score. For example, a child can be affected by the way he or she is feeling, the setting in the classroom, and the attitude of the teacher. Remember, also, that one test is simply one test.

- Meet with your child's teacher as often as possible to discuss his/her progress. Ask the teacher to suggest activities for you and your child to do at home to help prepare for tests and improve your child's understanding of schoolwork. Parents and teachers should work together to benefit students.

- Make sure your child attends school regularly. Remember, tests do reflect children's overall achievement. The more effort and energy a child puts into learning, the more likely he/she will do well on tests.

- Provide a quiet, comfortable place for studying at home.

- Make sure that your child is well rested on school days and especially the day of a test. Children who are tired are less able to pay attention in class or to handle the demands of a test.

- Give your child a well rounded diet. A healthy body leads to a healthy, active mind. Most schools provide free breakfast and lunch for economically disadvantaged students. If you believe your child qualifies, talk to the school principal.

- Provide books and magazines for your youngster to read at home. By reading new materials, a child will learn new words that might appear on a test. Ask your child's school about a suggested outside reading list or get suggestions from the public library.

After the Test

It's important for children to review test results. This is especially true when they take teacher-made tests. They can learn from a graded exam paper. It will show where they had difficulty and, perhaps, why. This is especially important for classes where the material builds from

264

one section to the next, as in math. Students who have not mastered the basics of math will be unable to work with fractions, square roots, beginning algebra, and so on.

Discuss the wrong answers with your children and find out why they answered as they did. Sometimes a child misunderstands the way a question is worded or misinterprets what was asked. The child may have known the correct answer but failed to express it effectively.

It's important, too, for children to see how well they used their time on the test and whether guessing was a good idea. This helps them to change what they do on the next test, if necessary. You and the child should read and discuss all comments written by the teacher. If there are any comments that aren't clear, the child should ask the teacher to explain.

Help Your Child Learn to Write Well

American children must be ready to learn from the first day of school. And of course, preparing children for school is a historic responsibility of parents. Should you help your child with writing? Yes, if you want your child to do well in school, enjoy self-expression, and become more self-reliant. You know how important writing will be to your child's life. It will be important from first-grade through college and throughout adulthood.

Writing is practical. Most of us make lists, jot down reminders, and write notes and instructions at least occasionally.

Writing is job-related. Professional and white-collar workers write frequently—preparing memos, letters, briefing papers, sales reports, articles, research reports, proposals, and the like. Most workers do some writing on the job.

Writing is stimulating. Writing helps to provoke thoughts and to organize them logically and concisely.

Writing is social. Most of us write thank-you notes and letters to friends at least now and then.

Writing is therapeutic. It can be helpful to express feelings in writing that cannot be expressed so easily by speaking.

Unfortunately, many schools are unable to give children sufficient instruction in writing. There are various reasons: teachers aren't trained to teach writing skills, writing classes may be too large, it's often difficult to measure writing skills, etc. Study after study shows that students' writing lacks clarity, coherence, and organization. Only a few students can write persuasive essays or competent business letters. As many as one out of four have serious writing difficulties. And students say they like writing less and less as they go through school.

That's why the Office of Educational Research and Improvement (OERI) suggests that you help your child with writing. OERI believes you, a parent, can make a big difference. You can use helping strategies that are simple and fun. You can use them to help your child learn to write well—and to enjoy doing it!

Things to Know

Writing is more than putting words on paper. It's a final stage in the complex process of communicating that begins with thinking. Writing is an especially important stage in communication, the intent being to leave no room for doubt. Has any country ratified a verbal treaty?

One of the first means of communication for your child is through drawing. Do encourage the child to draw and to discuss his/her drawings. Ask questions: What is the boy doing? Does the house look like ours? Can you tell a story about this picture?

Most children's basic speech patterns are formed by the time they enter school. By that time children speak clearly, recognize most letters of the alphabet, and may try to write. Show an interest in, and ask questions about, the things your child says, draws, and may try to write. Writing well requires:

- Clear thinking. Sometimes the child needs to have his/her memory refreshed about a past event in order to write about it.

- Sufficient time. Children may have stories in their heads but need time to think them through and write them down. School class periods are often not long enough.

- Reading. Reading can stimulate a child to write about his/her own family or school life. If your child reads good books, (s)he will be a better writer.

- A Meaningful Task. A child needs meaningful, not artificial writing tasks.

- Interest. All the time in the world won't help if there is nothing to write, nothing to say. Some of the reasons for writing include: sending messages, keeping records, expressing feelings, or relaying information.

- Practice. And more practice.

- Revising. Students need experience in revising their work— i.e., seeing what they can do to make it clearer, more descriptive, more concise, etc.

Pointers for Parents

In helping your child to learn to write well, remember that your goal is to make writing easier and more enjoyable.

Provide a place. It's important for a child to have a good place to write—a desk or table with a smooth, flat surface and good lighting.

Have the materials. Provide plenty of paper—lined and unlined—and things to write with, including pencils, pens, and crayons.

Allow time. Help your child spend time thinking about a writing project or exercise. Good writers do a great deal of thinking. Your child may dawdle, sharpen a pencil, get papers ready, or look up the spelling of a word. Be patient—your child may be thinking.

Respond. Do respond to the ideas your child expresses verbally or in writing. Make it clear that you are interested in the true function of writing which is to convey ideas. This means focusing on what the child has written, not how it was written. It's usually wise to ignore minor errors, particularly at the stage when your child is just getting ideas together.

Don't you write it! Don't write a paper for your child that will be turned in as his/her work. Never rewrite a child's work. Meeting a writing deadline, taking responsibility for the finished product, and feeling ownership of it are important parts of writing well.

Praise. Take a positive approach and say something good about your child's writing. Is it accurate? Descriptive? Thoughtful? Interesting? Does it say something?

Things to Do

Make it real. Your child needs to do real writing. It's more important for the child to write a letter to a relative than it is to write a one-line note on a greeting card. Encourage the child to write to relatives and friends. Perhaps your child would enjoy corresponding with a pen pal.

Suggest note-taking. Encourage your child to take notes on trips or outings and to describe what (s)he saw. This could include a description of nature walks, a boat ride, a car trip, or other events that lend themselves to note-taking.

Brainstorm. Talk with your child as much as possible about his/her impressions and encourage the child to describe people and events to you. If the child's description is especially accurate and colorful, say so.

Encourage keeping a journal. This is excellent writing practice as well as a good outlet for venting feelings. Encourage your child to write about things that happen at home and school, about people (s)he likes or dislikes and why, things to remember or things the child wants to do. Especially encourage your child to write about personal feelings— pleasures as well as disappointments. If the child wants to share the journal with you, read the entries and discuss them—especially the child's ideas and perceptions.

Write together. Have your child help you with letters, even such routine ones as ordering items from an advertisement or writing to a business firm. This helps the child to see firsthand that writing is important to adults and truly useful.

Use games. There are numerous games and puzzles that help a child to increase vocabulary and make the child more fluent in speaking and writing. Remember, building a vocabulary builds confidence. Try crossword puzzles, word games, anagrams and cryptograms designed especially for children. Flash cards are good, too, and they're easy to make at home.

Suggest making lists. Most children like to make lists just as they like to count. Encourage this. Making lists is good practice and helps a child to become more organized. Boys and girls might make lists of their records, tapes, baseball cards, dolls, furniture in a room, etc. They could include items they want. It's also good practice to make lists of things to do, schoolwork, dates for tests, social events, and other reminders.

Encourage copying. If a child likes a particular song, suggest learning the words by writing them down—replaying the song on your stereo/tape player or jotting down the words whenever the song is played on a radio program. Also encourage copying favorite poems or quotations from books and plays.

What Does It Mean to Be Ready for School?

There is no one quality or skill that children need to do well in school, but a combination of things contributes to success. These include good health and physical well-being, social and emotional maturity, language skills, an ability to solve problems and think creatively, and general knowledge about the world.

As you go about helping your child develop in each of these areas, remember children develop at different rates, and most children are stronger in some areas than in others. Remember, too, that being ready for school depends partly on what the school expects. One school may think it's very important for children to sit quietly and know the alphabet. Another may believe it's more important for children to get along well with others.

Children who match the school's expectations may be considered better prepared. You may want to visit your child's school to learn what the principal and teachers expect and discuss any areas of disagreement. While schools may have different priorities, most educators agree that the following areas are important for success.

Good Health and Physical Well-Being

Young children need nutritious food, enough sleep, safe places to play, and regular medical care. These things help children get a good start in life and lessen the chances that they will later have serious health problems or trouble learning.

Good health for children begins before birth with good prenatal care. Visit a doctor or medical clinic throughout your pregnancy. In addition, eat nourishing foods, avoid alcohol, tobacco, and other harmful drugs, and get plenty of rest. Pregnant women who don't take good

269

care of themselves increase their chances of giving birth to children who are low in birth weight, making them more likely to have life-long health and learning problems, who develop asthma, are mentally retarded, develop speech and language problems, have short attention spans, or become hyperactive.

If your child already has some of these problems, it is a good idea to consult with your doctor, your school district, or community agencies as soon as possible. Many communities have free or inexpensive services to help you and your child.

Good health for children continues after birth with a balanced diet. School-aged children can concentrate better in class if they eat nutritionally balanced meals. These should include breads, cereals, and other grain products; fruits; vegetables; meat, poultry, fish and alternatives (such as eggs and dried beans and peas); and milk, cheese, and yogurt. Avoid too many fats and sweets.

Children aged 2-5 generally can eat the same foods as adults but in smaller portions. Your child's doctor or clinic can provide advice on feeding babies and toddlers under the age of 2.

Federal, state, and local aid is available for parents who need food in order to make sure their children get a balanced diet. The federal nutrition program, called the Special Supplemental Food Program for Women, Infants, and Children (WIC), distributes food to more than 5.4 million low-income women and their children through about 8,200 service centers across the country. Food stamps also are available for many families with children. For information and to find out if you are eligible, contact your local or state health department.

Preschoolers require regular medical and dental checkups and immunizations. It's important to find a doctor or a clinic where children can receive routine health care as well as special treatment if they are sick or injured.

Children need immunizations beginning around the age of 2 months to prevent nine diseases: measles, mumps, German measles (rubella), diphtheria, tetanus, whooping cough, Hib (*Haemophilus influenzae* type b), polio, and tuberculosis. These diseases can have serious effects on physical and mental development. Regular dental checkups should begin at the latest by the age of 3.

Preschoolers need opportunities to exercise and develop physical coordination. To learn to control large muscles, children need to throw balls, run, jump, climb, and dance to music. To learn to control small muscles, particularly in the hands and fingers, they need to color with crayons, put together puzzles, use blunt-tipped scissors, and zip jackets. In kindergarten, they will build upon these skills.

Parents of youngsters with disabilities should see a doctor as soon as a problem is suspected. Early intervention can help these children develop to their full potential.

Social and Emotional Preparation

Young children are often very excited about entering school. But when they do, they can face an environment that's different from what they are used to at home or even in preschool. In kindergarten, they will need to work well in large groups and get along with new adults and other children. They will have to share the teacher's attention with other youngsters. The classroom routines may also be different.

Most 5-year-olds do not start school with good social skills or much emotional maturity. These take time and practice to learn. However, children improve their chances for success in kindergarten if they have had opportunities to begin developing these qualities:

- Confidence. Children must learn to feel good about themselves and believe they can succeed. Confident children are more willing to attempt new tasks—and try again if they don't succeed the first time.

- Independence. Children need to learn to do things for themselves.

- Motivation. Children must want to learn.

- Curiosity. Children are naturally curious and must remain so in order to get the most out of learning opportunities.

- Persistence. Children must learn to finish what they start.

- Cooperation. Children must be able to get along with others and learn to share and take turns.

- Self-control. Preschoolers must understand that some behaviors, such as hitting and biting, are inappropriate. They need to learn that there are good and bad ways to express anger.

- Empathy. Children must learn to have an interest in others and understand how others feel.

Parents, even more than child care centers and good schools, help children develop these skills. Following are some ways you can help your child acquire these positive qualities.

271

Youngsters must believe that, no matter what, someone will look out for them. Show that you care about your children. They thrive when they have parents or other caregivers who are loving and dependable. Small children need attention, encouragement, hugs, and plenty of lap time. Children who feel loved are more likely to be confident.

Set a good example. Children imitate what they see others do and what they hear others say. When parents exercise and eat nourishing food, children are more likely to do so. When parents treat others with respect, their children probably will, too. If parents share things, their children will learn to be thoughtful of others' feelings.

Have a positive attitude toward learning and toward school. Children come into this world with a powerful need to discover and to explore. Parents need to encourage this curiosity if children are to keep it. Enthusiasm for what children do ("You've drawn a great picture!") helps to make them proud of their achievements.

Children also become excited about school when their parents show excitement. As your child approaches kindergarten, talk to him about school. Talk about the exciting activities in kindergarten, such as going on field trips and making fun art projects. Be enthusiastic as you describe what he will learn in school—how to read and measure and weigh things, for example.

Provide opportunities for repetition. It takes practice to crawl, pronounce new words, or drink from a cup. Children don't get bored when they repeat things. Instead, repeating things until they are learned helps youngsters build the confidence needed to try something new.

Use appropriate discipline. All children need to have limits set for them. Children whose parents give firm but loving discipline are generally more skilled socially and do better in school than children whose parents set too few or too many limits.

- Direct children's activities, but don't make unnecessary restrictions or try to dominate.

- Offer reasons when asking your child to do something (For example, say, "Please move the toy truck off the stairs so no one falls over it"—not, "Do it because I said so.").

- Listen to your children to find out how they feel and whether they need any special support.

- Show love and respect when you are angry. Criticize a child's behavior but not the child (For example, say, "I love you, but it is not okay for you to draw pictures on the walls. I get angry when you do that.").

- Help your children make choices and work out problems (You might ask your 4-year-old, "What can we do to keep Kevin from knocking over your blocks?").

- Be positive and encouraging. Praise your child for a job well done. Smiles and encouragement go much further to shape good behavior than harsh punishment.

Let children do many things by themselves. Young children need to be closely watched. But they learn to be independent and to develop confidence by doing tasks such as dressing themselves and putting their toys away. It's also important to let them make choices, rather than deciding everything for them. Remember to give them a choice only when there really is one.

Encourage your children to play with other children and be with adults who are not family members. Preschoolers need these social opportunities to learn to see the point of view of others. Young children are more likely to get along with teachers and classmates if they already have had experiences with different adults and children.

Language and General Knowledge

Kindergartners participate in many activities that require them to use language and to solve problems. Children who can't or don't communicate easily may have problems in school. There are many things you can do to help children learn to communicate, solve problems, and develop an understanding of the world.

Give your child opportunities to play. Play is how children learn. It is the natural way for them to explore, to become creative, and to develop academic and social skills. Play helps them learn to solve problems—for example, a wagon tips over, and children must figure out how to get it upright again. Children learn about geometry, shapes, and balance when they stack up blocks. Playing with others helps children learn how to negotiate.

Talk to your children, beginning at birth. Babies need to hear your voice. A television or the radio can't take the place of your voice because it doesn't respond to coos and babbles. The more you talk to your baby, the more he will have to talk about as he gets older. Talking with children broadens their understanding of language and of the world.

Everyday activities, such as eating dinner or taking a bath, provide opportunities to talk, sometimes in detail, about what's happening and respond to your child. "First let's stick the plug in the drain. Now we'll turn on the water. I see you want to put your rubber duck in the bathtub. That's a good idea. Look, it's yellow, just like the rubber duck on 'Sesame Street.'"

Listen to your children. Children have their own special thoughts and feelings, joys and sorrows, hopes and fears. As their language skills develop, encourage them to talk. Listening is the best way to learn what's on their minds and to discover what they know and don't know, and how they think and learn. It also shows children that their feelings and ideas are valuable.

Answer questions and ask questions, particularly ones that require more than a "yes" or "no" response. While walking in a park, for example, most 2- and 3-year-olds will stop to pick up leaves. You might point out how the leaves are the same, and how they are different. With older children you might ask, "What else grows on trees?"

Questions can help children learn to compare and classify things. Answer your children's questions thoughtfully and, whenever possible, encourage them to answer their own questions. If you don't know the answer to a question, say so. Then together with your child try to find the answer.

Read aloud to your children every day. Reading can begin with babies and continue throughout the preschool years. Even though they don't understand the story or the poem, reading together gives children a chance to learn about language, enjoy the sound of your voice, and be close to you. You don't have to be an excellent reader for your child to enjoy this time together. You may also want to take your child to a local library that offers special story hours.

Make reading materials available. Children develop an interest in language and in reading much sooner if they have books and other reading materials around their homes.

Monitor television viewing. Next to parents, television may be our children's most influential teacher. Good television can introduce children to new worlds and promote learning, but poor or too much TV can be harmful.

Be realistic about your children's abilities and interests. Children usually do best in school when parents estimate their abilities correctly.

Parents must set high standards and encourage their preschoolers to try new things. Children who aren't challenged become bored. But ones who are pushed along too quickly, or are asked to do things that don't interest them, can become frustrated and unhappy.

Try to keep your children from being labeled. Labels such as dumb or stupid have a powerful effect on a child's confidence and school performance. Remember to praise your child for a job well done.

Provide opportunities to do and see things. The more varied the experiences that children have, the more they learn about the world. No matter where you live, your community can provide new experiences. Go for walks in your neighborhood, or go places on the bus. Visit museums, libraries, zoos, and other community resources.

If you live in the city, spend a day in the country (or if you live in the country, spend a day in the city). Let your children hear and make music, dance, and paint. Let them participate in activities that help to develop their imaginations and let them express their ideas and feelings.

Chapter 29

The "No Child Left Behind" Education Reform Agenda

"If a nation expects to be ignorant and free, in a state of civilization, it expects what never was and never will be."

— by Thomas Jefferson, 1816

Transforming the Federal Role in Education So That No Child Is Left Behind

As America enters the 21st Century full of hope and promise, too many of our neediest students are being left behind.

Today, nearly 70 percent of inner city fourth graders are unable to read at a basic level on national reading tests. Our high school seniors trail students in Cyprus and South Africa on international math tests. And nearly a third of our college freshmen find they must take a remedial course before they are able to even begin regular college level courses.

Although education is primarily a state and local responsibility, the federal government is partly at fault for tolerating these abysmal results. The federal government currently does not do enough to reward success and sanction failure in our education system.

Since 1965, when the federal government embarked on its first major elementary-secondary education initiative, federal policy has strongly influenced America's schools. Over the years Congress has

"No Child Left Behind," U.S. Department of Education, 2001; available online at http://www.ed.gov/inits/nclb/part2.html.

created hundreds of programs intended to address problems in education without asking whether or not the programs produce results or knowing their impact on local needs. This program for every problem solution has begun to add up—so much so that there are hundreds of education programs spread across 39 federal agencies at a cost of $120 billion a year. Yet, after spending billions of dollars on education, we have fallen short in meeting our goals for educational excellence. The academic achievement gap between rich and poor, Anglo and minority is not only wide, but in some cases is growing wider still.

We have a genuine national crisis. More and more, we are divided into two nations. One that reads, and one that doesn't. One that dreams, and one that doesn't.

In reaction to these disappointing results, some have decided that there should be no federal involvement in education. Others suggest we merely add new programs into the old system. Surely, there must be another way—a way that points to a more effective federal role. The priorities that follow are based on the fundamental notion that an enterprise works best when responsibility is placed closest to the most important activity of the enterprise, when those responsible are given greatest latitude and support, and when those responsible are held accountable for producing results. This education blueprint will:

- *Increase Accountability for Student Performance:* States, districts and schools that improve achievement will be rewarded. Failure will be sanctioned. Parents will know how well their child is learning, and that schools are held accountable for their effectiveness with annual state reading and math assessments in grades 3-8.

- *Focus on What Works:* Federal dollars will be spent on effective, research based programs and practices. Funds will be targeted to improve schools and enhance teacher quality.

- *Reduce Bureaucracy and Increase Flexibility:* Additional flexibility will be provided to states and school districts, and flexible funding will be increased at the local level.

- *Empower Parents:* Parents will have more information about the quality of their child's school. Students in persistently low-performing schools will be given choice.

Though these priorities do not address reforms in every federal education program, they do address a general vision for reforming the Elementary and Secondary Education Act (ESEA) and linking federal dollars to specific performance goals to ensure improved results.

The priorities in this blueprint consist of seven performance-based titles:

1. Improving the academic performance of disadvantaged students
2. Boosting teacher quality
3. Moving limited English proficient students to English fluency
4. Promoting informed parental choice and innovative programs
5. Encouraging safe schools for the 21st Century
6. Increasing funding for Impact Aid
7. Encouraging freedom and accountability

There will be additional funds targeted to needy schools and districts. States and school districts will have the flexibility to produce results, and may lose funds if performance goals are not met.

In America, no child should be left behind. Every child should be educated to his or her full potential. This proposal sets forth the President's proposed framework to accomplish that goal. This Administration will work with Congress to ensure that this happens quickly, and in a bipartisan manner.

The Policy

The Administration's education reform agenda is comprised of the following key components, many of which would be implemented during the re-authorization of the Elementary and Secondary Education Act (ESEA).

Closing the Achievement Gap

Accountability and High Standards. States, school districts, and schools must be accountable for ensuring that all students, including disadvantaged students, meet high academic standards. States must develop a system of sanctions and rewards to hold districts and schools accountable for improving academic achievement.

Annual Academic Assessments. Annual reading and math assessments will provide parents with the information they need to know how well their child is doing in school, and how well the school is educating their child. Further, annual data is a vital diagnostic tool for schools to achieve continuous improvement. With adequate time for

279

planning and implementation, each state may select and design assessments of their choosing. In addition, a sample of students in each state will be assessed annually with the National Assessment of Educational Progress (NAEP) 4th and 8th grade assessment in reading and math.

Consequences for Schools that Fail to Educate Disadvantaged Students. Schools that fail to make adequate yearly progress for disadvantaged students will first receive assistance, and then come under corrective action if they still fail to make progress. If schools fail to make adequate yearly progress for three consecutive years, disadvantaged students may use Title I funds to transfer to a higher-performing public or private school, or receive supplemental educational services from a provider of choice.

Improving Literacy by Putting Reading First

Focus on Reading in Early Grades. States that establish a comprehensive reading program anchored in scientific research from kindergarten to second grade will be eligible for grants under a new Reading First initiative.

Early Childhood Reading Instruction. States participating in the Reading First program will have the option to receive funding from a new Early Reading First program to implement research-based pre-reading methods in pre-school programs, including Head Start centers. Too many of our children cannot read. Reading is the building block, and it must be the foundation, for education reform.

Expanding Flexibility, Reducing Bureaucracy

Title I Flexibility. More schools will be able to operate Title I schoolwide programs and combine federal funds with local and state funds to improve the quality of the entire school.

Increased Funds to Schools for Technology. E-rate funds and technology grant funds will be consolidated and distributed to schools through states and local districts based on need. This will also ensure that schools no longer have to submit multiple grant applications and incur the associated administrative burdens to obtain education technology funding.

Reduction in Bureaucracy. Overlapping and duplicative categorical grant programs will be consolidated and sent to states and school districts.

New State and Local Flexibility Options. A charter option for states and districts committed to accountability and reform will be created. Under this program, charter states and districts would be freed from categorical program requirements in return for submitting a five-year performance agreement to the Secretary of Education and being subject to especially rigorous standards of accountability.

The federal government must be wise enough to give states and school districts more authority and freedom. And it must be strong enough to require proven performance in return.

Rewarding Success and Sanctioning Failure

Rewards for Closing the Achievement Gap. High performing states that narrow the achievement gap and improve overall student achievement will be rewarded.

Accountability Bonus for States. Each state will be offered a one-time bonus if it meets accountability requirements, including establishing annual assessments in grades 3-8, within two years of enacting this plan.

No Child Left Behind School Rewards. Successful schools that have made the greatest progress in improving the achievement of disadvantaged students will be recognized and rewarded with No Child Left Behind bonuses.

Consequences for Failure. The Secretary of Education will be authorized to reduce federal funds available to a state for administrative expenses if a state fails to meet their performance objectives and demonstrate results in academic achievement.

Promoting Informed Parental Choice

School Reports to Parents. Parents will be enabled to make informed choices about schools for their children by being given access to school-by-school report cards on student achievement for all groups of students.

Charter Schools. Funding will be provided to assist charter schools with start-up costs, facilities, and other needs associated with creating high-quality schools.

Innovative School Choice Programs and Research. The Secretary of Education will award grants for innovative efforts to expand parental choice, as well as to conduct research on the effects of school choice.

Improving Teacher Quality

All Students Taught by Quality Teachers. States and localities will be given flexibility in the use of federal funds so that they may focus more on improving teacher quality. States will be expected to ensure that all children are taught by effective teachers.

Funding What Works. High standards for professional development will be set to ensure that federal funds promote research-based, effective practice in the classroom.

Strengthening Math and Science Education. K-12 math and science education will be strengthened through math and science partnerships for states to work with institutions of higher education to improve instruction and curriculum.

Making Schools Safer for the 21st Century

Teacher Protection. Teachers will be empowered to remove violent or persistently disruptive students from the classroom.

Promoting School Safety. Funding for schools will be increased to promote safety and drug prevention during and after school. States will be allowed to give consideration to religious organizations on the same basis as other nongovernmental organizations when awarding grants for after-school programs.

Rescuing Students from Unsafe Schools. Victims of school-based crimes or students trapped in persistently dangerous schools will be provided with a safe alternative. States must report to parents and the public whether a school is safe.

Supporting Character Education. Additional funds will be provided for Character Education grants to states and districts to train teachers in methods of incorporating character-building lessons and activities into the classroom.

Chapter 30

AD/HD Under the Individuals with Disabilities Education Act

Educational Rights for Children with AD/HD

Two federal laws—the Individuals with Disabilities Education Act (IDEA) and Section 504 of the Rehabilitation Act of 1973 (Section 504), guarantee children with attention-deficit/hyperactivity disorder (AD/HD) a free and appropriate public education (FAPE). Both laws also require that children with disabilities be educated to the maximum extent appropriate with children who do not have disabilities. Because there are different criteria for eligibility, different services available, different procedures for implementing the laws, and different procedural safeguards, it is important for parents, educators, clinicians and advocates to be well aware of the variations between these laws and to be fully informed about their respective advantages and disadvantages.

Perhaps the most substantial difference between these two laws is that eligibility for IDEA mandates that a child have a disability requiring special education services, while eligibility for Section 504 may occur when the child needs special education or related services. Because of this distinction, children covered under Section 504 include those who typically either have less severe disabilities than those

Text in this chapter is from "Educational Rights for Children with AD/HD," *CHADD Facts*, and "What You Need to Know about AD/HD Under the Individuals with Disabilities Education Act," by Matthew Cohen, JD, © 1996-2001 CHADD; reprinted with permission. For more information write to CHADD at 8181 Professional Place, Suite 201, Landover, MD 20875, or visit CHADD at their website at www.chadd.org.

covered under IDEA, or have disabilities that do not neatly fit within the categories of eligibility under IDEA.

IDEA: Who's Eligible?

IDEA is the law that governs all special education services in the United States. IDEA provides federal funding to school districts to support special education and related services. Thus, a need for special education is a requirement of IDEA. IDEA provides special education for those children who meet the eligibility criteria for one of a number of categories. If the child meets the criteria listed under one of these categories, the disabling condition adversely affects educational performance, and he requires special education, the child may be eligible to receive services under this law.

AD/HD is listed under the IDEA category Other Health Impairment. To receive services, the child must have a diagnosis of AD/HD that results in limited alertness to academic tasks, due to heightened alertness to environmental stimuli; must be chronic (long-lasting) or acute (have a substantial impact); this must result in an adverse effect on educational performance; and the student must require special education services in order to address the AD/HD and its impact.

Evaluation

A multidisciplinary evaluation procedure is required to determine if a child is eligible for special education under IDEA and requires that the child who is eligible be considered for full or partial reevaluation at least every three years. The evaluation team must also consider whether the child requires assistive technology devices or services.

IDEA requires that the school district considers the findings of outside evaluators and, under some circumstances, pay for independent evaluations. Parental consent is required before any evaluation begins.

A parent's suspicion that a child has AD/HD is not sufficient to require a school system evaluation under the IDEA—an adverse effect on educational performance must also be reflected in the child's school work or school behavior. If an evaluation is warranted, it must be provided at no cost to the parents. This includes any medical component of the evaluation; parents are not financially responsible for the evaluation. If they have health insurance, the school must ensure that there is no out-of-pocket expense, nor impact on caps and premiums.

What Does It Provide?

Under IDEA, once an AD/HD child is determined to be eligible for special education, the child is entitled to have an individualized education plan (IEP) that includes annual goals and short-term objectives, and is developed with the participation of the parents. Once the IEP is completed, parents or the school can request changes to it, but no changes can be made without the parents being informed and having an opportunity to request an impartial due process hearing to challenge the decision. The IEP will be reviewed each year with any needed changes made. Parents are members of their child's eligibility, IEP and placement teams.

IDEA provides procedural safeguards that Section 504 does not. It specifies that a child must be educated in the class that he would be in if that child did not have a disability, and as close to home as possible, unless the IEP requires otherwise. All states and local education agencies must make a mediation process available to resolve disputes about a child's special education.

For children with more severe behavioral problems that lead to suspension and expulsion, IDEA also has two important provisions. Even when suspended or expelled, children covered by IDEA are still entitled to education services that meet the standards of a free appropriate education. Parents can request an impartial due process hearing when they disagree with the school's decision in such matters. Under a separate provision, the child can remain in the then-current educational placement until all administrative proceedings are concluded (with the exception of cases where the child has brought a weapon or drugs to school, or is proven to be substantially likely to harm himself or others).

Section 504: Who's Eligible?

Section 504 is a civil rights statute requiring that schools not discriminate against children with disabilities and that they provide children with reasonable accommodations. Under some circumstances, these reasonable accommodations may include the provision of services.

Eligibility for Section 504 is based on the existence of an identified physical or mental condition that substantially limits a major life activity. As learning is considered a major life activity, children diagnosed with AD/HD are entitled to the protections of Section 504 if the disability is substantially limiting their ability to learn. Children who are not eligible for special education may still be guaranteed access to related services if they meet the Section 504 eligibility criteria.

Evaluation

Although Section 504 requires testing and requires that testing be non-discriminatory, there are far fewer regulations placed on the testing procedure than are found with IDEA. In addition, unlike IDEA, Section 504 does not discuss the frequency of testing; the role outside evaluations may play, and does not require parental consent for testing. It does require that an evaluation be conducted before a child receives a 504 plan and before any changes are made to the plan.

What Does It Provide?

If the child is eligible under Section 504, the school district must develop a Section 504 plan. However, the regulations do not dictate the frequency of review of the 504 plan, and do not specify the right of parents to participate in its development.

Which One Is Right for My Child?

In general, Section 504 provides a faster, more flexible and less stigmatizing procedure for obtaining some accommodations and services for children with disabilities. By virtue of the looser eligibility criteria, some children may receive protection who are not eligible for services or protection under IDEA, and less information is needed to obtain eligibility. Thus, Section 504 can provide an efficient way to obtain limited assistance without the stigma and bureaucratic procedures attached to IDEA.

On the other hand, IDEA offers a wider range of service options, the procedures for parent participation and procedural safeguards are far more extensive, and the degree of regulation is far more specific than that found in Section 504. If a child has behavioral challenges that could lead to the possibility of excessive discipline, suspension and expulsion, parents should be particularly aware of the less rigorous safeguards provided by Section 504.

This chapter is designed to summarize various legal issues affecting the education of children with AD/HD and should not be construed as legal advice or a legal opinion on specific facts. Readers with particular questions should seek the assistance of their own legal counsel.

What You Need to Know about AD/HD Under the Individuals with Disabilities Education Act

Is AD/HD covered under the Other Health Impaired category of IDEA?

Yes. According to the U.S. Department of Education, children diagnosed with AD/HD who meet the eligibility criteria under Other Health Impaired (OHI) have always been eligible for special education services. While this was clarified by the 1991 Policy Memorandum issued by the U.S. Department of Education, the new regulations implementing the Individuals with Disabilities Education Act (IDEA) Amendments of 1997, issued March 12, 1999, for the first time explicitly incorporate AD/HD within the definition of Other Health Impaired.

What are the criteria for eligibility for special education under the OHI category due to AD/HD?

In order for a student to qualify for special education under the OHI category, the following criteria must be met:

a) the student must be diagnosed with AD/HD by the school district, or the school must accept the diagnosis rendered by another qualified professional;

b) the AD/HD must result in limited alertness to academic tasks, due to heightened alertness to environmental stimuli;

c) the effects of the AD/HD must be chronic (long-lasting) or acute (have a substantial impact);

d) this must result in an adverse effect on educational performance;

e) the student must require special education services in order to address the AD/HD and its impact.

What does "adversely affects educational performance" mean?

An adverse effect on educational performance can incorporate all aspects of the child's functioning at school, including educational performance as measured by grades or achievement test scores. It can also be manifested through behavioral difficulties at school; and impaired or inappropriate social relations; impaired work skills, such as being disorganized, tardy, having trouble getting to work on time and difficulty with following the rules. Schools are required to address the effects of a child's disability in all areas of functioning, including academic, social/emotional, cognitive, communication, vocational and independent living skills.

Does my child have to be failing in order to qualify for special education under the OHI category?

No. In fact, under the new 1999 regulations, the fact that a child is progressing from grade to grade is not by itself a basis to determine that he or she does not have a suspected disability. Failing grades may be evidence of a disability, but are not a prerequisite to establishing a disability. Conversely, the fact that a child is getting failing grades does not automatically mean the child has a disability or is entitled to special education.

If the child must need special education services in order to qualify under OHI, does this mean my child needs to be put in a special education class in order to qualify for services?

No. Special education services are defined in the statute as specially designed instruction, which may be available within a range of settings, including specially designed instruction within the regular classroom. The term special education services refers to the specially designed services contained in the Individual Education Plan (IEP). Special education is not a place or a classroom.

If my doctor diagnoses my child with AD/HD, does that mean he or she will automatically qualify for special education?

No. The school district is required to consider your outside evaluation, but is not obligated to follow it. If a referral is made by you, your outside clinician, or a member of the school staff, the school district must determine if an evaluation is indicated because of a suspicion that the child may have a disability. If the school decides not to conduct an evaluation, they must notify you of the decision, inform you of the reasons behind the decision, and give you information regarding your right to request a due process hearing to challenge that decision. On the other hand, before the school determines eligibility, it must conduct a multidisciplinary evaluation, which must include consideration of any outside evaluations you have obtained. Once that evaluation is complete the school will use the criteria described above to determine if the child meets the eligibility criteria for OHI. Consult your state's special education regulations for timelines within which an evaluation must be completed after a referral is made. These regulations are available at your state's Department of Education, or you can obtain a brief statement of your special education rights from your school district.

What type of information should be considered in determining an adverse effect on educational performance?

Both the school district evaluation team and any outside clinician should obtain as much information as possible about the child's school functioning. This would include an interview with the child; an interview with the parent; an observation of the child in the learning environment; review of grades, academic records, disciplinary records (if any) and other school records. In addition, this may also include the completion of behavioral rating scales by the parents, the teachers, and sometimes the student, as well as anecdotal reports from teachers. Consideration should be given to the child's current and historical functioning. The use of behavior rating scales which address AD/HD symptoms can be especially helpful because they can provide quantitative data for evaluating the severity of the problems.

Who is responsible for evaluating whether my child has AD/HD?

If you or the school staff suspect your child has AD/HD or any disability adversely affecting his or her school performance, a referral to the school for an evaluation for special education should be made. The parents, private professionals, and school staff all have the right to make a referral for evaluation for eligibility for special education. The school must then do the evaluation, or explain to the parents the reasons the school is not doing the evaluation and inform the parents of their right to request a hearing to challenge the school's decision. If the school agrees to do the evaluation, it must be done at no cost to the parents. Some schools require a medical evaluation, as a component of the school evaluation, to determine if a child has AD/HD. If the school requires a medical evaluation, it must be provided at no cost to the parent. Parents have the right to obtain a private evaluation at any time, at their own expense. Parents may request a private evaluation at district expense if the district has conducted an evaluation that the parents are dissatisfied with. The school then must either agree to pay for the private evaluation or request an impartial due process hearing to prove that the district evaluation was appropriate.

Is a medical evaluation required in order to determine if my child has AD/HD?

No. For educational purposes, local school district policy determines whether a medical evaluation is required. The school may require an evaluation, in which case it must pay for it. Alternatively, the school district may utilize its multidisciplinary team, including a psychologist or other professional qualified to diagnose AD/HD, to make the determination for educational purposes. Of course, a medical evaluation may also be desirable, as it can rule out other causes for the problem and determine if medication would be an appropriate of the child's treatment.

Speaking of medication, can a school district require my child to take medication, or to take it as a prerequisite for getting special services?

No to both questions. Parents have the exclusive legal right to determine if their child should receive medication. Special function-education services can not be predicated on your agreement to have your child take special medication.

My child has been determined eligible for a Section 504 plan. Does that mean he or she is automatically eligible for services under OHI under IDEA?

No. The standard for eligibility under Section 504 is broader and more flexible than the standard under IDEA. Of particular importance: in order to qualify for IDEA services under OHI, the child must need special education services. By contrast, a child may be eligible under Section 504 if they have a diagnosed physical or mental impairment, including AD/HD, which substantially limits (affects) learning and requires special education or related services. This means that children who need assistance with preferential seating, untimed tests, or help in taking medication from the school nurse may qualify for protection under Section 504, even though they do not need special education so as to qualify for services under IDEA.

My child is already eligible for accommodations under Section 504. What can OHI eligibility offer that is not available under Section 504?

Technically, a child is entitled to a free appropriate public education (FAPE) under both laws. This means that both can offer a range of interventions, from minor accommodations in the classroom (such as preferential seating), to substantial services (such as special education services and social work services). However, all school districts have an established special education delivery system, while many school districts have little or any dedicated 504 delivery systems. For more expensive services, IDEA also offers advantages, because the school districts are reimbursed for a substantial portion of their cost by the state and federal governments, while no 504 expenses are reimbursed with either state or federal funds. Most importantly, however, the procedural safeguards available under IDEA are far more extensive and protective of parents' rights than those under Section 504. For example, IDEA contains extensive rules relating to the rights of parents to participate in the decision making concerning their child's Individual Education Plan and placement. These rules also enumerate in detail what the content of the IEP must be, including requirements for regular reporting to the parents and specific time periods in which they must be reviewed and updated. By contrast, Section 504 contains little detail on implementation of the Section 504 plan. In addition, for children who are having behavioral difficulties, IDEA requires that the IEP contain positive behavioral intervention strategies and sets out very detailed safeguards limiting the types of disciplinary action that schools can take, particularly for behavior that is related to the child's disability. By comparison, Section 504 offers far fewer procedural safeguards.

Is it always better for my child to be eligible under OHI, rather than Section 504?

No. Some children with AD/HD do not need services under either Section 504 or IDEA. Some children may need accommodations, but do not have a sufficient level of educational interference from their AD/HD to warrant eligibility under IDEA. In addition, if accommodations available under Section 504 are sufficient for the child, Section 504 may be an easier way to get the help the child needs.

Part Four

AD/HD Facts for Specific Populations

Chapter 31

AD/HD and Children Who Are Gifted

Howard's teachers say he just isn't working up to his ability. He doesn't finish his assignments, or just puts down answers without showing his work; his handwriting and spelling are poor. He sits and fidgets in class, talks to others, and often disrupts class by interrupting others. He used to shout out the answers to the teachers' questions (they were usually right), but now he daydreams a lot and seems distracted. Does Howard have attention deficit hyperactivity disorder (AD/HD), is he gifted, or both?

Frequently, bright children have been referred to psychologists or pediatricians because they exhibited certain behaviors (e.g., restlessness, inattention, impulsivity, high activity level, day-dreaming) commonly associated with a diagnosis of AD/HD. Formally, the *Diagnostic and Statistical Manual of Mental Disorders (DSM)* (American Psychiatric Association) lists 14 characteristics that may be found in children diagnosed as having AD/HD. At least 8 of these characteristics must be present, the onset must be before age 7, and they must be present for at least six months.

Sometimes, professionals have diagnosed AD/HD by simply listening to parent or teacher descriptions of the child's behaviors along with

"AD/HD and Children Who Are Gifted," by James T. Webb and Diane Latimer, from *ERIC Digests,* U.S. Department of Education, ERIC Identifier ED358637, 1993. ERIC (Educational Resources Information Center) is a service of the U.S. Department of Education. Online databases are available at www.ed.gov/databases. Despite the age of this document, readers seeking to understand how giftedness in children can produce symptoms that may be confused with AD/HD will still find the information useful.

a brief observation of the child. Other times, brief screening questionnaires are used, although these questionnaires only quantify the parents' or teachers' descriptions of the behaviors. Children who are fortunate enough to have a thorough physical evaluation (which includes screening for allergies and other metabolic disorders) and extensive psychological evaluations, which include assessment of intelligence, achievement, and emotional status, have a better chance of being accurately identified. A child may be gifted and have AD/HD. Without a thorough professional evaluation, it is difficult to tell.

How Can Parents or Teachers Distinguish between AD/HD and Giftedness?

Seeing the difference between behaviors that are sometimes associated with giftedness but also characteristic of AD/HD is not easy, as Table 31.1 shows.

Table 31.1. Difference between Behaviors Associated with AD/HD and Giftedness

Behaviors Associated with AD/HD	Behaviors Associated with Giftedness
Poorly sustained attention in almost all situations	Poor attention, boredom, daydreaming in specific situations
Diminished persistence on tasks not having immediate consequences	Low tolerance for persistence on tasks that seem irrelevant
Impulsivity, poor delay of gratification	Judgment lags behind development of intellect
Impaired adherence to commands to regulate or inhibit behavior in social contexts	Intensity may lead to power struggles with authorities
More active, restless than normal children	High activity level; may need less sleep
Difficulty adhering to rules and regulations	Questions rules, customs and traditions

Consider the Situation and Setting

It is important to examine the situations in which a child's behaviors are problematic. Gifted children typically do not exhibit problems in all situations. For example, they may be seen as AD/HD-like by one classroom teacher, but not by another; or they may be seen as AD/HD at school, but not by the scout leader or music teacher. Close examination of the troublesome situation generally reveals other factors which are prompting the problem behaviors. By contrast, children with AD/HD typically exhibit the problem behaviors in virtually all settings including at home and at school though the extent of their problem behaviors may fluctuate significantly from setting to setting, depending largely on the structure of that situation. That is, the behaviors exist in all settings, but are more of a problem in some settings than in others.

In the classroom, a gifted child's perceived inability to stay on task is likely to be related to boredom, curriculum, mismatched learning style, or other environmental factors. Gifted children may spend from one-fourth to one-half of their regular classroom time waiting for others to catch up—even more if they are in a heterogeneously grouped class. Their specific level of academic achievement is often two to four grade levels above their actual grade placement. Such children often respond to non-challenging or slow-moving classroom situations by off-task behavior, disruptions, or other attempts at self-amusement. This use of extra time is often the cause of the referral for an AD/HD evaluation.

Hyperactive is a word often used to describe gifted children as well as children with AD/HD. As with attention span, children with AD/HD have a high activity level, but this activity level is often found across situations. A large proportion of gifted children are highly active too. As many as one-fourth may require less sleep; however, their activity is generally focused and directed, in contrast to the behavior of children with AD/HD. The intensity of gifted children's concentration often permits them to spend long periods of time and much energy focusing on whatever truly interests them. Their specific interests may not coincide, however, with the desires and expectations of teachers or parents.

While the child who is hyperactive has a very brief attention span in virtually every situation (usually except for television or computer games), children who are gifted can concentrate comfortably for long periods on tasks that interest them, and do not require immediate completion of those tasks or immediate consequences. The activities of children with AD/HD tend to be both continual and random; the gifted child's activity usually is episodic and directed to specific goals.

While difficulties and adherence to rules and regulations has only begun to be accepted as a sign of AD/HD, gifted children may actively question rules, customs and traditions, sometimes creating complex rules which they expect others to respect or obey. Some engage in power struggles. These behaviors can cause discomfort for parents, teachers, and peers.

One characteristic of AD/HD that does not have a counterpart in children who are gifted is variability of task performance. In almost every setting, children with AD/HD tend to be highly inconsistent in the quality of their performance (i.e., grades, chores) and the amount of time used to accomplish tasks. Children who are gifted routinely maintain consistent efforts and high grades in classes when they like the teacher and are intellectually challenged, although they may resist some aspects of the work, particularly repetition of tasks perceived as dull. Some gifted children may become intensely focused and determined (an aspect of their intensity) to produce a product that meets their self-imposed standards.

What Teachers and Parents Can Do

Determining whether a child has AD/HD can be particularly difficult when that child is also gifted. The use of many instruments, including intelligence tests administered by qualified professionals, achievement and personality tests, as well as parent and teacher rating scales, can help the professional determine the subtle differences between AD/HD and giftedness. Individual evaluation allows the professional to establish maximum rapport with the child to get the best effort on the tests. Since the test situation is constant, it is possible to make better comparisons among children. Portions of the intellectual and achievement tests will reveal attention problems or learning disabilities, whereas personality tests are designed to show whether emotional problems (e.g., depression or anxiety) could be causing the problem behaviors. Evaluation should be followed by appropriate curricular and instructional modifications that account for advanced knowledge, diverse learning styles, and various types of intelligence.

Careful consideration and appropriate professional evaluation are necessary before concluding that bright, creative, intense youngsters like Howard have AD/HD. Consider the characteristics of the gifted/ talented child and the child's situation. Do not hesitate to raise the possibility of giftedness with any professional who is evaluating the child for AD/HD; however, do not be surprised if the professional has had little training in recognizing the characteristics of gifted/talented children. It is important to make the correct diagnosis, and parents and teachers may need to provide information to others since giftedness is often neglected in professional development programs.

Chapter 32

AD/HD in Females: From Childhood to Adulthood

The majority of writing and research on AD/HD has traditionally focused on males, who were believed to make up 80 percent of all those with AD/HD. Today, more and more females are being identified, especially now that we are more aware of the non-hyperactive subtype of AD/HD. Girls and women with AD/HD face a variety of issues that are gender specific. This chapter will highlight some of those differences, and will explore some of the unique struggles faced by females with AD/HD.

Childhood Issues for Girls with AD/HD

Let's start with the recollections of childhood and adolescence by two women with AD/HD: Marie and Lauren. Marie is an introverted, "primarily inattentive" 34-year-old woman with AD/HD, who has struggled with anxiety and depression in addition to AD/HD, both in childhood and in adulthood:

"The thing I remember the most was always getting my feelings hurt. I was a lot happier when I played with just one friend. When someone teased me I never knew how to defend myself. I really tried in school, but I hated it when the teacher called on

"AD/HD in Females: From Childhood to Adulthood," by Kathleen Nadeau, Ph.D., in *Attention!* © 1996 CHADD, available online at www.chadd.org; reprinted with permission. For more information write to CHADD at 8181 Professional Place, Suite 201, Landover, MD 20875, or visit CHADD at their website at www.chadd.org.

me. Half the time I didn't even know what the question was. Sometimes I would get stomach aches and beg my mother to let me stay home from school."

These recollections are very different from those of a typical elementary school-age boy with AD/HD. Marie was hypersensitive to criticism, had difficulty with the rapid give-and-take of group interactions, and felt socially out of it, except in the company of her one best friend. She was a compliant girl whose greatest desire was to conform to teacher expectations and not to draw attention to herself. Her distractibility created agony because of teacher disapproval and the resulting embarrassment in front of her peers.

On the other hand, Lauren's hyperactive-impulsive AD/HD patterns are more similar to those seen in many boys with AD/HD. Now twenty-seven, she recalls being stubborn, angry, defiant and rebellious, and physically hyperactive. She was also hypersocial:

"I can remember in grade school that everything felt frantic. I had a fight with my mom almost every morning. At school I was always jumping around, talking, and passing notes. Some of my teachers liked me, but some of them—the really strict ones— didn't like me. And I hated them. I argued a lot and lost my temper. I cried really easily too, and some of the mean kids in the class liked to tease me and make me cry."

Although we see the argumentativeness and defiance in Lauren, which we see more often in boys who have AD/HD, we also see that, like many girls with AD/HD she was hyper-social and hyper-emotional. Life for Lauren, as for some other girls with AD/HD, was an emotional roller coaster. She was very disorganized, and had very low tolerance for stress.

Adolescent Girls with AD/HD

Let's take a look at Marie and Lauren's recollections of adolescence. Life for each of them seemed to become even more difficult. Adolescence is difficult enough as it is—when AD/HD is added to the mix, problems are amplified and stresses are intensified.

"High school just overwhelmed me. None of my teachers knew me because I never spoke up in class. Exams terrified me. I hated to study and write papers. They were really hard for me and I put them off until the last minute. I didn't date at all in high school. People didn't dislike me, but I bet if I went back to a class reunion that no one would remember who I was. I was pretty emotional, and it got ten times worse just before my period."

"I was totally out of control in high school. I was smart, but a terrible student. I guess I worked on being a party animal to make up for all the things I wasn't good at. At home I was angry, totally rebellious. I snuck out of the house after my parents went to sleep at night. I lied all the time. My parents tried to control me or punish me, but nothing worked. I couldn't sleep at night, and was exhausted all day in school. Things were bad most of the time, but when I had PMS I really lost it. School meant nothing to me."

Marie and Lauren presented very different pictures during their teenage years. Marie was shy, withdrawn, a daydreamer who was disorganized and felt overwhelmed. Lauren was hyperactive, hyper-emotional, and lived her life in a high stimulation, high risk mode. The differences in Marie's and Lauren's behaviors are obvious, but what do they have in common?

Severe Pre-Menstrual Syndrome

In teenage years, the neurochemical problems caused by AD/HD are greatly compounded by hormonal fluctuations. These combined dysregulated systems can result in tremendous mood swings, hyper-irritability, and emotional over-reaction.

Tremendous Concern with Peer Acceptance

Girls with AD/HD seem to suffer more as a result of peer problems than do boys with AD/HD. Although Lauren had many friends, her emotionality repeatedly got in the way. Marie, by contrast, felt overwhelmed and withdrew, and felt most comfortable in the company of one close friend. Both, however, had a strong sense of being different from their peers.

Among Impulsive-Hyperactive Girls, a Sense of Shame

Adolescent boys who are impulsive and hyperactive may be viewed as simply sowing their oats. They may even gain peer approval as they rebel against authority, or as a result of their hard drinking, fast driving, and sexually-active lifestyle. Girls, however, tend to receive much more negative feedback from parents, teachers, and peers when they behave in such a manner. Later, as young women, they often join the chorus of accusation and outrage, blaming themselves and feeling a strong sense of shame for their earlier behavior.

Raising Girls with AD/HD—Some Helpful Approaches

Just like adolescent boys with AD/HD, these girls need structure and guidelines at home. While males with AD/HD may behave in a very angry and rebellious fashion, for many girls, their life is an emotional roller coaster. They may withdraw and become depressed if they feel overwhelmed and socially rejected at school. Highly hyperactive-impulsive girls may engage in constant, dramatic screaming battles at home, where it feels much safer to release their fears and frustrations. Helping them to re-establish emotional equilibrium, especially in relation to hormonal fluctuations, is critical. For girls, more so than for many boys, home needs to become a place to calm down and to refuel emotionally. All too often, however, parents are drawn into tumultuous battles, rather than providing a much needed calming influence. How can you help as a parent?

Teach your daughters to establish a quiet zone in their lives. Whether shy and withdrawn, or hyper and impulsive, girls with AD/HD often feel emotionally overwhelmed. They need to learn stress management techniques from an early age, and to understand that they need emotional time out to regroup after an upset.

Try to minimize corrections and criticism. Too often, parents—with the best of intentions—shower girls who have AD/HD with corrections and criticisms. "Don't let them hurt your feelings like that." "You'd forget your head if it wasn't attached to your shoulders." "How do you expect to go to college with grades like that?" "If you just relaxed, dressed a little better..." These girls, whether loud and rebellious, or shy and retiring, typically suffer from low self-esteem. Home is not only an important place to refuel, it is where confidence—so frequently eroded during the day at school—must be rebuilt.

Help them look for ways to excel. Girls with AD/HD typically feel that they are not good at anything. Their distractibility, impulsivity, and disorganization often result in mediocre grades. Likewise, they often don't have the persistence, the stick-to-it-iveness, to develop skills and talents like many of their friends. Helping girls with AD/HD find a skill or ability, and then praising and recognizing them for it are terrific positive boosts. Often, the life of an adolescent girl with AD/HD reaches a positive turning point when she is lucky enough to find an activity that can raise her self-esteem.

Seek medical treatment if PMS is severe. PMS is something that many females with AD/HD may need to carefully manage throughout their lives. If PMS is severe in adolescence it should be taken seriously, and managed carefully. Sometimes severe PMS is managed through the use of anti-depressants with the dosage level being varied according to the menstrual cycle.

Special Issues Faced by Women with AD/HD

The same themes of social and physiological differences between males and females with AD/HD continue to play themselves out as adolescent girls become women with jobs, marriages, and families.

For a woman with AD/HD, her most painful challenge may be created by her own overwhelming sense of inadequacy at fulfilling the roles she feels that her family and society expect her to play. Both on the job and at home, women are often placed in the role of caretaker. While men with AD/HD are advised to build a support system around themselves, not only do few women have access to such a support system, society had traditionally expected women to be the support system.

The emergence of dual career couples have intensified the struggles for women with AD/HD. Over the past two decades, more and more women have been required to fulfill not only the more traditional roles of wife and mother, but also to function efficiently and tirelessly as they juggle the demands of a full time career. Divorce is also hitting women with AD/HD harder than their peers who do not have AD/HD. Divorce rates are close to fifty percent among all marriages in the United States; divorce becomes even more likely when AD/HD is added to the list of marital stressors. Following divorce, it continues to be predominantly mothers who act as primary parent for children. By adding AD/HD to the huge burden of single-parenting, the result is often chronic exhaustion and emotional depletion.

The hormonal fluctuations that commence at puberty continue to play a strong role in the lives of women with AD/HD. The problems they experience due to AD/HD are greatly exacerbated by their monthly hormonal fluctuations. Some women report that the stresses of parenting their children—who may have AD/HD—while attempting to struggle with their own AD/HD, reaches crisis proportions on a monthly basis as they go through their premenstrual phase, often lasting as long as a week.

Although the number of older women yet identified with AD/HD is small, it seems quite reasonable to assume that the hormonal changes associated with menopause would be expected to, once again, exacerbate AD/HD symptoms of emotional reactivity.

Managing Your Life

Here's a list of twelve actions (and attitude changes) that could help make your life more manageable and, therefore, less stressful:

Give yourself a break! Often the biggest struggle is an internal one. Societal expectations have been deeply ingrained in many women. Even if a loving husband said, "Don't worry about it," women would place demands upon themselves. Breaking out of a mold that doesn't fit can take time and effort. Working with a therapist who really understands issues related to AD/HD may help shed the impossible expectations that you have of yourself.

Educate your husband about AD/HD and how it affects you. Your husband may feel anger and resentment about an ill-kept house or badly behaved children, assuming that you just don't care. He needs to appreciate the full brunt of AD/HD's impact upon you. Get him on your side; strategize how to make your life at home more AD/HD-accommodating and AD/HD-friendly.

It's only spilled milk! Try to create an AD/HD-friendly environment in your home. If you can approach your AD/HD and that of your children with acceptance and good humor, explosions will decrease and you'll save more energy for the positive side of things.

Simplify your life. You are probably over-booked and chances are your children are too. Look for ways to reduce commitments so that you're not always pressed for time and hurried.

Choose supportive friends. So many women describe friends or neighbors who make them feel terrible by comparison—whose houses are immaculate, whose children are always clean, neat, and well-behaved. Don't put yourself in situations that will send you back to impossible expectations and negative comparisons.

Build a support group for yourself. One woman with AD/HD related that housework was such drudgery for her that she often couldn't bring herself to do it. One of her techniques, however, was to invite a friend, who shared similar tendencies, to keep her company while she completed some particularly odious task.

Build in time-outs daily. Time-out's are essential when you have AD/HD and are raising children. It's easy to not find time for time-outs, though, because they require planning. Make them routine so that you don't have to keep planning and juggling. For example, ask your husband to commit to two blocks of time each weekend when he will take the kids away from the house without you. Arrange for a regular baby-sitter several times a week.

Don't place yourself in burn-out. One mother with AD/HD, who is doing a great job of parenting her two children who also have AD/HD, is able to recognize her limitations. With two such challenging children she arranges for a month-long, summer sleep-away camp each summer. She also arranges for brief visits, one at a time, to grandparents. This allows her to spend time with each son without him having to compete with his brother.

Eliminate and delegate. Look at things that you require of yourself at home. Can some of these things be eliminated? Can you afford to hire someone to do some of them?

Learn child behavior management techniques. On the outside looking in, it may be easy for other parents to judge you if your children misbehave. What any parent of a child with AD/HD knows is that they don't respond to the usual admonishments and limits the way other children do. You have a super-challenging job. Get the best training you can find. There are excellent books on behavior management techniques for children with AD/HD.

Get help for PMS or Menopausal Symptoms. They are likely to be more severe in women with AD/HD than they may be in other women. Managing the destabilizing effect of your hormonal fluctuations is a critical part of managing your AD/HD.

Focus more on the things you love. There are many aspects of keeping a house and raising children that are rewarding and creative. Look for positive experiences to share with your children.

Women with AD/HD need to understand and accept themselves. They need to quit blaming themselves for not meeting the expected demands of two of life's most AD/HD-unfriendly jobs—that of house-wife and mother. They also need the understanding and acceptance of their husbands, their families, and friends. These are women who are struggling valiantly against demands which are difficult, if not impossible, to meet. Instead of measuring success in terms of clean dishes and folded laundry, women with AD/HD must learn to celebrate their gifts—their warmth, their creativity, their humor, their sensitivity, and their spirit—and to look for others who can appreciate the best in them as well.

This chapter is adapted from *Adventures in Fast Forward*, by Kathleen G. Nadeau, a book on life, love and work for adults with AD/HD, published by Brunner/Mazel in the spring of 1996.

Kathleen G. Nadeau, Ph.D. is Director of Chesapeake Psychological Services of Maryland, a private clinic that specializes in diagnosing and treating adolescents and adults with AD/HD. She is the editor of *A Comprehensive Guide to Attention Deficit Disorder in Adults: Research, Diagnosis, and Treatment,* the first guide for professionals on adults with AD/HD and is the author of several books on AD/HD.

Chapter 33

A Teenager's Guide to AD/HD

Are you tired of hearing "you're just lazy" and "I know you can do better if you wanted to?" If so, read on. This chapter is written for teenagers with attention deficit hyperactivity disorder (AD/HD or ADD). It describes what AD/HD is, how it is diagnosed, how it is treated, and what you can do to cope with it.

What Is AD/HD?

AD/HD (also called ADD) stands for attention deficit hyperactivity disorder. It is thought to be a brain disorder that makes it difficult to sit still and pay attention. Between 3 and 5 percent of children are thought to have AD/HD. It is more common in males, though many girls also have it. AD/HD is characterized by hyperactivity (e.g. being too active, being fidgety, talking too much, being restless, or having your mind be always racing with thoughts); inattentiveness (e.g. difficulty paying attention, mind wandering, forgetting or losing things); and impulsivity (e.g. acting first without thinking, interrupting others, not thinking about the consequences of your words or actions).

You may not have all three types of symptoms. If you only have problems with paying attention, this is called AD/HD—Inattentive

From "Attention Deficit Hyperactivity Disorder in Teenagers," by James J. Crist, Ph.D., © 2000 James J. Crist, Ph.D.; reprinted with permission. Additional information about Dr. Crist is included at the end of this chapter.

Type. This type of AD/HD used to be called ADD, though some people still use this term. If you mostly have problems with hyperactivity/impulsivity, this is called AD/HD—Hyperactive/Impulsive Type. If you have both sets of symptoms, this is called AD/HD—Combined Type. Many teens mostly have trouble with inattentiveness, which creates lots of problems with paying attention in class, getting homework done, and finishing chores at home. You may have good intentions to finish things, but somehow you often end up being distracted by something else.

AD/HD can also cause trouble in relationships. For instance, you may be more likely to interrupt others, to lose your temper and overreact to things, to forget what you promised to do, and to not pay attention when someone is talking to you. It can be harder to maintain friendships and relationships as a result.

Many teens with AD/HD also have learning disabilities (LD). This means that you have trouble learning certain subjects, such as reading, math, writing, and spelling. It does not mean that you are not smart. Some teens with AD/HD and LD are placed in LD classes to help them learn more effectively.

What Causes AD/HD?

While we do not know for sure, research suggests that people with AD/HD may not have enough of certain brain chemicals (called neurotransmitters) that are needed for paying attention and controlling behavior. Two of these neurotransmitters are norepinephrine and dopamine. Recent studies are also demonstrating difference between brain activity of people with AD/HD, as compared to people without AD/HD. People with AD/HD have less activity in certain areas of the brain that help you to pay attention. The medications that are used to treat AD/HD work by increasing the levels of these neurotransmitters in the brain.

How Can I Tell if I Have AD/HD?

AD/HD must be diagnosed by a qualified mental health professional. Such professionals may include a psychologist, psychiatrist, social worker, or a pediatrician. The therapist or doctor will ask you, your parents, and your teachers to complete some questionnaires. Sometimes, computer tests are used to see how well you can pay attention. One commonly used computer test is the Test of Variables of Attention (TOVA).

AD/HD can be difficult to diagnose because the symptoms are often inconsistent. In addition, some of the symptoms are also common in other disorders. For instance, depression and anxiety can also cause difficulties in concentration and activity level. If you are taking medications for other conditions, or if you have certain physical problems, these can cause symptoms similar to those of AD/HD.

If you are smart or gifted, chances are you got by pretty well in the earlier grades, when homework wasn't such a big issue. Often, gifted students are not identified as having AD/HD until middle school or high school, when the workload increases and you are penalized a lot more for not completing homework. You are also expected to work more independently, and that can be a big problem if you have trouble concentrating and staying organized.

Finally, the use of marijuana also tends to decrease your ability to concentrate and remember things. For these reasons, it is very important to be evaluated properly. If you are using drugs, try to stop for at least a month before being evaluated.

What Are the Effects of Having AD/HD?

People with AD/HD are at greater risk for school failure, having other learning disabilities, and abusing alcohol or other drugs. You may have more difficulty maintaining friendships and getting along with your family. You may be more irritable and have a quick temper. People with AD/HD are at higher risk for developing depression because of the frustrations that go along with having AD/HD.

Some people go on to develop Oppositional Defiant Disorder (ODD). People with this disorder often defy and are hostile toward anyone in authority. They are argumentative and blame others. This makes things more difficult because of the negative way in which people with ODD treat those who could help them.

You may have trouble maintaining your responsibilities at work. For instance, you may show up late because you are disorganized or plan poorly, or may blurt out something to your boss or coworkers that you later regret.

We are also finding that there may be subtypes of AD/HD. For example, you can be anxious and have AD/HD. Gifted students can also have AD/HD. Some people with AD/HD can be hyperfocused, which means when they do focus on something that interests them, they get so absorbed that they tune out everything else. For all of these reasons, proper treatment is essential. Failure to get the appropriate help now can lead to more problems later on.

How Is AD/HD Treated?

A combination of counseling and medication is often used. The most commonly used medication is Ritalin (also called methylphenidate, its generic form). Sometimes, Dexedrine (d-amphetamine) or Adderall is used. A new medicine, Concerta, has just been released. It is a time-release brand of methylphenidate that can last all day—about 10-12 hours. It comes in 18, 36, or 54 milligram capsules. Adderall and sustained-release Ritalin can also last for most of the day. This eliminates the need to take medicine at school. Cylert (pemoline) has also been used, but is used much less often now because of some evidence that it may damage your liver. These are all stimulant drugs, and they appear to stimulate certain centers in the brain which are responsible for motivation, behavior control, and attention.

In some cases, antidepressant medications are used. Examples include Tofranil (imipramine), Prozac (fluoxetine), Zoloft (sertraline), and Wellbutrin (bupropion). Wellbutrin is probably the most commonly prescribed antidepressant medication for teenagers with AD/HD. Sometimes, Catapres (clonidine) or Tenex (guanfacine) are used. Both are actually blood pressure medications but can be helpful in treating the hyperactivity and aggressiveness that is often associated with AD/HD. They can also help with tics, which can be made worse with stimulant medications.

When needed, combinations of the three types of medications noted are used. This is often done in more difficult to treat cases. Be sure to ask your doctor if you have any questions about medications.

Some side effects may occur with these medications. The most common side effects of stimulants such as Ritalin include upset stomach, difficulty sleeping, loss of appetite, and irritability. Some people also have a rebound effect, which means that the AD/HD symptoms come back pretty quickly and intensely when the medicine is wearing off. Common side effects of antidepressant medications include headaches, dry mouth, blurry vision, and drowsiness. These side effects will often decrease after awhile. Make sure you tell your doctor if you experience these or any other side effects. If the side effects bother you, your doctor may change the dose, switch medications, or possibly add another medication.

These medicines are not addictive when used at the prescribed doses. They make it easier for you to control your own behavior and make better choices. Some evidence suggests that teens who are properly treated for AD/HD are less likely to abuse alcohol and other drugs. Make sure you take the medicine as prescribed. Do not skip doses or take more than you are supposed to unless advised to do so by your doctor.

If you are thinking about stopping, talk to your doctor or therapist first. Do not stop taking your medicine suddenly. If you are taking a stimulant such as Ritalin or Adderall, you may not need to take it on weekends and holidays—again, ask your doctor about this. Remember also that while you may not think the medicine is helpful, others around you may see an improvement even when you cannot.

Counseling is also often recommended to help you develop better organizational strategies for home and school. If you also suffer from depression, low self-esteem, family conflict, or other problems, counseling can help you work these problems out. It could also prevent problems from occurring later in life.

Will I Always Have AD/HD?

While some people may outgrow it, most people have at least some AD/HD symptoms well into adulthood. Frequently, teenagers are less hyperactive than are children with AD/HD—they tend to be fidgety and impatient—but they still have problems paying attention, getting organized, and acting impulsively. Some adults may still need to take medicine, though not all do. If you are an older teenager or adult and are still experiencing AD/HD symptoms, you may want to consider being evaluated by a psychologist or psychiatrist with expertise in adult AD/HD. The same medicines that work with children and teens can also help adults.

How Can I Deal with Having AD/HD?

There are many strategies you can use to help you. In terms of school, use an assignment notebook. Write down all assignments, due dates, test dates, appointments, etc. Make sure you check the book on a daily basis. Tell your teachers you have AD/HD and ask them if they would be willing to help you do your best. Ask to be seated near the teacher, away from distractions such as the door or windows. Ask for written instructions whenever possible. Check with friends to make sure you did not miss what was assigned in class. When studying, use a multisensory approach. This means you use all of your senses—read chapters, write down notes, tape record the highlights, play them back, and quiz yourself. The more ways you try to get the information in, the better you will remember it.

At home, use to do lists as much as possible. Prioritize your tasks (highlight or put a star next to them), so that you do the most important ones first. Cross tasks off when you complete them. Make time to let off steam. Being physically active is very important when you have AD/HD, especially if you have the hyperactivity symptoms. Keep your room as simple as possible—otherwise, the clutter can cause you a lot of aggravation. Learn to express your feelings appropriately. People with AD/HD sometimes blurt out things without thinking about the consequences, and end up hurting family members (and other). Use "I" statements. Example: "I feel upset when you nag at me, because it makes me feel stupid. Please tell me only once, or leave me a note."

With friends, you may want to tell them you have AD/HD. They may be willing to give you feedback if you are talking too much, interrupting, or forgetting things (a common problem with AD/HD). They may also be able to support you when you get frustrated because of your problems. Remember that AD/HD also has its advantages. AD/HD can give you lots of energy, which can help with sports. The high need for stimulation can be helpful in entertaining others and doing emergency work. Talkativeness can help in sales positions. Many people with AD/HD are very creative, since AD/HD may allow you to think of many different possibilities at once.

Is Help Available from My School?

Yes. You may qualify for extra services if it can be demonstrated that your AD/HD is interfering with your ability to learn. If a learning disability is suspected, a child study team will be organized. This involves getting information from your teachers and doing some psychological testing, such as IQ and achievement testing. If evidence of a learning disability in a certain area such as math, reading, or writing is found, you may qualify for special services, ranging from in-class help to being put in a special class for certain periods. If your problems are severe, especially with your behavior, you may be placed in a smaller class, which is more structured.

If you do not qualify based on testing alone, you may qualify for help based on Section 504 of the Rehabilitation Act. This means that the school may be required to make accommodations to help you learn. Examples could include being given shorter assignments, having a tutor, having tests be given orally, being placed in front of the class, and being allowed to tape record classes. You may even qualify for accommodations for standardized testing, such as the SAT's.

It is important for you to participate in this process. Sometimes you have to make a strong case to get the services you need. By giving your input, and knowing your rights, you may be happier with the final decision. If your school is not willing to provide help, see if there is a special advocate who can help you and your parents get the services your need. In some cases, legal advice may be needed.

If you are planning on attending college, it helps to plan ahead of time. You may qualify for accommodations on testing. Also, some colleges offer specific programs for students with AD/HD or learning disabilities. A good website is the Heath Resource Center of the American Council on Education. This is a national clearinghouse on college education for students with disabilities, including AD/HD. Information on financial aid is also listed!

Conclusion

AD/HD can cause significant problems in your life. However, with proper treatment, it can become much more manageable. Learning as much as you can about the disorder will help you to cope. Don't forget that having AD/HD is not all bad. People with AD/HD often have lots of energy, can be entertaining, and can be very creative too. Many famous people have been diagnosed as having AD/HD.

About Dr. Crist

James J. Crist, Ph.D. is a licensed Clinical Psychologist and Certified Substance Abuse Counselor in practice at the Child and Family Counseling Center of Woodbridge, Virginia, where he works with children, teenagers, adults, couples, and families.

Dr. Crist is the author of *ADHD: A Teenager's Guide* (Childswork/ Childsplay 1997) and *Alcoholics and Families: A Guide for Kids* (Continental Press 2000). Questions and comments for Dr. Crist may be directed to DrJCrist@aol.com.

Chapter 34

Youth with Disabilities in the Juvenile Justice System

When Oliver was very young, both of his parents struggled with drug abuse, his older brother was killed, and his father ultimately left the family. Oliver changed schools often, ended up repeating several grades, and eventually became chronically truant. Early in his school career, he became known as a behavior problem. When he was twelve or thirteen years old, Oliver began to use drugs. He was convicted of several juvenile offenses, and was committed to a maximum-security juvenile facility at the age of fourteen. Coincident with his incarceration, Oliver was referred for special education testing and identified as suffering from an emotional disturbance, as well as a AD/HD and a speech/language disorder.

As a result of his identification as a child with disabilities, Oliver was finally able to receive needed services to address his emotional/behavioral needs, speech/language disorders and learning disabilities. He also received individual and group counseling, as well as vocational training and transition services. With these services, Oliver soon began to improve his academic performance in school and started making progress toward getting his GED. He hopes to repair computers when he is released from the correctional facility, and with the training he is receiving, he should be able to realize his goal.

"Youth with Disabilities in the Juvenile Justice System," an undated document prepared by the Office of Special Education Programs (OSEP) of the U.S. Department of Education; cited January 2002.

An estimated 30 to 50 percent of youth in juvenile corrections are identified as youth with disabilities. While the factors associated with overrepresentation of youth with disabilities in juvenile corrections are complex, evidence suggests that school failure, poorly developed social skills, and inadequate school and community supports are related to this phenomenon. Research suggests that effective community-based and school-based interventions can prevent antisocial behavior, reduce risk factors, and enhance protective factors for youth. Yet prevention efforts are often deterred by a general lack of collaboration on the part of the various agencies, schools, and community organizations involved with this population. Many youth, including those with disabilities, do not receive the collaborative prevention services, graduated sanctions, education services while incarcerated, and transition services that would deter future offending.

Why This Issue Is Important

Research has shown that school wide prevention activities, mobilization of neighborhoods, after school recreation, and interagency collaboration and support can reduce delinquency. Effective prevention, appropriate treatment of disabled youths who are incarcerated, and effective transition systems would be expected to lead to a decline in the disproportionate representation in the delinquency system of children with disabilities and a coincident decline in overall rates of incarceration for children.

Key Principles of Practice

- A three-pronged approach for working with youth with disabilities and who are either at risk for or currently involved in the juvenile justice system includes:

  Preventing antisocial behavior among youth

  Providing appropriate special education services in juvenile corrections and related systems

  Facilitating the process of transition as youth leave correctional facilities and reenter their home schools and communities

- Collaboration among education, mental health, social services, and other child-serving agencies as well as families is important to effective prevention, as well as effective treatment of youth who are incarcerated.

- Many youth who are involved in the juvenile justice system have not been provided with the services they need to address their disabilities. The Individuals with Disabilities Education Act requires that eligible youths be identified, located, evaluated, and have appropriate services made available to them in accordance with the law.

- In many cases, youth who are involved in the juvenile justice system failed to be identified as disabled for a number of years, and as a result may have increasingly fallen behind in academic achievement and repeated several grades. Early identification of children who are eligible for special education services can help prevent not only academic failure but also delinquency.

- If a child is determined to be eligible for special education and related services, school personnel, including teachers and evaluators, together with the parent and with the child, as appropriate, must develop an Individualized Education Program (IEP) to address the child's individual needs. The IEP is a written document that includes among other components, the specific special education, related services, and depending on the age of the child, transition services to which the child is entitled.

- A majority of individuals in both juvenile and adult correctional facilities are marginally literate or are illiterate and many have experienced school failure and retention. Research also suggests that among youth on parole or probation after they leave juvenile facilities, rates of recidivism and re-offending are inversely related to reading ability. Teaching reading and writing to youth who are disabled is, therefore, a crucial component of any prevention program, as well as key to assuring a smooth transition for those who are incarcerated as they reenter their schools and communities.

Where to Go for More Information

Office of Special Education Programs
Office of Special Education and Rehabilitative Services
U.S. Department of Education
400 Maryland Avenue
Washington, DC 20202
Tel: 202-205-5507
Internet: http://www.ed.gov/offices/OSERS/OSEP/index.html

The National Center on Education, Disability and Juvenile Justice (EDJJ)

University of Maryland Department of Special Education
1224 Benjamin Building
College Park, MD 20742
Tel: 301-405-6462
Fax: 301-314-5757
Internet: http://www.edjj.org
E-Mail: edjj@umail.umd.edu

EDJJ is a collaborative research, training, technical assistance and dissemination program designed to develop more effective responses to the needs of youth and disabilities in the juvenile justice system (JJS) or those at-risk for involvement with the JJS.

Chapter 35

Substance Abusers and AD/HD

In February 1999, the National Center on Addiction and Substance Abuse (CASA) at Columbia University hosted a conference with the National Center for Learning Disabilities and the National Institute on Drug Abuse. The objective of the conference was to better understand the relationship between substance abuse and learning disabilities. The CASA conference and subsequent white paper attempted to answer the following questions:

- Does having a learning disability increase an individual's vulnerability to start using drugs?

- Does a learning disability increase the chance that a person will become addicted to drugs?

- Do drugs compound existing learning disabilities?

The conferees, representing the medical, education, and treatment communities, agreed that while learning disabilities may increase the risk for substance abuse, they were not able to identify the precise

"Substance Abuse and Learning Disabilities: Is There a Link?" by Peggy Patten, from *Parent News* for March-April 2001, National Parent Information Network (NPIN); "Boys Treated with Ritalin and the Relationship to Substance Abuse Later in Life," from *Parent News* for November/December 1999, National Parent Information Network (NPIN); and "AOD Use and Attention Deficit/Hyperactivity Disorder," by Timothy E. Wilens, M.D., from *Alcohol Health and Research World,* Volume 22, Number 2, 1998, produced by the National Institute on Alcohol Abuse and Alcoholism (NIAAA).

nature of the link between substance abuse and learning disabilities. After examining existing research, they did, however, concur on the following:

• The link between learning disabilities and substance abuse begins in the womb.

• Prenatal smoking and drug or alcohol abuse can seriously damage the fetus and result in learning disabilities.

• Children with learning disabilities are at a higher risk for academic failure and for peer rejection risk factors associated with substance abuse.

• Children with learning disabilities are twice as likely to have attention deficit hyperactivity disorder, a behavioral disorder that often appears in combination with a learning disorder. Individuals with ADD/AD/HD are twice as likely to abuse substances and have greater difficulty shaking addiction.

Authors of the CASA white paper make clear that correlation is not causation and that having a learning disability does not insure that a child will abuse drugs. Yet, the authors contend that the high statistical coincidence occurring in these two conditions warrants further attention. They recommend the following next steps:

• Conduct needed research, particularly with older children, to further our understanding of the linkages between substance abuse, learning disabilities, and behavior disorders.

• Refine diagnostic criteria that help identify specific learning disabilities and behavior disorders.

• Inform parents so they can: (1) understand the risks involved in abusing alcohol, cigarettes, and other drugs during pregnancy; (2) identify and respond to children's learning disabilities and behavior disorders early on; and (3) respond to children's academic difficulties and peer rejection that may lead to increased risk for substance abuse.

• Educate physicians, teachers, guidance counselors, and treatment professionals so they understand the relationship between substance abuse, learning disabilities, and behavior disorders, and so they can accurately identify and respond to each condition alone and in combination. The white paper, "Substance

Abuse and Learning Disabilities: Peas in a Pod or Apples and Oranges?" can be read online at the Web site of the National Center on Addiction and Substance Abuse at Columbia University (http://www.casacolumbia.org/index.htm).

Boys Treated with Ritalin and the Relationship to Substance Abuse Later in Life

In an August 2, 1999, news release, the National Institute on Drug Abuse (NIDA) reported the findings of a study conducted jointly with the National Institute of Mental Health (NIMH). The study compared the susceptibility to substance use disorder among three groups of boys: 56 boys with attention deficit hyperactivity disorder (AD/HD) who had been treated with stimulants for an average of 4 years, 19 boys with AD/HD who had not been treated with stimulants, and 137 boys without AD/HD. AD/HD, the NIDA news release explained, is characterized by difficulties in paying attention, in keeping still, and in suppressing impulsive behaviors. It is usually treated with stimulants, such as methylphenidate (Ritalin) or dextroamphetamine (Dexedrine, Adderall) because these drugs reduce the behavioral and attentional problems connected to AD/HD.

All boys in the study were at least 15 years old when they were evaluated for substance abuse involving alcohol, marijuana, hallucinogens, stimulants, or cocaine. Results of the study showed that 75% of the nonmedicated AD/HD boys had at least one substance use disorder, compared to 25% of the medicated AD/HD boys and 18% of the boys without AD/HD.

The study researchers at Massachusetts General Hospital, Harvard School of Public Health, and Harvard Medical School calculated that treating AD/HD with medication (stimulants were used in over 90% of the cases) was associated with an 84% reduction in risk of developing a substance use disorder. The researchers will continue to study this entire group of boys in a follow-up study funded by the NIDA.

NIDA Director Alan Leshner says, "while some clinicians have expressed concern about giving stimulants to children with AD/HD because they fear it might increase the risk that these children will abuse stimulants and other drugs when they get older, this study seems to show the opposite. Treating the underlying disorder, even if with stimulants," says Leshner, "significantly reduces the probability they will use drugs later on."

Alcohol and Other Drug (AOD) Use and Attention Deficit/Hyperactivity Disorder

Children with attention deficit/hyperactivity disorder (AD/HD) often continue to exhibit significant impairment in academic, occupational, and social functioning throughout adulthood. In addition, children with AD/HD are at increased risk for developing alcoholism and other drug addictions, especially if alcoholism or AD/HD exists in other family members.

Alcohol and other drug (AOD) abuse may develop earlier in life (i.e., in mid adolescence) when AD/HD is accompanied by certain behavioral or mood disorders. The nature of the link between AD/HD and AOD use disorder is unknown, although the association may be mediated by co-occurring disorders. In addition, AD/HD-related AOD abuse may develop initially as an attempt to alleviate symptoms of mental distress associated with chronic failure, feelings of inadequacy, and conflict with parents and peers. Therapeutic intervention should incorporate both addiction and mental health treatment, including appropriate use of psychiatric medications.

Since the beginning of the century, terms such as hyperactive have been used to define a heterogeneous group of restless and inattentive children who display learning difficulties. Many such children exhibit the condition now known as attention deficit/hyperactivity disorder (AD/HD).

Children with AD/HD may run about aimlessly, fidget and squirm when seated, and talk excessively. They are often irritable, impatient, and impulsive. Additional symptoms may include difficulty concentrating, forgetfulness, daydreaming, and easy distractibility. The disorder may persist into adulthood, accompanied by significant academic, occupational, and social impairment.

The presence of AD/HD is an important risk factor for the development of alcoholism and other disorders associated with the use of alcohol and other drugs (AODs).[1] In addition, AOD use disorders (AODDs) tend to appear earlier and to progress more rapidly in persons with AD/HD. Alcoholics with AD/HD also are less likely than those without AD/HD to remain in alcoholism treatment programs or to achieve moderation or abstinence (Tarter and Edwards 1988). The identification of specific risk factors for AODD in persons with AD/HD may permit more targeted prevention and treatment programs for both disorders at earlier stages of their development.

322

Extent of Comorbidity of AD/HD and AODD

AD/HD and AODD occur together in the same person, either simultaneously or sequentially, more often than would be expected by chance (Wilens et al. 1996). Symptoms of AD/HD appear years before the development of AODD, often as early as infancy (APA 1994).

Studies have identified comorbid AD/HD in 25 to 30 percent of certain adolescents with AODD. However, the subjects of the studies were repeat criminal offenders and patients in residential settings who were undergoing treatment for psychiatric and addictive disorders (Wilens et al. 1996). Consequently, the applicability of those results to the general population is uncertain. Among adults with AODD, rates of AD/HD range from 15 to 25 percent (Wilens et al. 1996).[2] Conversely, approximately 50 percent of adults with AD/HD exhibit AOD abuse or dependence (Wilens et al. 1996). Data suggest that the risk of AODD developing at any time over the life span of an adult with AD/HD is twice that of adults without AD/HD (52 percent versus 27 percent, respectively) (Biederman et al. 1995).

Evidence from family studies confirms an association between co-occurring AD/HD and AODD. Elevated rates of alcoholism are consistently found in parents of youth with AD/HD (Wilens et al. 1996). Conversely, child and adolescent offspring of alcoholics, compared with children of nonalcoholics, exhibit lower attention spans; higher levels of impulsivity, aggressiveness, and hyperactivity; and elevated rates of AD/HD (Wilens et al. 1996). Those data support the hypothesis that both disorders are familial and probably genetically transmitted.

The interpretation of family studies is complicated by the possible influence of prenatal exposure to AODs. For example, the offspring of alcohol- and cocaine-dependent mothers are at increased risk for psychiatric abnormalities, including AD/HD (Wilens et al. 1996). Family genetic data in those studies are generally insufficient to determine the relative contributions of AOD exposure; parental psychopathology; and the interaction of genetic and environmental factors, such as the effects of poverty and poor prenatal care.

Course and Remission

AODD appears at an earlier age among adults with, compared with those without, AD/HD (mean age 19 versus 22) (Wilens et al. 1997). In addition, adults with AODD exhibit increased severity of AOD use problems when AD/HD is also present (Carroll and Rounsaville 1993). The presence of AD/HD appears to accelerate the transition from AOD abuse to dependence (Wilens et al. 1998) and increases the risk for developing a drug use disorder among subjects already abusing alcohol (Biederman et al. in press).

AD/HD also affects the rate of recovery from AODD. In one study, adults with AD/HD took more than twice as long as subjects without AD/HD to recover from comorbid AODD (144 versus 60 months, respectively). In addition, AODD lasted more than 3 years longer in the subjects with AD/HD (Wilens et al. 1998).

Possible Mechanisms

The underlying mechanisms that link AD/HD to AODD remain unknown but may involve complex interactions among biological and psychological factors. Two possible contributory factors of particular significance to risk evaluation and treatment strategy are comorbidity with additional psychiatric disorders and the use of AODs to self-medicate psychological distress.

Comorbid Psychiatric Disorders

Certain psychiatric conditions frequently co-occur in youth with combined AD/HD and AODD (Wilens et al. 1996). Among those conditions are bipolar disorder and conduct disorder. Juvenile bipolar disorder is characterized by irritability and mood swings. Conduct disorder is characterized by a persistent pattern of aggressive behavior, criminality, or violation of social norms (APA 1994). Childhood AD/HD is associated with the development of AODD in adolescence independent of other comorbid psychiatric conditions. However, the presence of conduct disorder or bipolar disorder confers a risk for an even younger onset of AODD (i.e., at age 16 or younger) independent of AD/HD (Wilens et al. 1997; Biederman et al. 1997). Although anxiety and depressive disorders may co-occur with AD/HD, they do not appear to confer additive risk for the development of AODD during adolescence in AD/HD youth (Biederman et al. 1997).

Self-Medication

Evidence suggests that some use of AODs represents in part an attempt to ameliorate psychiatric symptoms and their associated subjective states of distress (Khantzian 1997). The academic under-achievement and behavioral problems associated with AD/HD may result in conflicts with adults and peers, chronic failure, and demoralization. It is plausible that some people with AD/HD may develop

AODD in response to the emotional effects of social, occupational, and emotional impairment and accompanying poor self-image. Consistent with this theory, adolescents with AD/HD report using AODs for mood adjustment rather than to achieve a high (Biederman et al. 1995; Wilens et al. 1996).

Treatment Considerations

Treatment of patients with comorbid AD/HD and AODD should be based on a thorough evaluation of relevant psychiatric, social, cognitive, educational, and family factors, along with a history of the patient's AOD use and treatment. The clinician should rule out medical and neurological conditions whose symptoms may overlap with AD/HD (e.g., the restlessness and emotional lability of hyperthyroidism) or result from use (e.g., agitation associated with withdrawal) (Riggs 1998).

The treatment of AD/HD and AODD must be considered simultaneously; however, if the addiction is active, it must be treated immediately (Riggs 1998). Depending on the severity and duration of the AODD, patients may require treatment in a residential facility. Psychosocial therapies aimed at co-occurring AD/HD and AODD may be combined with patient and family education, attendance at self-help groups (e.g., Alcoholics Anonymous), and the use of appropriate medications (i.e., pharmacotherapy) (Riggs 1998).

Pharmacotherapy

Medications play an important role in the long-term treatment of AD/HD. The influence of such treatment on the subsequent development of AODD remains unclear and may depend in part on the severity of the underlying condition. Nevertheless, results of preliminary studies suggest that certain medications can alleviate AD/HD symptoms in adolescents and adults while reducing co-occurring AOD use or cravings (Levin et al. 1997; Riggs 1998).

The most commonly used medications for treating AD/HD are the psychostimulants, a class of medications that promote increased ability to concentrate, wakefulness, and alertness. Psychostimulants prescribed for AD/HD include amphetamine (Dexedrine), methylphenidate (Ritalin), and pemoline (Cylert) (Riggs 1998). Children with AD/HD treated with those medications may exhibit increased ability to pay attention in class as well as improved academic and social performance.

Psychostimulants themselves are subject to abuse. Of the three psychostimulants previously mentioned, pemoline has the lowest potential for abuse, followed by methylphenidate and amphetamine (Riggs 1998; Drug Enforcement Administration [DEA] 1995). The use of psychostimulants as prescribed for AD/HD does not promote subsequent misuse of stimulants themselves or of other potentially addictive drugs (Hechtman 1985). In one study, patients with AD/HD who were untreated and those who had poorer responses to psychostimulants exhibited more illegal AOD use than did patients treated successfully (Loney et al. 1981). However, patients with AD/HD and their families should be instructed not to give psychostimulants to persons to whom they are not prescribed (DEA 1995).

Additional medications used to treat AD/HD include various antidepressants (e.g., bupropion [Wellbutrin], imipramine [Tofranil and others], and venlafaxine [Effexor]) and certain medications commonly prescribed to treat high blood pressure (e.g., clonidine [Catapres]) (Spencer et al. 1996). The choice of such medications depends in part on potential adverse interactions with AODs that the patient may be using. During the course of pharmacotherapy, the clinician should frequently monitor compliance with treatment, perform random urine analyses to detect AOD use, and coordinate treatment with other caregivers.

Conclusions

Research supports a relationship between AD/HD and AODD, with symptoms of AD/HD appearing many years before the earliest onset of AOD abuse. AODDs that begin in adolescence run a more severe course than those that appear in adulthood. Therefore, prevention and early treatment strategies should be directed at children with AD/HD before AOD use problems develop and become chronic (Wilens et al. 1997). More studies that follow disease development over the life span are needed to distinguish the relative contributions of causal factors linking these disorders and to identify youth at increased risk for AD/HD-AODD comorbidity.

Notes

1. AOD disorders considered here include addiction (i.e., dependence) and abuse.

2. By comparison, between 10 and 30 percent of adults in the United States exhibit alcohol use disorders (Kessler et al. 1997).

References

Biederman, J. Attention-deficit/hyperactivity disorder: A life span perspective. *Journal of Clinical Psychiatry* 59(Suppl. 7):4–16, 1998.

Biederman, J.; Wilens, T.E.; Mick, E.; Milberger, S.; Spencer, T.J.; and Faraone, S.V. Psychoactive substance use disorders in adults with attention deficit hyperactivity disorder AD/HD: Effects of AD/HD and psychiatric comorbidity. *American Journal of Psychiatry* 152:1652–1658, 1995.

Biederman, J.; Wilens, T.; Mick, E.; Faraone, S.; Weber, W.; Curtis, S.; Thornell, A.; Pfister, K.; Jetton, J.; and Soriano, J. Is AD/HD a risk for psychoactive substance use disorder? Findings from a four year follow-up study. *Journal of the American Academy of Child and Adolescent Psychiatry* 36:21–29, 1997.

Biederman, J.; Wilens, T.; Mick, E.; Faraone, S.V.; and Spencer, T. Attention deficit hyperactivity disorder influences the path to substance use disorders. *Biological Psychiatry*, in press.

Carroll, K.M., and Rounsaville, B.J. History and significance of childhood attention deficit disorder in treatment-seeking cocaine abusers. *Comprehensive Psychiatry* 34:75–82, 1993.

Drug Enforcement Administration (DEA). Methylphenidate review document. Washington, DC: DEA Office of Diversion Control, Drug and Chemical Evaluation Section, 1995.

Hechtman, L. Adolescent outcome of hyperactive children treated with stimulants in childhood: A review. *Psychopharmacology Bulletin* 21:178–191, 1985.

Kessler, R.C.; Crum, R.; Warner, L.; Nelson, C.; Schulenberg, J.; And Anthony, J. Lifetime co-occurrence of *DSM IV* alcohol abuse and dependence with other psychiatric disorders in the national comorbidity survey. *Archives of General Psychiatry* 54:313–321, 1997.

Khantzian, E.J. The self-medication hypothesis of substance use disorders: A reconsideration and recent applications. *Harvard Review of Psychiatry* 4:231–244, 1997.

Levin, F.R.; Evans, S.M.; McDowell, D.; and Kleber, H.D. Methylphenidate treatment for cocaine abusers with adult attention-deficit/hyperactivity disorder: A pilot study. *Journal of Clinical Psychiatry* 58:1–21, 1997.

Loney, J.; Kramer, J.; and Milich, R. The hyperactive child grows up: Predictors of symptoms, delinquency and achievement at follow-up. In: Gadow, K., and Loney, J., eds. *Psychosocial Aspects of Drug Treatment for Hyperactivity.* Boulder, CO: Westview Press, 1981. pp. 381–415.

Riggs, P. Clinical approach to treatment of AD/HD in adolescents with substance use disorders and conduct disorder. *Journal of the American Academy of Child and Adolescent Psychiatry* 37: 331–332, 1998.

Spencer, T.; Biederman, J.; Wilens, T.; Harding, M.; O'Donnell, D.; and Griffin, S. Pharmacotherapy of attention deficit disorder across the life cycle. *Journal of the American Academy of Child and Adolescent Psychiatry* 35:409–432, 1996.

Tarter, R.E., and Edwards, K. Psychological factors associated with the risk for alcoholism. *Alcoholism: Clinical and Experimental Research* 12:471–480, 1988.

Wilens, T.E.; Biederman, J.; and Spencer, T. Attention deficit hyperactivity disorder and the psychoactive substance use disorders. In: Jaffee, S., ed. *Pediatric Substance Use Disorders: Child Psychiatric Clinics of North America.* Philadelphia: Saunders, 1996. pp. 73–91.

Wilens, T.E.; Biederman, J.; Mick, E.; Faraone, S.V.; and Spencer, T. Attention deficit hyperactivity disorder (AD/HD) is associated with early onset substance use disorders. *Journal of Nervous and Mental Disease* 185:475–482, 1997.

Wilens, T.; Biederman, J.; and Mick, E. Does AD/HD affect the course of substance abuse? Findings from a sample of adults with and without AD/HD. *American Journal on Addictions* 7:156–163, 1998.

Chapter 36

Advice for College Students with AD/HD

Chapter Contents

Section 36.1

Legal Rights of the College Student with AD/HD

From "Attention Deficit Disorder in College: Faculty and Students, Partners in Education," by Patricia H. Latham, J.D., and Peter S. Latham, J.D., with information and assistance from Kathleen G. Nadeau, Ph.D., Patricia O. Quinn, M.D., and Mary MacDonald Richard. © 2001 Patricia Latham and Peter Latham; reprinted with permission.

ADD which substantially limits a major life activity such as learning is a disability under two important federal statutes that apply to most colleges: the Rehabilitation Act of 1973 (RA) and the Americans with Disabilities Act (ADA).

Section 504 of the RA prohibits discrimination against otherwise qualified students with ADD that substantially limits a major life activity such as learning. The RA applies to all colleges that receive federal funds: all public colleges and most private colleges. The RA requires that students with disabilities that substantially limit a major life activity be provided with academic adjustments and auxiliary aids so that the courses, examinations and activities will be accessible to them.

The ADA prohibits discrimination against otherwise qualified students with ADD that substantially limits a major life activity and requires that those students be provided with reasonable accommodations. The ADA applies generally to public and private colleges, regardless of whether or not they receive federal funds.

Many colleges are offering programs and/or support services for students with learning disabilities and ADD. Most require standardized admissions tests—SAT or ACT—but some waive these tests as an accommodation in the admissions process. Students with ADD and/or learning disabilities who take standardized admissions tests may be eligible for test accommodations, e.g. extra time, breaks, alternative format. To establish eligibility, the disability must be documented in accordance with the requirements of the testing service.

Students with ADD may choose if and when to disclose their disabilities. If admissions and/or test accommodations are not needed, a student may elect to disclose the disability after admission. Remember, if the college is not aware of the disability, the college would not be required to provide accommodations.

In disclosing disabilities and requesting college accommodations, the student should consult with professionals to determine what documentation to provide to the college. The particular accommodations that a student may need is an individual matter. Some students may have one or more learning disabilities in addition to ADD. The request for accommodations should take into account how the disabilities impact on the student's learning. If a student has questions about confidentiality of information regarding the disability, he or she may consult with independent professionals and/or college personnel.

Colleges must provide legally required services at no additional charge to a student with a disability. Generally, the college must provide services necessary to make courses, examinations and activities accessible to a student with a disability but is not required to provide remedial services to improve the skill level of the student in the area of his or her disability. For example, test accommodations and note takers would be provided free of charge to students in need of those accommodations. Colleges may charge supplemental fees for services that are over and above legal requirements. For example, a fee may be charged for the services of a remedial reading tutor.

There are various mechanisms to enforce these statutes. Complaints may be filed with the Office for Civil Rights of the Department of Education. The ADA may be enforced by the Department of Justice as well as by private action.

Possible Accommodations by Colleges

In general, accommodations should provide the student with structure and reduced distractions, assistance with organizing and prioritizing, clear guidance as to expectations, and specific and repeated instructions, as needed. As with any disability, particular accommodations should be tailored to the needs of the individual to maximize success in learning. Some possible specific accommodations are:

1. Provide structure and reduce distraction in class.

2. Simplify and repeat instructions, as needed, both orally and in writing.

3. Give frequent and specific feedback from faculty and disability services staff.

4. Accommodations in courses may include: priority registration, reduced course load, taped textbooks, tape recorders, course modifications, tailoring assignments, modified text books, priority seating in the front of the room, study guide and summary of important points.

5. Accommodations in examinations may include: extra time, quiet room, alternative format and opportunity to seek clarification.

6. Allow course substitutions to fulfill certain requirements, e.g. for foreign language and mathematics.

7. Offer as electives alternative learning style courses, e.g.. history through film and internships to emphasize hands on learning.

8. Educate the student regarding ADD, coping strategies and advocacy techniques.

9. Encourage the use of support groups, counselors and advisors to assist with academic, career and other issues.

10. Review rules and expectations and use behavioral management techniques as needed.

Possible Strategies for Students

As with any disability, strategies should be tailored to the needs of each student to maximize success in college. Some possible strategies are:

1. Continue to educate yourself regarding ADD, strategies, and accommodations that might be useful and legal rights and advocacy techniques.

2. Sit toward the front of the class to help you focus.

3. Use note takers or a tape recorder in classes.

4. Take time to get to know faculty and disability support staff and seek them out to request any assistance you need. Seek help as soon as you experience difficulties. Consider working with a counselor or advisor to help you learn coping strategies.

5. Keep a planner (assignment book or electronic scheduler) in which you record your assignments, due dates for papers and

projects, your plans for completion, your personal deadlines for steps to completion, dates of quizzes, mid terms and finals exams, and your plans for study periods.

6. Pick a quiet and comfortable study place (e.g. your room, library or an available classroom), schedule study periods and take frequent breaks to get physical movement and refresh yourself.

7. Set aside 15 minutes at the end of your study time to review where you are on your various projects and to plan the next day.

8. Select courses that are high interest and a good fit for your learning style. Consider taking a reduced course load. If possible, request course substitutions to fulfill requirements that pose great difficulty for you because of your disability. If you must take a difficult course, consider taking it during the summer or during a semester in which you have a light load.

9. Request needed accommodations in advance in courses, examinations and activities.

10. Ask questions if you do not understand an assignment or an exam question, and, if you remain unsure, you may note in writing your question and then proceed to complete the task to the best of your ability and understanding.

Section 36.2

Ways that Students Can Help Themselves

This text is reprinted from *College Students with Learning Disabilities: A Handbook, Seventh Edition,* by Susan A. Vogel, Ph.D. © 2000 Susan A. Vogel. Reprinted with permission. To obtain a complete copy of the Handbook, contact the Learning Disabilities Association of America, LDA Bookstore, 4156 Library Road, Pittsburgh, PA 15234-1349, 412-341-1515 (voice), 412-344-0224 (fax), or visit their website at www.idanatl.org.

General Strategies

1. Many students with LD come to college and do not anticipate needing any accommodations or support services. However, if you have been previously diagnosed as having a learning disability, secure a copy of the most recent evaluation or Individualized Education Plan (IEP). You will need to provide this documentation or be reevaluated in order to be eligible for services.

2. Learn about Section 504. Find out what accommodations and support services your college provides, and, should you need them, where to find them.

3. Increase your understanding of the nature of learning disabilities in general and specifically the type and severity of your own learning disability by discussing your test results with an LD specialist.

4. Rehearse your explanation of the previous information with your LD specialist or a friend so that you can explain fully to faculty the reason for requesting an accommodation such as extended time on an examination.

5. Based on your self-understanding, identify the accommodations you need and in what courses you will need them. Discuss these with the LD coordinator/specialist in the DSS office and request an official letter describing the accommodations that you can use if needed. If you require classroom accommodations

of some kind, schedule an appointment with your instructor early in the semester to discuss the accommodations you need.

6. If you need to tape record lectures, ask permission of the instructor before doing so as a courtesy to the instructor. Be sure to explain why you need this modification and how you will use the tape to enhance your learning.

7. Take notes simultaneously while tape recording. Indicate questions in the margin when material is unclear. If your tape recorder has a counter, begin it at zero in the beginning of the lecture, and note the counter number in the margin next to your question.

8. Listen to tape, rewrite notes, and highlight key concepts, as soon after class as possible. Compare your notes with a study partners.

9. Apply the following principles of effective learning when you study. They will increase your chances of success. Included are:

   - Complete the reading assignments prior to class. Associating the lecture with the readings is a lot easier than listening to the lecture cold. In addition, you will be better prepared to ask the instructor for clarification and/or elaboration and to participate in class discussion, should the opportunity arise. Most instructors value the active participation of students who come to class prepared.

   - Attend all classes. Other students can get by missing an occasional class, but for you, hearing the lecture may be a critical factor in learning new material.

   - Preview new material and review the previous lecture before each class.

   - Sit toward the front of the class so you can hear and see well and be more easily recognized if you have a question or want to participate in the discussion.

   - If you tape record in class, carefully label every tape (for example, Side 1, Intro to Psychology, 2/8/00) before you insert it into the recorder. Set the counter to zero and if you are unsure of a concept during the lecture, jot down the counter number in the margin of your notes for easy review and clarification later.

- Review tapes and/or notes as soon after the lecture as possible. Compare your notes with a study partner's notes. Copy notes over, if necessary. Highlight and summarize the main points. Keep a glossary of important terms, lists of key concepts, major events, contributors and their theories, or formulas.

10. Keep a master calendar. Make sure it's large enough to enter assignments, exams, social events, and important appointments. Use other calendars for specific tasks, e.g., a wall calendar for long-range assignments.

11. Work backwards from due date on long-range assignments and build in extra time. Go over this time line with your instructor and ask for feedback on your progress periodically.

12. Make sure you have understood the assignment correctly and completely before plunging in or soon after you have started by scheduling an appointment with your instructor early. Don't wait till you have finished the assignment to find out you have not fulfilled the requirements.

13. Often, the hardest part of getting your work done on time and keeping up with the workload is getting started on a new assignment. Start by making a commitment of 30 minutes and then lengthen the studying periods gradually.

14. Because most college students with LD have trouble recognizing and correcting spelling errors in their handwriting, it is important to use a word processor with a spell checker and grammar check to identify misspelled words and incorrect grammar. However, proper nouns and homonym errors may not be identified. Use the grammar check to identify inappropriate prepositions and word choices, errors of punctuation, or poor sentence structure. If your instructor agrees to the plan, request a writing tutor, friend, roommate, or relative proofread your paper and assist you in error identification and correction as a final step.

15. Reach out for assistance early, if needed. Schedule an appointment with your instructor when you begin to get confused or flounder. Do not wait until you are already in danger of failing the course. Speak to the coordinator of the Office for Disabled Student Services and/or your advisor and find out what help is available.

16. Be aware of Drop-Add and Pass-Fail options and deadlines to adjust your schedule. Use them to your advantage to enhance success.

17. Make yourself available to speak to the student body, faculty, administration, and staff about learning disabilities. Organize public lectures, student panels, films, and videos. Write articles for the student newspaper on your campus.

18. Become a student member of and/or provide input to policy making university committees.

19. Find out if there is a support group for students with learning disabilities on your campus and become an active member in this group. At such group meetings you will find out your problems are not unique and you are not alone in your struggles. In addition to the comfort that provides, you will learn studying and test taking strategies and about instructors whose teaching style will be most compatible with your learning style.

20. Call the International Dyslexia Association at 412-296-0232 and find out how your student support group for those with learning disabilities (or if you do not presently have one, how you could start a student group) could become affiliated with a national network of student support groups. Official student organizations on campus receive financial support from the student government. Find out how your group could be recognized as an official student organization and qualify for funding.

21. Provide peer counseling and support to other students with learning disabilities on an individual basis or through a support group on campus.

22. Join professional organizations as a student member advocating for rights of adults with learning disabilities and other persons with disabilities (e.g., Learning Disabilities Association, The Association of Higher Education and Disabilities (AHEAD), and the International Dyslexia Association).

Memory Strategies

1. Learning is synonymous with reviewing and for you, reviewing frequently and regularly throughout the semester is essential.

2. Color code, enlarge, underline, and highlight your notes to strengthen your visual memory of the material.

3. Copy your notes over, if for you, the act of writing facilitates memorizing.

4. Read aloud (tape recording while reading) if hearing with or without seeing words helps you remember what you've read.

5. Tape record lectures and listen to them while driving, exercising, eating, grocery shopping, etc.

6. Rehearse material to be mastered either orally or in writing. Write out concepts in full. Read your notes silently or aloud whichever works best for you. Paraphrase or explain concepts to a friend.

7. Review frequently and commit material to memory using strategies that aid recall such as listing, categorizing, drawing, imaging, revisualizing, alphabetizing, devising acronyms, and associations.

Test-Taking Strategies

1. Find out what examination format your professor will use (e.g., long-answer essay questions, multiple choice, short-answer essay questions). Ask your professor for practice exams or find out if old exams are available. Take as many as you can and check your answers against the answer key, with a tutor, study partner, or graduate assistant.

2. If no prior exams or questions are provided, and if essay-type exams will be given, try to anticipate the questions that will be asked on the exam. Write out your answers to the anticipated questions.

3. Be sure to go into exams rested and not having just consumed a large amount of sugar or caffeine; complex carbohydrates and some protein will provide the best source of energy over an extended period of time.

4. If you have memorized specific formula, dates, names, or terminology for an exam, before you begin working on the exam, write down all that you have committed to memory and use, as needed, later in the exam.

5. Read test directions carefully, underlining the verb that describes what you are to do: describe, compare, summarize, list. Then follow the directions precisely.

6. Begin by answering the easiest questions first. Circle the hard ones and come back to them after you have answered the easy ones.

7. Pace yourself. Even if you have extended time, it is not unlimited.

8. If you come to a question you don't understand, paraphrase it for the proctor in order to get confirmation that you have understood what the question meant.

Self-Confidence Building Strategies

Building self-confidence is not an easy task. Many people benefit from the assistance of a counselor, psychologist, or therapist on a one-to-one basis or in a support group. You should explore such options in the counseling center on campus. In addition, the following strategies may prove helpful:

1. After preparing as well as you could, tell yourself as you go into an exam or to make a presentation, you will succeed and you are well prepared, rather than you are going to fail.

2. Identify a realistic goal and work toward it. When you succeed in accomplishing it, identify the strategies that you developed that contributed to your success. Building self confidence is a step by step process in which you meet increasingly difficult challenges and take credit as you accomplish each one.

3. If you don't achieve your goal on the first attempt, sit down with a family member, friend, teacher, or counselor and analyze and refine your strategies. Identify new strategies and intermediate goals that will prepare you better to achieve your final goal. Tell yourself, "Next time I know I'll do better."

4. Develop a time line to accomplish each goal, building in extra time for the unexpected. Remember, there is no point rushing toward failure. Take a long range perspective on your life, rather than focusing on just one semester.

5. Keep a list of your past successes and accomplishments and read this list over frequently.

6. Take credit for your achievements and work well done. Accept compliments with a simple thank you. A compliment is like a gift. When you reject a compliment, you are rejecting not only the compliment but also the person giving it. How would you feel if you brought a gift for someone and it was rejected? If your performance did not meet your expectations, you can critique it at a later time with your teacher, coach, counselor, or friend.

7. Identify your strengths and keep expanding the list of what you do well. Your learning disability gave you some special talents as well as difficulties. Identify your talents, develop them, and enjoy them.

8. Keep disappointments in perspective; a D on one quiz does not mean you will fail the course; a D in one course does not mean you will be dismissed from college.

9. If you do poorly on a paper or exam, find out why rather than condemning yourself or rejecting the good along with the ineffective strategies that you may have used. Chalk it up to experience. Mistakes are often the best teachers. By analyzing what went wrong, you will be better able to avoid such mistakes in the future.

10. Look at your friends. What do you admire and respect in them? Because they also chose you as a friend, you share in their attributes and have other qualities that they admire and respect as well.

11. Dress for success. If you are not sure of the appropriate dress code for a specific occasion, setting, or social event, check ahead of time with a knowledgeable person.

12. Smile. People who smile send a message to others that they are comfortable with themselves and are self confident. Smiling is contagious. You will find people around you will reflect your facial expression, be much more pleasant, and have confidence in you when you smile.

13. Look at those who have expressed confidence in you, provided you with opportunities, and given you responsibilities. These people know you well, have observed your past performance, and have confidence in your abilities and potential to succeed. As you accept new challenges, keep them and their confidence in you clearly in mind.

Part Five

Adults with AD/HD

Chapter 37

Diagnosing AD/HD in Adults

Hyperactivity is more difficult to diagnose in adults than children, according to researchers. More studies are needed in this area. Studies have also determined that adults with AD/HD have lower brain metabolism than normal adults. Hyperactive adults are generally not nearly as fidgety as children or teens, but they do have the symptoms such as restlessness, attention difficulties, and impulsiveness.

As we continue to search for answers and to conduct research to unravel the mystery of hyperactivity, we are uncovering more and more about the disorder that strikes not only children, but teens and adults as well.

Research continues to reveal how stimulant medications affect brain metabolism; how early intervention or identification might affect the long-term outcome and prognosis for these children; whether or not training and behavior modification are useful; and how researchers can use PET scans to study hyperactive children and teens, and possibly diagnose AD/HD.

From "Diagnosing AD/HD in Adults," and undated fact sheet from the National Institute of Mental Health (NIMH), available online at http://www.nimh.nih.gov; cited January 2002; and text beginning at the heading "Adult Woman and AD/HD," from "Feeling Overwhelmed, Disorganized, Scattered? Is It Just Stress, or Could You Be a Woman Struggling with Undiagnosed Attention Deficit Disorder?" by Kathleen G. Nadeau. Ph.D. © 1998 Kathleen G. Nadeau. Reprinted with permission.

Some Symptoms of AD/HD in Adults

You may have ADD if you: Have trouble completing projects and jump from one activity to another. Were told by parents and teachers that you should have tried harder in school. Are frequently forgetful; have trouble remembering to do the things you intended. Frequently rushing, over-committed, often late. Make impulsive purchases, impulsive decisions. Feel overwhelmed and disorganized in your daily life. Have a disorderly purse, car, closet, household, etc. Are easily distracted from the task you are doing. Go off on tangents in conversations; may tend to interrupt. Have trouble balancing your checkbook; difficulty with paperwork.

Having difficulty with one or two of these things doesn't mean you have ADD. This list isn't meant as a questionnaire for self-diagnosis; but if you find yourself answering yes to many of the questions listed above, it may be very helpful to seek an evaluation from a professional very experienced in diagnosing ADD in adults. (A good place to begin your hunt for such a professional is to call the child ADD experts in your community.)

Adult Women and AD/HD

Most of us are familiar with hyperactivity and attentional problems in kids, and the debate over whether Ritalin is being over-prescribed. You may have also read an article here or there about ADD in adults. John Ratey and Ned Hallowell's book on ADD, *Driven to Distraction*, made its way to the *New York Times* best seller's list. But chances are that you haven't read much about girls or women with ADD. Why not? Because ADD has long been considered a male problem that affects only a few girls and women.

What are the signs of ADD in women? ADD in females can often be masked. Women with ADD are most often diagnosed as depressed. And many women with ADD do struggle with depression, however that is only part of the picture. For most women with ADD their lives are filled with disorder which can feel overwhelming—piles and clutter out of control. There are some women with ADD who have successfully compensated for their ADD, but the price they pay is to expend most of their waking energy combating their natural tendency to be disorganized. Many women with ADD feel a powerful sense of shame and inadequacy. They feel constantly behind, overwhelmed and frazzled. Some women with ADD feel that their lives are so out of control that they rarely invite others into their home—too ashamed to allow anyone to see the disorder, too overwhelmed to combat the disorder that pervades their lives.

ADD can be mild, moderate or severe. Some women are able to cope with the demands of daily life until they become a mother. For other women, their coping abilities don't collapse until baby number two comes along. The job of housewife and mother is especially difficult for women with ADD because of its very nature. To raise children and to run a household well we are required to function in multiple roles at the same time, to cope with constant, unpredictable interruptions, to function with little structure, little support or encouragement, and to not only keep ourselves on track, but also be the scheduler of everyone else in the family. Who has soccer practice? Who has a dentist appointment? Who needs new shoes? Who needs a permission slip signed? Where is the permission slip? Who needs to go to the library? Who needs us to drop everything this minute because they skinned their knee or because they have an ear ache and want to come home from school? And in the midst of all this we are supposed to keep on track, planning meals, doing housework, laundry, planning social events, and, for the majority of mothers, working full time.

ADD has become a more challenging problem for women as the demands in our late twentieth century lifestyles become greater and greater. Now we are expected to juggle homemaking, child care and full time employment, along with a full complement of extra-curricular activities for our children. What is highly stressful for a woman without ADD, becomes a continuing crisis for a woman with ADD. These women frequently suffer from anxiety, depression and low self-esteem because they find they can't live up to the superwoman image that so many women attempt today.

What is the difference between ADD and stress? Stress is temporary or cyclical. A woman who feels disorganized and overwhelmed due to stress will heave a huge sigh of relief when the holidays are over or when the crunch at work has passed, and will set about returning her life to order. For a woman with ADD, the stressful times are bad, but even in the best of times there is a feeling that the wave of to do's is about to crash over her head.

If you are an undiagnosed woman with ADD, help could be just around the corner. Women who have blamed themselves for years as lazy or incompetent have received help, through ADD-oriented psychotherapy, medication and ADD coaching and are now feeling and functioning much better.

Chapter 38

Coping and Compensatory Strategies for Adults with AD/HD

A study was conducted to determine if adults who experience attention problems but obtain higher degrees and achieve occupational success use different coping strategies than those who do not. We also hoped to gather a list of coping strategies that might help improve functioning. Thirty-seven adults (12 men, 25 women) with significant symptoms of attention-deficit/hyperactivity disorder (as measured by an AD/HD symptom checklist) served as the study sample. These adults, whose average age was 42 years, met with one of the investigators for a one-on-one interview that included completing a coping inventory, a brief demographic profile and an intelligence test. They also answered questions about actual strategies they used to minimize the impact of AD/HD symptoms at home, school and work.

Findings indicated that the sample was composed of bright (average IQ=112) individuals who attained an average of 15 years of schooling and achieved an average occupational rank of semi-professional. Individuals with higher levels of occupational achievement used approach strategies (logical analysis, positive reappraisal, seeking guidance and support, and problem solving) more frequently than their less achieving peers.

From "AD/HD and Issues for Adults: Coping and Compensatory Strategies Used by Adults with Attentional Problems," by Robert D. Wells, Ph.D., Barbara B. Dahl, M.A., and David Snyder, M.D. This article originally appeared in *Attention!* Magazine, Volume 6, Number 5, Page 22. © 1996-2001 CHADD; reprinted with permission. For more information write to CHADD at 8181 Professional Place, Suite 201, Landover, MD 20875, or visit CHADD at their website www.chadd.org.

Higher achieving adults were more likely to try to approach a situation in a positive fashion and to logically analyze it. They were likely to seek help from others, use problem solving to generate possible solutions, think of different ways to deal with the problem, and to step back from the situation and be more objective. They were more likely to review in their mind what they would say or do, to anticipate how things would turn out, to find some personal meaning in the situation, and to anticipate new demands. In addition, they were more likely to talk to a spouse, friend, relative or professional about the problem, and to pray for guidance and strength. Participants who achieved higher levels of academic achievement also used more coping strategies than their less achieving peers did. Interestingly, those who were more academically successful were significantly less likely to use acceptance/resignation as a coping strategy.

Participants who had been previously professionally diagnosed with AD/HD used less acceptance and resignation and attained higher levels of education than those who were not diagnosed. Those who reported having been treated with medication for attentional problems used less acceptance and resignation and more positive appraisal and problem solving than did participants who had never been medically treated. Differences were also found between adults based on their level of education and occupation as to what strategies they used to compensate for attention difficulties. Adults who had attained higher levels of education were more likely to report that they used strategies, while those with lower educational achievement were more commonly unaware of any strategies that might help. For example, 47 percent of adults with relatively low educational achievement did not know how to make themselves feel more successful, whereas only seven percent of the more highly educated group were similarly unaware.

The researchers concluded that in this study, when managing an important problem, individuals with attention problems who are more achieving engage in greater efforts to actively approach and cope with their difficulties. These higher achieving adults were also less likely to simply accept or become resigned to their difficulties. Achieving adults devised a variety of strategies showing creative problem-solving solutions to deal with their AD/HD symptoms.

Because developing such solutions requires an awareness of one's difficulties and an ability to use trial and error problem-solving strategies to find ways that increase personal effectiveness, it is possible that children and teenagers who believe they can control their destiny are more likely to use approach coping and complex strategies. Those who become demoralized may rely too heavily on avoidance coping strategies and feel resigned to academic and occupational difficulties. The finding that adults who had been diagnosed and treated for AD/HD used less acceptance and resignation is interesting and supports the growing wealth of data that early treatment leads to better outcomes.

Compensatory Strategies Used by Adults with Attention Problems

What helps you get through repetitive tasks?

- Using deadlines for structure
- Using last-minute pressure to get energized
- Delegating to another person
- Doing a small amount of the task at a time
- Working with another person
- Varying tasks—doing several things at the same time
- Setting up rituals
- Persisting

What helps you control your impulses?

- Talking to yourself (in-your-head conversations)
- Switching gears mentally, thinking of something else
- Switching gears physically, leaving the situation

What helps you avoid environmental distractions?

- Going to a quiet place, isolating yourself
- Using background white noise such as music or television
- Hyper-focusing

What helps you control the intensity of unpleasant feelings?

- Taking time out mentally to talk to yourself or with another person
- Taking time out physically, going for a walk or exercise
- Leaving the situation

349

What helps you when you try to fix a problem and fail?

- Getting away, putting it out of your mind and re-focusing on the problem later
- Talking to others or to yourself
- Delegating the task to someone else

What helps you retain large amounts of information?

- Taking notes
- Using flash cards for schoolwork
- Watching someone else and then doing it, not relying on written instructions
- Asking questions and linking the idea or task to something that is already known
- Going to a quiet place and hyper-focusing
- Working on chunks of material at a time

What helps you stay organized?

- Making notes to yourself (lists, post-its, calendar, daily planner)
- Goal setting—structure each day (use mental mapping)
- Prioritizing
- Doing lots of projects at any one time
- Piling things and paper
- Delegating
- Pressure to get it done

What do you need in a job to help you feel satisfied in it?

- Action every day—every day has a new routine
- Many tasks at one time
- Dealing with different people all the time
- Sense of accomplishment—pats on the head
- Being creative
- Being in charge of myself and my time

- Quick fixes—work that can be accomplished with quick bursts of energy
- Structure
- Quotas and pressure

What helps you maintain relationships with family and friends?

- Maintaining eye contact when talking
- Asking questions so they know you are listening and interested
- Talking out your feelings with someone else
- Stepping back mentally and physically, going to another room

Chapter 39

Adult AD/HD and Social Skills

At the recent CHADD Conference in Washington, D.C. they came in large numbers. They quickly filled the room and then sat on the floor in the aisles until there wasn't an inch of carpet showing. They filled the hallway outside the room. They filled the adjoining tiny kitchen area and the bathroom. Yes, even the bathroom people stood in the tub and sat on the commode to listen to the lecture. Others were angry that they were unable to get near enough the lecture to listen. What was all this fuss about?

Social skills. They came to hear about adult AD/HD and social skills. According to Richard Lavoie, "Social competence, not academic skill, is the primary determiner of adult success." Many adults with AD/HD have learned ways to compensate in their jobs and activities of daily living. But many continue to struggle with a lack of social connections in their life.

Social skills are not specifically taught, and yet the penalties are harsh for those who violate these unwritten social rules. Often, most don't even know what they're doing wrong, so there's little chance to improve. People struggle quietly with social isolation or social rejection, longing for connections with others, yet unsure how to proceed.

From "Adult AD/HD and Social Skills: What Does Everybody Else Know That I Don't?" by Michele Novotni, Ph.D. This article was originally in *Attention!* Magazine, Volume 6, Number 3, Page 24. © 1996-2001 CHADD. For more information write to CHADD at 8181 Professional Place, Suite 201, Landover, MD 20875, or visit CHADD at their website www.chadd.org.

My son Jarryd had worked hard to overcome the academic diffi-culties associated with AD/HD. He had become an academic success, but he desperately struggled in the area of social relationships. Al-though I had been a behavior management consultant for over 15 years and had helped teach many people social skills, I had never been as painfully aware of the consequences of social skill difficulties as I was when the problem hit home.

At the age of 10, Jarryd had not been invited to a birthday party out-side of our family. No one at school wanted to come over to play when he would call. No one invited him over to play. He was overwhelmed with frustration and sadness. My heart broke to see my child in such emo-tional pain. Jarryd did not seem to be committing any overt social viola-tions. He wasn't aggressive or obviously rude. But somehow he was doing or not doing something that had others choosing not to be with him. I began to notice similar social difficulties in many of the adults with AD/HD with whom I worked. Often social difficulties at home and work caused a great deal of emotional pain in their lives. Many were strug-gling with the weight of social isolation or rejection.

Little has been written to date on social skills especially in the area of adult AD/HD and social skills. Review of the existing literature was not encouraging regarding the effectiveness of teaching of social skills, but I knew from my years of work in other settings that it could be done. This began my journey into the world of AD/HD and social skills. In this chapter I'll share with you some of the key concepts in improv-ing social skills.

Attribution Theory

Although many people struggle with social skill difficulties, those with AD/HD have additional difficulties because of the attributions others often make regarding their AD/HD characteristics. According to attribution theory, people try to make sense of their world so they make explanations of behaviors based upon what they already know and understand (Taylor et al, 1997). Therefore, many times the AD/HD symptoms of inattention, impulsivity, hyperactivity or disorgani-zation are attributed to a lack of caring, a lack of motivation, rude-ness, being self-centered and the like. The title of the Kelly Ramundo book, *So You Mean I'm Not Lazy, Stupid, or Crazy?!* captures the misattributions all too well.

Unless people in your life understand AD/HD, there is a tendency for them to attribute your social difficulties to all sorts of negative characteristics. However, once they understand AD/HD they then have something else to attribute your behaviors to and are much less likely to see you in a negative light.

Subtext

A social skill difficulty for many with AD/HD involves missing the subtle nuances of communication. Unfortunately, what is said is often not what is actually meant. You may have a difficult enough time trying to hear what is being said. Often there is not the energy to figure out if that is what is actually meant. It would be great if our world had little pop-up bubbles like those on music videos to tell you what is really going on, but until that happens, following are some tips.

Assessment

In order to improve your social skills, you'll need a realistic picture of your strengths as well as areas that need improvement. It's difficult to work on improving your social skills if you don't understand what it is that you are or are not doing. Self-assessment, along with assessments by others, can help you see blind spots that others can see clearly. However, others will usually not tell you about your social errors unless you specifically and openly ask. For example, Jarryd discovered that his excessive talking often drove others away. He asked a simple question. "Why didn't they just tell me I was talking too much? I can't believe they think that it's rude to tell me that I talk too much. I think it's much ruder to not play with me." Although I agree with him, and perhaps you do too, we don't make the rules.

Take a few minutes to go over the following brief checklist. Ask others to also fill out a copy. When you know what areas you need to improve, you'll have a sense of direction and you'll no longer feel blindsided by these mysterious social errors.

Becoming a subtext detective:

1. Look for clues in your environment to help you decipher the subtext. Be mindful of alternative possibilities. Be observant.

2. Be aware of body language, tone of voice, behavior and the look in someone's eyes to help you interpret what is really being said.

3. Look at the choice of words the person uses to help you detect the subtext. ("I'd love to go" probably means yes. "If you want to," probably means I'd rather not, but I'll do it.)

4.   Actions speak louder than words. If someone's words say one thing but his actions reveal another, it would be wise to consider that his actions might be revealing his true feelings.

5.   Find someone to act as a guide to help you with this hidden language. Compare your understanding of reality with the guide's understanding of reality. If there is a discrepancy, you might want to try the other person's interpretation and see what happens, especially if you usually get it wrong.

6.   Learn to interpret polite behavior. Polite behavior often disguises actual feelings.

7.   Be alert to what others are doing. Look around for clues about proper behavior, dress, seating, parking and the like.

Strategies

Attitude: Be open to growing in the area of social skills. Be open to feedback from others.

One Goal: Using your assessment and the assessments of others, pick one goal at a time to work on. Yes, pick only one. You'll be much more successful if you tackle the skill areas one at a time.

If, for example, you struggle with missing pieces of information due to attentional difficulties, you may develop a system of checking what you heard with others. "I heard you say that....Did I get it right? Is there more?" Or you could ask others to check with you after they give you important information: "Please tell me what you heard me say." In this way, social errors aren't committed because you missed important information.

Observe others: You can learn a great deal by watching others do what you need to learn to do. Use people in your life as well as people on television to serve as role models.

Role play: Practice the skill you need with others. Get their feedback on how you are doing.

Visualization: Gain additional practice and improve the ability to apply this skill in other settings by using visualization. Once you know what you want to do, rehearse this in your mind. Imagine actually using the skill in the setting you will be in, with the people you will be interacting with. Repeat this as many times as possible to help you overlearn the skill. In this manner, you can gain experience in the real world, which will greatly increase the likelihood of your success.

Prompts: Set yourself up for success by using prompts to help you stay focused on your social skill goal. The prompts can be visual (an index card), verbal (someone telling you to be quiet), physical (a vibrating watch set every four minutes reminding you to be quiet), or a gesture (someone rubbing his head) to help remind you to work on your social skill.

Learn skills of anger management, negotiation and compromise: Even though you may not get exactly what you want all the time, if you are able to be included socially with a group of people you want to be with—you still win.

Increase your likeability: Social exchange theory states that we maintain relationships based on how well those relationships meet our needs (Taylor, et al., 1997). People are not exactly social accountants, but people do on some level weigh the costs and benefits of being in relationships. Many with AD/HD are considered high maintenance. Therefore, it is helpful to see what you can bring into relationships to help balance the equation. Researchers (Anderson, 1968) have found that the following traits are characteristic of highly likeable people:

• sincere	• dependable	• happy
• honest	• thoughtful	• unselfish
• understanding	• considerate	• humorous
• loyal	• reliable	• responsible
• truthful	• warm	• cheerful
• trustworthy	• kind	• trustful
• intelligent	• friendly	

Any of the likeability characteristics you can develop or improve upon should help your social standing.

There are specific things you can learn about yourself as well as specific skills you can learn to help improve your social skills. Seek help through reading, counseling or coaching. You can improve social connections in your life. Social skills can be learned; they do not need to remain a mystery. You too can learn the skills that everybody else seems to know.

About the Author

Michele Novotni, Ph.D., is author of *What Does Everybody Else Know That I Don't? Social Skills Help for Adults with AD/HD—A Reader Friendly Guide* (1999, Specialty Press) and co-authored, *Adult ADD: A Reader-Friendly Guide to Identifying, Understanding, and Treating Adult Attention Deficit Disorder* (1995, Pinion Press). She lectures extensively on AD/HD. She has more than 20 years of experience as a psychologist working with children and adults with AD/HD and a lifetime of experience living with AD/HD as both her son, Jarryd, and her father have AD/HD. She is an assistant professor in the graduate counseling department of Eastern College, Saint Davids, Pennsylvania.

References

Anderson, N.H. (1968). "Likeableness ratings of 555 personality-trait words." *Journal of Social Psychology*, 9, 272-279. Cited in S. Taylor, L. Peplau, and D. Sears, *Social Psychology, 9th ed.* (1997). Upper Saddle River, New Jersey: Prentice Hall. p. 235.

Ramundo, Kelly, Kate, and Peggy (1996). *So You Mean I'm Not Lazy, Stupid or Crazy?!*, New York: Fireside.

Lavoie, R. (1994). Learning disabilities and social skills: last one picked...first one picked on. Washington, D.C.: WETA-TV.

Novotni, Michele (1999). *What Does Everybody Else Know That I Don't? Social Skills Help for Adults with AD/HD*. Specialty Press: Plantation, Florida.

Taylor, S., Peplau, L., and Sears, D. (1997). *Social Psychology, 9th ed.* Upper Saddle River, New Jersey: Prentice Hall,. p. 235.

Whiteman, Thomas, and Novotni, Michele (1995). *Adult ADD: A reader-friendly guide to identifying, under-standing, and treating adult attention deficit disorder*. Colorado Springs, Colorado: Pinion Press.

Chapter 40

Couples and AD/HD

When one partner in the relationship has ADD, it's critically important for both of them to understand not just how the ADD effects that person, but also how it effects the relationship.

The partner with ADD is likely to be less organized, less predictable, and less attentive than the other one. It can be easy for the non-ADD partner to misinterpret those behaviors as not caring or as being passive-aggressive......that's simply not true in most cases.

Most of the time ADD behaviors which cause problems are not malicious behaviors—usually it's just a case of the ADD not being managed well and the person needing to learn more coping skills. It helps to keep in mind a biological perspective though—that the basis for most ADD behavior is biological in nature—it has to do with how the brain works—and is not usually due to bad intentions or lack of caring.

It's also easy for the non-ADD partner to become frustrated and fall into a critical/blaming mode of behavior—that usually just makes things worse. Sit down and discuss specific behaviors which are causing problems and then make some changes in how things are done—like any couple must do, with or without ADD. Focus on the behavior as the problem though, not the person—a very important distinction.

Another problem is if the non-ADD partner becomes the rescuer in the relationship, and the person with ADD takes on the helpless victim role. This is very bad for both partners involved and will only lead to more problems.

The couple needs to clearly delegate responsibility for certain duties or jobs, and each of them has to follow through on their end without being babied or bullied by the other. The person with ADD needs to structure the environment in whatever way he/she needs to make sure that those things get done.

People with ADD are not crippled in any sense and should never use ADD as an excuse for irresponsible behavior. If some behavior is a problem.....fix it. Never make excuses.

In their book *Driven to Distraction*, Edward Hallowell M.D. and John Ratey M.D. provide some great suggestions for couples living with ADD:

- Make sure you have an accurate diagnosis—it could be ADD, or something else

- Keep a sense of humor!!

- Declare a truce after the diagnosis...i.e. end the squabbling and fighting

- Set up a time for talking

- Spill the beans—tell each other what's on your mind!

- Write down your complaints and your recommendations

- Make a treatment plan

- Follow through on the plan

- Make lists!

- Use bulletin boards for messages

- Put notepads in strategic places—by the bed, in the car, etc.

- Consider writing down what you want the person to do and give it to them on the day it's supposed to get done

- Pay attention to your sex life

- Avoid the pattern of mess-maker and cleaner-upper

- Avoid the pattern of pesterer and tuner-outer

- Avoid the pattern of victim and victimizer

- Avoid the pattern of sadomasochistic struggle as a routine was of interacting

- In general, watch out for the dynamics of control and dominance
- Break the negativity cycle
- Use praise and encouragement frequently
- Learn about mood management
- Let the one who is the better organizer take on the job of organization
- Make time for each other
- Don't use ADD as an excuse

Chapter 41

20 Things Adults with Attention Deficit Disorder (ADD) Would Like Their Partners to Know

Submitted by adults with AD/HD:

1. There is no correlation between AD/HD and intelligence!

2. I am not selfish or lazy.

3. I may have to take notes, and if I write something that's irrelevant to the discussion, it's because I want to get it out of my brain so it doesn't distract me from what you're saying.

4. I'm not deliberately misunderstanding you. I do tend to latch on to a picture of what you're saying, and it can be wrong. If I ask interminable questions, it's because I want to be sure I get what you're saying. It's a sign of respect for you.

5. If I'm out of order, just tell me that. I get conclusions mixed in with facts easily, and with a little patience, we can work out what needs to come first, middle, and last.

6. I want my partner to allow me to win (Don't focus on what I did not get done or what I did incorrectly, look for what I have completed and accomplished and ignore the rest.)

7. Have the patience to allow me to learn what they are trying to teach.

8. You are one of the people who sustain me, and quirks or no quirks—I have every intention of meeting your needs.

9. I try. Even if it looks like I'm not. I am also as tired of failures (maybe more) than you are. Just remember I try.

10. I am frustrated with my abhorrent short term memory.

11. I prefer to refer to ADD as Multi Focal Cognition a term that better describes my drifting thoughts and tangential conversations.

12. The answer to the question: "Why can't you just get your act together and do things like normal people?" is: "Normal is a selection on a washing machine, imagine how boring we'd all be if we were all normal."

13. ADD is not something that gets cured, but that gets treated and something that one lives with every day.

14. I will probably always forget things, lose things, miss details and have difficulty paying attention. Some days will be better than others.

15. We think a little different, just as it is tough to understand how we think in your mind, so it is with us to understand how your mind works. It doesn't make us stupid or uncaring, just different!

16. No two ADDers' symptoms and main problems are going to be exactly alike.

17. No one ADDer is going to be exactly the same in magnitude of problems from day to day.

18. Never forget that we're in this together. to support, teach and learn from one another, always remembering that we all have challenges to conquer and we need to keep a positive attitude in meeting our challenges.

19. This is not anyone's fault, it just is.

20. Accept me for who I am and relish my uniqueness.

Chapter 42

Close Relationships, Intimacy, and AD/HD

AD/HD is no longer viewed as a children's illness, but as a syndrome continuing into adulthood. The adult symptom picture usually includes less pronounced hyperactivity and more problems with inattention, distractibility and forgetfulness. AD/HD adults are also likely to have frequent mood swings. Possibly because of the difficulty in coping with AD/HD, many adults become involved with drugs and alcohol. Many AD/HD adults report this is the only way that they can slow down and feel halfway normal. Adults with AD/HD often develop depression. In view of these symptoms, it is not surprising that many adults with attentional problems are referred by their spouse for AD/HD evaluation and treatment. These adults may arrive at the office with a frustrated, angry husband or wife who voices complaints such as: "He never remembers family outings." "She won't follow through on errands." "He doesn't finish projects in the house." "She won't sit and formulate a plan for dealing with the kids." Often, spouses have given the AD/HD adult an ultimatum—"find out what is wrong with you, get treated, or else..."

While most of the descriptive information on AD/HD is focused on the classroom and work setting, these same symptoms can lead to frequent emotional outbursts, destructive anger, and dissolved relationships

"Close Relationships, Intimacy, and AD/HD," by H. Russell Searight, Ph.D., originally published in *Attention!* Magazine, Volume 6, Number 2, Page 44. © 1996-2001 CHADD. For more information write to CHADD at 8181 Professional Place, Suite 201, Landover, MD 20875, or visit CHADD at their website at www.chadd.org.

at home. Some researchers report that AD/HD adults are more likely to be divorced than those without AD/HD.

Many of us in choosing a long-term partner may unconsciously be looking for someone who complements our own personality. A shy, withdrawn man may feel drawn to a vivacious, outgoing woman to fill a personal void.

While AD/HD is often described in negative terms—a lack of attention, memory and life direction—AD/HD often has some positive characteristics such as spontaneity, creativity and a zest for new experiences. These are often the qualities that were attractive to the non-AD/HD partner. Similarly, AD/HD adults may have initially been drawn to their husband or wife because of their patience, endurance and goal-directed focus. As one AD/HD man put it, "I was really drawn to Susan because she knew what she wanted out of life and knew how to get there. I thought that she could provide me with the focus I've never had." While differences may be some of the sparks that begin a relationship, with time they often become a source of considerable conflict.

Forgotten anniversaries, missed children's birthday parties, impulse buying, and bouts of short-lived anger and irritability may quickly take a toll on even the most loving relationship. Partners of AD/HD adults complain that their spouses make major purchases such as a new refrigerator or car without consulting them first. Family activities may be chosen in the same way. A vacation cruise, to begin next week, may be reserved without consulting wife or children, and without appreciating that family members may have their own work or school schedules.

The AD/HD adult's distractibility and problems focusing may unintentionally distance them from their spouses and children. Intense, brief, angry outbursts may be frightening—particularly to children. When the AD/HD adult puts a fist through a glass door panel because the key doesn't work, or becomes frustrated with the ice maker and breaks it further rather than fixing it, family members become anxious and confused. Typically the AD/HD individual is genuinely surprised and puzzled about the impact these episodes have on those closest to them: "C'mon get over it, let's move on," they say.

Intimacy may be difficult because AD/HD adults may have difficulty genuinely knowing their partners. They may be drawn in part because of the novelty of a new person. This initial attraction may be based on superficial attraction, (appearance, a shared hobby) rather than their values or personality. Over a brief time, the attraction wanes and the AD/HD adult is often in search of someone else with the explanation that the relationship just didn't feel right without knowing why. This impressionistic approach to relationships leaves the other partner feeling confused, frustrated and alone. This feeling of being alone may also permeate the AD/HD adult's social life, "There's an emptiness in me—I don't know how to fill it." "I have many acquaintances but no one really knows me—it's lonely to be in a house full of people or on a date and feel a wall between me and everyone else."

Problems with distractibility and maintaining focus may also create frustration in the bedroom. The AD/HD adult may have difficulty paying close attention to their partner during sex. This inattention may leave the partner feeling alone—"it's like he's not with me." As a result, the deeper meaning of sexuality in a long-term relationship may not occur. Stimulation, rather than an underlying expression of closeness to the partner, may be the primary force in sexual intimacy. This pattern may in turn lead the AD/HD adult to seek multiple partners in an undirected drive for novelty and new sensations. Hallowell and Ratey also noted that this drive for stimulation may contribute to extramarital affairs among AD/HD adults. Again, these are likely to be impulsive, brief relationships that occur independently of their ongoing commitment to their spouse.

When AD/HD Becomes Part of an Unhealthy Relationship

When evaluating children for AD/HD, it is not uncommon to hear a parent to say, "I'm worried about my son's distractibility because his father is AD/HD." The verb "is" implies that the symptoms are the husband's personality. The challenge posed by inattention and distractibility overshadow the partner's identity, including their positive characteristics.

In long-term relationships that include a partner with previously diagnosed AD/HD, the syndrome may become an unhealthy defining feature of the couple. Because of one or both partners' personal conflicts around dependency and control, relationships may develop into a one-up one-down pattern. The non-AD/HD partner becomes the rational adult in relation to the AD/HD partner who is erroneously perceived as chronically irresponsible and undependable. The partner's forgetfulness, impulsiveness and difficulties with task completion may become magnified to stabilize the marriage as a patient-caregiver relationship.

Over time, a spouse may give up on their AD/HD partner and develop a separate life while remaining physically, but not emotionally engaged in the relationship. Hallowell and Ratey note that the AD/HD adult, after years of criticism for forgetfulness, not listening, and poor communication, may also give up and develop a separate lifestyle from a life partner.

Relationship Skills

How can AD/HD adults have satisfying relationships? The answer: communication! While love may play an important role in choosing a long-term partner, romantic feelings alone will not sustain a relationship. Enduring and satisfying marriages include partners committed to the daily effort required for relationship success. Richard Stuart, a marriage and family therapist, emphasizes the importance of clear, concrete and specific communication. A good first step is using "I" statements in which the partner speaks from his or her own frame of reference. ("The trash can in the kitchen is overflowing. I would appreciate it if you would take the trash out.")

Distressed couples often communicate with "you" statements. "You" statements automatically create a climate of defensiveness. ("You haven't taken the trash out! You're so lazy, you don't think you need to lift a finger around this house...") A common expectation, particularly of couples who have been together a long time, is that one person should be able to read the other's mind. While many of us in long-term relationships are able to respond to our partner's unspoken needs and wishes, periodically we fail miserably. In relationships in which mind-reading is expected, anger and resentment will frequently build to destructive accusatory explosions.

Couples should also avoid criticizing their partner's personality. Statements such as "You're never interested in me, you don't care about my needs," or "You are so selfish and self-centered," will by themselves create conflict. These labels also have a degree of permanence, making it difficult for a spouse to see alternative, generous, thoughtful behavior. It's important to remember that the AD/HD adult typically has suffered a long history of negative labels such as "lazy," "irresponsible," "never follows through" or "no direction in life," beginning in childhood. When a spouse uses these labels, they may unfortunately become self-fulfilling prophecies in a marriage.

One of the most difficult skills to learn is conflict containment. When emotions are high, it becomes challenging to use many of these common skills. In addition, if one partner feels angry or irritable about something else such as a hard day at work or a flat tire, it is best for them to cool down before discussing a serious problem. This guideline should not be an excuse to stonewall and refuse to address an issue. Instead, a wife should say, "I'm sorry, right now I can't really talk about this, I'm still very upset about what happened today at work. I'd like to wait and talk about it after dinner." However, it's very important that the person who wants to delay be able to state specifically when they will have this discussion. Simply saying, "Not now! I'm just really fed up with everything!" is not helpful.

In the process of conflict resolution, it is important that the more distressed partner be able to speak openly without interruption. Typically, the degree of anger, frustration or hurt will gradually dissipate if they can simply listen closely and try to understand the feelings expressed. Once the feelings have begun to wind-down, the listener should factually summarize the issues causing distress. The next step should be trying to find an agreed upon solution for the problem so the same conflict does not arise over and over.

A final skill is to be sure to attend to the small affirmations that make relationships work. The AD/HD adult, while genuinely wanting to do things for a spouse, may have difficulty prioritizing. They should use their day planner or appointment book to remember to do small things to show they care. ("Bring flowers home today." "Call husband at work and tell him I love him.") While this may seem to take the romance and spontaneity out of a relationship, relying solely upon spur of the moment loving feelings may not be practical in a long-term relationship with busy spouses, particularly in a family with children.

As many happily married people remind us, relationships are hard work. This job is even more challenging when one or both partners have AD/HD. It's particularly important that the disorder is not used as a way of devaluing or putting down an AD/HD partner. In particular, because of their history of feeling misunderstood, criticized and socially isolated, the AD/HD adult deeply appreciates the love and caring of a life partner. Fortunately, the heart of a successful relationship, communication, is a skill that can be learned. The sustained work required to listen well and clearly convey one's desire to support is well worth the effort.

About the Author

H. Russell Searight, Ph.D., is the director of Behavioral Medicine for Family Medicine of St. Louis. He is also adjunct associate professor of Community and Family Medicine for the St. Louis University

School of Medicine and adjunct professor of Psychology for St. Louis University.

Chapter 43

Advice from an Adult with AD/HD

Ok, so you have been diagnosed with AD/HD. You have been given a prescription for medication and you've read the bible according to Hallowell and Ratey. In my case, after the initial sense of relief subsided, I had to ask myself an important question—what do I do next?

Before I continue with my offerings of wisdom on this subject, let me first qualify my remarks by saying that I am not a health care professional. I am not qualified to offer professional advice on this neuro-psychiatric condition and/or its treatment. I am, however, someone with AD/HD who wishes to share some coping strategies that work for me and to offer some encouragement to those who are still searching.

Medication can make a big difference in focusing on-task and reducing distractions, but it only goes so far with respect to the whole problem. Perhaps the biggest disappointment in medication on the whole is that it can truly give a false sense of security. After an initial honeymoon period, I realized that there was a lot of hard work ahead of me. When I first began taking medication over a year ago, the initial response was nothing short of astounding. I felt focused, driven and productive. It took a while to get the dosage correct, and eventually my doctor and I found that it was a combination of medications

"AD/HD and Issues for Adults: Advice from a Certified Non-Expert," by Robert Tudisco, Esq., from *Attention!* Magazine, Volume 7, Number 2, Page 39, © 1996-2001 CHADD. For more information write to CHADD at 8181 Professional Place, Suite 201, Landover, MD 20875 or visit CHADD at their website at www.chadd.org.

at different times of the day that worked best for me. In the months that passed, I also realized that there are many facets of AD/HD that are not aided by medication and that my challenges were just beginning.

After reading anything and everything that I could get my hands on and taking my medication religiously, it was somewhat frustrating when I would slip into situations that had AD/HD written all over them. On the one hand, the education I had received from my reading and research helped me to understand why this was happening. On the other hand, they made it all the more frustrating. I became my own worst critic—I was constantly thinking, "I should know better now," or "This should not be happening to me." This is a very easy and frustrating trap to fall into, and the only thing to do is to shake it off and keep plugging away.

While medication is invaluable in the treatment of AD/HD, its role is limited. So I began to look at the coping skills that got me through Catholic school, college and law school. I highlighted what has worked in the past and what can work in the future.

The highly structured and inflexible environment of my Catholic elementary was very helpful in keeping me moving. While this environment wreaked havoc on an already low sense of self-esteem and confidence, I believe that people with AD/HD need that structure to point us in the right direction and to push us forward. In the highly structured environment of a Catholic school, the consequences of inaction or mistakes were severe enough to keep me moving. I imagine that life in the military would work the same way.

In college, especially during the semesters when my grades were the highest, I examined what was going on in my life and what my routines were. Exercise was a major part of my daily routine—not only did it help me focus, but the discipline of doing it religiously carried over into my schoolwork. When I was stressed out I would run, regardless of the time of day. I found solitude and was able to think clearly. It was my time to put my thoughts in perspective and mentally file things. Physical fitness wasn't the goal—I literally needed to take my mind out for a run.

Nowadays, I wake up at 5 a.m. three days a week and run four to five miles, hopefully in the dark, and always alone. It accomplishes many things for me. It clears my head, organizes my thoughts, maps out my day, but most importantly it does something very important for my AD/HD. I have always felt plagued by the lack of control over my life. Feelings of no control or a lack of self-esteem are common symptoms of AD/HD. My run is my time—period—for that hour, three days of the week. I am the master of my own universe. It may not be much, but it is something I look forward to. Running also helps me in that it sets a very positive tone for my day. I think that the discipline of going out religiously carries over into the rest of my life. I find that habits, once formed, are easy to maintain. After all, we are creatures of habit. The problem with AD/HD adults is that, all too often, it was undiagnosed in childhood. As a result, AD/HD adults rarely developed good habits as children.

Does this mean that running is a cure for AD/HD? Hardly. Does this mean that it will benefit every one? Probably not. The important thing is that it appears to have an effect for me. Each of us is different, yet we have a common theme of concerns. The important thing is to find what works for you and make it part of your life.

Another technique that I discovered in college helped me to cope with my terrible reading comprehension. As we all know, especially inattentive types like myself, the ability to read anything is virtually impossible. The AD/HD mind wanders quickly either out of boredom or as it is distracted by external stimuli. A friend of mine who worked in an accounting office introduced me to foam earplugs. They were distributed at her office to aid the employees in reading difficult (and boring) portions of the tax code. I tried them and was amazed at my ability to literally climb into whatever I was reading. I could create an artificial tunnel in which to focus on my task. From that day on, I always carried a pair in my book bag. I used earplugs to take all of my exams. I found I could actually create a situation in which I could completely shut out the rest of the world and concentrate on the task at hand. Years later, during the bar exam, I had several pairs of earplugs and made good use of them during the two-day exam. I don't know if I could have gotten through without them.

The problem with earplugs, while great in school, is that the modern office environment is not at all conducive to completely shutting yourself off from the rest of the world. Phones ring, people drop into your office and so this presented a more difficult problem. A modified solution that works for me is to play music in my office during the day to help me concentrate on-task—not just any music. I play instrumental music, either classical music, Spanish guitar or some other type of background music and it aids me tremendously in focusing. I have heard about studies that have been done in which certain types of music promote focus and attention. I have heard about something known as the Mozart effect. The term is very interesting in that Mozart himself is thought to have had AD/HD. I do not know why this works, although I have my own theories. Perhaps, the music serves as a white noise, which filters out distractions and keeps me on-task. Perhaps, the music serves to be more boring than the task at hand, thereby inducing concentration or perhaps the music serves to occupy the part of my mind that tends to wander. I prefer this explanation most of all. I visualize the inattentive child inside of my head. I picture that the music entertains him and allows me to concentrate. Whatever the reason, it doesn't matter, it works for me and so I do it.

Another thing that helps me to cope with my AD/HD is to outline everything. I always try, if possible, to think in terms of outlines. It is important for me to visualize a hierarchy of things if for no other reason than it organizes the chaos in my brain. I am a trial attorney and when I am on trial, I outline the case, the questioning of each and every witness, my opening statement, summation and even jury selection. The funny thing is that when I am actually on trial and in front of the jury, I rarely use these outlines. They serve as an organizational tool in preparing my thoughts before hand. Once I stand to address the court or the jury, my free flow and my AD/HD (the good part of my AD/HD) take over. I become a man possessed, only now, my free flow has direction and there is order to it.

In preparing for trials, I developed another coping mechanism which grew directly out of my natural disorganization. Early on in my career, I was plagued by disorganization. I believed that I had good instincts, but a mountain of papers in front of me masked them. I was concerned that my chaos translated into a lack of confidence in me as an advocate. With perception being everything, I had to find a solution, so I devised a system—my form of a trial notebook that kept everything at my fingertips. It was perfect. I could put my outlines in it, as well as all of the reports and exhibits so I could find everything at a second's notice. I bought some transparent sheet protectors and put all of the reports in chronological order inside. They were labeled and indexed. I found that not only was I organized inside of the courtroom, but also more importantly, preparing the book was much like the map that I made for myself when I outlined things. It helped me organize the case in my head before having to perform. It served as a solid foundation for the time in front of the jury when my AD/HD would take over. The funny thing about it was that when my adversaries and colleagues would see me flipping through this notebook, and say things like, "Wow, I wish I could be organized like that," or "You must be one of those super organized people." I always laugh when I hear that.

The trial notebook I just mentioned evolves with every case I try. Perhaps the evolution of the system keeps it fresh and exciting. Like the notebook, these coping skills will develop if you keep at them. Find what works for you and do it. Remember, the rule of thumb I have found invaluable is to keep it as simple as possible. If it is difficult at all, chances are you will not do it or won't stick with it. Keep it easy and fun. I constantly search for mechanisms that will help me in managing my life.

The search never ends, but it gets easier as you start to develop the tools that increase your productivity and self confidence, and make them part of a routine. Once you find something that works for you, think about why and how it worked. I guarantee it will lead you to another. Remember that like medication, know your limitations, work around them and capitalize on your strengths. Trust me, you have many. Good luck, and remember there are others out there just like you.

Chapter 44

ADD in the Workplace

There is much talk these days about being differently abled rather than disabled—about the importance of reframing, in a positive manner, the set of strengths and weaknesses which characterize an individual with a disability. There is no more appropriate disability than attention deficit disorder for which to do this reframing. In our fast paced, high-pressure late 20th century lifestyle, the deficit side of ADD is overemphasized. Few of us can remain focused, organized and efficient while bombarded with multiple demands of fast changing workplace environments, the multiple distractions of our workplace cubicle existence, and the need for constant updating and retraining, while simultaneously coping with the demands of dual career marriages and the simultaneous complications of child rearing in such a high stress environment. In fact, there are those who say that our contemporary American lifestyle is ADD inducing.

To really understand our overemphasis of the negative side of ADD, perhaps, for a moment, we should over emphasize the negative, or underdeveloped side of those who are considered to be high functioning in other respects. For example, we could label many accountants as suffering from Imagination Deficit Disorder; we could label many hard driving CEO's as having Empathy Deficit Disorder; and we could assign the label of Spontaneity Deficit Disorder to those who live a highly regulated 9 to 5 existence. In other words, by labeling an individual with attention deficit disorder we are only looking at an area of weakness, with little or no recognition of the cluster of strengths, and even giftedness that are often associated with individuals who may be distractible and less detail focused.

Ironically, this country was built by individuals who share many traits of attention deficit disorder—they were high-energy, impulsive, risk-taking, good in a crisis, jump-in-with-both-feet and figure-it-out-as-they-went-along people. These were the people who took a leap of faith to come to the new world, then risked it again to leave the security of the east coast states and forge out into the American wilderness. They were the '49ers who bet their last dollar chasing the promise of riches in California. They were the Thomas Edisons, who had no sense of time and yet had endless ingenuity and creativity. A study of successful business entrepreneurs today will show a great over representation of individuals with ADD. People in sales, inventors, politicians, comedians, pilots, entertainers and all manner of other high profile people have strong ADD characteristics.

So why do some in the business community hold a largely negative view of people with ADD? Because of that disability frame which has been placed around them. Because so many work environments today—with windowless cubicles in noisy workspaces—are so intolerable to those who are more distractible or who are more sensitive to environmental stressors. Because we live more inactive, stressed, time pressed lives these days. Because many managers don't know how to recognize the strengths of these often highly intelligent and creative employees, who may also have difficulty with time management or mundane, detailed paperwork.

Put an ADD employee in an appropriate ADD-friendly work environment, pair him or her with a more detail oriented person, give him projects which interest and challenge him, and you may suddenly find that you have a highly motivated, top performing employee.

One ADD-savvy supervisor was very receptive to his employee's request to attend fewer meetings. This gifted computer specialist found himself feeling restless and distracted in slow moving meetings. He asked his boss to only invite him to critical meetings, explaining that his time could be much more productively used working alone in his office. This flexible boss recognized the creative brainpower of his employee, and was flexible enough to rethink the standard operating procedure of the work environment.

Another ADD employee in a large accounting firm changed from a bored, restless, under functioning accountant to a top-performing employee when his enlightened supervisor understood his discontent.

He had little patience or tolerance for the predictable, routine paperwork of his first job assignment, but became a superstar when he was allowed to help develop specialized software, and to teach other accountants how to use it. Once again, his very real gifts were recognized and taken advantage of. A less enlightened firm might have let him go after poor performance reviews, as this accountant's previous firm had done.

A woman with ADD was functioning very poorly as an administrative assistant to an executive. She was frustrated with the many mundane tasks of the job, had difficulty arriving at work exactly on time, and sometimes handled problem inappropriately—jumping to a solution rather than conferring with her boss beforehand. Once again, her savvy boss recognized an intelligent, frustrated person who showed many ADD characteristics. A large fund-raising project had begun, in which she showed great interest. Her boss consulted with her, asking if she would rather work on this project instead of remaining in the front office job. She leapt at the chance for more autonomy and an opportunity to use her creativity and problem solving ability. Her frequent lateness on the fund-raising project was more than compensated for by working long past normal working hours as she threw herself into the project. She was teamed up with a highly organized, detail oriented person. This employee's organizational skills, paired with the ADD employee's creativity and dynamism, formed an unbeatable team which was highly successful in their fund raising mission.

The moral—the part of the elephant you're looking at determines how you'll describe it. If you only look at a tendency to be 10 minutes late, paired with disorganized paperwork, you will conclude you have a less than desirable employee. If you look at their energy, their willingness to work overtime, and their creative problem solving, then you've got a superior employee. So, instead of bemoaning ADD employees who can't sit still for hours or fill out their time sheets in a timely manner, employers would do better to celebrate the untapped ingenuity, creativity and energy waiting to be mined by the savvy manager. The employer who creates an ADD-friendly work environment creates a win/win situation. Put an ADD employee in the right job with the right supports and then stand back! You'll be amazed at the motivation and productivity that is unleashed.

About the Author

Kathleen G. Nadeau, Ph.D. is a nationally recognized expert on attention deficit disorder in adults, and the author of several books on adult ADD, including the recently released *ADD in the Workplace, Choices, Changes and Challenges*, published by Brunner/Mazel. She is a frequent lecturer and consultant on issues relating to ADD in the workplace. Dr. Nadeau is co-editor of *ADDvance Magazine*.

Chapter 45

Finding Your AD/HD-Friendly Job

Doing what you are interested in, what you are good at and being governed by your strengths can lead to career fulfillment.

ADD is different in each person, so what may seem like a great ADD-friendly job to you, may be a disaster for another individual with ADD. There are some common complaints of adults with ADD, including time management problems and organization. However, some adults with ADD have compensated by structuring their day and are extremely organized. Many people have asked what specific jobs are best for individuals with AD/HD, but each person is unique and ADD brings out different strengths and weaknesses in each person. Every industry also provides a wide array of jobs so that for any interest, a job can be found. While an engineer with ADD might find it to be boring and tedious working in a large office, he might do well as an independent contractor where each job he undertakes is new and refreshing. So, how do you determine what job is best for you?

Understand that this is a process and will not be completed in a day or a week. It may take a month or longer. Your goal is to find a career that suits your lifestyle, your personality and your interests. Buy a notebook to keep all of your notes as you will refer to them in order to determine in which direction your career should go. Take as much time to work on the following steps as you need.

Write an interest inventory. Start with as many items as you want. List all of your interests and likes. A list might look something like this:

Likes:

- Reading books
- Talking with people
- Spectator sports, especially basketball
- Swimming
- Internet
- Web site development
- Health care
- Solving problems

Dislikes:

- Answering phones
- Paperwork
- Large crowds
- Early mornings
- Working with numbers
- Tedious projects
- Public speaking

Add to the list as you think of more interests and dislikes. Put a check next to the interests that sound really exciting to you and a check next to the dislikes that you really detest.

Write a work experience inventory. Think of every job that you have had. (It might be easier to work your way backwards, one job at a time.) List all of the functions and responsibilities that you had.

Skills Inventory

- *Office Skills:* Filing, answering phones, customer service, telemarketing, sales, bookkeeping, typing 60wpm, receptionist Duties

- *Computer Skills:* Desktop publishing, web site development, programming

- *Software:* MS Word, MS Publisher, MS Front Page, Lotus
- *Office Equipment:* Typewriter, computer, cash register
- *Additional Skills:* Accurate typist and proofreader, great spelling skills, quick learner

Take a few days to think about all the experience and skills you have had over the years. Add as much detail and information as possible to the list. (The previous examples are not complete examples. Include education, personal experience and volunteer work. Yours should be much more detailed.)

Life Skills Inventory

Your next inventory sheet should include all of the day-to-day skills you have. You want to write down those that you are great at and those that could use some additional work.

Great:

- Very creative, can usually find creative solutions to problems that arise.
- Life of the party
- Good in small gatherings
- Work well on my own
- Work well in small groups
- Love to give and organize parties
- Willingly make sacrifices for something I really want

Could Use Some Work:

- Getting up and to work on time
- Intimidated by large crowds
- Forgetful
- Disorganized
- Sometimes work very slow to make sure it is done right

Decide which of these items you are willing to work to change and which are not changeable. Don't accept a position where success would depend on an item that you have not yet strengthened.

Make an inventory of what you have liked best about previous positions that you held.

- Flexible hours
- Lots of contact with the public
- Worked without much supervision
- Allowed creativity to come through
- Received sense of accomplishment at completion of project
- Boss gave credit for jobs well done
- Deadlines forced me to complete work on time

Put a star next to the items you really liked.

Make an inventory of what you did not like in previous positions.

- Did not get along with boss
- Got talked to about lack of organization
- Panic of upcoming deadlines caused me to miss the deadlines
- Tedious and boring
- Too unstructured
- Too many people around

Mark those that you do not feel you would be able to deal with again in a work environment.

Take a break—by now you should be totally overwhelmed with all of these ideas and facts running around your head and you should probably put your notebook somewhere safe for a couple days and not look at it. When you come back to it, you might be surprised to see that you have even more to add to it.

Ask some close friends/relatives to help you complete the lists if you are having a difficult time with them. Ask them to be objective and to help your memory of events and jobs so that you can get an accurate view of what has worked and what hasn't in your past employment.

Compare the results of your interests and your experiences. If you put down that you were interested in photography, but you haven't yet picked up a camera—you just think it might be fun—now is the time to cross photography off your list. What interests do you have left that are backed up by some type of experience or education?

Look at the interests that are left and begin to write down all of the jobs that are available in those interests. About.com "Guide to Career Planning" has details on many of the major industries and professions.

You should now have in front of you a list of several jobs for which you have an interest and some experience/education in. Work with your list of life skills to determine if any of those positions would not fit your personality. Does a job require you to be on the road visiting companies and you are terrible at following a map and always end up getting lost? This might cause undue stress and you will end up leaving the job. Is there a job that always starts at 7 a.m. and you can't seem to get up and moving much before 9 a.m.? Match the positions with your strengths to find a position where you will be able to grow instead of feeling frustration.

Look again at what you disliked and liked in previous positions to determine what is important to you. Do you like the structure of a large company, where each day you know exactly what you are going to do and how long it will take you to do it? Do you like the excitement of a new company, being there on the ground floor and watching and being a part of the growth of the company? Do you want someone in the background to oversee your work, yet leave you alone to complete it? Use these to determine which type of company you would like to work for (or whether you would prefer to be self-employed).

Using all of information you compiled should help you immensely during the interview process. You will know what you want and why you should have a job. You will know what to look for in a company. This knowledge will allow you to show your confidence and make decisions based on what is best for you, rather than on the impulse of "Wow, this sounds terrific, when do I start?" If needed, take notes during the interview and bring them home to compare with your inventories to see if you and the position are a good match.

Doing what we are interested in, what we are good at and in a position, which will be governed by our strengths, rather than pointing out our weaknesses will lead to fulfillment in our careers.

Chapter 46

Should You Tell Your Employer You Have AD/HD?

The answer is, it depends on the facts of the individual case. Generally, we recommend disclosure of AD/HD to an employer if (1) you can document AD/HD, and AD/HD is a disability under the law in your case, (2) you are qualified for the job, and (3) you need job accommodations that are reasonable.

When You Should Not Disclose AD/HD

There are many instances in which disclosure of AD/HD to an employer is not the best course of action. Let's look at some examples.

The Successful Employee

Recently, a woman with an excellent job called to say that she wanted to tell her employer she has AD/HD. We asked if she wanted to request workplace accommodations. She replied no and added that she was not experiencing any problems on her job. We then asked why she wanted to tell her employer that she had AD/HD. She thought about it and then said she was excited about her diagnosis at the age of 45 because it gave her an explanation as to why she had struggled

"Legal Briefs: Should You Tell Your Employer You Have AD/HD?" by Peter S. Latham, J.D. and Patricia H. Latham, J.D., from *Attention!* Magazine, Volume 7, Number 3, © 1996-2001 CHADD. For more information write to CHADD at 8181 Professional Place, Suite 201, Landover, MD 2087, or visit CHADD at their website at www.chadd.org.

over the years, and she wanted to share her happiness with her employer. We suggested that it would be fine to share her happiness with family and friends, if she felt so inclined, but that, in the case of her employer, there is no upside to telling and there is a possible downside.

There is no upside because she doesn't need special accommodations at this time. Furthermore, while she has a diagnosis of AD/HD, which is recognized as an impairment under the Americans with Disabilities Act (ADA), it is not likely that she would be considered an individual with a disability under the ADA, and so she would not be protected under it. To be an individual with a disability, one must have an impairment that substantially limits a major life activity, such as learning or working. In evaluating whether or not a person is substantially limited, it is necessary to look at the person's performance of the major life activity compared to that of the average person and to take into account the positive and negative effects of the person's medication and compensatory strategies. Some individuals with AD/HD have less severe symptoms and/or great strengths that enable them to develop excellent compensatory strategies and to function as well or better than the average person in learning and working. A woman who has an excellent job and performs it well, most likely would be unable to show that she is substantially limited in working compared to the average person. Other individuals with more severe symptoms of AD/HD, who have been unable to benefit from medication and have been unable to develop effective compensatory strategies, might be able to show that AD/HD substantially limits a major life activity and thus that such individuals do have a disability under the ADA.

There is a downside to disclosing her AD/HD. Her employer might be puzzled as to why she is disclosing a medical condition and may assume that she is having some problem with her job and wants understanding or specific accommodations. She may actually cause her employer to become concerned when in reality there is no reason for any concern about her functioning in the workplace.

The Social Worker Who Wants Understanding

A social worker with AD/HD was experiencing workplace difficulties and wished to disclose the condition to his employer, not to seek specific accommodations, but rather to receive understanding as to why he was sometimes late to work and late completing reports. It is important to be aware that, even if the social worker has a disability under the ADA, the ADA does not require an employer to be understanding as to why an individual with a disability is not completing work assignments or is coming in late. On the contrary, the ADA is very clear that even if an individual has a disability, the individual must be qualified for the job. Part of being qualified is completing work assignments and coming in on time.

Instead of disclosing AD/HD in order to receive understanding, the social worker should first explore whether there are strategies he could use to address the difficulties. For example, if his office has flex time available to employees, he could consider arranging to start one hour later in the morning and work one hour later at the end of the day. Advantages to this change would be better traffic conditions for his commute to work and so more predictability as to his arrival time and a quieter hour at the end of the day to handle report preparation and to plan the work for the next day.

When and How to Disclose

If strategies and medication are not enough, and you conclude that you must request reasonable accommodations, it would be advisable to consult with an attorney to determine whether or not you can establish that you are a qualified individual with a disability and thus entitled to reasonable accommodations.

If the answer is that you do have a strong argument that you are a person with a disability, then you can work with your attorney and your mental health professional to draft a request for specific reasonable accommodations. If the company denies your request, you may decide to challenge the denial through processes that may include: internal processes in the company, mediation, arbitration, complaint to an appropriate governmental agency, and/or filing in court. In making a decision to litigate, keep in mind that in 1999, employers won 95.7 percent of ADA employment court cases. It is difficult for employees to win these cases. Many employee plaintiffs have impairments, but courts find that these impairments simply do not substantially limit a major life activity compared to the average person. Other employees meet the substantially limited test, but courts find that the employees are not qualified for their jobs.

If the answer is that your legal claim to ADA disability status is weak, you may opt to continue to use strategies in your current job, to seek a new job that is a better match for you, or to proceed with disclosure and request reasonable accommodations in your current job. If you choose to request accommodations, it may be wise to draft a request for minimal reasonable accommodations and to invite the employer's input as to what would work best from the employer's point of view. Some employers are quite willing to provide a few accommodations that pose no problem to the employer, even if there is some question as to disability status under the ADA. These employers reason that providing the accommodations simply makes good business sense.

About the Authors

Peter S. Latham, J.D., and Patricia Horan Latham, J.D., are partners in the Washington, D.C. law firm Latham & Latham, and authors of eight books, including *Attention-Deficit Disorder and the Law*. Peter Latham has produced the video, *The ABCs of ADD*. Patricia Latham serves on the Board of Directors of LDA and the Professional Advisory Board of ADDA.

Chapter 47

AD/HD in the Military

Ritalin is not welcome in the Armed Services.

During World War II, Japanese, Russian and German armies used Ritalin as a means of combating battle fatigue. They discovered that soldiers using Ritalin followed directions more easily and focused better on their tasks. Although we may not agree with the intent of these armies, we can certainly agree with the positive effects of Ritalin on those soldiers. Today, the U.S. Armed Forces faces another enemy and the entire military service is gearing up for a long war. Ritalin, however, has no place in the military.

The outcry and heartwarming tales of Americans coming together in this hour of need has brought tears to our eyes. Together, our country will fight this invisible enemy and we will prevail. Each of us, no matter where we live, has been deeply affected and has tried to find a way that we can help. Donations of clothes, money, blood, and time has overwhelmed the Red Cross and the Salvation Army. New York officials are turning away people that have come to help as they can not use any more volunteers at this time. As in any family, Americans will reach deep within themselves to continue to help and defend our great nation.

The next step is fighting a war. It is estimated that 3%-5% of our population has AD/HD. It would follow that 3%-5% of individuals wanting to serve our country in the Armed Forces also have AD/HD. How will this diagnosis effect their ability to serve their country?

Talking with a recruiter for the U.S. Navy gave me some insight. This recruiter wishes to remain anonymous and is clear in that he could only provide information on how the recruiting process is today, in a volunteer Armed Services. He also indicated that the information he provided me was specific to the U.S. Navy, although he believes that this information would be similar, if not the same, in all other branches of the Military. The answers following are paraphrased from the responses that were received during this interview.

Can an individual taking prescription medication for AD/HD enter the Armed Forces?

No, although this is not limited to AD/HD, many disorders/illnesses that require prescription medication would create ineligibility.

Does a diagnosis of AD/HD prevent an individual from serving in the Military?

The diagnosis itself does not prevent service, however, the need for medication would. Individuals with AD/HD that do not take medication can be accepted into military service. Individuals who are currently on medication for AD/HD are not eligible to enlist in the Armed Forces.

What if a person is on medication for AD/HD, yet would like to serve in the Military?

Although the official documentation could not be found during the interview with the Naval Recruiting Officer, he believed that operating procedures would call for an individual to be off of prescription medication for a period of six months. A doctor would need to certify that the individual no longer needed medication and could function without medication.

Many times other diagnosis and disorders accompany AD/HD, such as depression, bi-polar disorder and other behavioral disorders. How do these diagnosis effect the ability to enter the Armed Services?

Again, medication seems to the key. If an individual has a mental disorder and does not require any medication, the situation will be taken under review. Documentation from a doctor stating current health conditions may be needed. If prescription medication is currently part of the treatment process and is needed to maintain stability, then most likely, the individual would not be eligible to serve.

A few examples of other diagnosis that would make an individual not eligible would be diabetes and sleepwalking.

Would any of this change should a draft be put into place?

This question was difficult as speculation into the need for a draft is really not possible at this time. There has to be reservists called upon for duty, however, no talk of a possible draft has been reported. The draft would not be considered unless a tremendous loss of military personnel occurred. At this time no military personnel has been lost and therefore speculation of a draft is just that—speculation. Should the need for a draft become apparent, the officials would need to decide if exceptions/changes should be made.

How can someone that is currently on medication serve their country?

By doing those things that the general public is now doing:

- Donating blood
- Volunteering in rescue efforts
- Donating items/money that is needed to help victims and rescue workers
- Becoming a Red Cross/Salvation Army/United Way volunteer
- Working or volunteering in civil positions within the government

For additional questions or details, contact the Armed Forces recruiting office near you.

Chapter 48

When ADD Adults Learn English as a Second Language

Some adult English language learners experience difficulty in sustaining employment and showing progress on assessment measures. This may be due, in part, to learning disabilities. According to the federal Interagency Committee on Learning Disabilities, learning disabilities are disorders "that create difficulty in acquiring and using skills such as listening, speaking, reading, writing, and reasoning. These disorders can also inhibit mathematical abilities and social interactions" (Brown & Ganzglass, 1998, p. 2). Learning disabilities are generally thought to be caused by a dysfunction in the central nervous system, and people who have learning disabilities are considered to possess average or above-average intelligence (Seattle-King County Private Industry Council, 2000). Little is known about how these disabilities affect the adult learner of English as a second language (ESL).

This chapter reviews what is known about adult ESL learners and learning disabilities, suggests ways to identify and assess ESL adults who may have learning disabilities, and offers practical methods for both instruction and teacher training.

"ESL Instruction and Adults with Learning Disabilities," by Robin Schwarz and Lynda Terrill, *ERIC Digest*, ERIC Identifier: ED443298. Publication Date: 2000-06-00, from National Clearinghouse for ESL Literacy Education Washington DC, 2000. ERIC (Educational Resources Information Center) is a service of the U.S. Department of Education. Online databases are available at www.ed.gov/databases.

Learning Disabilities in a Second Language

Learners may show learning disabilities in a second language when they do not in their first. A learning disability may be so subtle in a first language that it is masked by an individual's compensatory strategies, e.g., getting general information through the overall context when specific words or concepts are not understood, and substituting known words for words that cause difficulty. These strategies may not be available to the learner in the new language (Ganschow & Sparks, 1993). Sometimes a learning disability does not manifest itself in the learner's first language "because of the systematic structure or transparent nature of his native language versus English" (D. Shewcraft, *Personal Communication*, June 2000). For example, a reading disability may be more pronounced in English than in Spanish, where the sound/symbol correspondence system is more predictable.

Identifying Learning Disabled ESL Adults

It is thought that the percentage of learning disabled students in adult education classes may exceed the percentage in the population as a whole, with some estimates as high as 80% (Seattle-King County Private Industry Council, 2000). Although it is not known if this is true in ESL classes, there is a general sense in the field that it may not be true. Unlike native speakers in adult education programs, many ESL learners were not unsuccessful in their previous educational experience. Rather, they are enrolled in programs to learn to speak, read, and write in a new language. Therefore, care should be taken before labeling ESL learners as learning disabled.

Being identified as learning disabled can be stigmatizing for anyone—adult, child, native English speaker, or ESL learner (McCormick, 1991). Educators stress the importance of weighing the advantages of identifying adult learners as learning disabled (planning instruction to help learners, making them eligible for services, and so forth) against the possible stigma of the label (Almanza, Singleton, & Terrill, 1995/96).

Before testing and labeling an adult ESL student as learning disabled, other reasons for lack of expected progress should be considered. Educators (Adkins, Sample, & Birman, 1999; Almanza, Singleton, & Terrill, 1995/96; Grognet, 1997; Schwarz & Burt, 1995) have noted the following reasons for slow progress in learning English:

- Limited academic skills in a learner's native language due to limited previous education

- Lack of effective study habits

- The interference of a learner's native language, particularly if the learner is used to a non-Roman alphabet

- A mismatch between the instructor's teaching style and the learner's expectations of how the class will be conducted

- Stress or trauma that refugees and other immigrants have experienced, causing symptoms such as difficulty in concentration and memory dysfunction

- Sociocultural factors such as age, physical health, social identity, and even diet

- External problems with work, health, and family

- Sporadic attendance

- Lack of practice outside the classroom

These behaviors or problems will most likely affect all learning, whereas a learning disability usually affects only one area of learning.

Assessing the Learner

The use of standardized testing to identify learning disabilities presents problems. First, instruments designed to diagnose learning disabilities are usually normed on native English speakers, so the results cannot be reliably used with learners whose first language is not English. Second, since the concepts and language being tested may have no direct translation, the validity of tests translated into the native language is questionable. Third, most tests are primarily designed for and normed on younger students and may not be suitable for adults.

No single assessment technique is sufficient to diagnose a learning disability; multiple assessment measures are necessary. Even before an interview or other assessments are administered, instructors should answer the following questions about a learner:

1. Has the problem persisted over time?

2. Has the problem resisted normal instruction?

3. Does the learner show a clear pattern of strengths and weaknesses in class?

4. Does the learner show a clear pattern of strengths and weaknesses outside of class?

5. Does the problem interfere with learning or a life activity in some way to a significant degree?

If the responses to these questions are affirmative, there is probably a learning problem that should be looked into more closely. The following are suggestions on how to do this.

Interview learners. This can provide a variety of useful information, such as educational and language history and social background, the learner's strengths, and the learner's perception on the nature of the suspected problem.

Collect information about the learner's work. Portfolio assessment, where measurements of learner progress in reading and writing are considered along with attendance data, writing samples, autobiographical information, and work on class assignments, can provide a broad picture of the learner's performance. Keeping a learner portfolio is helpful in documenting the persistence of problems as well as which teaching strategies have worked or not worked.

Use visual screening and routine hearing tests. What appears to be a learning disability may be due in part to developmental visual problems or correctable auditory problems.

Instructional Methods and Materials

Learning disabilities affect learning in any language and must therefore be a guiding factor in designing instruction for the adult learner with disabilities. Educators of learning disabled children and adults (Almanza, Singleton, & Terrill, 1995/96; Baca & Cervantes, 1991; Ganschow & Sparks, 1993) give the following suggestions for providing instruction.

- Be highly structured and predictable.

- Teach small amounts of material at one time in sequential steps.

- Include opportunities to use several senses and learning strategies.

- Provide multisensory reviews.

- Recognize and build on learners' strengths and prior knowledge.

- Simplify language but not content.

- Emphasize content words and make concepts accessible through the use of pictures, charts, maps, etc.

- Reinforce main ideas and concepts through rephrasing rather than through verbatim repetition.

- Be aware that learners often can take in information, but may experience difficulty retrieving it and sorting it appropriately.

- Provide a clean, uncluttered, quiet, and well-lit learning environment.

In adult basic education and adult ESL instruction where little time or money is spent on program capacity building through research and teacher training, there are few instructional models to look toward (Burt & Keenan, 1998). However, some programs are developing their own practical guides and disseminating them to a wider audience (Hatt & Nichols, 1995; Shewcraft & Witkop, 1998).

Technology has potential for assisting adult learners with learning disabilities to acquire a second language; computers have proven to be particularly useful (Gerber & Reiff, 1994; Riviere, 1996). In fact, adult ESL learners who have had limited success in learning English report that working one-on-one in the computer lab with a teacher seems more comfortable and productive than being one of many students in a crowded classroom (Almanza, Singleton, & Terrill, 1995/96). Using assistive technology can build self-esteem as well as provide immediate feedback, two things all adult language learners can benefit from.

Conclusion

Although a learning disability does not effect all areas of learning, it may have a significant impact on the social and work life of the learner. Therefore, the field of adult ESL must intensify its efforts to assist learning disabled adult ESL learners and their teachers. Such efforts require greater and more long-term sources of funding for research, specifically in the areas of assessment and instruction, training, and assistive technology.

References

Adkins, M.A., Sample, B., & Birman, D. (1999). "Mental health and the adult ESL refugee: The role of the ESL teacher." *ERIC Digest*. Washington, DC: National Clearinghouse for ESL Literacy Education.

Almanza, D., Singleton, K., & Terrill, L. (1995/96). Learning disabilities in adult ESL: Case studies and directions. *The Year in Review*, 5, 1-6.

Baca, L., & Cervantes, H.T. (1991). "Bilingual special education." *ERIC Digest*. Reston, VA: Clearinghouse on Handicapped and Gifted Children. (ED 333 618)

Brown, R., & Ganzglass, E. (1998). "Serving welfare recipients with learning disabilities in a work first environment." On-line at (http://www.nga.org/pubs/issuebriefs/1998/980728learning.asp)

Burt, M., & Keenan, F. (1998). "Trends in staff development for adult ESL instructors." *ERIC Q&A*. Washington, DC: National Clearinghouse for ESL Literacy Education. (ED 423 711)

Ganschow, L., & Sparks, R. (1993). Foreign language and learning disabilities: Issues, research and teaching implications. In S.A. Vogel & P.B. Adelman (Eds.), *Success for College Students with Learning Disabilities* (pp. 283-322). New York: Springer-Verlag.

Gerber, P.J., & Reiff, H.B. (Eds.). (1994). *"Learning Disabilities In Adulthood: Persisting Problems and Evolving Issues,* Stoneham, MA: Butterworth-Heineman.

Grognet, A.G. (1997). "Elderly refugees and language learning." Denver, CO: Spring Institute for International Studies. (ED 416 721)

Hatt, P., & Nichols, E. (1995). "Links in learning." West Hill, Ontario, Canada: MESE Consulting, Ltd.

McCormick, K. (1991). Myth #14: All literacy problems are the result of learning disabilities. *The Literacy Beat 4* (2), 1-4.

Riviere, A. (1996). "Assistive technology: Meeting the needs of adults with learning disabilities." Washington, DC: National Adult Literacy and Learning Disabilities Center.

Seattle-King County Private Industry Council. (2000). Learning Disabilities Project Website. http://www.skcpic.org

Schwarz R., & Burt, M. (1995). "ESL instruction for learning disabled adults." *ERIC Digest*. Washington, DC: National Clearinghouse for ESL Literacy Education. (ED 379 966)

Shewcraft, D.F., & Witkop, E. (1998). "Do my ESOL students have learning disabilities?" Pittsfield, MA: Western Massachusetts Young Adults With Learning Disabilities (YALD) Project.

Part Six

Additional Help
and Information

Chapter 49

Glossary of Related Terms

The following terms will be useful to those seeking information about AD/HD and learning disabilities.

Accommodations: Techniques and materials that allow individuals with learning disabilities (LD) to complete school or work tasks with greater ease and effectiveness. Examples include spellcheckers, tape recorders, and expanded time for completing assignments.

ADA: Americans with Disabilities Act.

Assistive Technology: Equipment that enhances the ability of students and employees to be more efficient and successful. For individuals with LD, computer grammar checkers, an overhead projector used by a teacher, or the audiovisual information delivered through a CD-ROM would be typical examples.

Attention Deficit Disorder (ADD): A severe difficulty in focusing and maintaining attention. Often leads to learning and behavior problems at home, school, and work. Also called attention deficit hyperactivity disorder (AD/HD).

"Learning Disabilities: Glossary of Some Important Terms," by Jean Lokerson, from *ERIC Digest* #E517, ERIC Identifier: ED352780, Publication Date: 1992. ERIC (Educational Resources Information Center) is a service of the U.S. Department of Education. Online databases are available at www. ed.gov/databases. Despite the older date of this document, readers will find the terms in this chapter helpful.

Brain Imaging Techniques: Recently developed, noninvasive techniques for studying the activity of living brains. Includes brain electrical activity mapping (BEAM), computerized axial tomography (CAT), and magnetic resonance imaging (MRI).

Brain Injury: The physical damage to brain tissue or structure that occurs before, during, or after birth that is verified by EEG, MRI, CAT, or a similar examination, rather than by observation of performance. When caused by an accident, the damage may be called Traumatic Brain Injury (TBI).

Collaboration: A program model in which the LD teacher demonstrates for or team teaches with the general classroom teacher to help a student with LD be successful in a regular classroom.

Developmental Aphasia: A severe language disorder that is presumed to be due to brain injury rather than because of a developmental delay in the normal acquisition of language.

Direct Instruction: An instructional approach to academic subjects that emphasizes the use of carefully sequenced steps that include demonstration, modeling, guided practice, and independent application.

Dyscalculia: A severe difficulty in understanding and using symbols or functions needed for success in mathematics.

Dysgraphia: A severe difficulty in producing handwriting that is legible and written at an age-appropriate speed.

Dyslexia: A severe difficulty in understanding or using one or more areas of language, including listening, speaking, reading, writing, and spelling.

Dysnomia: A marked difficulty in remembering names or recalling words needed for oral or written language.

Dyspraxia: A severe difficulty in performing drawing, writing, buttoning, and other tasks requiring fine motor skill, or in sequencing the necessary movements.

FAPE: Free and Appropriate Education.

Learned Helplessness: A tendency to be a passive learner who depends on others for decisions and guidance. In individuals with LD, continued struggle and failure can heighten this lack of self-confidence.

Learning Modalities: Approaches to assessment or instruction stressing the auditory, visual, or tactile avenues for learning that are dependent upon the individual.

Learning Strategy Approaches: Instructional approaches that focus on efficient ways to learn, rather than on curriculum. Includes specific techniques for organizing, actively interacting with material, memorizing, and monitoring any content or subject.

Learning Styles: Approaches to assessment or instruction emphasizing the variations in temperament, attitude, and preferred manner of tackling a task. Typically considered are styles along the active/passive, reflective/impulsive, or verbal/spatial dimensions.

Locus of Control: The tendency to attribute success and difficulties either to internal factors such as effort or to external factors such as chance. Individuals with learning disabilities tend to blame failure on themselves and achievement on luck, leading to frustration and passivity.

Metacognitive Learning: Instructional approaches emphasizing awareness of the cognitive processes that facilitate one's own learning and its application to academic and work assignments. Typical metacognitive techniques include systematic rehearsal of steps or conscious selection among strategies for completing a task.

Minimal Brain Dysfunction (MBD): A medical and psychological term originally used to refer to the learning difficulties that seemed to result from identified or presumed damage to the brain. Reflects a medical, rather than educational or vocational orientation.

Multisensory Learning: An instructional approach that combines auditory, visual, and tactile elements into a learning task. Tracing sandpaper numbers while saying a number fact aloud would be a multisensory learning activity.

Neuropsychological Examination: A series of tasks that allow observation of performance that is presumed to be related to the intactness of brain function.

Perceptual Handicap: Difficulty in accurately processing, organizing, and discriminating among visual, auditory, or tactile information. A person with a perceptual handicap may say that "cap/cup" sound the same or that "b" and "d" look the same. However, glasses or hearing aids do not necessarily indicate a perceptual handicap.

Prereferral Process: A procedure in which special and regular teachers develop trial strategies to help a student showing difficulty in learning remain in the regular classroom.

Resource Program: A program model in which a student with LD is in a regular classroom for most of each day, but also receives regularly scheduled individual services in a specialized LD resource classroom.

Self-Advocacy: The development of specific skills and understandings that enable children and adults to explain their specific learning disabilities to others and cope positively with the attitudes of peers, parents, teachers, and employers.

Specific Language Disability (SLD): A severe difficulty in some aspect of listening, speaking, reading, writing, or spelling, while skills in the other areas are age-appropriate. Also called Specific Language Learning Disability (SLLD).

Specific Learning Disability (SLD): The official term used in federal legislation to refer to difficulty in certain areas of learning, rather than in all areas of learning. Synonymous with learning disabilities.

Subtype Research: A recently developed research method that seeks to identify characteristics that are common to specific groups within the larger population of individuals identified as having learning disabilities.

Transition: Commonly used to refer to the change from secondary school to postsecondary programs, work, and independent living typical of young adults. Also used to describe other periods of major change such as from early childhood to school or from more specialized to mainstreamed settings.

Chapter 50

Support Groups and Organizations

ADD Warehouse
300 NW 70th Avenue, Suite 102
Plantation, FL 33317-2360
Toll Free: 800-233-9273
Phone: 954-792-8100
Fax: 954-792-8545
Website: http://addwarehouse.com
E-Mail: sales@addwarehouse.com

Distributes books, tapes, videos, assessment on attention deficit hyperactivity disorders.

Attention Deficit Information Network (AD-IN)
475 Hillside Avenue
Needham, MA 02494
Phone: 781-455-9895
Fax: 781-444-5466
Website: www.addinfonetwork.com
E-Mail: adin@gis.net

Attention Deficit Information Network (AD-IN), continued

Provides up-to-date information on current research, regional meetings. Offers aid in finding solutions to practical problems faced by adults and children with an attention disorder.

Center for Mental Health Services
Office of Consumer, Family, and Public Information
5600 Fishers Lane
Room 17-99
Rockville, MD 20857
Phone: 301-443-2792
Website: www.mentalhealth.org/cmhs/default.asp

This national center, a component of the U.S. Public Health Service, provides a range of information on mental health, treatment, and support services.

Children and Adults with Attention Deficit Disorders (CH.A.D.D.)
8181 Professional Place, Suite 201
Landover, MD 20785-7221
Toll Free: 800-233-4050
Phone: 301-306-7070
Fax: 301-306-7090
Website: http://www.chadd.org
E-Mail: national@chadd.org

A nonprofit parent-based organization formed to better the lives of individuals with attention deficit disorder and those who care for them. Through family support and advocacy, public and professional education and encouragement of scientific research, CH.A.D.D works to ensure that those with attention deficit disorder are given the opportunity to reach their inherent potential.

Council for Exceptional Children
1110 North Glebe Road, Suite 300
Arlington, VA 22201-4795
Toll Free: 888-CEC-SPED
Phone: 703-620-3660
TTY: (text only) 703-264-9447
Fax: 703-263-9494
Website: www.cec.sped.org

Provides publications for educators. Can also provide referral to ERIC (Educational Resource Information Center) Clearinghouse for Handicapped and Gifted Children.

Council for Learning Disabilities (CLD)
P.O. Box 40303
Overland Park, KS 66204-4303
Phone: 913-492-8755

Federation of Families for Children's Mental Health
1101 King Street, Suite 420
Alexandria, VA 22314-2944
Phone: 703-684-7710
Fax: 703-836-1040
Website: www.ffcmh.org
E-Mail: ffcmh@ffcmh.org

Provides information, support, and referrals through federation chapters throughout the country. This national parent-run organization focuses on the needs of children with broad mental health problems.

HEATH Resource Center
American Council on Education
1 Dupont Circle
Washington, DC 20036
Toll Free: 800-544-3284 (V/TTY)
Phone: 202-939-9300
Fax: 202-833-4760

A national clearinghouse on post-high school education for people with disabilities.

Learning Disabilities Association of America
4156 Library Road
Pittsburgh, PA 15234
Phone: 412-341-1515
Fax: 412-344-0224
Website: www.ldanatl.org
E-Mail: info@ldaamerica.org

Provides information and referral to state chapters, parent resources, and local support groups. Publishes news briefs and a professional journal.

National Association of Private Special Education Centers (NAPSEC)

1522 K Street, NW, Suite 1032
Washington, DC 20005
Phone: 202-408-3338
Fax: 202-408-3340
Website: www.napsec.com
E-Mail: napsec@aol.com

Provides referrals to private special education programs.

National Attention Deficit Disorder Association (National A.D.D.A.)

1788 Second Street, Suite 200
Highland Park, IL 60035-3279
Phone: 847-432-ADDA
Fax: 847-432-5874
Website: www.add.org
E-Mail: mail@add.org

A nonprofit organization with a mission to help people with ADD lead happier, more successful lives through education, research, and public advocacy. A.D.D.A. is especially focused on the needs of adults and young adults with ADD, such as work and career issues, legal issues, college and higher education, and relationship issues. Parents of children with ADD, teachers, and professionals who treat and counsel people with ADD are also welcome.

National Center for Learning Disabilities

381 Park Avenue South, Suite 1401
New York, NY 10016-8806
Toll Free: 888-575-7373
Phone: 212-545-7510
Fax: 212-545-9665
Website: www.ncld.org

Provides referrals and resources. Publishes *Their World* magazine describing true stories on ways children and adults cope with LD.

National Clearinghouse for Alcohol and Drug Information

P.O. Box 2345
Rockville, MD 20847-2345
Toll Free: 800-729-6686

Website: www.health.org
E-Mail: info@health.org

Provides information on the risks of alcohol during pregnancy, and fetal alcohol syndrome.

National Information Center for Children and Youth with Disabilities (NICHCY)
P.O. Box 1492
Washington, DC 20013-1492
Toll Free: 800-695-0285
Website: www.nichcy.org
E-Mail: nichcy@aed.org

Publishes free, fact-filled newsletters. Arranges workshops. Advises parents on the laws entitling children with disabilities to special education and other services.

Tourette Syndrome Association
4240 Bell Boulevard
Bayside, NY 11361-2874
Phone: 718-224-2999
Fax: 718-279-9596
Website: www.tsa-usa.org
E-Mail: ts@tsa-usa.org

State and local chapters provide national information, advocacy, research, and support.

Chapter 51

Toll Free Resources and Hotlines

This chapter contains toll free phone numbers for various AD/HD and mental health related resources.

Action, Parent & Teen Support Program (Rosemead CA)
Toll Free: 800-282-5660

Alcohol/Drug Help Line
Toll Free: 800-562-1240

American Health Assistance Foundation (Rockville MD)
Toll Free: 800-437-2423

Attorney Referral Network
Toll Free: 800-624-8846 (24 hrs)

Child Help USA Hotline
Toll Free: 800-422-4453 (24 hrs)

Emotional Distress
Toll Free: 800-LIFENET

Family Support Network of North Carolina (Chapel Hill NC)
Toll Free: 800-852-0042

Medicare Hotline
Toll Free: 800-638-6833

Provides general information and publications on Medicare. Answers questions on claims or fraud.

NAMI (National Alliance for the Mentally Ill) Helpline
Toll Free: 800-950-NAMI (6264)

An information & referral service. You can discuss mental illness and the medications that treat them.

National Mental Health Association (Alexandria, VA)
Mental Health Information Center
Toll Free: 800-969-NMHA

National OCD Information Hotline
Toll Free: 800-NEWS-4-OCD

Provides information on obsessive-compulsive disorder.

National Runaway Switchboard
Toll Free: 800-621-4000 (24 hrs)

Information and referrals for runaways re: shelter, counseling; food pantries; transportation. Suicide and crisis counseling.

National Youth Crisis Hotline (San Diego CA)
Toll Free: 800-448-4663

Teen Help Inc. (LaVerkin, UT)
Toll Free: 800-400-0900

Teenline (Oklahoma City, OK)
Toll Free: 800-522-8336

Tourette Syndrome Association
Toll Free: 800-237-0717

Chapter 52

AD/HD Resources on the Internet

This chapter contains websites which you may find useful.

ADD.About.com
http://add.about.com

A wealth of information on many topics related to ADD, also developing stories and coverage of legislation and political issues. Developed and managed by Bob Seay, a veteran in the ADD community.

ADD and Addiction
http://www.addandaddiction.com

Wendy Richardson presents information on addictions.

ADDitude Magazine
http://www.additudemag.com

ADD News for Christian Families
http://members.aol.com/addnews

ADDvance Magazine
http://www.addvance.com

A resource for women and girls with ADD.

"A.D.D. on the WWW!!" this material is reprinted with permission from the website of the National Attention Deficit Disorder Association (www.add.org). Copyright © 1996-2002 National Attention Deficit Disorder Association.

415

Beth's Little Corner of Cyberspace
http://www.pcnet.com/~dodge

CH.A.D.D.
http://www.chadd.org

Edward Hallowell M.D.
http://www.drhallowell.com

The Hallowell Center

Family Education Network
http://www.familyeducation.com

FamilyEducation Network's mission is to help parents help their children succeed.

For the Attentionally Disenfranchised
http://www.geocities.com/HotSprings/6502

Greater Rochester ADD Association
http://www.netacc.net/~gradda

KidSource
http://www.kidsource.com/kidsource/pages/dis.add.html

LD/ADD articles, self-esteem, teachers.

LD Learning
http://www.ldlearning.com

Very nice website covers LD and ADD topics.

LD Pride Online
http://www.ldpride.net

An online community for youth and adults with learning disabilities and attention deficit disorder.

Taming The Triad
http://home.att.net/~tamingthetriad

The Mining Company
http://add.miningco.com

Great ADD info— lots of links and resources.

Thom Hartmann
http://www.thomhartmann.com

UnnaWhim with ADD
http://members.aol.com/UnnaWhim/index.html

ADD information presented with humor and wonderful graphics.

ADD—Adult Specific

ADD Articles
http://www.geocities.com

Paul Elliot, MD

ADDult Support of Washington
http://www.addult.org

Adult support group in Washington State

Bob's Little Corner of the World
http://www.ruralnet.net/~bobseay/homepageversion2.htm

Good site with links to pages from other sites.

Born To Explore! The Other Side of ADD
http://borntoexplore.org

Stressing positive and alternative aspects of ADD.

FDISK's ADD Page
http://www.fdisk.com/cgi-bin/add/youknow.pl

Humor

Learning Disabilities Research & Training Center
http://www.rit.edu/~easi/easisem/ldnoelbw.html

University of Georgia—National informational resource guide for and about adolescents/adults with LD and ADD

Health Links
http://www.healthlinks.net

General health information including ADD

Co-Morbidities and ADD

Anxiety-Panic Internet Resource
http://www.algy/com/anxiety/contents.html

Articles, books, humor, stories, pen pals, and chat.

At Health
http://www.athealth.com

Articles on health issues.

Bipolar Disorder Information Network
http://www.frii.com~parrot/bip.html

Book/film list, articles, and organizations.

Depression Central
http://www.psycom.net/depression.central/html

Information on dysthymia, depression and mood disorders.

Society for the Autistically Handicapped
http://www.autismuk.com

History, theories, diagnosis, and treatment.

Tourette Syndrome Association
http://www.tsa-usa.org

Frequently Asked Questions, myths, diagnosis and treatment.

Medication Information

ADDMed
http://www.addmed.com

HealthGuide Online
http://www.adhdlivingguide.com

Lifeskills/Coaching

Counseling Center
http://www.couns.uiuc.edu

Articles on procrastination, time management, stress, etc.

ADD Coaching
http://www.addcoaching.com

ADD Coaching
http://www.sandymaynard.ocm

Schools for Children and Teens with ADD or LD

Paladin Academy
http://www.nobellearning.com/paladinlhtm

Day school, summer camp, and tutoring programs.

Kids and Creativity

Help with Homework Hassles
http://www.Delphi.com/ADD/homework.html

How Can I Say No?
http://www.health.org/features/kidsarea/sayno/index.htm

Alcohol, tobacco, and other drugs.

Asthma Tutorial
http://galen.med.Virginia.edu/~smb4v/tutorials/asthma/asthma1.html

Many kids with ADD also have asthma.

Neuroscience for Kids — The Brain
http://faculty.Washington.edu/chudler/neurok.html

Good information on how the brain works.

Berit's Best Sites for Children
http://www.beritsbest.com

The Global Show and Tell Museum
http://www.telenaut.com/gst

KidZone on LD Online
http://ldonline.org

Women Issues

National Women's Health Resource Center (NWHRC)
http://www.healthywomen.org

A one-stop shop for women's health information.

Chapter 53

Suggested Additional Reading

This chapter contains listings and mini-reviews of many books on ADD. The listings are broken down into several categories: books for parents, children and teens with ADD, adults with ADD, and professionals.

Books for Parents

Negotiating the Special Education Maze: A Guide for Parents and Teachers

Anderson, W., Chitwood S., & and Hayden, D. (1990). Bethesda: Woodbine House. Paperback, 267pp.

Comments: A must-have for any parent who's child needs special education or services in the public school system. Clearly walks the parent through the entire process of how to build an individual education plan for their child, and does a good job explaining the ins and outs of the legal rights and responsibilities of the schools.

Taking Charge of AD/HD: The Complete, Authoritative Guide for Parents

Barkley, R.A. (1995). New York: Guilford Press. Paperback, 294pp.

Comments: Becoming a classic. Well-written, very readable, comprehensive guide to AD/HD for parents by one of the leading experts in the field.

ADD and Adolescence: Strategies for Success from CHADD.
Plantation, FL: CHADD. Paperback, 134pp. Can only be ordered from CHADD's distributor Caset by calling 1-800-545-5583, or from the ADD WareHouse Catalog at 1-800-233-9273.

Comments: A collection of articles and documents by the top experts and leaders in the field of attention deficit disorders covering diagnosis, treatment, education, social skills, family issues, advocacy, beyond high school and other challenges.

Teenagers with ADD: A Parent's Guide
Dendy, C.A.Z. (1995). Bethesda: Woodbine House. Paperback, 370pp.

Comments: The definitive reference/resource for any parent with an adolescent with ADD. Almost every issue is discussed. Lots of great lists that can be copied and used at school meetings. Extremely comprehensive and helpful.

Maybe You Know My Kid: A Parent's Guide to Identifying, Understanding, and Helping Your Child with Attention Deficit Hyperactivity Disorder
Fowler, M.C. (1990). New York: Birch Lane Press.

Comments: A classic. Written for parents by a parent of a child with AD/HD.

Educators Manual: Attention Deficit Disorders. An In-Depth Look from an Educational Perspective
Fowler, M. (in collaboration with Russell A. Barkley, Ron Reeve and Sydney Zentall). (1992). Plantation: CHADD. Paperback, 80pp. Can only be ordered from CHADD's distributor, Caset by calling 1-800-545-5583, or from the ADD WareHouse Catalog at 1-800-233-9273.

Comments: A most important document about what schools should know and do. It is very important for parents to know what the school knows so they can safeguard their child's education. This manual is therefore an essential document to own.

When You Worry about the Child You Love: Emotional and Learning Problems in Children
Hallowell, E. (1996). New York: Simon & Schuster. Hardcover, 280pp.

Comments: This is a warm, informative and moving book by one of the best and most knowledgeable communicators of childhood problems. Hallowell manages to guide parents through the most significant causes of problems in childhood in a sensitive, caring way. Highly recommended.

Answers to Distraction
Hallowell, E. & Ratey, J. (1996). New York: Bantam Books. Paperback, 334 pgs.

Comments: A comprehensive guide to AD/HD, written in an easy to read question/answer format. The sequel to their classic *Driven To Distraction*.

Attention Deficit Disorder and Learning Disabilities: Realities, Myths and Controversial Treatments
Ingersoll, B. & Goldstein, S. (1993). New York: Bantam Doubleday. Paperback, 246pp.

Comments: An important book by two of the best in the field. Accurate, factual information about ADD, LD and their treatments.

Fathering the AD/HD Child: A Book for Fathers, Mothers, and Professionals
Jacobs, E.H. (1998). Northvale, NJ: Jason Aronson, 294 pp.

Comments: Fathers and mothers experience parenting differently, and with the AD/HD child, the differences in the way parents regard discipline, behavior, and the nature of AD/HD itself, interferes with working effectively as a team. This book explores how fathers and mothers can use their differences creatively to parent their AD/HD child more effectively.

I Can't Sit Still
Johnson, K. (1991). Santa Cruz: ETR Associates. Paperback, 178pp.

Comments: Written by a neuropediatrician, complete and readable, translates complicated medical jargon into simple, down-to-earth language that both caregivers and children can understand and feel good about. Only available from the publisher.

Survival Strategies for Parenting Your ADD Child
Lynn, G.T. (1996). Grass Valley, CA: Underwood Books. Paperback, 268pp.

Comments: Offers concise and practical information for parents on dealing with oppositional behavior, dangerous and destructive behavior, depression, obsessions and compulsions, rage, school-related stress, etc.

Taming the Dragons: Real Help for Real School Problems
Setley, S. (1995). St. Louis: Starfish Publishing Co. Paperback, 241pp.

Comments: A very practical hands-on guide for parents on helping students with academic problems, homework, and specific suggestions for improving skills in reading, math, spelling.

Books for Children and Teens with AD/HD

AD/HD: A Teenagers Guide
Crist, J. (1996). King of Prussia, PA: Center for Applied Psychology. Paperback, 173pp.

Comments: Written specifically for teens with AD/HD, presents information and practical advice.

Succeeding in College with Attention Deficit Disorders
Bramer, J.S. (1996). Paperback, 189 pages. Plantation, FL: Specialty Press.

Comments: A very practical, well written, useful book for college students with ADD and those planning on going to college. Also recommended for counselors and educators.

The Survival Guide for Teenagers with LD (*Learning Differences)*
Cummings, R. & Fisher, G. (1993). Minneapolis: Free Spirit. Paperback, 190pp.

Comments: Provides information and advise to young people who have different learning styles on such topics as dating, driving, getting a job and planning for the future.

The Other Me: Poetic Thoughts on ADD for Adults, Kids, and Parents
Fellman, W. R. (1997). Plantation, FL: Specialty Press. Paperback, 121 pp.

Comments: Touching, funny, insightful poems about living with ADD.

Keeping A Head in School: A Student's Book about Learning Abilities and Learning Disorders
Levine, M. (1994). Cambridge: Educators Publishing Service. Paperback, 297pp.

Comments: For the motivated high school student, this book can be the answer to learning about how they learn and for building strategies to enhance their education. This book is highly recommended for parents of teens and for school professionals.

Shelly the Hyperactive Turtle
Moss, D. (1989). Rockville, MD: Woodbine Press. Hardcover, 24pp.

Comments: An illustrated story, for young children ages 3-7.

Help4ADD@High School
Nadeau, K. (1998). Bethesda, MD: Advantage Press. Paperback, 117 pages.

Comments: A terrific book for high school students written in a very readable website format that is fun and easy to navigate. Give it to a teen with ADD and watch them read though it, helped along by sharp graphics and cartoons. Even kids in junior high will benefit from it. Very highly recommended!

Survival Guide for College Students with ADD or LD
Nadeau, K. (1994). New York: Magination Press. Paperback, 56pp.

Comments: Provides information needed to survive and thrive in the college setting. Filled with practical suggestions and useful information.

Learning to Slow Down and Pay Attention
Nadeau, K., & Dixon, E. Paperback, 70pp.

Comments: For ages 6-12, provides age-appropriate information and practical suggestions.

Making the Grade: An Adolescent's Struggle with A.D.D.
Parker, R.A. (1992). Plantation, FL: ADD Warehouse.

Comments: A classic, on managing AD/HD behaviors for ages 9-12.

Adolescents and ADD: Gaining the Advantage
Quinn, P. (1995). New York: Magination Press. Paperback, 81pp.

Comments: Addresses the particular concerns of adolescents diagnosed with ADD and offers coping strategies as well as personal stories from teens with the disorder.

ADD and the College Student: A Guide for High School and College Students with Attention Deficit Disorder
Quinn, P. (Ed.) (1994). New York: Magination Press. Paperback, 113pp.

Comments: Filled with practical wisdom of both specialist and those who have ADD themselves, this reassuring book is full of practical information and advise to help students effectively navigate the difficult transition to college life.

Putting on the Brakes

Quinn, P. (1992). New York: Magination Press. Paperback, 64pp.

Comments: General information and coping strategies for AD/HD, well written, for ages 8-12.

Books for Adults with AD/HD

The Other Me: Poetic Thoughts on ADD for Adults, Kids, and Parents

Fellman, W. R. (1997). Plantation, FL: Specialty Press. Paperback, 121 pp.

Comments: Touching, funny, insightful poems about living with ADD.

Attention Deficit Disorder: A Different Perception

Hartmann, T. (1993; revised 1997). Grass Valley, CA: Underwood.

Comments: An interesting hunter/farmer metaphor for ADD which emphasizes the positive aspects of having and living with ADD.

Answers to Distraction

Hallowell, E. & Ratey, J. (1996). New York: Bantam Books. Paperback, 334 pgs.

Comments: A comprehensive guide to AD/HD, written in an easy to read question/answer format. The sequel to their classic *Driven To Distraction*.

Driven to Distraction

Hallowell, E. & Ratey, J. (1994). New York: Pantheon Books. Paperback, 319 pgs.

Comments: A classic, considered by many as the bible of ADD books. Covers general AD/HD issues from childhood to adulthood, with lots of practical information and suggestions.

You Mean I'm Not Lazy, Stupid, or Crazy?!

Kelly, K., & Ramundo, P. (1995). Cincinnati, OH: Scribner.

Comments: A classic by two women with ADD, clearly written, provides practical advice.

The ADDed Dimension: Everyday Advice for Adults with ADD
Kelly, K., & Ramundo, P. (1997).

Comments: More practical advice and coping skills from two pioneers in adult ADD.

Adventures in Fast Forward: Life, Love, and Work for the A.D.D. Adult
Nadeau, K. (1996). Paperback, 219pp.

Comments: Well written, readable, with clear information and practical suggestions for ADD adults. Highly recommended for Adults with AD/HD and those who wish to understand Adult with AD/HD behaviors better.

The Link between ADD and Addiction: Getting the Help You Deserve
Richardson, W. (1997). Paperback, 315pp.

Comments: A review of ADD, substance abuse, and addictive behaviors, useful and well written by a certified addiction specialist.

Women with Attention Deficit Disorder
Solden, S. (1995). Paperback, 288pp.

Comments: Focus on particular issues for women with AD/HD, by a female therapist. Highly recommended by many women with ADD.

Books for Professionals and Teachers

Attention Deficit Hyperactivity Disorder: A Handbook for Diagnosis and Treatment
Barkley, R.A. (1990). New York: Guilford Press. Hardback, 747pp.

Comments: Despite its publication date still the classic source of comprehensive information on the etiology, diagnosis, and treatment of AD/HD.

Succeeding in College with Attention Deficit Disorders
Bramer, J.S. (1996). Paperback, 189 pages. Plantation, FL: Specialty Press.

Comments: A very practical, well written, useful book for college students with ADD and those planning on going to college. Also recommended for counselors and educators.

Medications for Attention Deficit Disorders and Related Medical Problems: A Comprehensive Handbook
Copeland, E. D., & Copps, S.C. (1995). Plantation, FL: Specialty Press. Hardcover, 406pp.

Comments: Accurate and authoritative information on the medication selection and dosing of medications for ADD and related disorders.

AD/HD in the Schools: Assessment and Intervention Strategies
DuPaul, G. J. & Stoner, G. (1994). New York: Guildford Press. Hardcover, 269pp.

Comments: Presents solid research to support effective and appropriate assessment and interventions in the schools.

Managing Attention and Learning Disorders in Late Adolescence and Adulthood: A Guide for Practitioners
Goldstein, S. (1997). New York: John Wiley & Sons. Hardcover, 496pp.

Comments: With contributions by Rob Crawford, M.Ed., Michael Goldstein, M.D., Barbara D. Ingersoll, Ph.D., Patrician H. Latham,. J.D., Peter S. Latham, J.D., and Mary McDonald Richard this book is designed to be an accurate and authoritative guide for professionals on the subject matter covered.

Sourcebook for Children with Attention Deficit Disorder: A Management Guide for Early Childhood Professionals and Parents
Jones, C. B. Published by Communication Skill Builders (The Psychological Corporation) 1-800-763-2306.

Comments: Packed with information on identification and management tips for parents and teachers of preschoolers with ADD. Includes specific activities with goals, materials needed and clear directions. A must-have for early childhood programs.

Educational Care: A System for Understanding and Helping Children with Learning Problems at Home and in School
Levine, M. (1994). Cambridge: Educators Publishing Service. Hardcover, 325pp.

Comments: Dr. Levine dedicates his book to innocent children whose stifled struggles to succeed have been misinterpreted.

The Attention Deficit Disorders Intervention Manual

McCarney, S.B. (1989). Columbia, MO: Hawthorne Educational Services. Paperback, 404pp.

Comments: Provides a wealth of practical guidelines and suggestions for school based accommodations, for both learning and behavioral problems. Should be required reading for anyone attending an IEP conference for a child with AD/HD.

A Comprehensive Guide to Attention Deficit Disorder in Adults

Nadeau, K. (1995). New York: Brunner/Mazel. Hardcover, 408 pgs.

Comments: Well written, research based, and comprehensive review of adult ADD issues.

All about AD/HD: The Complete Practical Guide for Classroom Teachers

Pfiffner, L. J. (1996). Jefferson City, MO: Scholastic Professional Books. Paperback, 173 pp.

Comments: An excellent, well written, comprehensive manual for classroom teachers on identifying and managing AD/HD behaviors. Very practical information from one of our leading researchers in the area of classroom management and family-based interventions for AD/HD.

Index

Index

Page numbers followed by 'n' indicate a footnote. Page numbers in *italics* indicate a table or illustration.

A

433

445

Health Reference Series

COMPLETE CATALOG

Adolescent Health Sourcebook

Basic Consumer Health Information about Common Medical, Mental, and Emotional Concerns in Adolescents, Including Facts about Acne, Body Piercing, Mononucleosis, Nutrition, Eating Disorders, Stress, Depression, Behavior Problems, Peer Pressure, Violence, Gangs, Drug Use, Puberty, Sexuality, Pregnancy, Learning Disabilities, and More

Along with a Glossary of Terms and Other Resources for Further Help and Information

Edited by Chad T. Kimball. 658 pages. 2002. 0-7808-0248-9. $78.

AIDS Sourcebook, 1st Edition

Basic Information about AIDS and HIV Infection, Featuring Historical and Statistical Data, Current Research, Prevention, and Other Special Topics of Interest for Persons Living with AIDS

Along with Source Listings for Further Assistance

Edited by Karen Bellenir and Peter D. Dresser. 831 pages. 1995. 0-7808-0031-1. $78.

"One strength of this book is its practical emphasis. The intended audience is the lay reader . . . useful as an educational tool for health care providers who work with AIDS patients. Recommended for public libraries as well as hospital or academic libraries that collect consumer materials."
— *Bulletin of the Medical Library Association, Jan '96*

"This is the most comprehensive volume of its kind on an important medical topic. Highly recommended for all libraries."
— *Reference Book Review, '96*

"Very useful reference for all libraries."
— *Choice, Association of College and Research Libraries, Oct '95*

"There is a wealth of information here that can provide much educational assistance. It is a must book for all libraries and should be on the desk of each and every congressional leader. Highly recommended."
— *AIDS Book Review Journal, Aug '95*

"Recommended for most collections."
— *Library Journal, Jul '95*

AIDS Sourcebook, 2nd Edition

Basic Consumer Health Information about Acquired Immune Deficiency Syndrome (AIDS) and Human Immunodeficiency Virus (HIV) Infection, Featuring Updated Statistical Data, Reports on Recent Research and Prevention Initiatives, and Other Special Topics of Interest for Persons Living with AIDS, Including New Antiretroviral Treatment Options, Strategies for Com-

bating Opportunistic Infections, Information about Clinical Trials, and More

Along with a Glossary of Important Terms and Resource Listings for Further Help and Information

Edited by Karen Bellenir. 751 pages. 1999. 0-7808-0225-X. $78.

"Highly recommended."
— *American Reference Books Annual, 2000*

"Excellent sourcebook. This continues to be a highly recommended book. There is no other book that provides as much information as this book provides."
— *AIDS Book Review Journal, Dec-Jan 2000*

"Recommended reference source."
— *Booklist, American Library Association, Dec '99*

"A solid text for college-level health libraries."
— *The Bookwatch, Aug '99*

Cited in *Reference Sources for Small and Medium-Sized Libraries, American Library Association, 1999*

Alcoholism Sourcebook

Basic Consumer Health Information about the Physical and Mental Consequences of Alcohol Abuse, Including Liver Disease, Pancreatitis, Wernicke-Korsakoff Syndrome (Alcoholic Dementia), Fetal Alcohol Syndrome, Heart Disease, Kidney Disorders, Gastrointestinal Problems, and Immune System Compromise and Featuring Facts about Addiction, Detoxification, Alcohol Withdrawal, Recovery, and the Maintenance of Sobriety

Along with a Glossary and Directories of Resources for Further Help and Information

Edited by Karen Bellenir. 613 pages. 2000. 0-7808-0325-6. $78.

"This title is one of the few reference works on alcoholism for general readers. For some readers this will be a welcome complement to the many self-help books on the market. Recommended for collections serving general readers and consumer health collections."
— *E-Streams, Mar '01*

"This book is an excellent choice for public and academic libraries."
— *American Reference Books Annual, 2001*

"Recommended reference source."
— *Booklist, American Library Association, Dec '00*

"Presents a wealth of information on alcohol use and abuse and its effects on the body and mind, treatment, and prevention."
— *SciTech Book News, Dec '00*

"Important new health guide which packs in the latest consumer information about the problems of alcoholism."
— *Reviewer's Bookwatch, Nov '00*

SEE ALSO Drug Abuse Sourcebook, Substance Abuse Sourcebook

449

Allergies Sourcebook, 1st Edition

Basic Information about Major Forms and Mechanisms of Common Allergic Reactions, Sensitivities, and Intolerances, Including Anaphylaxis, Asthma, Hives and Other Dermatologic Symptoms, Rhinitis, and Sinusitis

Along with Their Usual Triggers Like Animal Fur, Chemicals, Drugs, Dust, Foods, Insects, Latex, Pollen, and Poison Ivy, Oak, and Sumac; Plus Information on Prevention, Identification, and Treatment

Edited by Allan R. Cook. 611 pages. 1997. 0-7808-0036-2. $78.

■

Allergies Sourcebook, 2nd Edition

Basic Consumer Health Information about Allergic Disorders, Triggers, Reactions, and Related Symptoms, Including Anaphylaxis, Rhinitis, Sinusitis, Asthma, Dermatitis, Conjunctivitis, and Multiple Chemical Sensitivity

Along with Tips on Diagnosis, Prevention, and Treatment, Statistical Data, a Glossary, and a Directory of Sources for Further Help and Information

Edited by Annemarie S. Muth. 598 pages. 2002. 0-7808-0376-0. $78.

■

Alternative Medicine Sourcebook, First Edition

Basic Consumer Health Information about Alternatives to Conventional Medicine, Including Acupressure, Acupuncture, Aromatherapy, Ayurveda, Bioelectromagnetics, Environmental Medicine, Essence Therapy, Food and Nutrition Therapy, Herbal Therapy, Homeopathy, Imaging, Massage, Naturopathy, Reflexology, Relaxation and Meditation, Sound Therapy, Vitamin and Mineral Therapy, and Yoga, and More

Edited by Allan R. Cook. 737 pages. 1999. 0-7808-0200-4. $78.

"Recommended reference source."
—Booklist, American Library Association, Feb '00

"A great addition to the reference collection of every type of library." *—American Reference Books Annual, 2000*

■

Alternative Medicine Sourcebook, Second Edition

Basic Consumer Health Information about Alternative and Complementary Medical Practices, Including Acupuncture, Chiropractic, Herbal Medicine, Homeopathy, Naturopathic Medicine, Mind-Body Interventions, Ayurveda, and Other Non-Western Medical Traditions

Along with Facts about such Specific Therapies as Massage Therapy, Aromatherapy, Qigong, Hypnosis, Prayer, Dance, and Art Therapies, a Glossary, and Resources for Further Information

Edited by Dawn D. Matthews. 618 pages. 2002. 0-7808-0605-0. $78.

Alzheimer's, Stroke & 29 Other Neurological Disorders Sourcebook, 1st Edition

Basic Information for the Layperson on 31 Diseases or Disorders Affecting the Brain and Nervous System, First Describing the Illness, Then Listing Symptoms, Diagnostic Methods, and Treatment Options, and Including Statistics on Incidences and Causes

Edited by Frank E. Bair. 579 pages. 1993. 1-55888-748-2. $78.

"Nontechnical reference book that provides reader-friendly information."
—Family Caregiver Alliance Update, Winter '96

"Should be included in any library's patient education section." *—American Reference Books Annual, 1994*

"Written in an approachable and accessible style. Recommended for patient education and consumer health collections in health science center and public libraries." *—Academic Library Book Review, Dec '93*

"It is very handy to have information on more than thirty neurological disorders under one cover, and there is no recent source like it." *—Reference Quarterly, American Library Association, Fall '93*

SEE ALSO *Brain Disorders Sourcebook*

■

Alzheimer's Disease Sourcebook, 2nd Edition

Basic Consumer Health Information about Alzheimer's Disease, Related Disorders, and Other Dementias, Including Multi-Infarct Dementia, AIDS-Related Dementia, Alcoholic Dementia, Huntington's Disease, Delirium, and Confusional States

Along with Reports Detailing Current Research Efforts in Prevention and Treatment, Long-Term Care Issues, and Listings of Sources for Additional Help and Information

Edited by Karen Bellenir. 524 pages. 1999. 0-7808-0223-3. $78.

"Provides a wealth of useful information not otherwise available in one place. This resource is recommended for all types of libraries."
—American Reference Books Annual, 2000

"Recommended reference source."
—Booklist, American Library Association, Oct '99

■

Arthritis Sourcebook

Basic Consumer Health Information about Specific Forms of Arthritis and Related Disorders, Including Rheumatoid Arthritis, Osteoarthritis, Gout, Polymyalgia Rheumatica, Psoriatic Arthritis, Spondyloarthropathies, Juvenile Rheumatoid Arthritis, and Juvenile Ankylosing Spondylitis

Along with Information about Medical, Surgical, and Alternative Treatment Options, and Including Strategies for Coping with Pain, Fatigue, and Stress

Edited by Allan R. Cook. 550 pages. 1998. 0-7808-0201-2. $78.

"... accessible to the layperson."
— *Reference and Research Book News, Feb '99*

Asthma Sourcebook

Basic Consumer Health Information about Asthma, Including Symptoms, Traditional and Nontraditional Remedies, Treatment Advances, Quality-of-Life Aids, Medical Research Updates, and the Role of Allergies, Exercise, Age, the Environment, and Genetics in the Development of Asthma

Along with Statistical Data, a Glossary, and Directories of Support Groups, and Other Resources for Further Information

Edited by Annemarie S. Muth. 628 pages. 2000. 0-7808-0381-7. $78.

"A worthwhile reference acquisition for public libraries and academic medical libraries whose readers desire a quick introduction to the wide range of asthma information."
— *Choice, Association of College & Research Libraries, Jun '01*

"Recommended reference source."
— *Booklist, American Library Association, Feb '01*

"Highly recommended." — *The Bookwatch, Jan '01*

"There is much good information for patients and their families who deal with asthma daily."
— *American Medical Writers Association Journal, Winter '01*

"This informative text is recommended for consumer health collections in public, secondary school, and community college libraries and the libraries of universities with a large undergraduate population."
— *American Reference Books Annual, 2001*

Attention Deficit Disorder Sourcebook, First Edition

Basic Consumer Health Information about Attention Deficit/Hyperactivity Disorder in Children and Adults, Including Facts about Causes, Symptoms, Diagnostic Criteria, and Treatment Options Such as Medications, Behavior Therapy, Coaching, and Homeopathy

Along with Reports on Current Research Initiatives, Legal Issues, and Government Regulations, and Featuring a Glossary of Related Terms, Internet Resources, and a List of Additional Reading Material

Edited by Dawn D. Matthews. 470 pages. 2002. 0-7808-0624-7. $78.

Back & Neck Disorders Sourcebook

Basic Information about Disorders and Injuries of the Spinal Cord and Vertebrae, Including Facts on Chiropractic Treatment, Surgical Interventions, Paralysis, and Rehabilitation

Along with Advice for Preventing Back Trouble

Edited by Karen Bellenir. 548 pages. 1997. 0-7808-0202-0. $78.

"The strength of this work is its basic, easy-to-read format. Recommended."
— *Reference and User Services Quarterly, American Library Association, Winter '97*

Blood & Circulatory Disorders Sourcebook

Basic Information about Blood and Its Components, Anemias, Leukemias, Bleeding Disorders, and Circulatory Disorders, Including Aplastic Anemia, Thalassemia, Sickle-Cell Disease, Hemochromatosis, Hemophilia, Von Willebrand Disease, and Vascular Diseases

Along with a Special Section on Blood Transfusions and Blood Supply Safety, a Glossary, and Source Listings for Further Help and Information

Edited by Karen Bellenir and Linda M. Shin. 554 pages. 1998. 0-7808-0203-9. $78.

"Recommended reference source."
— *Booklist, American Library Association, Feb '99*

"An important reference sourcebook written in simple language for everyday, non-technical users. "
— *Reviewer's Bookwatch, Jan '99*

Brain Disorders Sourcebook

Basic Consumer Health Information about Strokes, Epilepsy, Amyotrophic Lateral Sclerosis (ALS/Lou Gehrig's Disease), Parkinson's Disease, Brain Tumors, Cerebral Palsy, Headache, Tourette Syndrome, and More

Along with Statistical Data, Treatment and Rehabilitation Options, Coping Strategies, Reports on Current Research Initiatives, a Glossary, and Resource Listings for Additional Help and Information

Edited by Karen Bellenir. 481 pages. 1999. 0-7808-0229-2. $78.

"Belongs on the shelves of any library with a consumer health collection."
— *E-Streams, Mar '00*

"Recommended reference source."
— *Booklist, American Library Association, Oct '99*

SEE ALSO Alzheimer's, Stroke & 29 Other Neurological Disorders Sourcebook, 1st Edition

Breast Cancer Sourcebook

Basic Consumer Health Information about Breast Cancer, Including Diagnostic Methods, Treatment Options, Alternative Therapies, Self-Help Information, Related Health Concerns, Statistical and Demographic Data, and Facts for Men with Breast Cancer

Along with Reports on Current Research Initiatives, a Glossary of Related Medical Terms, and a Directory of Sources for Further Help and Information

Edited by Edward J. Prucha and Karen Bellenir. 580 pages. 2001. 0-7808-0244-6. $78.

"Recommended reference source."
— Booklist, American Library Association, Jan '02

"This reference source is highly recommended. It is quite informative, comprehensive and detailed in nature, and yet it offers practical advice in easy-to-read language. It could be thought of as the 'bible' of breast cancer for the consumer." *— E-Streams, Jan '02*

"The broad range of topics covered in lay language make the *Breast Cancer Sourcebook* an excellent addition to public and consumer health library collections."
— American Reference Books Annual 2002

"From the pros and cons of different screening methods and results to treatment options, *Breast Cancer Sourcebook* provides the latest information on the subject."
— Library Bookwatch, Dec '01

"This thoroughgoing, very readable reference covers all aspects of breast health and cancer. . . . Readers will find much to consider here. Recommended for all public and patient health collections."
— Library Journal, Sep '01

SEE ALSO Cancer Sourcebook for Women, 1st and 2nd Editions, Women's Health Concerns Sourcebook

■

Breastfeeding Sourcebook

Basic Consumer Health Information about the Benefits of Breastmilk, Preparing to Breastfeed, Breastfeeding as a Baby Grows, Nutrition, and More, Including Information on Special Situations and Concerns Such as Mastitis, Illness, Medications, Allergies, Multiple Births, Prematurity, Special Needs, and Adoption

Along with a Glossary and Resources for Additional Help and Information

Edited by Jenni Lynn Colson. 388 pages. 2002. 0-7808-0332-9. $78.

SEE ALSO Pregnancy & Birth Sourcebook

■

Burns Sourcebook

Basic Consumer Health Information about Various Types of Burns and Scalds, Including Flame, Heat, Cold, Electrical, Chemical, and Sun Burns

Along with Information on Short-Term and Long-Term Treatments, Tissue Reconstruction, Plastic Surgery, Prevention Suggestions, and First Aid

Edited by Allan R. Cook. 604 pages. 1999. 0-7808-0204-7. $78.

"This is an exceptional addition to the series and is highly recommended for all consumer health collections, hospital libraries, and academic medical centers."
— E-Streams, Mar '00

"This key reference guide is an invaluable addition to all health care and public libraries in confronting this ongoing health issue."
— American Reference Books Annual, 2000

"Recommended reference source."
— Booklist, American Library Association, Dec '99

SEE ALSO Skin Disorders Sourcebook

■

Cancer Sourcebook, 1st Edition

Basic Information on Cancer Types, Symptoms, Diagnostic Methods, and Treatments, Including Statistics on Cancer Occurrences Worldwide and the Risks Associated with Known Carcinogens and Activities

Edited by Frank E. Bair. 932 pages. 1990. 1-55888-888-8. $78.

Cited in *Reference Sources for Small and Medium-Sized Libraries, American Library Association, 1999*

"Written in nontechnical language. Useful for patients, their families, medical professionals, and librarians."
— Guide to Reference Books, 1996

"Designed with the non-medical professional in mind. Libraries and medical facilities interested in patient education should certainly consider adding the *Cancer Sourcebook* to their holdings. This compact collection of reliable information . . . is an invaluable tool for helping patients and patients' families and friends to take the first steps in coping with the many difficulties of cancer."
— Medical Reference Services Quarterly, Winter '91

"Specifically created for the nontechnical reader . . . an important resource for the general reader trying to understand the complexities of cancer."
— American Reference Books Annual, 1991

"This publication's nontechnical nature and very comprehensive format make it useful for both the general public and undergraduate students."
— Choice, Association of College and Research Libraries, Oct '90

■

New Cancer Sourcebook, 2nd Edition

Basic Information about Major Forms and Stages of Cancer, Featuring Facts about Primary and Secondary Tumors of the Respiratory, Nervous, Lymphatic, Circulatory, Skeletal, and Gastrointestinal Systems, and Specific Organs; Statistical and Demographic Data; Treatment Options; and Strategies for Coping

Edited by Allan R. Cook. 1,313 pages. 1996. 0-7808-0041-9. $78.

"An excellent resource for patients with newly diagnosed cancer and their families. The dialogue is simple, direct, and comprehensive. Highly recommended for patients and families to aid in their understanding of cancer and its treatment."

— *Booklist Health Sciences Supplement, American Library Association, Oct '97*

"The amount of factual and useful information is extensive. The writing is very clear, geared to general readers. Recommended for all levels." — *Choice, Association of College & Research Libraries, Jan '97*

■

Cancer Sourcebook, 3rd Edition

Basic Consumer Health Information about Major Forms and Stages of Cancer, Featuring Facts about Primary and Secondary Tumors of the Respiratory, Nervous, Lymphatic, Circulatory, Skeletal, and Gastrointestinal Systems, and Specific Organs

Along with Statistical and Demographic Data, Treatment Options, Strategies for Coping, a Glossary, and a Directory of Sources for Additional Help and Information

Edited by Edward J. Prucha. 1,069 pages. 2000. 0-7808-0227-6. $78.

"This title is recommended for health sciences and public libraries with consumer health collections." — *E-Streams, Feb '01*

". . . can be effectively used by cancer patients and their families who are looking for answers in a language they can understand. Public and hospital libraries should have it on their shelves." — *American Reference Books Annual, 2001*

"Recommended reference source." — *Booklist, American Library Association, Dec '00*

■

Cancer Sourcebook for Women, 1st Edition

Basic Information about Specific Forms of Cancer That Affect Women, Featuring Facts about Breast Cancer, Cervical Cancer, Ovarian Cancer, Cancer of the Uterus and Uterine Sarcoma, Cancer of the Vagina, and Cancer of the Vulva; Statistical and Demographic Data; Treatments, Self-Help Management Suggestions, and Current Research Initiatives

Edited by Allan R. Cook and Peter D. Dresser. 524 pages. 1996. 0-7808-0076-1. $78.

". . . written in easily understandable, non-technical language. Recommended for public libraries or hospital and academic libraries that collect patient education or consumer health materials." — *Medical Reference Services Quarterly, Spring '97*

"Would be of value in a consumer health library. . . . written with the health care consumer in mind. Medical jargon is at a minimum, and medical terms are explained in clear, understandable sentences." — *Bulletin of the Medical Library Association, Oct '96*

"The availability under one cover of all these pertinent publications, grouped under cohesive headings, makes this certainly a most useful sourcebook." — *Choice, Association of College & Research Libraries, Jun '96*

"Presents a comprehensive knowledge base for general readers. Men and women both benefit from the gold mine of information nestled between the two covers of this book. Recommended." — *Academic Library Book Review, Summer '96*

"This timely book is highly recommended for consumer health and patient education collections in all libraries." — *Library Journal, Apr '96*

SEE ALSO *Breast Cancer Sourcebook, Women's Health Concerns Sourcebook*

■

Cancer Sourcebook for Women, 2nd Edition

Basic Consumer Health Information about Gynecologic Cancers and Related Concerns, Including Cervical Cancer, Endometrial Cancer, Gestational Trophoblastic Tumor, Ovarian Cancer, Uterine Cancer, Vaginal Cancer, Vulvar Cancer, Breast Cancer, and Common Non-Cancerous Uterine Conditions, with Facts about Cancer Risk Factors, Screening and Prevention, Treatment Options, and Reports on Current Research Initiatives

Along with a Glossary of Cancer Terms and a Directory of Resources for Additional Help and Information

Edited by Karen Bellenir. 604 pages. 2002. 0-7808-0226-8. $78.

SEE ALSO *Breast Cancer Sourcebook, Women's Health Concerns Sourcebook*

■

Cardiovascular Diseases & Disorders Sourcebook, 1st Edition

Basic Information about Cardiovascular Diseases and Disorders, Featuring Facts about the Cardiovascular System, Demographic and Statistical Data, Descriptions of Pharmacological and Surgical Interventions, Lifestyle Modifications, and a Special Section Focusing on Heart Disorders in Children

Edited by Karen Bellenir and Peter D. Dresser. 683 pages. 1995. 0-7808-0032-X. $78.

". . . comprehensive format provides an extensive overview on this subject." — *Choice, Association of College & Research Libraries, Jun '96*

". . . an easily understood, complete, up-to-date resource. This well executed public health tool will make valuable information available to those that need it most, patients and their families. The typeface, sturdy non-reflective paper, and library binding add a feel of quality found wanting in other publications. Highly recommended for academic and general libraries. " — *Academic Library Book Review, Summer '96*

SEE ALSO *Healthy Heart Sourcebook for Women, Heart Diseases & Disorders Sourcebook, 2nd Edition*

Caregiving Sourcebook

Basic Consumer Health Information for Caregivers, Including a Profile of Caregivers, Caregiving Responsibilities and Concerns, Tips for Specific Conditions, Care Environments, and the Effects of Caregiving

Along with Facts about Legal Issues, Financial Information, and Future Planning, a Glossary, and a Listing of Additional Resources

Edited by Joyce Brennfleck Shannon. 600 pages. 2001. 0-7808-0331-0. $78.

"Essential for most collections."
— Library Journal, Apr 1, 2002

"An ideal addition to the reference collection of any public library. Health sciences information professionals may also want to acquire the *Caregiving Sourcebook* for their hospital or academic library for use as a ready reference tool by health care workers interested in aging and caregiving." *—E-Streams, Jan '02*

"Recommended reference source."
—Booklist, American Library Association, Oct '01

■

Colds, Flu & Other Common Ailments Sourcebook

Basic Consumer Health Information about Common Ailments and Injuries, Including Colds, Coughs, the Flu, Sinus Problems, Headaches, Fever, Nausea and Vomiting, Menstrual Cramps, Diarrhea, Constipation, Hemorrhoids, Back Pain, Dandruff, Dry and Itchy Skin, Cuts, Scrapes, Sprains, Bruises, and More

Along with Information about Prevention, Self-Care, Choosing a Doctor, Over-the-Counter Medications, Folk Remedies, and Alternative Therapies, and Including a Glossary of Important Terms and a Directory of Resources for Further Help and Information

Edited by Chad T. Kimball. 638 pages. 2001. 0-7808-0435-X. $78.

"A good starting point for research on common illnesses. It will be a useful addition to public and consumer health library collections."
— American Reference Books Annual 2002

"Will prove valuable to any library seeking to maintain a current, comprehensive reference collection of health resources. . . . Excellent reference."
— The Bookwatch, Aug '01

"Recommended reference source."
— Booklist, American Library Association, July '01

■

Communication Disorders Sourcebook

Basic Information about Deafness and Hearing Loss, Speech and Language Disorders, Voice Disorders, Balance and Vestibular Disorders, and Disorders of Smell, Taste, and Touch

Edited by Linda M. Ross. 533 pages. 1996. 0-7808-0077-X. $78.

"This is skillfully edited and is a welcome resource for the layperson. It should be found in every public and medical library." *—Booklist Health Sciences Supplement, American Library Association, Oct '97*

■

Congenital Disorders Sourcebook

Basic Information about Disorders Acquired during Gestation, Including Spina Bifida, Hydrocephalus, Cerebral Palsy, Heart Defects, Craniofacial Abnormalities, Fetal Alcohol Syndrome, and More

Along with Current Treatment Options and Statistical Data

Edited by Karen Bellenir. 607 pages. 1997. 0-7808-0205-5. $78.

"Recommended reference source."
— Booklist, American Library Association, Oct '97

SEE ALSO *Pregnancy & Birth Sourcebook*

■

Consumer Issues in Health Care Sourcebook

Basic Information about Health Care Fundamentals and Related Consumer Issues, Including Exams and Screening Tests, Physician Specialties, Choosing a Doctor, Using Prescription and Over-the-Counter Medications Safely, Avoiding Health Scams, Managing Common Health Risks in the Home, Care Options for Chronically or Terminally Ill Patients, and a List of Resources for Obtaining Help and Further Information

Edited by Karen Bellenir. 618 pages. 1998. 0-7808-0221-7. $78.

"Both public and academic libraries will want to have a copy in their collection for readers who are interested in self-education on health issues."
—American Reference Books Annual, 2000

"The editor has researched the literature from government agencies and others, saving readers the time and effort of having to do the research themselves. Recommended for public libraries."
— Reference and User Services Quarterly, American Library Association, Spring '99

"Recommended reference source."
— Booklist, American Library Association, Dec '98

■

Contagious & Non-Contagious Infectious Diseases Sourcebook

Basic Information about Contagious Diseases like Measles, Polio, Hepatitis B, and Infectious Mononucleosis, and Non-Contagious Infectious Diseases like Tetanus and Toxic Shock Syndrome, and Diseases Occurring as Secondary Infections Such as Shingles and Reye Syndrome

Along with Vaccination, Prevention, and Treatment Information, and a Section Describing Emerging Infectious Disease Threats

Edited by Karen Bellenir and Peter D. Dresser. 566 pages. 1996. 0-7808-0075-3. $78.

Death & Dying Sourcebook

Basic Consumer Health Information for the Layperson about End-of-Life Care and Related Ethical and Legal Issues, Including Chief Causes of Death, Autopsies, Pain Management for the Terminally Ill, Life Support Systems, Insurance, Euthanasia, Assisted Suicide, Hospice Programs, Living Wills, Funeral Planning, Counseling, Mourning, Organ Donation, and Physician Training

Along with Statistical Data, a Glossary, and Listings of Sources for Further Help and Information

Edited by Annemarie S. Muth. 641 pages. 1999. 0-7808-0230-6. $78.

"Public libraries, medical libraries, and academic libraries will all find this sourcebook a useful addition to their collections."
— *American Reference Books Annual, 2001*

"An extremely useful resource for those concerned with death and dying in the United States."
— *Respiratory Care, Nov '00*

"Recommended reference source."
— *Booklist, American Library Association, Aug '00*

"This book is a definite must for all those involved in end-of-life care." — *Doody's Review Service, 2000*

Diabetes Sourcebook, 1st Edition

Basic Information about Insulin-Dependent and Non-insulin-Dependent Diabetes Mellitus, Gestational Diabetes, and Diabetic Complications, Symptoms, Treatment, and Research Results, Including Statistics on Prevalence, Morbidity, and Mortality

Along with Source Listings for Further Help and Information

Edited by Karen Bellenir and Peter D. Dresser. 827 pages. 1994. 1-55888-751-2. $78.

". . . very informative and understandable for the layperson without being simplistic. It provides a comprehensive overview for laypersons who want a general understanding of the disease or who want to focus on various aspects of the disease."
— *Bulletin of the Medical Library Association, Jan '96*

Diabetes Sourcebook, 2nd Edition

Basic Consumer Health Information about Type 1 Diabetes (Insulin-Dependent or Juvenile-Onset Diabetes), Type 2 (Noninsulin-Dependent or Adult-Onset Diabetes), Gestational Diabetes, and Related Disorders, Including Diabetes Prevalence Data, Management Issues, the Role of Diet and Exercise in Controlling Diabetes, Insulin and Other Diabetes Medicines, and Complications of Diabetes Such as Eye Diseases, Periodontal Disease, Amputation, and End-Stage Renal Disease

Along with Reports on Current Research Initiatives, a Glossary, and Resource Listings for Further Help and Information

Edited by Karen Bellenir. 688 pages. 1998. 0-7808-0224-1. $78.

"An invaluable reference." — *Library Journal, May '00*

Selected as one of the 250 "Best Health Sciences Books of 1999." — *Doody's Rating Service, Mar-Apr 2000*

"This comprehensive book is an excellent addition for high school, academic, medical, and public libraries. This volume is highly recommended."
— *American Reference Books Annual, 2000*

"Provides useful information for the general public."
— *Healthlines, University of Michigan Health Management Research Center, Sep/Oct '99*

". . . provides reliable mainstream medical information . . . belongs on the shelves of any library with a consumer health collection." — *E-Streams, Sep '99*

"Recommended reference source."
— *Booklist, American Library Association, Feb '99*

Diet & Nutrition Sourcebook, 1st Edition

Basic Information about Nutrition, Including the Dietary Guidelines for Americans, the Food Guide Pyramid, and Their Applications in Daily Diet, Nutritional Advice for Specific Age Groups, Current Nutritional Issues and Controversies, the New Food Label and How to Use It to Promote Healthy Eating, and Recent Developments in Nutritional Research

Edited by Dan R. Harris. 662 pages. 1996. 0-7808-0084-2. $78.

"Useful reference as a food and nutrition sourcebook for the general consumer." — *Booklist Health Sciences Supplement, American Library Association, Oct '97*

"Recommended for public libraries and medical libraries that receive general information requests on nutrition. It is readable and will appeal to those interested in learning more about healthy dietary practices."
— *Medical Reference Services Quarterly, Fall '97*

"An abundance of medical and social statistics is translated into readable information geared toward the general reader." — *Bookwatch, Mar '97*

"With dozens of questionable diet books on the market, it is so refreshing to find a reliable and factual reference book. Recommended to aspiring professionals, librarians, and others seeking and giving reliable dietary advice. An excellent compilation." — *Choice, Association of College and Research Libraries, Feb '97*

SEE ALSO Digestive Diseases & Disorders Sourcebook, Gastrointestinal Diseases & Disorders Sourcebook

Diet & Nutrition Sourcebook, 2nd Edition

Basic Consumer Health Information about Dietary Guidelines, Recommended Daily Intake Values, Vitamins, Minerals, Fiber, Fat, Weight Control, Dietary Supplements, and Food Additives

Along with Special Sections on Nutrition Needs throughout Life and Nutrition for People with Such Spe-

cific Medical Concerns as Allergies, High Blood Cho-
lesterol, Hypertension, Diabetes, Celiac Disease,
Seizure Disorders, Phenylketonuria (PKU), Cancer, and
Eating Disorders, and Including Reports on Current
Nutrition Research and Source Listings for Additional
Help and Information

Edited by Karen Bellenir. 650 pages. 1999. 0-7808-0228-
4. $78.

"This book is an excellent source of basic diet and
nutrition information." — Booklist Health Sciences
Supplement, American Library Association, Dec '00

"This reference document should be in any public
library, but it would be a very good guide for beginning
students in the health sciences. If the other books in
this publisher's series are as good as this, they should all
be in the health sciences collections."
—American Reference Books Annual, 2000

"This book is an excellent general nutrition reference
for consumers who desire to take an active role in their
health care for prevention. Consumers of all ages who
select this book can feel confident they are receiving
current and accurate information." — Journal of
Nutrition for the Elderly, Vol. 19, No. 4, '00

"Recommended reference source."
—Booklist, American Library Association, Dec '99

SEE ALSO Digestive Diseases & Disorders Sourcebook,
Gastrointestinal Diseases & Disorders Sourcebook

Digestive Diseases
& Disorders Sourcebook

Basic Consumer Health Information about Diseases
and Disorders that Impact the Upper and Lower Digestive System, Including Celiac Disease, Constipation,
Crohn's Disease, Cyclic Vomiting Syndrome, Diarrhea,
Diverticulosis and Diverticulitis, Gallstones, Heartburn, Hemorrhoids, Hernias, Indigestion (Dyspepsia),
Irritable Bowel Syndrome, Lactose Intolerance, Ulcers,
and More

Along with Information about Medications and Other
Treatments, Tips for Maintaining a Healthy Digestive
Tract, a Glossary, and Directory of Digestive Diseases
Organizations

Edited by Karen Bellenir. 335 pages. 2000. 0-7808-0327-
2. $78.

"This title would be an excellent addition to all public
or patient-research libraries."
—American Reference Books Annual, 2001

"This title is recommended for public, hospital, and
health sciences libraries with consumer health collections." — E-Streams, Jul-Aug '00

"Recommended reference source."
—Booklist, American Library Association, May '00

SEE ALSO Diet & Nutrition Sourcebook, 1st and 2nd
Editions, Gastrointestinal Diseases & Disorders
Sourcebook

Disabilities Sourcebook

Basic Consumer Health Information about Physical
and Psychiatric Disabilities, Including Descriptions of
Major Causes of Disability, Assistive and Adaptive
Aids, Workplace Issues, and Accessibility Concerns

Along with Information about the Americans with
Disabilities Act, a Glossary, and Resources for Additional Help and Information

Edited by Dawn D. Matthews. 616 pages. 2000. 0-7808-
0389-2. $78.

"It is a must for libraries with a consumer health section." — American Reference Books Annual 2002

"A much needed addition to the Omnigraphics Health
Reference Series. A current reference work to provide
people with disabilities, their families, caregivers or
those who work with them, a broad range of information
in one volume, has not been available until now. . . . It
is recommended for all public and academic library reference collections." — E-Streams, May '01

"An excellent source book in easy-to-read format covering many current topics; highly recommended for all
libraries." — Choice, Association of College
and Research Libraries, Jan '01

"Recommended reference source."
—Booklist, American Library Association, Jul '00

"An involving, invaluable handbook."
— The Bookwatch, May '00

Domestic Violence &
Child Abuse Sourcebook

Basic Consumer Health Information about Spousal/
Partner, Child, Sibling, Parent, and Elder Abuse,
Covering Physical, Emotional, and Sexual Abuse, Teen
Dating Violence, and Stalking; Includes Information
about Hotlines, Safe Houses, Safety Plans, and Other
Resources for Support and Assistance, Community Ini-
tiatives, and Reports on Current Directions in Research
and Treatment

Along with a Glossary, Sources for Further Reading,
and Governmental and Non-Governmental Organizations Contact Information

Edited by Helene Henderson. 1,064 pages. 2001. 0-7808-
0235-7. $78.

"This is important information. The Web has many
resources but this sourcebook fills an important societal need. I am not aware of any other resources of this
type." — Doody's Review Service, Sep '01

"Recommended for all libraries, scholars, and practitioners." — Choice,
Association of College & Research Libraries, Jul '01

"Recommended reference source."
— Booklist, American Library Association, Apr '01

"Important pick for college-level health reference libraries." — The Bookwatch, Mar '01

"Because this problem is so widespread and because
this book includes a lot of issues within one volume,
this work is recommended for all public libraries."
— American Reference Books Annual, 2001

Drug Abuse Sourcebook

Basic Consumer Health Information about Illicit Substances of Abuse and the Diversion of Prescription Medications, Including Depressants, Hallucinogens, Inhalants, Marijuana, Narcotics, Stimulants, and Anabolic Steroids

Along with Facts about Related Health Risks, Treatment Issues, and Substance Abuse Prevention Programs, a Glossary of Terms, Statistical Data, and Directories of Hotline Services, Self-Help Groups, and Organizations Able to Provide Further Information

Edited by Karen Bellenir. 629 pages. 2000. 0-7808-0242-X. $78.

"Containing a wealth of information, this book will be useful to the college student just beginning to explore the topic of substance abuse. This resource belongs in libraries that serve a lower-division undergraduate or community college clientele as well as the general public." — Choice, Association of College and Research Libraries, Jun '01

"Recommended reference source."
— Booklist, American Library Association, Feb '01

"Highly recommended." — The Bookwatch, Jan '01

"Even though there is a plethora of books on drug abuse, this volume is recommended for school, public, and college libraries."
— American Reference Books Annual, 2001

SEE ALSO Alcoholism Sourcebook, Substance Abuse Sourcebook

Ear, Nose & Throat Disorders Sourcebook

Basic Information about Disorders of the Ears, Nose, Sinus Cavities, Pharynx, and Larynx, Including Ear Infections, Tinnitus, Vestibular Disorders, Allergic and Non-Allergic Rhinitis, Sore Throats, Tonsillitis, and Cancers That Affect the Ears, Nose, Sinuses, and Throat

Along with Reports on Current Research Initiatives, a Glossary of Related Medical Terms, and a Directory of Sources for Further Help and Information

Edited by Karen Bellenir and Linda M. Shin. 576 pages. 1998. 0-7808-0206-3. $78.

"Overall, this sourcebook is helpful for the consumer seeking information on ENT issues. It is recommended for public libraries."
— American Reference Books Annual, 1999

"Recommended reference source."
— Booklist, American Library Association, Dec '98

Eating Disorders Sourcebook

Basic Consumer Health Information about Eating Disorders, Including Information about Anorexia Nervosa, Bulimia Nervosa, Binge Eating, Body Dysmorphic Disorder, Pica, Laxative Abuse, and Night Eating Syndrome

Along with Information about Causes, Adverse Effects, and Treatment and Prevention Issues, and Featuring a Section on Concerns Specific to Children and Adolescents, a Glossary, and Resources for Further Help and Information

Edited by Dawn D. Matthews. 322 pages. 2001. 0-7808-0335-3. $78.

"Recommended for health science libraries that are open to the public, as well as hospital libraries. This book is a good resource for the consumer who is concerned about eating disorders." — E-Streams, Mar '02

"This volume is another convenient collection of excerpted articles. Recommended for school and public library patrons; lower-division undergraduates; and two-year technical program students."
— Choice, Association of College & Research Libraries, Jan '02

"Recommended reference source." — Booklist, American Library Association, Oct '01

Emergency Medical Services Sourcebook

Basic Consumer Health Information about Preventing, Preparing for, and Managing Emergency Situations, When and Who to Call for Help, What to Expect in the Emergency Room, the Emergency Medical Team, Patient Issues, and Current Topics in Emergency Medicine

Along with Statistical Data, a Glossary, and Sources of Additional Help and Information

Edited by Jenni Lynn Colson. 600 pages. 2002. 0-7808-0420-1. $78.

Endocrine & Metabolic Disorders Sourcebook

Basic Information for the Layperson about Pancreatic and Insulin-Related Disorders Such as Pancreatitis, Diabetes, and Hypoglycemia; Adrenal Gland Disorders Such as Cushing's Syndrome, Addison's Disease, and Congenital Adrenal Hyperplasia; Pituitary Gland Disorders Such as Growth Hormone Deficiency, Acromegaly, and Pituitary Tumors; Thyroid Disorders Such as Hypothyroidism, Graves' Disease, Hashimoto's Disease, and Goiter; Hyperparathyroidism; and Other Diseases and Syndromes of Hormone Imbalance or Metabolic Dysfunction

Along with Reports on Current Research Initiatives

Edited by Linda M. Shin. 574 pages. 1998. 0-7808-0207-1. $78.

"Omnigraphics has produced another needed resource for health information consumers."
— American Reference Books Annual, 2000

"Recommended reference source."
— Booklist, American Library Association, Dec '98

Environmentally Induced Disorders Sourcebook

Basic Information about Diseases and Syndromes Linked to Exposure to Pollutants and Other Substances in Outdoor and Indoor Environments Such as Lead, Asbestos, Formaldehyde, Mercury, Emissions, Noise, and More

Edited by Allan R. Cook. 620 pages. 1997. 0-7808-0083-4. $78.

"Recommended reference source."
— *Booklist, American Library Association, Sep '98*

"This book will be a useful addition to anyone's library." — *Choice Health Sciences Supplement, Association of College and Research Libraries, May '98*

". . . a good survey of numerous environmentally induced physical disorders . . . a useful addition to anyone's library."
— *Doody's Health Sciences Book Reviews, Jan '98*

". . . provide[s] introductory information from the best authorities around. Since this volume covers topics that potentially affect everyone, it will surely be one of the most frequently consulted volumes in the *Health Reference Series*." — *Rettig on Reference, Nov '97*

Ethnic Diseases Sourcebook

Basic Consumer Health Information for Ethnic and Racial Minority Groups in the United States, Including General Health Indicators and Behaviors, Ethnic Diseases, Genetic Testing, the Impact of Chronic Diseases, Women's Health, Mental Health Issues, and Preventive Health Care Services

Along with a Glossary and a Listing of Additional Resources

Edited by Joyce Brennfleck Shannon. 664 pages. 2001. 0-7808-0336-1. $78.

"Recommended for health sciences libraries where public health programs are a priority."
— *E-Streams, Jan '02*

"Not many books have been written on this topic to date, and the *Ethnic Diseases Sourcebook* is a strong addition to the list. It will be an important introductory resource for health consumers, students, health care personnel, and social scientists. It is recommended for public, academic, and large hospital libraries."
— *American Reference Books Annual 2002*

"Recommended reference source."
— *Booklist, American Library Association, Oct '01*

"Will prove valuable to any library seeking to maintain a current, comprehensive reference collection of health resources. . . . An excellent source of health information about genetic disorders which affect particular ethnic and racial minorities in the U.S."
— *The Bookwatch, Aug '01*

Family Planning Sourcebook

Basic Consumer Health Information about Planning for Pregnancy and Contraception, Including Traditional Methods, Barrier Methods, Hormonal Methods, Permanent Methods, Future Methods, Emergency Contraception, and Birth Control Choices for Women at Each Stage of Life

Along with Statistics, a Glossary, and Sources of Additional Information

Edited by Amy Marcaccio Keyzer. 520 pages. 2001. 0-7808-0379-5. $78.

"Recommended for public, health, and undergraduate libraries as part of the circulating collection."
— *E-Streams, Mar '02*

"Information is presented in an unbiased, readable manner, and the sourcebook will certainly be a necessary addition to those public and high school libraries where Internet access is restricted or otherwise problematic." — *American Reference Books Annual 2002*

"Recommended reference source."
— *Booklist, American Library Association, Oct '01*

"Will prove valuable to any library seeking to maintain a current, comprehensive reference collection of health resources. . . . Excellent reference."
— *The Bookwatch, Aug '01*

SEE ALSO Pregnancy & Birth Sourcebook

Fitness & Exercise Sourcebook, 1st Edition

Basic Information on Fitness and Exercise, Including Fitness Activities for Specific Age Groups, Exercise for People with Specific Medical Conditions, How to Begin a Fitness Program in Running, Walking, Swimming, Cycling, and Other Athletic Activities, and Recent Research in Fitness and Exercise

Edited by Dan R. Harris. 663 pages. 1996. 0-7808-0186-5. $78.

"A good resource for general readers." — *Choice, Association of College and Research Libraries, Nov '97*

"The perennial popularity of the topic . . . make this an appealing selection for public libraries."
— *Rettig on Reference, Jun/Jul '97*

Fitness & Exercise Sourcebook, 2nd Edition

Basic Consumer Health Information about the Fundamentals of Fitness and Exercise, Including How to Begin and Maintain a Fitness Program, Fitness as a Lifestyle, the Link between Fitness and Diet, Advice for Specific Groups of People, Exercise as It Relates to Specific Medical Conditions, and Recent Research in Fitness and Exercise

Along with a Glossary of Important Terms and Resources for Additional Help and Information

Edited by Kristen M. Gledhill. 646 pages. 2001. 0-7808-0334-5. $78.

"This work is recommended for all general reference collections."

—*American Reference Books Annual 2002*

"Highly recommended for public, consumer, and school grades fourth through college."

—*E-Streams, Nov '01*

"Recommended reference source."   — *Booklist, American Library Association, Oct '01*

"The information appears quite comprehensive and is considered reliable. . . . This second edition is a welcomed addition to the series."

—*Doody's Review Service, Sep '01*

"This reference is a valuable choice for those who desire a broad source of information on exercise, fitness, and chronic-disease prevention through a healthy lifestyle."   —*American Medical Writers Association Journal, Fall '01*

"Will prove valuable to any library seeking to maintain a current, comprehensive reference collection of health resources. . . . Excellent reference."

— *The Bookwatch, Aug '01*

Food & Animal Borne Diseases Sourcebook

Basic Information about Diseases That Can Be Spread to Humans through the Ingestion of Contaminated Food or Water or by Contact with Infected Animals and Insects, Such as Botulism, E. Coli, Hepatitis A, Trichinosis, Lyme Disease, and Rabies

Along with Information Regarding Prevention and Treatment Methods, and Including a Special Section for International Travelers Describing Diseases Such as Cholera, Malaria, Travelers' Diarrhea, and Yellow Fever, and Offering Recommendations for Avoiding Illness

Edited by Karen Bellenir and Peter D. Dresser. 535 pages. 1995. 0-7808-0033-8. $78.

"Targeting general readers and providing them with a single, comprehensive source of information on selected topics, this book continues, with the excellent caliber of its predecessors, to catalog topical information on health matters of general interest. Readable and thorough, this valuable resource is highly recommended for all libraries."

— *Academic Library Book Review, Summer '96*

"A comprehensive collection of authoritative information."   — *Emergency Medical Services, Oct '95*

Food Safety Sourcebook

Basic Consumer Health Information about the Safe Handling of Meat, Poultry, Seafood, Eggs, Fruit Juices, and Other Food Items, and Facts about Pesticides, Drinking Water, Food Safety Overseas, and the Onset, Duration, and Symptoms of Foodborne Illnesses, Including Types of Pathogenic Bacteria, Parasitic Protozoa, Worms, Viruses, and Natural Toxins

Along with the Role of the Consumer, the Food Handler, and the Government in Food Safety; a Glossary, and Resources for Additional Help and Information

Edited by Dawn D. Matthews. 339 pages. 1999. 0-7808-0326-4. $78.

"This book is recommended for public libraries and universities with home economic and food science programs."   — *E-Streams, Nov '00*

"Recommended reference source."

—*Booklist, American Library Association, May '00*

"This book takes the complex issues of food safety and foodborne pathogens and presents them in an easily understood manner. [It does] an excellent job of covering a large and often confusing topic."

—*American Reference Books Annual, 2000*

Forensic Medicine Sourcebook

Basic Consumer Information for the Layperson about Forensic Medicine, Including Crime Scene Investigation, Evidence Collection and Analysis, Expert Testimony, Computer-Aided Criminal Identification, Digital Imaging in the Courtroom, DNA Profiling, Accident Reconstruction, Autopsies, Ballistics, Drugs and Explosives Detection, Latent Fingerprints, Product Tampering, and Questioned Document Examination

Along with Statistical Data, a Glossary of Forensics Terminology, and Listings of Sources for Further Help and Information

Edited by Annemarie S. Muth. 574 pages. 1999. 0-7808-0232-2. $78.

"Given the expected widespread interest in its content and its easy to read style, this book is recommended for most public and all college and university libraries."

— *E-Streams, Feb '01*

"Recommended for public libraries."

—*Reference & User Services Quarterly, American Library Association, Spring 2000*

"Recommended reference source."

—*Booklist, American Library Association, Feb '00*

"A wealth of information, useful statistics, references are up-to-date and extremely complete. This wonderful collection of data will help students who are interested in a career in any type of forensic field. It is a great resource for attorneys who need information about types of expert witnesses needed in a particular case. It also offers useful information for fiction and nonfiction writers whose work involves a crime. A fascinating compilation. All levels."   — *Choice, Association of College and Research Libraries, Jan 2000*

"There are several items that make this book attractive to consumers who are seeking certain forensic data. . . . This is a useful current source for those seeking general forensic medical answers."

—*American Reference Books Annual, 2000*

Gastrointestinal Diseases & Disorders Sourcebook

Basic Information about Gastroesophageal Reflux Disease (Heartburn), Ulcers, Diverticulosis, Irritable Bowel Syndrome, Crohn's Disease, Ulcerative Colitis, Diarrhea, Constipation, Lactose Intolerance, Hemorrhoids, Hepatitis, Cirrhosis, and Other Digestive Problems, Featuring Statistics, Descriptions of Symptoms, and Current Treatment Methods of Interest for Persons Living with Upper and Lower Gastrointestinal Maladies

Edited by Linda M. Ross. 413 pages. 1996. 0-7808-0078-8. $78.

". . . very readable form. The successful editorial work that brought this material together into a useful and understandable reference makes accessible to all readers information that can help them more effectively understand and obtain help for digestive tract problems."
— *Choice, Association of College & Research Libraries, Feb '97*

SEE ALSO *Diet & Nutrition Sourcebook, 1st and 2nd Editions, Digestive Diseases & Disorders*

■

Genetic Disorders Sourcebook, 1st Edition

Basic Information about Heritable Diseases and Disorders Such as Down Syndrome, PKU, Hemophilia, Von Willebrand Disease, Gaucher Disease, Tay-Sachs Disease, and Sickle-Cell Disease, Along with Information about Genetic Screening, Gene Therapy, Home Care, and Including Source Listings for Further Help and Information on More Than 300 Disorders

Edited by Karen Bellenir. 642 pages. 1996. 0-7808-0034-6. $78.

"Recommended for undergraduate libraries or libraries that serve the public."
— *Science & Technology Libraries, Vol. 18, No. 1, '99*

"Provides essential medical information to both the general public and those diagnosed with a serious or fatal genetic disease or disorder." —*Choice, Association of College and Research Libraries, Jan '97*

"Geared toward the lay public. It would be well placed in all public libraries and in those hospital and medical libraries in which access to genetic references is limited." —*Doody's Health Sciences Book Review, Oct '96*

■

Genetic Disorders Sourcebook, 2nd Edition

Basic Consumer Health Information about Hereditary Diseases and Disorders, Including Cystic Fibrosis, Down Syndrome, Hemophilia, Huntington's Disease, Sickle Cell Anemia, and More; Facts about Genes, Gene Research and Therapy, Genetic Screening, Ethics of Gene Testing, Genetic Counseling, and Advice on Coping and Caring

Along with a Glossary of Genetic Terminology and a Resource List for Help, Support, and Further Information

Edited by Kathy Massimini. 768 pages. 2001. 0-7808-0241-1. $78.

"Recommended for public libraries and medical and hospital libraries with consumer health collections."
— *E-Streams, May '01*

"Recommended reference source."
— *Booklist, American Library Association, Apr '01*

"Important pick for college-level health reference libraries." — *The Bookwatch, Mar '01*

■

Head Trauma Sourcebook

Basic Information for the Layperson about Open-Head and Closed-Head Injuries, Treatment Advances, Recovery, and Rehabilitation

Along with Reports on Current Research Initiatives

Edited by Karen Bellenir. 414 pages. 1997. 0-7808-0208-X. $78.

■

Headache Sourcebook

Basic Consumer Health Information about Migraine, Tension, Cluster, Rebound and Other Types of Headaches, with Facts about the Cause and Prevention of Headaches, the Effects of Stress and the Environment, Headaches during Pregnancy and Menopause, and Childhood Headaches

Along with a Glossary and Other Resources for Additional Help and Information

Edited by Dawn D. Matthews. 362 pages. 2002. 0-7808-0337-X. $78.

■

Health Insurance Sourcebook

Basic Information about Managed Care Organizations, Traditional Fee-for-Service Insurance, Insurance Portability and Pre-Existing Conditions Clauses, Medicare, Medicaid, Social Security, and Military Health Care

Along with Information about Insurance Fraud

Edited by Wendy Wilcox. 530 pages. 1997. 0-7808-0222-5. $78.

"Particularly useful because it brings much of this information together in one volume. This book will be a handy reference source in the health sciences library, hospital library, college and university library, and medium to large public library."
— *Medical Reference Services Quarterly, Fall '98*

Awarded "Books of the Year Award"
— *American Journal of Nursing, 1997*

"The layout of the book is particularly helpful as it provides easy access to reference material. A most useful addition to the vast amount of information about health insurance. The use of data from U.S. government agen-

cies is most commendable. Useful in a library or learning center for healthcare professional students."
— *Doody's Health Sciences Book Reviews, Nov '97*

■

Health Reference Series Cumulative Index 1999

A Comprehensive Index to the Individual Volumes of the Health Reference Series, Including a Subject Index, Name Index, Organization Index, and Publication Index

Along with a Master List of Acronyms and Abbreviations

Edited by Edward J. Prucha, Anne Holmes, and Robert Rudnick. 990 pages. 2000. 0-7808-0382-5. $78.

"This volume will be most helpful in libraries that have a relatively complete collection of the Health Reference Series." — *American Reference Books Annual, 2001*

"Essential for collections that hold any of the numerous *Health Reference Series* titles."
— *Choice, Association of College and Research Libraries, Nov '00*

■

Healthy Aging Sourcebook

Basic Consumer Health Information about Maintaining Health through the Aging Process, Including Advice on Nutrition, Exercise, and Sleep, Help in Making Decisions about Midlife Issues and Retirement, and Guidance Concerning Practical and Informed Choices in Health Consumerism

Along with Data Concerning the Theories of Aging, Different Experiences in Aging by Minority Groups, and Facts about Aging Now and Aging in the Future; and Featuring a Glossary, a Guide to Consumer Help, Additional Suggested Reading, and Practical Resource Directory

Edited by Jenifer Swanson. 536 pages. 1999. 0-7808-0390-6. $78.

"Recommended reference source."
— *Booklist, American Library Association, Feb '00*

SEE ALSO *Physical & Mental Issues in Aging Sourcebook*

■

Healthy Heart Sourcebook for Women

Basic Consumer Health Information about Cardiac Issues Specific to Women, Including Facts about Major Risk Factors and Prevention, Treatment and Control Strategies, and Important Dietary Issues

Along with a Special Section Regarding the Pros and Cons of Hormone Replacement Therapy and Its Impact on Heart Health, and Additional Help, Including Recipes, a Glossary, and a Directory of Resources

Edited by Dawn D. Matthews. 336 pages. 2000. 0-7808-0329-9. $78.

"A good reference source and recommended for all public, academic, medical, and hospital libraries."
— *Medical Reference Services Quarterly, Summer '01*

"Because of the lack of information specific to women on this topic, this book is recommended for public libraries and consumer libraries."
— *American Reference Books Annual, 2001*

"Contains very important information about coronary artery disease that all women should know. The information is current and presented in an easy-to-read format. The book will make a good addition to any library." — *American Medical Writers Association Journal, Summer '00*

"Important, basic reference."
— *Reviewer's Bookwatch, Jul '00*

SEE ALSO *Cardiovascular Diseases & Disorders Sourcebook, 1st Edition, Heart Diseases & Disorders Sourcebook, 2nd Edition, Women's Health Concerns Sourcebook*

■

Heart Diseases & Disorders Sourcebook, 2nd Edition

Basic Consumer Health Information about Heart Attacks, Angina, Rhythm Disorders, Heart Failure, Valve Disease, Congenital Heart Disorders, and More, Including Descriptions of Surgical Procedures and Other Interventions, Medications, Cardiac Rehabilitation, Risk Identification, and Prevention Tips

Along with Statistical Data, Reports on Current Research Initiatives, a Glossary of Cardiovascular Terms, and Resource Directory

Edited by Karen Bellenir. 612 pages. 2000. 0-7808-0238-1. $78.

"This work stands out as an imminently accessible resource for the general public. It is recommended for the reference and circulating shelves of school, public, and academic libraries."
— *American Reference Books Annual, 2001*

"Recommended reference source."
— *Booklist, American Library Association, Dec '00*

"Provides comprehensive coverage of matters related to the heart. This title is recommended for health sciences and public libraries with consumer health collections."
— *E-Streams, Oct '00*

SEE ALSO *Cardiovascular Diseases & Disorders Sourcebook, 1st Edition; Healthy Heart Sourcebook for Women*

■

Household Safety Sourcebook

Basic Consumer Health Information about Household Safety, Including Information about Poisons, Chemicals, Fire, and Water Hazards in the Home

Along with Advice about the Safe Use of Home Maintenance Equipment, Choosing Toys and Nursery Furniture, Holiday and Recreation Safety, a Glossary, and Resources for Further Help and Information

Edited by Dawn D. Matthews. 606 pages. 2002. 0-7808-0338-8. $78.

Immune System Disorders Sourcebook

Basic Information about Lupus, Multiple Sclerosis, Guillain-Barré Syndrome, Chronic Granulomatous Disease, and More

Along with Statistical and Demographic Data and Reports on Current Research Initiatives

Edited by Allan R. Cook. 608 pages. 1997. 0-7808-0209-8. $78.

■

Infant & Toddler Health Sourcebook

Basic Consumer Health Information about the Physical and Mental Development of Newborns, Infants, and Toddlers, Including Neonatal Concerns, Nutrition Recommendations, Immunization Schedules, Common Pediatric Disorders, Assessments and Milestones, Safety Tips, and Advice for Parents and Other Caregivers

Along with a Glossary of Terms and Resource Listings for Additional Help

Edited by Jenifer Swanson. 585 pages. 2000. 0-7808-0246-2. $78.

"As a reference for the general public, this would be useful in any library." — *E-Streams, May '01*

"Recommended reference source."
— *Booklist, American Library Association, Feb '01*

"This is a good source for general use."
— *American Reference Books Annual, 2001*

■

Injury & Trauma Sourcebook

Basic Consumer Health Information about the Impact of Injury, the Diagnosis and Treatment of Common and Traumatic Injuries, Emergency Care, and Specific Injuries Related to Home, Community, Workplace, Transportation, and Recreation

Along with Guidelines for Injury Prevention, a Glossary, and a Directory of Additional Resources

Edited by Joyce Brennfleck Shannon. 696 pages. 2002. 0-7808-0421-X. $78.

■

Kidney & Urinary Tract Diseases & Disorders Sourcebook

Basic Information about Kidney Stones, Urinary Incontinence, Bladder Disease, End Stage Renal Disease, Dialysis, and More

Along with Statistical and Demographic Data and Reports on Current Research Initiatives

Edited by Linda M. Ross. 602 pages. 1997. 0-7808-0079-6. $78.

Learning Disabilities Sourcebook

Basic Information about Disorders Such as Dyslexia, Visual and Auditory Processing Deficits, Attention Deficit/Hyperactivity Disorder, and Autism

Along with Statistical and Demographic Data, Reports on Current Research Initiatives, an Explanation of the Assessment Process, and a Special Section for Adults with Learning Disabilities

Edited by Linda M. Shin. 579 pages. 1998. 0-7808-0210-1. $78.

Named "Outstanding Reference Book of 1999."
— *New York Public Library, Feb 2000*

"An excellent candidate for inclusion in a public library reference section. It's a great source of information. Teachers will also find the book useful. Definitely worth reading."
— *Journal of Adolescent & Adult Literacy, Feb 2000*

"Readable . . . provides a solid base of information regarding successful techniques used with individuals who have learning disabilities, as well as practical suggestions for educators and family members. Clear language, concise descriptions, and pertinent information for contacting multiple resources add to the strength of this book as a useful tool." — *Choice, Association of College and Research Libraries, Feb '99*

"Recommended reference source."
— *Booklist, American Library Association, Sep '98*

"A useful resource for libraries and for those who don't have the time to identify and locate the individual publications." — *Disability Resources Monthly, Sep '98*

■

Liver Disorders Sourcebook

Basic Consumer Health Information about the Liver and How It Works; Liver Diseases, Including Cancer, Cirrhosis, Hepatitis, and Toxic and Drug Related Diseases; Tips for Maintaining a Healthy Liver; Laboratory Tests, Radiology Tests, and Facts about Liver Transplantation

Along with a Section on Support Groups, a Glossary, and Resource Listings

Edited by Joyce Brennfleck Shannon. 591 pages. 2000. 0-7808-0383-3. $78.

"A valuable resource."
— *American Reference Books Annual, 2001*

"This title is recommended for health sciences and public libraries with consumer health collections."
— *E-Streams, Oct '00*

"Recommended reference source."
— *Booklist, American Library Association, Jun '00*

Lung Disorders Sourcebook

Basic Consumer Health Information about Emphysema, Pneumonia, Tuberculosis, Asthma, Cystic Fibrosis, and Other Lung Disorders, Including Facts about Diagnostic Procedures, Treatment Strategies, Disease Prevention Efforts, and Such Risk Factors as Smoking, Air Pollution, and Exposure to Asbestos, Radon, and Other Agents

Along with a Glossary and Resources for Additional Help and Information

Edited by Dawn D. Matthews. 678 pages. 2002. 0-7808-0339-6. $78.

■

Medical Tests Sourcebook

Basic Consumer Health Information about Medical Tests, Including Periodic Health Exams, General Screening Tests, Tests You Can Do at Home, Findings of the U.S. Preventive Services Task Force, X-ray and Radiology Tests, Electrical Tests, Tests of Blood and Other Body Fluids and Tissues, Scope Tests, Lung Tests, Genetic Tests, Pregnancy Tests, Newborn Screening Tests, Sexually Transmitted Disease Tests, and Computer Aided Diagnoses

Along with a Section on Paying for Medical Tests, a Glossary, and Resource Listings

Edited by Joyce Brennfleck Shannon. 691 pages. 1999. 0-7808-0243-8. $78.

"Recommended for hospital and health sciences libraries with consumer health collections."
— E-Streams, Mar '00

"This is an overall excellent reference with a wealth of general knowledge that may aid those who are reluctant to get vital tests performed."
— Today's Librarian, Jan 2000

"A valuable reference guide."
—American Reference Books Annual, 2000

■

Men's Health Concerns Sourcebook

Basic Information about Health Issues That Affect Men, Featuring Facts about the Top Causes of Death in Men, Including Heart Disease, Stroke, Cancers, Prostate Disorders, Chronic Obstructive Pulmonary Disease, Pneumonia and Influenza, Human Immunodeficiency Virus and Acquired Immune Deficiency Syndrome, Diabetes Mellitus, Stress, Suicide, Accidents and Homicides; and Facts about Common Concerns for Men, Including Impotence, Contraception, Circumcision, Sleep Disorders, Snoring, Hair Loss, Diet, Nutrition, Exercise, Kidney and Urological Disorders, and Backaches

Edited by Allan R. Cook. 738 pages. 1998. 0-7808-0212-8. $78.

"This comprehensive resource and the series are highly recommended."
—American Reference Books Annual, 2000

"Recommended reference source."
— Booklist, American Library Association, Dec '98

Mental Health Disorders Sourcebook, 1st Edition

Basic Information about Schizophrenia, Depression, Bipolar Disorder, Panic Disorder, Obsessive-Compulsive Disorder, Phobias and Other Anxiety Disorders, Paranoia and Other Personality Disorders, Eating Disorders, and Sleep Disorders

Along with Information about Treatment and Therapies

Edited by Karen Bellenir. 548 pages. 1995. 0-7808-0040-0. $78.

"This is an excellent new book . . . written in easy-to-understand language."
— Booklist Health Sciences Supplement, American Library Association, Oct '97

". . . useful for public and academic libraries and consumer health collections."
— Medical Reference Services Quarterly, Spring '97

"The great strengths of the book are its readability and its inclusion of places to find more information. Especially recommended." — Reference Quarterly, American Library Association, Winter '96

". . . a good resource for a consumer health library."
—Bulletin of the Medical Library Association, Oct '96

"The information is data-based and couched in brief, concise language that avoids jargon. . . . a useful reference source." — Readings, Sep '96

"The text is well organized and adequately written for its target audience." — Choice, Association of College and Research Libraries, Jun '96

". . . provides information on a wide range of mental disorders, presented in nontechnical language."
— Exceptional Child Education Resources, Spring '96

"Recommended for public and academic libraries."
— Reference Book Review, 1996

■

Mental Health Disorders Sourcebook, 2nd Edition

Basic Consumer Health Information about Anxiety Disorders, Depression and Other Mood Disorders, Eating Disorders, Personality Disorders, Schizophrenia, and More, Including Disease Descriptions, Treatment Options, and Reports on Current Research Initiatives

Along with Statistical Data, Tips for Maintaining Mental Health, a Glossary, and Directory of Sources for Additional Help and Information

Edited by Karen Bellenir. 605 pages. 2000. 0-7808-0240-3. $78.

"Well organized and well written."
—American Reference Books Annual, 2001

"Recommended reference source."
—Booklist, American Library Association, Jun '00

Mental Retardation Sourcebook

Basic Consumer Health Information about Mental Retardation and Its Causes, Including Down Syndrome, Fetal Alcohol Syndrome, Fragile X Syndrome, Genetic Conditions, Injury, and Environmental Sources

Along with Preventive Strategies, Parenting Issues, Educational Implications, Health Care Needs, Employment and Economic Matters, Legal Issues, a Glossary, and a Resource Listing for Additional Help and Information

Edited by Joyce Brennfleck Shannon. 642 pages. 2000. 0-7808-0377-9. $78.

"Public libraries will find the book useful for reference and as a beginning research point for students, parents, and caregivers."
—American Reference Books Annual, 2001

"The strength of this work is that it compiles many basic fact sheets and addresses for further information in one volume. It is intended and suitable for the general public. This sourcebook is relevant to any collection providing health information to the general public."
—E-Streams, Nov '00

"From preventing retardation to parenting and family challenges, this covers health, social and legal issues and will prove an invaluable overview."
—Reviewer's Bookwatch, Jul '00

■

Obesity Sourcebook

Basic Consumer Health Information about Diseases and Other Problems Associated with Obesity, and Including Facts about Risk Factors, Prevention Issues, and Management Approaches

Along with Statistical and Demographic Data, Information about Special Populations, Research Updates, a Glossary, and Source Listings for Further Help and Information

Edited by Wilma Caldwell and Chad T. Kimball. 376 pages. 2001. 0-7808-0333-7. $78.

"The book synthesizes the reliable medical literature on obesity into one easy-to-read and useful resource for the general public."
—American Reference Books Annual 2002

"This is a very useful resource book for the lay public."
—Doody's Review Service, Nov '01

"Well suited for the health reference collection of a public library or an academic health science library that serves the general population." *—E-Streams, Sep '01*

"Recommended reference source."
—Booklist, American Library Association, Apr '01

" Recommended pick both for specialty health library collections and any general consumer health reference collection." *— The Bookwatch, Apr '01*

■

Ophthalmic Disorders Sourcebook

Basic Information about Glaucoma, Cataracts, Macular Degeneration, Strabismus, Refractive Disorders, and More

Along with Statistical and Demographic Data and Reports on Current Research Initiatives

Edited by Linda M. Ross. 631 pages. 1996. 0-7808-0081-8. $78.

■

Oral Health Sourcebook

Basic Information about Diseases and Conditions Affecting Oral Health, Including Cavities, Gum Disease, Dry Mouth, Oral Cancers, Fever Blisters, Canker Sores, Oral Thrush, Bad Breath, Temporomandibular Disorders, and other Craniofacial Syndromes

Along with Statistical Data on the Oral Health of Americans, Oral Hygiene, Emergency First Aid, Information on Treatment Procedures and Methods of Replacing Lost Teeth

Edited by Allan R. Cook. 558 pages. 1997. 0-7808-0082-6. $78.

"Unique source which will fill a gap in dental sources for patients and the lay public. A valuable reference tool even in a library with thousands of books on dentistry. Comprehensive, clear, inexpensive, and easy to read and use. It fills an enormous gap in the health care literature." *— Reference and User Services Quarterly, American Library Association, Summer '98*

"Recommended reference source."
—Booklist, American Library Association, Dec '97

■

Osteoporosis Sourcebook

Basic Consumer Health Information about Primary and Secondary Osteoporosis and Juvenile Osteoporosis and Related Conditions, Including Fibrous Dysplasia, Gaucher Disease, Hyperthyroidism, Hypophosphatasia, Myeloma, Osteopetrosis, Osteogenesis Imperfecta, and Paget's Disease

Along with Information about Risk Factors, Treatments, Traditional and Non-Traditional Pain Management, a Glossary of Related Terms, and a Directory of Resources

Edited by Allan R. Cook. 584 pages. 2001. 0-7808-0239-X. $78.

"This would be a book to be kept in a staff or patient library. The targeted audience is the layperson, but the therapist who needs a quick bit of information on a particular topic will also find the book useful."
—Physical Therapy, Jan '02

"This resource is recommended as a great reference source for public, health, and academic libraries, and is another triumph for the editors of Omnigraphics."
— American Reference Books Annual 2002

"Recommended for all public libraries and general health collections, especially those supporting patient education or consumer health programs."
—E-Streams, Nov '01

"Will prove valuable to any library seeking to maintain a current, comprehensive reference collection of health resources. . . . From prevention to treatment and associated conditions, this provides an excellent survey."
—The Bookwatch, Aug '01

■

Pain Sourcebook, 1st Edition

Basic Information about Specific Forms of Acute and Chronic Pain, Including Headaches, Back Pain, Muscular Pain, Neuralgia, Surgical Pain, and Cancer Pain

Along with Pain Relief Options Such as Analgesics, Narcotics, Nerve Blocks, Transcutaneous Nerve Stimulation, and Alternative Forms of Pain Control, Including Biofeedback, Imaging, Behavior Modification, and Relaxation Techniques

Edited by Allan R. Cook. 667 pages. 1997. 0-7808-0213-6. $78.

■

Pain Sourcebook, 2nd Edition

Basic Consumer Health Information about Specific Forms of Acute and Chronic Pain, Including Muscle and Skeletal Pain, Nerve Pain, Cancer Pain, and Disorders Characterized by Pain, Such as Fibromyalgia, Shingles, Angina, Arthritis, and Headaches

Along with Information about Pain Medications and Management Techniques, Complementary and Alternative Pain Relief Options, Tips for People Living with Chronic Pain, a Glossary, and a Directory of Sources for Further Information

Edited by Karen Bellenir. 670 pages. 2002. 0-7808-0612-3. $78.

■

Pediatric Cancer Sourcebook

Basic Consumer Health Information about Leukemias, Brain Tumors, Sarcomas, Lymphomas, and Other Cancers in Infants, Children, and Adolescents, Including Descriptions of Cancers, Treatments, and Coping Strategies

Along with Suggestions for Parents, Caregivers, and Concerned Relatives, a Glossary of Cancer Terms, and Resource Listings

Edited by Edward J. Prucha. 587 pages. 1999. 0-7808-0245-4. $78.

■

Physical & Mental Issues in Aging Sourcebook

Basic Consumer Health Information on Physical and Mental Disorders Associated with the Aging Process, Including Concerns about Cardiovascular Disease, Pulmonary Disease, Oral Health, Digestive Disorders, Musculoskeletal and Skin Disorders, Metabolic Changes, Sexual and Reproductive Issues, and Changes in Vision, Hearing, and Other Senses

Along with Data about Longevity and Causes of Death, Information on Acute and Chronic Pain, Descriptions of Mental Concerns, a Glossary of Terms, and Resource Listings for Additional Help

Edited by Jenifer Swanson. 660 pages. 1999. 0-7808-0233-0. $78.

■

Podiatry Sourcebook

Basic Consumer Health Information about Foot Conditions, Diseases, and Injuries, Including Bunions, Corns, Calluses, Athlete's Foot, Plantar Warts, Hammertoes and Clawtoes, Clubfoot, Heel Pain, Gout, and More

Along with Facts about Foot Care, Disease Prevention, Foot Safety, Choosing a Foot Care Specialist, a Glossary of Terms, and Resource Listings for Additional Information

Edited by M. Lisa Weatherford. 380 pages. 2001. 0-7808-0215-2. $78.

Pregnancy & Birth Sourcebook

Basic Information about Planning for Pregnancy, Maternal Health, Fetal Growth and Development, Labor and Delivery, Postpartum and Perinatal Care, Pregnancy in Mothers with Special Concerns, and Disorders of Pregnancy, Including Genetic Counseling, Nutrition and Exercise, Obstetrical Tests, Pregnancy Discomfort, Multiple Births, Cesarean Sections, Medical Testing of Newborns, Breastfeeding, Gestational Diabetes, and Ectopic Pregnancy

Edited by Heather E. Aldred. 737 pages. 1997. 0-7808-0216-0. $78.

"A well-organized handbook. Recommended."
— *Choice, Association of College and Research Libraries, Apr '98*

"Recommended reference source."
— *Booklist, American Library Association, Mar '98*

"Recommended for public libraries."
— *American Reference Books Annual, 1998*

SEE ALSO *Congenital Disorders Sourcebook, Family Planning Sourcebook*

∎

Prostate Cancer Sourcebook

Basic Consumer Health Information about Prostate Cancer, Including Information about the Associated Risk Factors, Detection, Diagnosis, and Treatment of Prostate Cancer

Along with Information on Non-Malignant Prostate Conditions, and Featuring a Section Listing Support and Treatment Centers and a Glossary of Related Terms

Edited by Dawn D. Matthews. 358 pages. 2001. 0-7808-0324-8. $78.

"Recommended reference source."
— *Booklist, American Library Association, Jan '02*

"A valuable resource for health care consumers seeking information on the subject....All text is written in a clear, easy-to-understand language that avoids technical jargon. Any library that collects consumer health resources would strengthen their collection with the addition of the *Prostate Cancer Sourcebook*."
— *American Reference Books Annual 2002*

∎

Public Health Sourcebook

Basic Information about Government Health Agencies, Including National Health Statistics and Trends, Healthy People 2000 Program Goals and Objectives, the Centers for Disease Control and Prevention, the Food and Drug Administration, and the National Institutes of Health

Along with Full Contact Information for Each Agency

Edited by Wendy Wilcox. 698 pages. 1998. 0-7808-0220-9. $78.

"Recommended reference source."
— *Booklist, American Library Association, Sep '98*

"This consumer guide provides welcome assistance in navigating the maze of federal health agencies and their data on public health concerns."
— *SciTech Book News, Sep '98*

∎

Reconstructive & Cosmetic Surgery Sourcebook

Basic Consumer Health Information on Cosmetic and Reconstructive Plastic Surgery, Including Statistical Information about Different Surgical Procedures, Things to Consider Prior to Surgery, Plastic Surgery Techniques and Tools, Emotional and Psychological Considerations, and Procedure-Specific Information

Along with a Glossary of Terms and a Listing of Resources for Additional Help and Information

Edited by M. Lisa Weatherford. 374 pages. 2001. 0-7808-0214-4. $78.

"An excellent reference that addresses cosmetic and medically necessary reconstructive surgeries. . . . The style of the prose is calm and reassuring, discussing the many positive outcomes now available due to advances in surgical techniques."
— *American Reference Books Annual 2002*

"Recommended for health science libraries that are open to the public, as well as hospital libraries that are open to the patients. This book is a good resource for the consumer interested in plastic surgery."
— *E-Streams, Dec '01*

"Recommended reference source."
— *Booklist, American Library Association, July '01*

∎

Rehabilitation Sourcebook

Basic Consumer Health Information about Rehabilitation for People Recovering from Heart Surgery, Spinal Cord Injury, Stroke, Orthopedic Impairments, Amputation, Pulmonary Impairments, Traumatic Injury, and More, Including Physical Therapy, Occupational Therapy, Speech/ Language Therapy, Massage Therapy, Dance Therapy, Art Therapy, and Recreational Therapy

Along with Information on Assistive and Adaptive Devices, a Glossary, and Resources for Additional Help and Information

Edited by Dawn D. Matthews. 531 pages. 1999. 0-7808-0236-5. $78.

"This is an excellent resource for public library reference and health collections."
— *American Reference Books Annual, 2001*

"Recommended reference source."
— *Booklist, American Library Association, May '00*

Respiratory Diseases & Disorders Sourcebook

Basic Information about Respiratory Diseases and Disorders, Including Asthma, Cystic Fibrosis, Pneumonia, the Common Cold, Influenza, and Others, Featuring Facts about the Respiratory System, Statistical and Demographic Data, Treatments, Self-Help Management Suggestions, and Current Research Initiatives

Edited by Allan R. Cook and Peter D. Dresser. 771 pages. 1995. 0-7808-0037-0. $78.

"Designed for the layperson and for patients and their families coping with respiratory illness. . . . an extensive array of information on diagnosis, treatment, management, and prevention of respiratory illnesses for the general reader." — *Choice, Association of College and Research Libraries, Jun '96*

"A highly recommended text for all collections. It is a comforting reminder of the power of knowledge that good books carry between their covers."
— *Academic Library Book Review, Spring '96*

"A comprehensive collection of authoritative information presented in a nontechnical, humanitarian style for patients, families, and caregivers."
— *Association of Operating Room Nurses, Sep/Oct '95*

■

Sexually Transmitted Diseases Sourcebook, 1st Edition

Basic Information about Herpes, Chlamydia, Gonorrhea, Hepatitis, Nongonoccocal Urethritis, Pelvic Inflammatory Disease, Syphilis, AIDS, and More

Along with Current Data on Treatments and Preventions

Edited by Linda M. Ross. 550 pages. 1997. 0-7808-0217-9. $78.

■

Sexually Transmitted Diseases Sourcebook, 2nd Edition

Basic Consumer Health Information about Sexually Transmitted Diseases, Including Information on the Diagnosis and Treatment of Chlamydia, Gonorrhea, Hepatitis, Herpes, HIV, Mononucleosis, Syphilis, and Others

Along with Information on Prevention, Such as Condom Use, Vaccines, and STD Education; And Featuring a Section on Issues Related to Youth and Adolescents, a Glossary, and Resources for Additional Help and Information

Edited by Dawn D. Matthews. 538 pages. 2001. 0-7808-0249-7. $78.

"Recommended for consumer health collections in public libraries, and secondary school and community college libraries."
— *American Reference Books Annual 2002*

"Every school and public library should have a copy of this comprehensive and user-friendly reference book."
— *Choice, Association of College & Research Libraries, Sep '01*

"This is a highly recommended book. This is an especially important book for all school and public libraries." — *AIDS Book Review Journal, Jul-Aug '01*

"Recommended reference source."
— *Booklist, American Library Association, Apr '01*

"Recommended pick both for specialty health library collections and any general consumer health reference collection." — *The Bookwatch, Apr '01*

■

Skin Disorders Sourcebook

Basic Information about Common Skin and Scalp Conditions Caused by Aging, Allergies, Immune Reactions, Sun Exposure, Infectious Organisms, Parasites, Cosmetics, and Skin Traumas, Including Abrasions, Cuts, and Pressure Sores

Along with Information on Prevention and Treatment

Edited by Allan R. Cook. 647 pages. 1997. 0-7808-0080-X. $78.

". . . comprehensive, easily read reference book."
— *Doody's Health Sciences Book Reviews, Oct '97*

SEE ALSO Burns Sourcebook

■

Sleep Disorders Sourcebook

Basic Consumer Health Information about Sleep and Its Disorders, Including Insomnia, Sleepwalking, Sleep Apnea, Restless Leg Syndrome, and Narcolepsy

Along with Data about Shiftwork and Its Effects, Information on the Societal Costs of Sleep Deprivation, Descriptions of Treatment Options, a Glossary of Terms, and Resource Listings for Additional Help

Edited by Jenifer Swanson. 439 pages. 1998. 0-7808-0234-9. $78.

"This text will complement any home or medical library. It is user-friendly and ideal for the adult reader."
— *American Reference Books Annual, 2000*

"A useful resource that provides accurate, relevant, and accessible information on sleep to the general public. Health care providers who deal with sleep disorders patients may also find it helpful in being prepared to answer some of the questions patients ask."
— *Respiratory Care, Jul '99*

"Recommended reference source."
— *Booklist, American Library Association, Feb '99*

Sports Injuries Sourcebook, First Edition

Basic Consumer Health Information about Common Sports Injuries, Prevention of Injury in Specific Sports, Tips for Training, and Rehabilitation from Injury

Along with Information about Special Concerns for Children, Young Girls in Athletic Training Programs, Senior Athletes, and Women Athletes, and a Directory of Resources for Further Help and Information

Edited by Heather E. Aldred. 624 pages. 1999. 0-7808-0218-7. $78.

"While this easy-to-read book is recommended for all libraries, it should prove to be especially useful for public, high school, and academic libraries; certainly it should be on the bookshelf of every school gymnasium." —*E-Streams, Mar '00*

"Public libraries and undergraduate academic libraries will find this book useful for its nontechnical language." —*American Reference Books Annual, 2000*

Sports Injuries Sourcebook, Second Edition

Basic Consumer Health Information about the Diagnosis, Treatment, and Rehabilitation of Common Sports-Related Injuries in Children and Adults

Along with Suggestions for Conditioning and Training, Information and Prevention Tips for Injuries Frequently Associated with Specific Sports and Special Populations, a Glossary, and a Directory of Additional Resources

Edited by Joyce Brennfleck Shannon. 600 pages. 2002. 0-7808-0604-2. $78.

Stress-Related Disorders Sourcebook

Basic Consumer Health Information about Stress and Stress-Related Disorders, Including Stress Origins and Signals, Environmental Stress at Work and Home, Mental and Emotional Stress Associated with Depression, Post-Traumatic Stress Disorder, Panic Disorder, Suicide, and the Physical Effects of Stress on the Cardiovascular, Immune, and Nervous Systems

Along with Stress Management Techniques, a Glossary, and a Listing of Additional Resources

Edited by Joyce Brennfleck Shannon. 610 pages. 2002. 0-7808-0560-7. $78.

Substance Abuse Sourcebook

Basic Health-Related Information about the Abuse of Legal and Illegal Substances Such as Alcohol, Tobacco, Prescription Drugs, Marijuana, Cocaine, and Heroin; and Including Facts about Substance Abuse Prevention Strategies, Intervention Methods, Treatment and Recovery Programs, and a Section Addressing the

Special Problems Related to Substance Abuse during Pregnancy

Edited by Karen Bellenir. 573 pages. 1996. 0-7808-0038-9. $78.

"A valuable addition to any health reference section. Highly recommended."
—*The Book Report, Mar/Apr '97*

". . . a comprehensive collection of substance abuse information that's both highly readable and compact. Families and caregivers of substance abusers will find the information enlightening and helpful, while teachers, social workers and journalists should benefit from the concise format. Recommended."
—*Drug Abuse Update, Winter '96/'97*

SEE ALSO Alcoholism Sourcebook, Drug Abuse Sourcebook

Surgery Sourcebook

Basic Consumer Health Information about Inpatient and Outpatient Surgeries, Including Cardiac, Vascular, Orthopedic, Ocular, Reconstructive, Cosmetic, Gynecologic, and Ear, Nose, and Throat Procedures and More

Along with Information about Operating Room Policies and Instruments, Laser Surgery Techniques, Hospital Errors, Statistical Data, a Glossary, and Listings of Sources for Further Help and Information

Edited by Annemarie S. Muth and Karen Bellenir. 600 pages. 2002. 0-7808-0380-9. $78.

Transplantation Sourcebook

Basic Consumer Health Information about Organ and Tissue Transplantation, Including Physical and Financial Preparations, Procedures and Issues Relating to Specific Solid Organ and Tissue Transplants, Rehabilitation, Pediatric Transplant Information, the Future of Transplantation, and Organ and Tissue Donation

Along with a Glossary and Listings of Additional Resources

Edited by Joyce Brennfleck Shannon. 628 pages. 2002. 0-7808-0322-1. $78.

Traveler's Health Sourcebook

Basic Consumer Health Information for Travelers, Including Physical and Medical Preparations, Transportation Health and Safety, Essential Information about Food and Water, Sun Exposure, Insect and Snake Bites, Camping and Wilderness Medicine, and Travel with Physical or Medical Disabilities

Along with International Travel Tips, Vaccination Recommendations, Geographical Health Issues, Disease Risks, a Glossary, and a Listing of Additional Resources

Edited by Joyce Brennfleck Shannon. 613 pages. 2000. 0-7808-0384-1. $78.

■

Vegetarian Sourcebook

Basic Consumer Health Information about Vegetarian Diets, Lifestyle, and Philosophy, Including Definitions of Vegetarianism and Veganism, Tips about Adopting Vegetarianism, Creating a Vegetarian Pantry, and Meeting Nutritional Needs of Vegetarians, with Facts Regarding Vegetarianism's Effect on Pregnant and Lactating Women, Children, Athletes, and Senior Citizens

Along with a Glossary of Commonly Used Vegetarian Terms and Resources for Additional Help and Information

Edited byChad T. Kimball. 375 pages. 2002. 0-7808-0439-2. $78.

■

Women's Health Concerns Sourcebook

Basic Information about Health Issues That Affect Women, Featuring Facts about Menstruation and Other Gynecological Concerns, Including Endometriosis, Fibroids, Menopause, and Vaginitis; Reproductive Concerns, Including Birth Control, Infertility, and Abortion; and Facts about Additional Physical, Emotional, and Mental Health Concerns Prevalent among Women Such as Osteoporosis, Urinary Tract Disorders, Eating Disorders, and Depression

Along with Tips for Maintaining a Healthy Lifestyle

Edited by Heather E. Aldred. 567 pages. 1997. 0-7808-0219-5. $78.

SEE ALSO *Breast Cancer Sourcebook, Cancer Sourcebook for Women, 1st and 2nd Editions, Healthy Heart Sourcebook for Women, Osteoporosis Sourcebook*

■

Workplace Health & Safety Sourcebook

Basic Consumer Health Information about Workplace Health and Safety, Including the Effect of Workplace Hazards on the Lungs, Skin, Heart, Ears, Eyes, Brain, Reproductive Organs, Musculoskeletal System, and Other Organs and Body Parts

Along with Information about Occupational Cancer, Personal Protective Equipment, Toxic and Hazardous Chemicals, Child Labor, Stress, and Workplace Violence

Edited by Chad T. Kimball. 626 pages. 2000. 0-7808-0231-4. $78.

■

Worldwide Health Sourcebook

Basic Information about Global Health Issues, Including Malnutrition, Reproductive Health, Disease Dispersion and Prevention, Emerging Diseases, Risky Health Behaviors, and the Leading Causes of Death

Along with Global Health Concerns for Children, Women, and the Elderly, Mental Health Issues, Research and Technology Advancements, and Economic, Environmental, and Political Health Implications, a Glossary, and a Resource Listing for Additional Help and Information

Edited by Joyce Brennfleck Shannon. 614 pages. 2001. 0-7808-0330-2. $78.

Teen Health Series

Helping Young Adults Understand, Manage, and Avoid Serious Illness

Diet Information for Teens
Health Tips about Diet and Nutrition

Including Facts about Nutrients, Dietary Guidelines, Breakfasts, School Lunches, Snacks, Party Food, Weight Control, Eating Disorders, and More

Edited by Karen Bellenir. 399 pages. 2001. 0-7808-0441-4. $58.

"Full of helpful insights and facts throughout the book. . . . An excellent resource to be placed in public libraries or even in personal collections."
—*American Reference Books Annual 2002*

"Recommended for middle and high school libraries and media centers as well as academic libraries that educate future teachers of teenagers. It is also a suitable addition to health science libraries that serve patrons who are interested in teen health promotion and education."
— *E-Streams, Oct '01*

"This comprehensive book would be beneficial to collections that need information about nutrition, dietary guidelines, meal planning, and weight control. . . . This reference is so easy to use that its purchase is recommended."
— *The Book Report, Sep-Oct '01*

"This book is written in an easy to understand format describing issues that many teens face every day, and then provides thoughtful explanations so that teens can make informed decisions. This is an interesting book that provides important facts and information for today's teens."
—*Doody's Health Sciences Book Review Journal, Jul-Aug '01*

"A comprehensive compendium of diet and nutrition. The information is presented in a straightforward, plain-spoken manner. This title will be useful to those working on reports on a variety of topics, as well as to general readers concerned about their dietary health."
— *School Library Journal, Jun '01*

Drug Information for Teens
Health Tips about the Physical and Mental Effects of Substance Abuse

Including Facts about Alcohol, Anabolic Steroids, Club Drugs, Cocaine, Depressants, Hallucinogens, Herbal Products, Inhalants, Marijuana, Narcotics, Stimulants, Tobacco, and More

Edited by Karen Bellenir. 400 pages. 2002. 0-7808-0444-9. $58.

Mental Health Information for Teens
Health Tips about Mental Health and Mental Illness

Including Facts about Anxiety, Depression, Suicide, Eating Disorders, Obsessive-Compulsive Disorders, Panic Attacks, Phobias, Schizophrenia, and More

Edited by Karen Bellenir. 406 pages. 2001. 0-7808-0442-2. $58.

"In both language and approach, this user-friendly entry in the *Teen Health Series* is on target for teens needing information on mental health concerns." — *Booklist, American Library Association, Jan '02*

"Readers will find the material accessible and informative, with the shaded notes, facts, and embedded glossary insets adding appropriately to the already interesting and succinct presentation."
—*School Library Journal, Jan '02*

"This title is highly recommended for any library that serves adolescents and parents/caregivers of adolescents." — *E-Streams, Jan '02*

"Recommended for high school libraries and young adult collections in public libraries. Both health professionals and teenagers will find this book useful."
— *American Reference Books Annual 2002*

"This is a nice book written to enlighten the society, primarily teenagers, about common teen mental health issues. It is highly recommended to teachers and parents as well as adolescents."
— *Doody's Review Service, Dec '01*

Sexual Health Information for Teens
Health Tips about Sexual Development, Human Reproduction, and Sexually Transmitted Diseases

Including Facts about Puberty, Reproductive Health, Chlamydia, Human Papillomavirus, Pelvic Inflammatory Disease, Herpes, AIDS, Contraception, Pregnancy, and More

Edited by Deborah A. Stanley. 400 pages. 2002. 0-7808-0445-7. $58.

Health Reference Series